THE SECOND CLASSIC ITALIAN COOKBOOK

Also by Marcella Hazan
The Classic Italian Cookbook

THE SECOND CLASSIC ITALIAN COOKBOOK

*

Marcella Hazan

Adapted by Anna Del Conte

ILLUSTRATIONS BY

Marisabina Russo

Jill Norman & Hobhouse

This revised and metricated edition first published 1982 by
Jill Norman & Hobhouse Ltd
90 Great Russell Street
London WCIB 3PY

The Second Classic Italian Cookbook was first published, under the title *More Classic Italian Cooking*, in 1978 in the United States of America by Alfred A Knopf Inc., New York, and simultaneously in Canada by Random House of Canada Ltd, Toronto

British Library Cataloguing in Publication Data
Hazan, Marcella
The second classic Italian cookbook
– Rev. & metricated ed.
1. Cookery, Italian
I. Title II. Hazan, Marcella. More classic
Italian cooking
641.5945 TX723

ISBN 0-90690-66-3

First printing

Printed in Great Britain by
Butler & Tanner Ltd
Frome and London

To
Julia and Jim
molto affettuosamente

Contents

Preface

WHEN the manuscript of my first book was finished and turned over to the publisher, my strongest feeling was one of immense relief that it was done and delivered at last. Mixed with the feeling of relief, however, was one of regret. There were still so many wonderful dishes one could do! But would I ever get the chance to work on another Italian cookbook? Not very likely, I thought.

My cooking was so different from the then current image of Italian food, it seemed impossible to me that there would be more than a very limited public for it. As it turned out, I was wrong, and *The Classic Italian Cookbook* continues to find its way into a surprisingly large number of kitchens. Apparently this cooking, in which the least complicated means are used to achieve the most satisfying results, was exactly the kind of cooking many people were ready to turn to. And so I have been encouraged to give them more of it.

Here is an entirely new collection of authentic gems from Italian kitchens. In doing research for this book, I have talked to cooks in nearly every province of Italy, from Valtellina, on the Swiss border, to Agrigento, on the southern coast of Sicily.

I went wherever I was told there was a gifted cook. I took down recipes the way one takes down unwritten folk songs and stories, travelling with a tape recorder slung beside my shoulder bag, a magic listening box so small and unobtrusive few people I talked to were aware it was there.

The cooking that interests me is living, contemporary cooking. It bubbles in the pots of different kinds of kitchens, from those of aristocratic houses to those of middle-class housewives to those of farmers, fishermen, and small, family *trattorie*.

What we have here is the authentic language of the kitchen that is spoken in Italy today. It is forthright and spontaneous; like colloquial speech, it has colour, vitality, and unpremeditated grace. As good cooking has always done, it can make the everyday business of survival not only bearable but worthwhile.

What will you find in this book?

There is an extensive section on Italian breads. In it you have three different table breads, including a biscuity, golden hard-wheat bread, and a selection of *focacce* – flat breads for snacks or for buffets, flavoured with bacon, onion, sage or rosemary. There is a recipe for pizza that is as close as one can come to the crispness and fresh flavour of the genuine Neapolitan original. And then, with the same dough, you will learn how to make three different kinds of *sfinciuni*, a delicious stuffed pizza that is made in Sicily and nowhere else.

There are splendid examples of the very best farmhouse cooking, such as *pizza rustica* (pork and cheese pie in a crust), *pizza di scarola*, stone-griddle bread, and different kinds of dumplings with tasty fillings. There are party dishes, and lovely cold dishes, such as spinach and tuna roll and *spaghetti* salad. If you have never had *spaghetti* salad or a *spaghetti frittata*, you are in for delectable surprises.

There is fragrant cooking from the Riviera: beautiful, inventive combinations of fish and vegetables. From the North there are several unusual veal dishes, as well as stews and braised meat dishes that can give, I think, as ample a measure of contentment as anything one can eat. From country kitchens everywhere there is a remarkable collection of roasts and fricassees of chicken and lamb, and marvellous soups. There are many spectacular and new sauces for pasta, and little-known fish, meat, and vegetable courses from that unjustly neglected reservoir of honest cooking, the South. And, of course, from my own region, there is an elegant selection of home-made pasta – *lasagne* with mushrooms and ham, *cappelletti* with fish stuffing, green *tortellini* – and a savoury assortment of pork dishes. Both pasta and pork are areas of cooking where Emilia-Romagna reigns supreme.

The chapter on making fresh pasta at home in *The Classic Italian Cookbook* was the first detailed discussion of the subject ever undertaken in English. It has here been expanded and revised. Its instructions should make it possible for anyone who has the time and patience to master one of the most rewarding skills any cook can possess – the art of making fresh Bolognese pasta by hand. And, for those without the time and patience, there are directions on how to get the best results from both the hand-cranked and the electric pasta machines.

Desserts are never the strong suit for an Italian cook, but you will find some very nice things here, all the same. Among others, there are *zuppa inglese*, almond and walnut cakes, an unusual fruitcake with polenta, irresistible ricotta fritters, and a cake handed down from my own family, made for dunking in sweet wine. This last is one of the perennial favourites of my students. In the ice-cream section, there is a recipe for custard cream ice-cream, the classic of the Italian repertoire, plus some other basic ice-creams, as well as some unusual ones, such as prune or black grape ice-cream. The book ends with a frozen tangerine surprise, which is the best of all Italian ices.

The beginning and end of this book are in the taste of the food with which it deals. The point of departure was the taste of the original version. Although I have talked, heard, and read about thousands of recipes, I have worked on no dish that I did not first taste at the source, in its native region.

Wherever I have gone, thanks to many friends and to the open-heartedness that good food begets, I have always found cooks willing to satisfy my curiosity about a dish.

As I worked on it in my kitchen, faithful as I tried to be to my recollections, to the instructions I had been given, and to my voluminous notes, I was guided by my own taste in the making of the dish. Now, as these recipes are turned over to you, it must be your taste that takes charge. The dish will become yours, as much as it became mine, as much as it was that of the cook who preceded me. The art of cooking never comes to a standstill. It is renewed each day, as we renew our lives.

In writing of poets, Emily Dickinson said they 'light but lamps, / Themselves go out.' The same can be said of cooks. We light but fires.

* * *

This book was originally written for American readers, and used American measurements and terminology. The original ingredients were in some cases unobtainable in the United States because pork products may not be imported and so locally available imitations or substitutes were suggested instead. For this new edition, the recipes have been converted back to metric measurements and their imperial equivalents and the terminology to that familiar to British and Commonwealth readers. I am most grateful to Anna Del Conte who has again painstakingly undertaken this task.

The coming of the E.E.C., the spread of foreign communities in our large towns and an upsurge in interest in, and enthusiasm for, food has meant that far more of the ingredients necessary for Italian cooking are readily available. For the best quality, though, you must still go to Italy, or at least insist on ingredients – for instance tinned tomatoes and pork products – imported from Italy.

Marcella Hazan

INTRODUCTION

La Buona Cucina

WHAT it is and how it is done – that is what I most want to know when it comes to cooking. The historical whys and wherefroms, intriguing though they are, have never interested me quite so much. Not that they would not make a fascinating story. No odyssey has been written so packed with incident as the annals of Italian cooking.

If the entire fabric of this most varied of all cuisines could be laid out before our mind's eye, we would be faced with a tapestry of unequalled intricacy. Weaving our way among its infinite patterns we would be tracing Italy's inexhaustible history, picking up threads that lead us to the Roman conquests, the foreign rulers, the great traders and explorers. Here our eye would be caught by the glittering tracery of court cooking in the city states; there it would fall upon the homespun of *la cucina povera*, peasants' cooking.

But no single pattern dominates the composition, nor can we unerringly follow any one thread to its beginning. No one can say we shall find the origin of Italy's greatest cooking in the North or in the South, in Bologna or Florence, in Venice or Genoa, in Naples or Rome. It is everywhere.

This is not the cooking of professional chefs. There is no such thing as Italian *haute cuisine* because there are no high or low roads in Italian cooking. All roads lead to the home, *la cucina casereccia* – home cooking, which is the only good cooking – *la buona cucina.*

La buona cucina comes to us from the once cloistered Italian family life, where it first flourished, and where it still survives. Although Italians are among the most sociable people on earth, genuinely hospitable, and powerfully attracted by the company of others, up to recent times it was quite unusual to be invited to anyone's home for dinner. It was possible, in fact even likely, to be friends for a lifetime yet never eat together, except when eating out.

The family table, worshipfully called *il sacro desco*, was an inviolable place, the one still spot in a turning world to which parents, children, and kin could safely cling. The food put on such a table did not strain for effect, was not meant to dazzle and impress, did not need to be elaborate. It only had to be good. This is still the essential character of *la buona cucina*, of good Italian cooking. Good is good enough.

In addressing themselves to the private satisfactions of the same family group, day after day, Italian cooks developed a relaxed cuisine, simple and resourceful enough to combine the comfort of the familiar with the sprightliness of improvisation. The result is the lively balance of a classic Italian meal, with its animated progression of small courses. It starts with soup, pasta, or rice, follows with frugal portions of meat or fish accompanied by seasonal vegetables, continues with salad, and concludes with fruit. It almost invariably abstains from cloying desserts. It is healthy cooking for healthy people.

Often, when people talk about cooking, they mean cooking for guests. We all like to share food and wine with friends, but why should entertaining become a synonym for cooking? What does the family do between one party and another? Doesn't it eat? And is there anything more valuable we can do with the time we spend with our children, brothers, sisters, or parents than to share the far-reaching joys of good food?

The memories associated with the meals of our youth are among the most deeply imbedded in our consciousness. Lin Yutang, a Chinese scholar and epicure, wrote, 'What is patriotism but the love of good things we ate in our childhood?' The joy of unpretentious food, prepared and consumed simply because it is good, leads to moments of pure well-being that are vital to leave only to guests and to Saturday nights. They should belong to us and to every day.

Somehow, we must eat. We can do it absent-mindedly, as a matter of routine. We can turn it into an occasion for romance; for filling in gaps in our social lives; for displaying our sophistication, or our means; for talking business. Or we can make it into a recurrent source of unhurried, intimate, deep-seated satisfaction. Good Italian cooking can serve most of these ends, but what it serves best is the last.

The Good Italian Cook

I know young people now who play the piano as ... one can't ... can't play it better. But then, when I hear them play it that way, I have my little question for them. I ask them, when will you start to make music?
From an interview given by Arthur Rubinstein on his ninetieth birthday

MUSIC and cooking are so much alike. There are people who, simply by working hard at it, become technically quite accomplished at either art. But it isn't until one connects technique to feeling, turning it into the outward thrust of that feeling, that one becomes a musician, or a cook.

The good Italian cook is an improviser, whose performance is each time a fresh response to the suggestions of an inner beat.

Those who set out to become accomplished Italian cooks have at least one advantage over others – there are no acrobatic movements to execute, no intricate arabesques to master. Italian cooking produces some of the most delectable food in the world, with astonishingly simple means. Except for rolling out pasta by hand, an Italian cook does not need to command special skills. There are none of the elaborate preliminaries one may find in other cuisines. *La buona cucina* is not an exercise in dexterity. It is an act of taste.

Taste, like rhythm, may be described, but it does not exist until it is experienced. Carefully annotated recipes are useful because they lead to the re-creation of an experience; they demonstrate what can be accomplished. But one must bear in mind that a recipe is only the congealed record of a once fluid and spontaneous act. It is this spontaneity that the good cook must recover. To attempt to reproduce any dish, time after time, through plodding duplication of a recipe's every step, is futile and tedious, like memorising a ditty in some foreign tongue.

As the Greek philosopher Heraclitus said, no one ever steps into the same river twice. One does not need to be a philosopher, only a cook, to know that no dish ever turns out again exactly the same. Cooking, like life itself, flows out of the experienced past, but belongs to the unique moment in which it takes place. From one occasion to the next you will not find vegetables at the identical stage of ripeness or freshness. No two cloves of garlic, no two bunches of celery, no two peppers in a basket have exactly the same flavour, no cuts of meat duplicate precisely the texture and tenderness of those of another day. Each time you bring your ingredients together, your own hand falls with a different cadence. The objective in good Italian cooking is not to achieve uniformity, or even absolute predictability of result. It is to express the values of the materials at hand, and the unrepeatable intuitions of the moment of execution.

All this does not mean there are no rules. Of course there are rules. There is structure to Italian cooking just as there is structure to the music of a dance. The brief suggestions that follow here and the recipes of the book will succeed, I hope, in making you aware of how Italian cooking is achieved. Even more, I hope that eventually the recipes will release you from their grasp, and allow you to cook through the unfettered exercise of your own taste. Once you have understood technique you must stop paying attention to it. You must stop counting teaspoons and begin to cook.

How I cook When I first started cooking, I had to learn in a hurry. I was newly married, just landed in New York, having no word of English, and no relatives or Italian-speaking friends to turn to for advice. All I had was a cookbook, and the remembered taste of the food which had always nourished me. As I stepped for the first time into a kitchen of my own, I realised with despair that I had to begin, but I had no idea where.

My husband, the man who would be coming home to dinner, could face life's greatest trials with splendid detachment, but became curiously heated over commonplace matters of taste. The one indignity he bore with least grace and understanding was that of an indifferent meal. Precarious was the word for the future of our union. Or, if I may borrow Winston Churchill's phrase out of another battle, the odds were great, my margins small, the stakes infinite.

The book I had brought took technique for granted, was vague about measurements, and skimped on explanations. It was a good cookbook – for good cooks.

My cooking became a process more of discovery than of invention, mixing memories with observation. Once past the first, and fortunately few, disasters, I began to respond to the materials with which I worked. I discovered how hot and quick fat had to be to make zucchini crisp; how slow and gentle a flame I needed to make a veal roast tender. I learned to balance the flavours and textures of the components in the stuffing for *tortellini*; I found that the less I fussed with a tomato sauce the fresher it tasted.

When we eventually returned to Italy to live, and I was once again surrounded by my native cooking, I was elated to find that the food I had learned to prepare in my New York kitchen was as unmistakably Italian as my speech. I was still teaching biology and mathematics then, but cooking had already become what I loved best to do. And, as I kept adding new dishes to my repertoire, I found that my most precious tool was the judgment I had developed when I had stood alone in my first kitchen in America.

I have now grown rather sceptical of books that promise to take all the guesswork out of cooking. What a sad thing it would be, assuming it could be done. To produce the simplest dish, even if it is just dressing some salad greens with oil and vinegar, judgment must be exercised, fine adjustments made. Of course, we all want to be told as explicitly as possible what to expect when starting an unfamiliar dish. That I have tried to do here. The recipes in this book are statements, set down as clearly as I was able, about how certain procedures and ingredients were combined to produce a particular result. They worked through my judgment. It is up to you to make them work through yours.

MARKETING

I chafe at shopping lists. What is the point of insisting you are going to make *fegato alla veneziana* if the liver you find is dark and gristly, and makes you think of steer rather than calf? Or why decide you want to do the striped bass with artichokes, until you've seen the artichokes?

The market is the place where the idea of a meal best takes place, as our eyes are caught by the good things of the day. No one loves cooking who is immune to the sudden enticement of perfect green beans. When I find firm young courgettes, or bosomy aubergines, taut, glossy, and unblemished, or ripe local tomatoes, I start to cook right there, in my mind. What a thrill to discover fresh sardines have come in, or that the butcher has a baby lamb or some lovely sweetbreads he has not yet had time to entomb in his freezer.

One should go marketing as frequently as possible, ideally every day, even if it is only to check up on fresh arrivals on the produce stands, or in the fish market. Whether or not I start out with an exact idea of what I'd like to do for dinner, I never really make up my mind until I see what is available. From the vegetables I find I may decide to do a soup, a stew, or a *risotto*. Or, as I walk through the fish market, I may discover it is the perfect day for fish soup. Then I would look for some tart and nutty greens for a salad to follow it, and some sweet ripe seasonal fruit for dessert.

Cooking, like any other art, is a form of love. Marketing is the wooing stage, which one must approach with a discerning eye and a ready heart. What takes place in the kitchen later is simply the development and conclusion of the same process.

USING THE REFRIGERATOR

The first 'refrigerator' I remember from my childhood was a wooden cabinet with side panels made of chicken wire to let air circulate. It was usually suspended from a hook set into a shaded wall by the back kitchen door, except for a few subfreezing winter days, when it was brought inside and kept in an unheated room. There was never too much in it, since everything perishable and fresh was cooked and consumed the same day it was bought; but the rare leftovers, soups, cold meats, cheeses it harboured stayed in fine condition.

I am not so foolishly nostalgic for our old air-cooled pantry as to want to trade in my fine modern refrigerator for it. At the same time, having lived and survived without refrigeration, I know it is not always the best solution for storing food. Sometimes it may be the worst.

When foods are going to be reheated, or consumed at room temperature, just a few hours after they've been cooked, they should never go into the refrigerator. This applies particularly to cooked green vegetables, which quickly acquire a sour, grassy taste in the fridge. It does not apply to vegetable soups, which actually improve after a day or two.

All things that are to be fried or sautéed should be taken out of the refrigerator some time in advance. First, to avoid a sharp drop in the temperature of the cooking fat; second, to spare them the shock of a sudden change in temperature, which sometimes adversely affects their taste and consistency.

Cold, and heat as well, can stunt and suppress flavour. Chilled seafood and vegetable appetisers or salads are so often a waste of time, I think, because they all have the same numb refrigerated taste. Conversely, while the ideal temperature for fried courgettes or grilled meats is piping hot, dishes with more complex flavours – such as some soups, *lasagne*, meat or vegetable pies, gratins, stews – must wait for part of the intense flush of cooking to subside before their character opens up.

It is terribly important in cooking to understand that temperature is a vehicle for flavour, much as air is for sound. At the correct temperature, flavour comes across as clear and unimpaired as voices that travel through the crisp, still air of a winter night. In my recipes I usually suggest whether dishes should be served warm, hot, or at room temperature. But there is no inflexible rule to follow. The only reliable thermometer is in one's palate.

ON FROZEN FOODS AND FREEZING

I know many eminent cooks who swear by the superior freshness of frozen vegetables. To me they all taste somewhat the same, the way smoked foods do. They may not taste bad. They simply don't taste fresh. Of all frozen vegetables, peas turn out the best, and I use them occasionally, although they are still no substitute for even 'reasonably fresh' raw peas.

The argument some people advance is that vegetables frozen minutes after they are picked are actually fresher than those that have travelled hundreds or thousands of miles, languishing in trains, in warehouses, in the local market's cold store. This misses the point, I think. Frozen vegetables have a precooked taste to them that just does not measure up to the flavour of knowingly selected fresh ones. It is true that there is a lot of stale, over-the-hill produce in the markets. But there is also some fine produce to be found, if you are willing to look for it. It takes time to pick and choose one's way to a good dinner. But is it not a more stimulating and even enjoyable exercise than filling a supermarket trolley with little waxed boxes from the unvarying and mummified display of the frozen-food counter?

Although I use my freezer less than most people I know, there are some things it does for me that I like very much.

Freezing broth, for instance. Homemade broth is an indispensable element of good Italian cooking, and I prepare great batches of it, which I pour into ice-cube trays. When it is frozen, I transfer the cubes to small plastic bags, so handy for taking the quantity I need, from a tablespoon to half a litre. Frozen broth keeps a very long time, about two to three months. But if you get into the habit of using it, you are not likely ever to keep a supply that long.

I also keep bones, chicken carcasses, and scraps of meat in the freezer, and I add them to the pot with fresh ingredients every time I make a new batch of broth.

Whenever a recipe calls for egg yolks, I freeze the whites, just as I do broth, in ice-cube trays.

I freeze meat sauce, tomato sauce (when I come across some ripe local tomatoes and can make a handsome quantity of it), and pesto. Pesto stays almost as fresh as the day it was made, and there is something bewitching about a steaming dish of pasta tempering a stern winter day with basil-scented summer vapours.

TIME AND THE KITCHEN

There are very few of us so fortunate today that we needn't worry about time when we think of cooking. Sometimes there just doesn't seem to be any. I have observed, however, that those who complain the most about time are often the same people who find it for activities not even remotely as vital, or as deeply connected with our happiness, as good cooking.

In the old, hackneyed image of Italian cooking, there were pasta sauces endlessly cooking, and endlessly being stirred. But that was pure fantasy. Most pasta sauces are ready in the time it takes for the pasta to boil. There are so many wonderful dishes that take just minutes to do. A most elegant dish of *scaloppine* can take less than 5 minutes. If you use odd moments to set up the preliminaries, the choice of dishes that take less than 30 minutes is infinite.

In talking to my students, I have found that the greatest problem is that many cooks waste a large part of the time they have available. They set out to do a specific dish and spend half the time looking at the pot or peering into the oven. And then they sigh about how time-consuming it all is! Actually most of the dishes that take longest are the ones that give you more free time to do something else. If you have a pan roast on that takes an hour or two, who is to stop you from starting a minestrone that you can finish or reheat a day or two later? Or putting on a stew at the same time, which will be even more delicious when warmed up later on in the week? Or slicing and pounding some *scaloppine* for *rollatini* the next day? Or peeling some asparagus for a *frittata*? Two hours in the kitchen can produce not one dish, but the makings of three or four meals.

ON USING SALT

When St Matthew used the phrase 'the salt of the earth', no one had any trouble understanding that he was talking about goodness. But there are many timorous cooks who do not take into account how essential to the goodness of their dishes is an adequate and properly administered dose of salt. As a budding flower unclenches in the sun, cooped-up flavours emerge at the call of salt.

While too much salt destroys a dish, too little may defeat it. In seasoning with salt you cannot let measuring spoons intercede for you. You must taste. This is especially true when preparing a dish for the first time. When I try something new, even after I have seasoned it to my satisfaction, I sprinkle a touch more salt on a separate biteful. On many occasions this has helped define some unfamiliar nuances of flavour I otherwise would have missed.

I have become accustomed in recent years to shaking salt directly from the packet, but I first learned to use salt pinching it from a bowl. It is a method I strongly recommend to those who are still laboriously dosing the salt with measuring spoons. A healthy pinch, using all 5 fingertips, amounts to about $\frac{1}{4}$ teaspoon. A thumb-and-forefinger pinch, perhaps half that. It may sound like a return to the Middle Ages, but it is a necessary thing, I believe, to develop a physical awareness of the amount of salt you are handling. When you add a little at time, and taste frequently, you cannot possibly go wrong.

When seasoning, bear in mind that some of the ingredients already present or to be added later, in the dish you are preparing, may be salty. This is often the case with sauces for pasta. If the sauce has in it prosciutto, sausages, anchovies, capers, you may need to hold back some of the salt you add to the water in which the pasta boils. When tasting a sauce, remember that its saltiness will be thinned out by the pasta with which it will be tossed. It should therefore be a few degrees more savoury than if you were eating it on its own. *Pecorino romano* cheese is sharper and saltier than Parmesan, and if it is going to be used, you must take this into account. When the reverse is true, that is, when the pasta is to be seasoned with a delicate sauce such as butter and cream, or a light tomato sauce, a bit more salt than usual should be added to the water in which the pasta boils. Adding salt at the table is seldom as effective in producing good flavour as cooking the food with it. The most sublime pasta may become quite ordinary if it has to be corrected with salt after serving.

There are certain things that lose as much as half or more of their bulk as they cook. In order not to be misled by their impressive initial volume and add a disproportionate amount of salt, it is a good idea to wait to season until after they have become substantially reduced through cooking.

Prolonged contact with salt draws out moisture. You may want to do this sometimes, as when preparing aubergines for cooking. But you definitely do not want to lose any precious moisture from veal *scaloppine*, chicken breasts, or thin slices of beef. In sautéing this, do not add salt until they are almost completely cooked.

I do not add salt to foods that are to be deep-fried because any escape of moisture it may provoke will diminish the crispness of their crust. And when I add salt to batter it is in minute amounts. Therefore, salt must be added to fried foods shortly after they have been removed from the pan, but not before you have given them a few seconds to firm up their crust. Unsalted fried food can never be adequately corrected at the table.

DEEP-FRYING

In the kitchen, I am happiest when I am frying. One reason is that frying takes the whole cooking process and condenses it into a continuously visible, uninterrupted sequence. It resembles those nature documentaries where the camera shows us tiny buds developing into full blooms, compressing weeks of growth into seconds. One is never out of touch with the food one is frying, even for a moment, and I find that very satisfying.

Another reason is that frying fixes like no other process the flavour and texture of food at their most appealing. When properly done, the food tastes fresh and clean, and never palls.

In deep-frying, the secrets of success are three. There must be enough fat so the food in it can float. The fat must be very hot. The pan must never be crowded. The soggy, greasy food that has given frying a bad name can almost invariably be attributed to a failure to observe these principles.

You should never, never have to add fat once you have started frying; the result would be a disastrously fatty coating on the food. If you find you need to, it means you did not have sufficient oil to start with. In properly conducted frying, there should be very nearly as much oil left in the pan at the end as there was at the beginning.

Frying oil can be used more than once, provided it does not become too dark and it is thoroughly skimmed or filtered clear of every single particle of solid matter. If any remain, they will burn the next time you use the oil, and contaminate the food with a bitter taste. It should go without saying that the subsequent times oil is used it should be used for the same kind of food, except for potato-frying oil, which can be used for other vegetables. Do not expect to recycle oil indefinitely, however. Each time you use it it absorbs some food flavour, and eventually will impart a stale, leaden taste. When reusing oil, each time I cook with it I add one part fresh oil to four parts used oil. After using it four or five times more, I discard it and start with entirely fresh oil.

In many parts of Italy, olive oil is the traditional frying medium. For deep-frying I prefer vegetable oil, specifically, corn oil. I cook with olive oil only when I want its taste in the dish – as in some sautéed vegetables, some pasta sauces, or in one of those slow-cooked, smothered dishes we call a *stufato*.

I also use lard, and strongly recommend it for such things as making fritters, where its flavour and the crispness it imparts are absolutely matchless.

I am not comfortable with pushbutton cooking, so I never use an electric frying pan. If you have one, you no doubt know better than I the proper setting for deep-frying. I use a straight-sided sauté pan. The way I tell when the oil is ready is to take one of the pieces to be fried and dip a corner of it into the fat. If it is instantly ringed with a burst of bubbles, the oil is hot enough. If I am using batter, I slip in a drop of batter instead. If the oil is hot, the batter quickly stiffens, and immediately floats to the surface.

Maintaining the oil at a steady temperature is so important that I never burden the pan all at once with a full load. This would cause the oil to cool off momentarily, and the food to become soggy. I slip in a few pieces at a time. When the pan is full, and I have more food left to fry, I take out the first pieces that went in, as soon as they are done, and replace them with uncooked pieces. If I were to clear the pan completely before putting in the next batch, the oil would become too hot. In other words, every piece of food that goes in absorbs some heat, every piece that goes out releases some heat. Put the food in and take it out at a pace that will neither deplete the frying heat available nor let it build up too rapidly.

We used to drain fried foods on brown butcher paper, which absorbed quite a lot of grease without becoming soggy, as kitchen paper quickly does. Even better for the purpose is a cooling rack, the kind you use in baking, set on a dish. If you use kitchen paper, and you are frying a large amount, replace the paper with fresh, dry sheets from time to time. Do not pile up too many pieces of just-fried food on top of each other.

Fried food must be eaten promptly, and cannot be reheated. In Naples they have a phrase for saying that one thing follows immediately upon another. It is *frienno magnanno*, which means, literally, frying and eating. And that is how it should be done.

PAN-ROASTING

In Italian cooking we very often roast veal, lamb, pork, chicken, game birds in a pot. We use a method that combines some of the features of braising, which is cooking with moist heat in a closed pot, and oven roasting, which is cooking with dry heat. The Italian term for it is *arrosto in tegame.* I call it pan-roasting, to distinguish it from braising or pot roasting. It is done entirely on top of the stove.

The initial technique is somewhat like that for a pot roast. The meat is browned on all sides with a little oil, or butter, or both. Occasionally some liquid is added – wine, broth, or milk – the heat is lowered, and the pot is covered with the lid slightly askew. The moisture is allowed to evaporate slowly. At the end there should be no liquid left in the pot, except for the condensed cooking juices. If there is liquid left, the hat is raised and it is boiled away.

The result is a roast with all the moist tenderness that braising imparts but with the texture and more concentrated flavour of dry oven roasting.

BOILING

The best way to boil vegetables is in a large pot with plenty of fast-boiling water. The more water there is surrounding the vegetable, the faster it cooks, the fresher it tastes, the brighter it becomes. Take a cauliflower for example. Cook it in a cramped pot with a skimpy amount of water and it will turn pinkish and sharp. Cook it as suggested above, and it will stay as white as when you put it in, and have a fine, sweet taste. Provided, of course, it is not an old stale head.

(The only exceptions to this method are the leafy vegetables such as spinach or Swiss chard, which cook in just the water clinging to their leaves after washing, and in the vapours produced by their own moisture.)

Bring the water to a rolling boil before putting in the vegetables. If you are cooking green vegetables such as French beans or broccoli, add salt to the water before the vegetables go in. It helps to keep them bright green. If part of the vegetable floats above the water, dunk it from time to time. Keep the pot covered and the heat under control so the water does not boil over.

When vegetables are to undergo further cooking, such as frying or gratinéing, they should be boiled very briefly, in a process known as blanching, and removed from the pot long before they are cooked through.

An important thing to remember is that cooking in cold water extracts the flavours of the ingredients, while boiling water seals them in. A useful application of this principle is in making broth (page 17), a key ingredient in Italian cooking. To produce a rich broth, start the cooking by putting all ingredients – meat bones, vegetables, etc. – in cold water.

If your object is to produce a fine boiled chicken, or brisket of beef or veal, and the broth is simply a byproduct, put them in water that has already been brought to a boil. The contact with the rapidly boiling water has the same flavour-sealing effect upon the meat that searing does when it is grilled, or browning when it is roasted.

SAUTÉING ONION AND GARLIC

A fundamental procedure in a vast number of Italian dishes is sautéing onion or garlic or both in hot fat before adding other ingredients. This provides background flavour, which may be faint or pronounced, sweetish or pungent, depending on how lightly or deeply the onion and garlic are browned.

Cookbooks, including my own first book, *The Classic Italian Cookbook*, instruct you to heat up the oil or butter first, then add the onion or garlic. I have since learned better. If through distraction or miscalculation you let the fat become too hot, when you drop in the onion or garlic they may quickly become browner than you need, or even burnt.

In order to control browning to the exact degree I want, I now put the fat in the pan *together* with the onion or garlic, and turn on the heat to high or medium high. The moment the fat becomes hot enough to make little bubbles dance around the onion and garlic, I turn down the heat, and continue sautéing until I have the colour I want – anywhere from light gold to deep amber for garlic or brown for onion.

Garlic colours more quickly than onion, so if a recipe calls for both, I put in the onion first. When it has turned a light gold, I add the garlic.

When chopping an onion or cloves of garlic, I cannot always predict with absolute precision how many teaspoons I am going to end up with. If I find

I have chopped up more than I actually need, I am certainly not going to throw out a half tablespoon of onion, or a teaspoon of garlic. It usually does not make much difference, but if I feel it matters, I simply brown it a little less. Or, if I have slightly less than I need, I let it colour more. In short, I adjust the browning to compensate for the difference in the amount.

CUTTING AND POUNDING SCALOPPINE

Some of the most justifiably popular of all Italian dishes are those with veal *scaloppine*. And there is no reason to pay exorbitant prices for them in restaurants when you can make far better *scaloppine* at home.

The first requirement is, of course, not just good veal but the right cut of veal. But that is between you and your butcher. When your relationship with the butcher enables you to obtain part of the top round of veal in one solid piece, you are well on your way to perfect *scaloppine*.

What you must do now is cut the meat in thin slices against the grain. I find that many people, including some butchers, have difficulty understanding what 'against the grain' means. The layers of muscle in meat are stacked and form a pattern a little like that of the different layers in a log of wood. This faint pattern is called the grain. If you cut a log in the same direction the tree grows, you are cutting *with* the grain. If you cut it across, as you would to cut the tree down, you are cutting *against* the grain. Think of the piece of meat you are holding as a log, observe the fine, closely packed layers of muscle, and cut *against* the direction in which they lie. Unless *scaloppine* are cut this way, no matter how pretty they look raw, they will curl, warp, shrink, and toughen in the cooking.

Once cut, *scaloppine* must be pounded flat. Pounding is an unfortunate word, because it makes one think of pummelling or thumping. Which is exactly what you must not do. If all you do is to bring the pounder down hard against the *scaloppine*, you will be mashing the meat between the weight and the board, breaking it up or punching holes in it. When you pound *scaloppine*, you should stretch them and thin them out. To do this, as you bring the punder down flat on the meat, you must let it slide from the centre outward in one continuous motion. Pound each *scaloppina* in this way until it is evenly thinned out. (*See illustration on following page.*)

HALVING OR DOUBLING RECIPES

When halving or doubling a recipe, all the ingredients, except for the cooking fat, can be divided in half or multiplied by two. Follow common sense in this, and try not to fuss about half of $\frac{1}{8}$ teaspoon of anything.

In halving a recipe, the cooking fat should not be reduced by more than

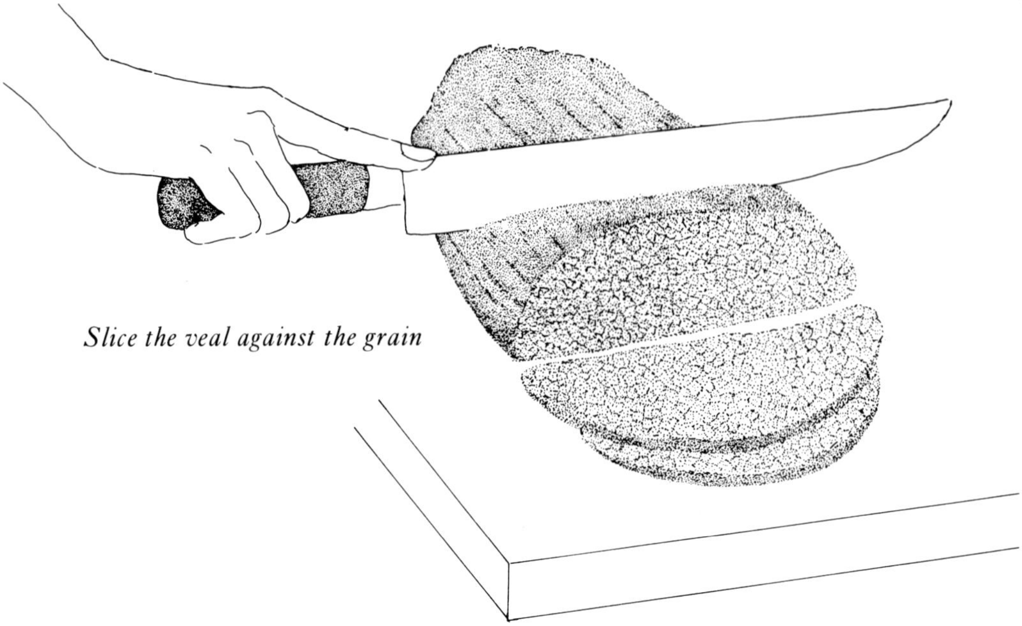

Slice the veal against the grain

Pound – stretching and thinning out the slice

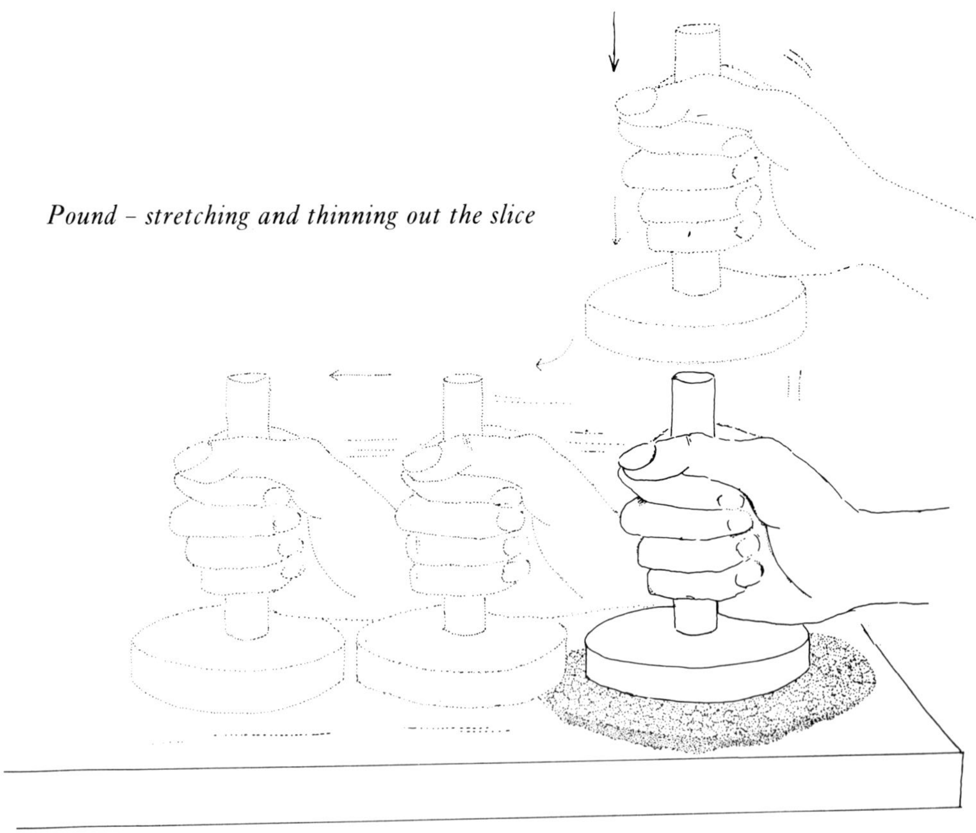

one third. For example, if a recipe calls for 50 g (2 oz) butter and 2 tablespoons oil, for a total of 75 g (3 oz) fat, reduce it to 40 g (1½ oz) butter and 1 tablespoon of oil. Or, if it calls for 40 g (1½ oz) of butter or oil, reduce it to 25 g (1 oz).

In doubling a recipe, the total cooking fat should be about one-third short of twice the original amount. Using the sample figures above as an example, 50 g (2 oz) butter and 2 tablespoons oil would become 85 g (3½ oz) butter and 3 of oil, for a total of 150 g (5 oz). This is valid if you are using one pan. If you are using two pans, then all the quantities, including the fat, are doubled exactly, just as though you were making two separate recipes.

The Good Italian Kitchen

Ingredients

THE general assumption on which good recipes are written is that when you have got the mechanics of it well worked out, when you have clearly described how, when, where, why the ingredients are put together, you have cleared the way for the reader to duplicate a dish successfully. But this does not take into account that it is the quality of the ingredients that go into the cooking that determines the taste of the food that goes to the table. This is a matter of some concern for an Italian cook, because high-quality Italian ingredients have not yet achieved broad and consistent distribution.

How much of a problem this can be one discovers only by travelling around the country, as I have had to do the last few years, giving lessons and doing demonstrations with locally available materials. It is all too easy to say, You must have that oil, You must use this cheese. I know only too well how discouraging the search can be, particularly if you live far from a large city.

Weeping and wailing over unattainable perfection is not the answer. But neither is settling for what first comes to hand on the supermarket shelf. Obtaining good ingredients takes patience and insistence. It may mean badgering your local Italian grocer into buying *pancetta* and real *parmigiano-reggiano*. Or growing your own sage, basil, or rosemary. Or ordering olive oil, Italian pasta, dried wild mushrooms by mail. You will not always reach your ideal, but you may come close enough. Fortunately, the interest in good Italian food is expanding so rapidly that every year one finds the materials one needs closer to home.

The following is a discussion of a few selected Italian ingredients and includes suggestions on how to use them, and, where pertinent, how to find them, make them, or conserve them.

Salsa Balsamella

BÉCHAMEL SAUCE

Béchamel is a white sauce of butter, flour, and milk that is a vital component of some of the most delectable Italian dishes: *lasagne*, gratins of vegetables, and many a *pasticcio* and *timballo* – succulent compounds of meat, cheese, and vegetables.

There is nothing complicated about making it. If there were, it would not appear so frequently in everyday home cooking in Italy. The following recipe is essentially the same one given in *The Classic Italian Cookbook*. It has always worked so well I see no reason to offer a different version here.

The 'secrets' of a smooth, luxuriantly creamy béchamel are three. First, you must not allow the flour to become coloured when you cook it with the butter, or it will acquire a burnt, pasty taste. Second, the hot milk must be added very gradually, and off the heat, to the flour-and-butter mixture. This will help to keep lumps from forming. Third, you must not get weary of stirring until the sauce is formed. It is all so basic and straightforward you can be making perfect sauce at the first try.

Makes approximately 300 ml (½ pint) medium-thick sauce

450 ml (¾ pt) milk
60 g (2 oz) butter
45 g (1½ oz) plain flour
¼ teaspoon salt

1 Put the milk in a saucepan, turn on the heat to medium low, and bring the milk just to the verge of boiling, when it begins to form a ring of small, pearly bubbles.

2 While you are heating the milk, put the butter in a heavy-bottomed, 1 to 1·5 litre (1¾ to 2½ pint) saucepan, and turn on the heat to low. When the butter has melted completely, add all the flour, stirring it in with a wooden spoon. Cook, while stirring constantly, for about 2 minutes. Do not allow the flour to become coloured. Remove from heat.

3 Add the hot milk to the flour-and-butter mixture, no more than 2 tablespoons of it at a time. Stir steadily and thoroughly. As soon as the first 2 tablespoons have been incorporated into the mixture, add 2 more, and continue to stir. Repeat this procedure until you have added 8 tablespoons of milk; then you can put in the rest of the milk 8 tablespoons at a time stirring steadfastly, until all the milk has been smoothly amalgamated with the flour and butter.

4 Place the pan over low heat, add the salt, and cook, stirring without interruption, until the sauce is as dense as thick cream. To make it even

thicker, if a recipe requires it, cook and stir a little longer. For a thinner sauce, cook it a little less. If you find any lumps forming, beat the béchamel rapidly with a whisk.

Note Béchamel takes so little time to prepare it is best to make it just when you need it, so you can spread it before it cools and stiffens. If you must make it in advance, reheat it slowly, in the upper half of a double boiler. Stir it constantly as it warms up, until it becomes soft and spreadable. If you are making béchamel one day in advance or more, store it in the refrigerator in a sealed container.

Increasing the recipe You can double or triple the quantities given here, but no more than that for any single batch. Choose a saucepan that is broader than it is tall, so that the sauce will cook more quickly and evenly.

BROTH

Broth is a liquid to which vegetables, meat and bones have given their essences through cooking. The broth used in Italian cooking, in braised dishes, in *risotto*, in soups, is not a dense reduction of these essences. If one may borrow wine terminology, it is light and flowery, rather than full-bodied and intense. Like a fruity, recently pressed young wine, it captures the first fresh rush of flavours that its ingredients release. This is in keeping with the spontaneous, uncomplicated, homey taste of Italian food.

Except when making a dish of boiled meats, the frugal Italian cook does not make broth with solid chunks of meat. Broth is the clearest illustration of the basic principle of good cooking, that nothing is ever wasted.

Bones are as useful as meat, because they contribute body as well as flavour. Of course, that does not mean they take the place of meat. If you are an active cook, you can accumulate meat for a broth from the boning and preparation of different cuts of veal, beef, and chicken, stealing here and there a juicy morsel from meat for a stuffing, from a beef or a veal stew. Whatever is missing, you can make up by buying an inexpensive odd piece of meat from your butcher.

Do not use lamb or pork, which give too strong a flavour to the broth. Don't make too liberal use of chicken giblets or carcasses. If not used sparingly, their sharp taste will taint the flavour of a broth.

As suggested on page 18, make a good quantity of broth in your spare time, freeze it in ice-cube trays, then wrap the cubes in several different plastic bags, and seal tightly. You will then have as much or as little broth as you may want, available the moment you need it.

Makes 1·5 to 2·5 litres (2½ to 4 pints) broth

1 teaspoon salt
1 carrot, peeled
1 small to medium onion, peeled
1 or 2 sticks celery
¼ to ½ green or red pepper, stripped of its seeds
1 small potato, peeled
1 tomato, preferably tinned Italian plum tomato, drained
2 kg (5 lb) assorted pieces of meat and bones, of which at least 1·35 kg (1½ lb) is all meat

1 Put all the ingredients in a stock pot, and add enough cold water to cover by 50 mm (2 inches). Set the cover askew, turn on the heat to medium, and bring to the boil. As soon as the liquid starts to boil, turn the heat down so that it bubbles at the gentlest of simmers.

2 Skim off the scum that floats to the surface, fairly frequently at first, then only from time to time. Cook for 3 hours, never any more rapidly than at a simmer.

3 Strain the broth through a large wire strainer lined with kitchen paper, pouring it into a nonmetallic bowl. Allow to cool completely, uncovered.

4 When cool, place in the refrigerator long enough for any fat to come to the surface and solidify. Remove the fat, and pour the clear broth below into ice-cube trays. Freeze, then divide up the cubes into four or five small plastic bags. Seal the bags tightly, and return to the freezer compartment until needed.

CAPERS

Capers are the small, green, unripe fruit of a plant that grows wild, clinging to walls and cliffs, all around the Mediterranean. It looks like a tiny, heart-shaped berry.

There are two sizes of capers. The larger is called *capote*, and the smaller, *nonpareil*. The smaller one is very much finer.

Capers are sold in jars, pickled in vinegar. If the vinegar is too strong, you may have to rinse the capers before using them. Once one could buy them packed in salt, and these used to be very much better than the pickled ones. But they are more perishable, and when there is little turnover they become rancid, so don't risk buying them.

Capers are a most appetising and tonic addition to a broad variety of pasta sauces, meat and vegetable dishes, salads, and *antipasti*. Unhappily, they are becoming very expensive, because of the manual labour required to pick them. For the same reason, the very small *nonpareil* capers are more expensive than the larger ones.

CHEESE

Fontina This is tender, gently savoury cheese that melts well in cooking. It is delicate, but unlike its imitations from Scandinavia it is not characterless. It's the kind of cheese you use when you want flavour but not sharpness.

True fontina, by Italian law, may be made only in the Val d'Aosta region, which is as far north as Italy goes before disappearing into Switzerland.

Parmesan Real Parmesan – *parmigiano-reggiano* – is produced under the strictest legal and technical supervision of any natural food product in the world. It is made with milk produced between the 1st April and the 11th November in the provinces of Parma, Reggio, Modena, Mantua, and Bologna. It takes 5 litres (2 gallons) of milk to make 450 g (1 lb) of cheese. It is aged a minimum of 18 months before being released for sale.

Parmesan is not a factory cheese. It is made by hand, by artisan cheesemakers following exactly the same methods that have been used for the past seven hundred years. Any other Italian grating cheese is simply *grana*. It is not *parmigiano-reggiano*. The taste, consistency, amd cooking qualities of the true Parmesan are unique.

There are several ways you can tell whether or not you are buying real Parmesan. The simplest is to look for the words *parmigiano-reggiano*. They should be etched in small dots in a continuously repeated pattern over the entire buff-coloured surface of the crust. Even a small piece of crust will bear a recognisable part of the name. If it does not, it is not Parmesan.

Parmigiano-reggiano is no longer coated on the outside with the once-familiar mixture of black earth and oil. The black wheels of cheese you may see in some groceries are *grana*.

Parmesan that has been kept in good condition should be straw yellow in colour, and crumble softly in the hand. It should taste faintly moist, mellow, rich, and a little salty. It should have neither a sharp bite nor a bland, lactic, 'dairy' taste. It must leave no lingering bitterness in the mouth. Before you buy a large piece of Parmesan, ask to taste a little piece. If it doesn't meet the description above, buy something else if you have to soothe the grocer's feelings, but don't buy the cheese.

Parmesan can be kept quite a long time, if properly wrapped. If you don't have an easily accessible source for it, once you come across a good piece of Parmesan, buy as much as you can afford or carry. So as not to have to open and close the wrapping too often, divide it into several wedge-shaped pieces, each large enough to satisfy your needs for about two weeks. Each piece should have some crust attached. Wrap each wedge in two or three thicknesses of aluminium foil. Wrap it tightly, making sure that the foil is not torn at any point, exposing the cheese. Store it on the bottom shelf of the refrigerator.

From time to time, check the cheese that you are not using. If you find it has begun to dry, and its golden colour is turning to white, wrap it in muslin that has been moistened and wrung out until it is just damp. Wrap foil around the muslin, and return the cheese to the refrigerator overnight. Then remove the muslin, and wrap it tightly again just in aluminium foil.

Grating Parmesan: In this book's recipes, 'grated cheese' means freshly grated. The flavour and aroma of cheese begin to die minutes after grating. The pulverised substance in supermarket jars, or sold loose at some groceries, is a waste of time and money. It will defeat the passion and sincerity you put into good cooking.

When grating Parmesan for pasta, use a grater that reduces the cheese to quick-melting fine flakes. My favourite gadget for the purpose is a two-piece hand-held grater that clamps the cheese against a revolving perforated drum.

When I need large quantities for cooking, I grind it in the food processor, using the steel blades. But this produces little grains of cheese that are too solid for use at the table, on pasta.

I have been asked how to grate cheese when it is extremely hard. Well, it shouldn't have been kept around long enough to get that hard, and it will have become too sharp for most uses. The best way to utilise it is to shave it very fine with a knife, and add it to a vegetable soup while it's cooking. But do try to avoid keeping Parmesan until it gets to that stage. Precious as it is, it is not an heirloom to hand down to posterity. Enjoy it while it is still soft and mellow.

If real Parmesan is absolutely unavailable, do not stop cooking. Use the best-tasting *grana* you can find, while you wait for the real thing to come along.

Pecorino *Pecorino* is cheese made from sheep's milk. It takes its name from *pecora*, the Italian for sheep. In Italy, you will find soft or hard *pecorino*, mild or sharp. When travelling in almost any region of Italy, look for fresh, tender, locally made, unbranded *pecorino*. It is likely to be the best cheese you will ever eat, particularly if you happen to be in Tuscany or Sardinia.

The *pecorino* we are most familiar with outside Italy is *romano*, a hard, pungent grating cheese from Rome. It is useful in some pasta sauces, but, except for pesto, it is out of place in any dish of the North.

Ricotta and mozzarella: When you get ricotta and mozzarella in the supermarket here, neither one of the products is quite like the Italian original, but they are the best we've got, and we must accept them as adequate, if not perfect, substitutes.

Ricotta is a by-product of cheese, made from the whey, a watery milk residue. Italian ricotta, when unpasteurised, has a richer, fresher, tarter taste than ours, and is less watery. English ricotta is quite acceptable for stuffings and some desserts, but it will not meet the standards for such luscious Sicilian sweets as *cannoli* and *cassata*. Cottage cheese is in no circumstances an eligible substitute for ricotta in Italian cooking.

In some Italian neighbourhoods, a runny, freshly made ricotta is sometimes available. Look for it and try it. If it is genuinely fresh, it will make perceptibly better sauces and fillings.

In the south of Italy, the best mozzarella is spun from the curd of water-buffalo milk. It is sometimes called *bufalina*, and it is a good table cheese, creamy and sweet-tasting, served as an *antipasto*. The mozzarella produced here is a rubbery, neutral-tasting factory product, whose most appropriate use is as a binding agent because of its characteristic melting qualities.

FACTORY-MADE PASTA

The best flour for the best factory-made pasta comes exclusively from selected hard, durum wheat. It produces pasta with a compact, resilent consistency that is most gratifying in the mouth, and is a perfect carrier for sauce. It goes further than other pasta, growing as much as an extra 20 per cent in bulk while cooking.

Most factory-made products are made to suit the taste of a public accustomed to soft, mushy pasta. It is more difficult to cook because at one moment it is very hard and the next it has given way and become irreparably overdone. If you are using it, watch it carefully, tasting it frequently, and stop the cooking when you think it is still slightly underdone. It will continue to soften as you drain, and later when you toss it in the bowl.

For the authentic taste of Italian *spaghetti* and macaroni dishes, try the pasta imported from Italy. On the box look for the words 'durum wheat' or, in Italian, '*pura semolina*'. One of the most reliable brands is De Cecco. Another is Agnesi, but it is less frequently found. Lay in a good stock, in different shapes and sizes of pasta; see page 386 for illustrations and definitions of the different shapes.

GARLIC

The garlic used by cooks in Italy is often fresh and tender, and always sweet. When working with garlic elsewhere, look at the cloves before you use them. If they are very dry and wrinkled, and have a dull, faded yellow colour, use a little less, because the garlic is likely to be fairly sharp. Try to buy heads of garlic that are large and full, with thick meaty cloves. Their sweetness is more long-lived. What you should avoid are those supermarket boxes with pathetic little shrivelled heads inside.

The presence of garlic in Italian cooking is much misunderstood. It can be a very gentle one; there is a place for it in almost every kind of dish, from the earthiest to the most delicate. It is all in how you use it. When, instead of being sautéed first, it cooks together with other ingredients, it is steamed in natural cooking juices, and its flavour is very understated. When it is chopped and sautéed, it is coloured lightly, and its flavour is developed only to the point where it acts as a support for the more prominent components of the dish. When it is used whole and coloured a light brown, the cloves are discarded before continued cooking, so that only an earthy but not overbearing fragrance lingers on. Garlic that is used in a crude and pungent manner is not characteristic of good Italian food.

HERBS

In Italian cooking, the use of herbs always suggests specific dishes and, like a regional accent, sometimes gives away their place of origin.

In any part of the country, the odour of rosemary immediately calls to mind meat roasting in a pan or on a spit. In Tuscany or on the Riviera it may make one think of special breads.

Sage, especially in the centre and north, perpetuates the flavours of the hunter's cuisine, invigorating the tamer resources of urban markets.

Oregano instantly evokes the generous, expansive cooking of the south. Its gentler cousin, marjoram, calls up the fragrances of garden cooking of the Riviera.

Basil is much used and should always be fresh. It is a very easy herb to grow. You can even keep a plant indoors all winter, using the leaves sparingly. But in spring and summer till the end of September it grows abundantly and can sometimes be found in greengrocers and on market stalls.

Fresh herbs make life easier for the cook. They make no difficult demands on one's judgment; they suit themselves to one's sense of proportions; there is no stiff price to pay for being a little bolder here, a little more hesitant there. You can use up to two or three sprigs of fresh rosemary per pound of meat in a roast, and rest easy about the result.

Dried herbs are less good-natured and reliable. They need to be used with care and a good nose.

Dried rosemary acquires with age an odour closer to the hayloft than the open fields. Sniff it before using it. Use a little less if it does not seem to you to smell quite as lovely as it should. If it is in good condition, chopping it a bit revives it even more. Do not stock a great deal of rosemary; buy it in whole leaves from a quality source that seems to have a rapid turnover.

While fresh sage can be one of the most charmingly fragrant of all herbs, dried sage can turn viciously pungent. Test a dried leaf by crumbling it between your fingertips and sniffing it. If it is very sharp, cut down the quantity in the recipe. Use only whole leaves, if using dried sage. Do not waste time or your good cooking with crumbled or powdered sage.

Dried oregano appears to be longer living than many other herbs. But it too can acquire a disagreeable musty odour with age. Do not buy great jars of it. Sniff it regularly. Throw it out when it no longer smells right, and buy a fresh jar from your trusty source.

The observations on oregano apply to marjoram, which is closely related to it.

Do try to buy or grow herbs, if you can. They are of incalculable value in achieving the light, natural taste of good Italian cooking.

LUGANEGA

Luganega is a mild pork sausage, stuffed into a long casing, then coiled, like a thick rope, not tied into links.

In its native version, it is made from pork shoulder, Parmesan, and a minimum of spice. It is available at some Italian delicatessens, and is the most desirable sausage to use for the recipes in this book. Otherwise, good-quality pork sausages, bratwurst, or other mild pork sausage are acceptable substitutes.

OLIVE OIL

Think of olive oil as the juice of a fruit. It should have the colour, fragrance and, above all, taste of the olive it comes from.

In those dishes in which oil is used only as cooking fat, neutral vegetable oils are not only acceptable but preferable. Where olive oil is part of the flavour of the dish, obviously the poorer the oil, the poorer will be the dish.

Unfortunately, in the great majority of olive oils on the market, most of the taste of the olive has been taken out. They are no more equivalent to the natural product than tinned fruit juice is to fresh. It is not even a question of price, since some of the costliest exported oils share the same lack of flavour.

Olive oil, once opened, does not last indefinitely. It may turn rancid. If you do not use it regularly, decant a 4-litre tin into two or more clean, dry glass bottles; any bottle will do, but the most practical ones are those from jug wines, with a handle. Do not cap the bottles, but, if you worried about dust, cover with a piece of muslin fastened to the neck with elastic. Do not risk keeping good olive oil in a plastic container, as it may alter the taste. Keep away from heat.

PANCETTA

Pancetta is bacon, but it is prepared in a manner that is very different from English or Danish bacon. It is not smoked, but is salted, lightly spiced, and rolled up tightly into a salami-like shape. It is cured meat, like prosciutto, and like prosciutto can be eaten without cooking. It makes a tasty sandwich.

The authentically Italian taste of many dishes is very difficult to achieve if you do not have pancetta. It is now much easier to find in Italian or Continental delicatessens than it used to be. But hardly any other kind of shop carries it, and not all Italian delicatessens yet do.

If you do not have a ready source for pancetta, but do manage to find some, buy a substantial quantity and freeze it. For freezing purposes, have some of it cut into thick 110 g (4 oz) slices, and part of it into thin, prosciutto-like slices. This is because some recipes call for pancetta sliced thin, others diced, others sliced thick. Wrap each lot separately, label it, and freeze. Do not keep it too long after it has thawed, or it will become rancid.

Pancetta substitutes Salt pork is too fatty to be a satisfactory substitute. Bacon has the right proportion of lean and fat, but it must be green, and green bacon is still not pancetta. One must settle for it, if one has no choice, but every other means should first be explored to obtain genuine pancetta. If you do have a grocer who carries Italian specialities, you may persuade them to order it for you. A whole pancetta weighs about 2½ kg (6 lb). You could take it all, have it cut as described above, and freeze it.

PROSCIUTTO

Prosciutto is salted and air-cured ham. The curing process makes it perfectly safe to eat as it is, without cooking.

It makes a delicious appetiser or snack, served with ripe figs or melon. The melon used in Italy is a variety of cantaloupe. It is interesting that the juiciest, sweetest cantaloupe is grown near Modena, not far from the town of Langhirano, where the finest of all prosciutto – Parma ham – is cured. Whenever I can find well-ripened, sweet cantaloupe, it is my first choice to go with prosciutto. If I cannot, honeydew melon is an agreeable substitute.

Contrary to prevalent opinion, good-quality prosciutto should not be sliced paper thin, when it becomes as insubstantial as plastic film. It should in fact be sliced by hand. Failing this, you should ask your grocer to adjust his machine a couple of notches so that it will slice the ham a little thicker than at the conventional setting. Prosciutto should be firm and chewy in the mouth.

It is also used extensively in cooking, for flavour, either diced or shredded. If it is absolutely unavailable, one can substitute cooked, unsmoked ham, if it is not too salty.

RICE

If you like the creamy density of *risotto*, with each grain of rice firm and toothy, the best way to achieve it is with stubby, thick Italian rice.

The name of the most widely exported grain variety is Arborio. Even if not available locally, Arborio is obtainable by mail from a large number of sources, both those that specialise in Italian products and the high-class food shops that exist in most major cities. At a pinch, substituting standard, plain rice does not lead to disaster.

TOMATOES

It would be such a relief to be able to say, at least once, look here, any old tomatoes will do, round or long, fresh or tinned. Alas, your tomato sauces are not likely to have that fresh, ripe tomato taste unless you use Italian San Marzano tomatoes. Fortunately, these are available, shipped by one packer or another, in many parts of the country. Do not be misled, in reading the label, by words in Italian such as *pomidori* or *pomodori pelati*. If you look at the fine print, you may discover they have been packed in South America or in Spain. Somewhere on the label it must say San Marzano, and 'imported from Italy'.

If you are trying a brand for the first time, buy only one tin. The tomatoes inside should be a deep, ripe red, firm, and whole. It shows that they are hand-picked, naturally ripened tomatoes.

When you've settled on a brand you like, it pays to buy the large tins, if you consume a lot of tomatoes. Pour what you don't use out of an opened tin into a refrigerator container, where it will keep for at least a week.

Of course, if you grow your own tomatoes, and you produce a variety chosen for flavour rather than looks, use these. See *The Classic Italian Cookbook*, pages 79–82.

VEAL

True veal is the meat from an 8- to 10-week-old so-called 'natural' calf that has never tasted grass. It is fed on a special diet of dried milk and eggs. This is fine-grained, sweet-tasting, delicate meat that only those who would eat beef steak exclusively could call bland.

It is very lean and consequently will become dry and tough if mishandled in cooking. It is most successful in sautéd dishes, where it is cooked very briefly, or in braised dishes, where it cooks very slowly in a moist environment.

The most celebrated cut of veal is *scaloppine*. The choicest *scaloppine* come from the top round, a solid tapered muscle in the hind leg. From a 70 to 90 kg (12 to 13 stone) calf one can extract just 4½ to 5½ kg (10 to 12 lb) of top round. This makes fine *scaloppine* the most expensive cut of meat you can buy. The consolation is that there is no waste. It is all beautiful lean meat, which takes to a great variety of sauces, and with 450 g (1 lb) you can serve four persons.

Do not expect to find this kind of veal everywhere. In many parts of the country you might have better luck looking for a unicorn. There is a great deal of other veal. It comes from much older calves, some of them grass-fed, others force-fed a milk diet long past their prime. It is usually a deep pink, although it can be, occasionally, as creamy in colour as the meat from natural calves. But the texture is coarser, and the taste less sweet. You can make good stews with it, pan roasts, and such things as stuffed breast of veal. But it makes less perfect chops and *scaloppine*.

WILD MUSHROOMS

Boletus edulis

If there were no other reason for leaving home in the spring or autumn and going to Italy, the wild mushrooms would be sufficient. Once you have had wild *porcini* mushrooms alone or in any dish, no other mushrooms, and no other dish with mushrooms, will taste quite the same again. Except for white truffles, there is no product of the earth with such a stirring intensity of fragrance and flavour.

Fresh wild mushrooms are not available here, except to those who know how to pick their own. But the dried ones, imported from Italy, are sold by a great number of shops, from Italian delicatessens to the food halls of major department stores. They come in little packets of 10 g (¾ oz). They are expensive, but a little goes a long way, because their flavour is highly concentrated through dehydration.

As you will find in any recipe in this book that uses them, dried mushrooms must be reconstituted by soaking in warm water for at least 30 minutes. The water is filtered and used in cooking along with the mushrooms, because there is so much of their flavour in it. Use reconstituted boletus mushrooms in sauces for pasta, and with any pan-roasted meat.

I have found that dried wild mushrooms have a magical effect when cooked with fresh, cultivated mushrooms. They act upon them like a call of the wild, drawing from them a flavour and an aroma of the woods you'd never imagine tame *champignons* could possess. To achieve this concentrated taste, one must abandon the customary rapid method of cooking *champignons*, and cook them slowly and at length, just as you would the wild mushrooms. The exact technique varies from dish to dish. It is all set out in detail in the recipes.

When buying dried wild mushrooms, make sure you are buying *Boletus edulis*, and not dried *champignons*. Since the packages are transparent, take a good look to make sure there are nice, large, meaty pieces of mushroom inside, and not a lot of dark brown crumbs. Dried boletus are exported by both Italy and France; they are equally satisfactory.

If you are going to go to Italy, one of the most precious things you can bring back is a pound or more of choice dried boletus (*porcini*). Dried boletus is admitted by customs. If you keep them in a tightly covered tin box, in a dry place, you can have several months' supply of dried mushrooms at a great saving over the small costly packets. When keeping them for a long time, it's advisable to store them in the refrigerator, always in a tightly sealed container.

Equipment

This is not the place, nor do I wish to be the one, to add to the voluminous literature on kitchen equipment. Those who want guidance on this subject should study the meticulously compiled appendix in Volume II of *Mastering the Art of French Cooking*.

I do like to work with good tools. I like solid, heat-retentive pots, such as enamelled cast iron or cast-aluminium alloys. And I like sharp knives. But I am more interested in food than I am in kitchen objects. I am very sceptical of the dream kitchen – not necessarily because of its elaborate equipment, but because of the spirit in which it has been assembled. It sometimes seems to reflect more of an interest in theatre than in the taste of cooking. Simple cooking requires simple attitudes. Some of the best food I have ever had has come from kitchens so bare that to use the word 'equipment' to describe their facilities would be an overstatement.

Good cooking is the successful exercise of the senses of touch, of time, of smell, of taste, of colour. Tools are an extension of these senses, not a substitute. All those devices that do the thinking for you, that turn themselves on or off, that slow this down or speed that up, that guarantee the same result each time, make me uneasy. Can there be cooking where there is no cook?

Now that I've delivered my homily, I had better turn to things that may be of practical help to the user of this book.

I assume that anyone interested in Italian cooking will have a pasta colander and a cheese grater. The colander with a self-supporting base is the simplest and most successful way of draining pasta. Freshly grated cheese is an ingredient without which much of Italian cooking could not exist, so a grater is nearly as indispensable as fire or water. (See page **20** for discussion of grater and grating.)

Another tool necessary to an Italian cook is a meat pounder for flattening *scaloppine*, chops, or *braciole*. The best-designed pounder is the simplest: a thick, heavy, smooth-bottomed disc of stainless steel, with a short handle rising perpendicularly from its centre. (See pages 13–14 for detailed explanation of pounding technique.)

Special tools, such as the pasta rolling-pin, the baking stone, an ice-cream freezer, are referred to in the appropriate recipe sections.

In many of the recipes I refer to a sauté pan. This is the workhorse of my kitchen. It is a broad pan with a flat bottom and low straight sides. You should have it in two or three sizes, of the heaviest, most solid construction you can afford. In it I cook everything that will fit, vegetables, fish, fricassees, tomato sauces. It will handle cooking of any speed, from a lazy simmer to deep-frying.

Another pan I find helpful, although in a more limited way, is an oval casserole made of enamelled cast iron, or other heavy material. A round pot is fine for a stew, a *risotto*, for boiling potatoes or pasta. But a roast of veal, pork, or beef has an unbending long shape. With an oval casserole, the shape of the pot fits the shape of the roast, which means there is no waste of cooking liquid – such as broth or good wine – and no waste of heat.

The proper pan for perfect *lasagne* has the following characteristics: it is made of heavy metal so that the *lasagne* do not come out scorched at the sides and bottom; the sides of the pan are not much less than 75 mm (3 inches) high so that when the pasta seethes and swells in the oven the sauce does not spill over the top; the corners are at sharp right angles because *lasagne*, which are cut straight, do not fit well into round corners.

THE FOOD PROCESSOR

There is no more fervent believer than a convert, and here I must confess my devotion to the food processor. With my scepticism about all machines, I probably never would have had one in my kitchen if James Beard hadn't asked me to contribute one or two recipes to the Magimix book he was editing. To test the recipes I had to borrow a machine, and I instantly saw the light.

I use the processor to knead dough for bread, pizza, *focaccia* (page 52), and *pasta frolla* (page 284). It is invaluable for chopping fatty substances such as *pancetta*, lard, and prosciutto, which are tricky to do by hand. It makes far better pesto than the blender, it handles all the ingredients for pasta stuffings, and it chops up everything you need for a meat sauce. It does a neater job of chopping parsley than a knife. It will shred a head of cabbage in no time. For smaller quantities of vegetables, I prefer slicing or chopping by hand. And there are two things for which I never use the processor: one is chopping onions – it forces out too much liquid, and instead of sautéing, the onions steam in their own moisture; the other is kneading dough for pasta. Some things are still done better by hand.

BREAD, PIZZA, SFINCIUNI & PASTIES

BREAD & PIZZA

The ways of making bread are infinite. Wherever I have stopped in Italy, I have talked to bakers, and for longer now than I wish to remember I have worked in my kitchen on every promising suggestion that turned up. Of all the methods I've tried, I have settled on two, one for bread, the other for pizza dough.

What I was interested in producing was a particular kind of bread, one that is firm, close-grained, and satisfyingly chewy, one whose appeal is not solely concentrated in the crust, a bread to enjoy all the way through. I grew up on such bread, but it is no longer found in large cities in Italy, only in a few small bakeries in provincial towns.

You will find three different table breads in the recipes that follow. One is my basic white bread, *pane all'olio*, the second, whole-wheat bread, *pane integrale*, and the third, golden hard-wheat bread, *pane giallo*. They use different flours, and sometimes other ingredients, such as olive oil, but the fundamental procedure remains the same.

The dough goes through two risings. For the first rising, half the flour is mixed with all the yeast and the water in which it is dissolved. The rising is complete when the dough has doubled in bulk. It usually takes about 3 hours in a moderately warm environment, between 23° and 27°C (75° and 80°F). This first batch of dough is called the 'sponge', because as the yeast goes to work on it, it begins to resemble the loose, open structure of a sponge. It also performs a spongelike action, in absorbing the flour and any other ingredients that will be added later.

At the end of the first rising, the rest of the flour and whatever else is to go into the bread are kneaded into the mass of dough. It is allowed to rise again until it has once more doubled in bulk. Depending on the temperature, it will take about 3 hours.

The same basic method is used to produce all the *focacce* – the flavoured snack breads – in this section.

The other basic yeast dough I have developed is the one used for pizza and *sfinciuni*. All the ingredients are kneaded together, and the dough needs but one rising, until it has doubled in bulk.

The rising should be fairly rapid, in a well-protected, warm environment, such as inside an unlit gas oven, where the pilot keeps the temperature at around 32° to 38°C (90° to 100°F). Of course, it can rise at a slower pace, but the speed at which the dough develops contributes to the compact and resilient consistency that is characteristic of good pizza dough.

For pizza and *sfinciuni* I use hard-wheat flour exclusively. You will find that this is quite different from the spongy, corner-pizza-shop product. Of all home-made pizzas, it comes as close as the limitations of a gas or electric oven allow to authentic Neapolitan pizza.

Flour Wherever white flour is required, I use unbleached flour.

For whole-wheat bread – *pane integrale* – I have been using a fine-textured stone-ground flour. Mixed with unbleached flour (see the recipe for proportions), it produces bread very close to *pane integrale*. Some whole-wheat flours are very coarsely ground and may even contain bits of bran or kernels. Avoid them. They will not work well in these recipes, and do not, in any event, make bread that has an Italian character.

For beautiful golden bread and for pizza I use only hard-wheat (durum) flour. This is not available in supermarkets, at least not yet, but it can be purchased in many health-food shops, in Italian groceries, and in some of those shops, now beginning to proliferate, where they sell fresh pasta.

Yeast These recipes have been tested with both fresh yeast and packaged active dry yeast, and they will work with either one. I prefer the fresh yeast. It seems to me to produce a warmer-tasting, less sour bread. This is wholly subjective, of course. I have not conducted, nor do I ever intend to conduct, large-scale tests to substantiate or disprove it. Fresh yeast works well for me, and I am satisfied with that. I am definitely convinced that an overdose of dry yeast taints the flavour of home-made bread. In my opinion, the conventionally accepted equivalent of 1 packet of dry yeast to 15 g ($\frac{1}{2}$ oz) fresh yeast is excessive. I have made all the breads and pizzas in this section using exactly half the amount of dry yeast, with completely satisfactory results.

Kneading Good kneading leads to good bread. It thoroughly integrates the flour with the water and yeast; it gets all the molecules moving together into a structure well able to support the upheaval and radical expansion to which it will be subjected.

If you are kneading a dough with up to 250 g or 400 g ($10\frac{1}{2}$ oz or 14 oz) of flour by hand – and it can be a most satisfying thing to do – it will take from 8 to 10 minutes to do a proper job. This is not as brief a span of time as you may think. If you do not have an accurate sense of time, or have not yet acquired a natural rhythm and feel for well-kneaded dough, go by the clock, at first.

The food processor takes all the time and problems out of kneading. It does a thorough job of it, producing moist, elastic, well-integrated dough in just a few seconds' whirring of its powerful steel blades. When the dough forms in one or more balls on top of the blades, it is done. Another minute or so of amalgamating it by hand afterwards does not do any harm.

I have never possessed, and consequently never tried, a heavy-duty mixer with a dough-hook attachment. I have it on the most reliable authority that it does an excellent job of kneading, so if you have one, by all means use it.

The baking stone or tiles for the oven A baking stone or quarry tiles transform a home oven into something very like a baker's brick oven.

Quarry tiles are unglazed reddish tiles such as one may still see on the floors of country kitchens. Four 150-mm (6-inch) square tiles will line the larger part of a standard oven rack. They are inexpensive and easily obtained. Look for a tile supplier in your telephone book.

Even better than tiles, and much closer to the heat-retentive qualities of a baker's oven brick surface, is a baking stone. It is a single slab of heavy, refractory material available in rectangular as well as round shapes. For bread, the rectangular shape is the most practical, while the round is made to order for pizza. I am much indebted to Julia Child for bringing the baking stone to my attention, just as I was beginning to develop the bread and pizza recipes for this book.

Baking stones are not commonly available, and they cost quite a bit more than quarry tiles, but if you are lucky enough to track one down, it is well worth the difference.

Both baking stones and tiles must be in place when the oven is turned on, and preheated at least 30 minutes in advance.

Variables in bread making One of the least-standardised items in general commerce in this country is flour. Even flour bearing the same nationally distributed brand may vary from one section of the country to the other, depending on the location of the plant where the flour is produced. This affects the flour's capacity to absorb liquids. So does the moisture or heat of the kitchen. Although these recipes have been tested to admit substantial latitude in the variables linked to flour or environment, use your own judgment when adding liquid. Your hands will tell you if the dough is too dry and needs more liquid, or too runny and needs more flour.

Rising times are also difficult to predict exactly. They vary according to temperature, humidity, and the yeast's appetite. Do not go by the time so much as by the increase in bulk. Provide yourself with a large bowl that can contain the sponge four or five times over, and you needn't worry about leaving the dough in the bowl once it has reached the desired volume. If you are not quite ready to use it, it will wait for you, a half hour, one hour, two hours. It makes little difference; it has nowhere else to go.

Ovens are another variable. They may be mass produced, but each one has its quirks. I have a sturdy oven of unimpeachable make, which I regulate not by the thermostat alone but with readings taken from a very accurate mercury thermometer. Nevertheless, although I always work with constant temperatures, I always get a slightly different loaf of bread from the right side of the oven than I do from the left.

If your bread is not rising fast enough when you first put it in, next time start at a slightly higher temperature than the recipe calls for. If you find at the end the crust is not the rich gold colour you expected, leave it in a little longer. An oven is an instrument, and like any instrument it possesses character. To get it to work well for you, you must adjust time and temperature to suit its temperament.

Pane all' olio

ITALIAN OLIVE-OIL BREAD

This is my favourite everyday bread. It is smooth and tasty, with a fine texture and a sturdy consistency it is a pleasure to sink one's teeth into. It used to be a very common bread in northern Italy, particularly in some parts of Emilia. The plump, oblong loaves were called *mantovane*, after Mantua. Today people seem to prefer cotton wadding to real bread, and the only ones still making bread of this type are local bakers in a few small towns.

Makes 2 small loaves

30 g (1 oz) fresh yeast or packet active dry yeast
225 ml (scant $\frac{1}{2}$ pint) lukewarm water
About 400 g (14 oz) plain flour
2 teaspoons salt
1 tablespoon olive oil
Unglazed quarry tiles or a baking stone, placed on the uppermost rack of the oven

1 Dissolve the yeast completely in 8 tablespoons of lukewarm water.

2 Pour 200 g (7 oz) flour onto a work surface, and shape it into a mound, making a shallow hollow in the centre. Pour the dissolved yeast into the hollow, draw the sides of the mound together, and knead steadily for about 10 minutes. Shape the kneaded dough into a ball. Or use the food processor (see below).

3 Choose an ample bowl, and lightly dust the inside with flour. Put the dough into the bowl. Wring out a wet tea-towel, fold it in two, and cover the bowl with it.

4 Place the bowl in a warm, draught-free place. I put mine on top of the refrigerator, where the temperature stays between 23° and 27°C (75° and 80°F). Let it rest for 3 hours or more, until the dough has approximately doubled in bulk. It should be well pocked with air bubbles.

5 Pour the remaining 200 g (7 oz) flour onto the work surface. Place the ball of dough on the flour, punching it down, flattening it, and opening it with your hands. Pour the remaining 8 tablespoons of lukewarm water over it, add the salt, and olive oil. Knead steadily, thoroughly integrating the newly added ingredients with the leavened dough, for 8 to 10 minutes. Or use the food processor (see below). Shape the mass into a ball.

6 Return the dough to the floured bowl, covering it with a damp towel; let it rest in the same warm corner until it has doubled in bulk again, about 3 hours.

7 At least 30 minutes before you are ready to bake, turn on the oven, with the tiles or baking stone in it, to 230°/450°F/Mark 7 to 8.

8 After the second rising, knead the dough by hand for a few seconds and place it on a floured paddle, sheet of cardboard, or piece of plywood. Make sure it is well floured so the dough can slip off easily when you put it into the oven. Divide the dough in half, and shape each half into a thick, cigar-shaped roll, plump at the middle, slightly tapered at the ends, and about 175 to 200 mm (7 to 8 inches) long.

9 Allow the dough to rest a few minutes. When the surface has dried slightly, make a single lengthwise slash along the top of each roll with a knife, going about 25 mm (1 inch) deep. Brush the surface of the rolls with a pastry brush lightly moistened with water.

10 Slide the dough from the paddle or cardboard onto the hot tiles or baking stone. Bake for 12 minutes at 230°/450°F/Mark 7 to 8, then turn the thermostat down to 190°C/375°F/Mark 5 and bake for 45 minutes more. Remove bread to a cooling rack, and allow it to cool completely, a minimum of 2 hours, before using it.

Note Both the first and second kneadings can be done with the food processor (see comment on page 32). Use the steel blades, and run the processor until one or more balls of dough form on the blades. On both occasions, pour in the liquid slowly, after the flour.

Pane integrale

ITALIAN WHOLE-WHEAT BREAD

In those Italian neighbourhoods in this country where good bread is found, one of the most popular is *pane integrale*. It is a gutsier, more substantial bread than the usual Italian loaf, but it is lighter and paler than most other ethnic whole-wheat breads. In *pane integrale* the proportions of whole-wheat flour to white are 1 part to 2. The bread in this recipe looks and turns out well when it is shaped into a single round loaf.

Follow all the directions given in the recipe for *pane all'olio*, page 33, using the same ingredients listed there except for the following quantities of flour:

Makes one 20- to 22-cm (8- to 9-inch) round loaf

130 g ($4\frac{1}{2}$ oz) stone-ground fine whole-wheat flour that does not contain coarse bits of bran or kernel

About 260 g ($8\frac{1}{2}$ oz) unbleached flour

After the second rising, when you've placed the dough on a floured paddle or board of some kind, shape it into a slightly domed, round loaf. When its surface has caked a little, cut a shallow cross in the centre. Brush the surface with a lightly moistened pastry brush. Bake as directed in the basic recipe, page 33.

Pane giallo di grano duro

HARD-WHEAT BREAD

James Beard, in his invaluable *Beard on Bread* (Knopf, 1973), says hard-wheat flour is 'the choicest for making bread'. It certainly makes a beautiful bread, golden bright and with a firm, fine-grained texture. It is so good when you toast it you can munch on it as you would on biscuits. It is the same hard wheat, incidentally, from which flour is ground for the finest Italian-made spaghetti and macaroni.

I like to make this bread in a ring shape, which yields a greater proportion of crust.

Hard-wheat – or durum-wheat – flour is easier to obtain than it used to be, although I have yet to find it in supermarkets. Many delicatessens, grocers and health food shops carry it.

Makes 1 ring-shaped loaf

About 400 g (14 oz) hard-wheat flour
30 g (1 oz) fresh yeast or 1 packet active dry yeast, dissolved in 16 tablespoons lukewarm water
$1\frac{1}{2}$ teaspoons salt
1 tablespoon olive oil
A baking stone or quarry tiles placed on the uppermost rack of the oven

1 Follow all the directions for making *pane all'olio*, page 33.

2 At least 30 minutes before you are ready to bake, turn on the oven, with the tiles or baking stone in it, to 230°C/450°F/Mark 7 to 8.

3 After the second rising, place the dough on a floured paddle or sheet of cardboard or plywood. Shape it into a doughnut-like large ring, with a hole about 90 mm ($3\frac{1}{2}$ inches) in diameter. Make a series of small diagonal cuts all around the upper side of the ring. Brush the dough with a pastry brush moistened in water.

4 Slide the ring onto the hot stone or tiles.

5 After 10 minutes, turn the thermostat down to 190°C/375°F/Mark 5. Bake for 40 minutes more. Remove to a cooling rack. Allow to cool completely – at least 2 hours – before using.

Note See page 32, for note on the use of the food processor.

Focaccia

FLAT BREAD

The thin, flat, crusty bread Italians call *focaccia* is a direct descendant of the earliest kind of bread. Its name comes from the Latin *focus*, which means 'hearth', and therein is its story. Long before anyone had invented the oven, bread was made by flattening out some dough upon a stone or terracotta slab, and cooking it on the hearth, under a cover of hot ashes. When done, the ashes were brushed off, and the hearth bread – *panis focacius* – was turned over.

Some varieties of *focaccia* are still made on heated stone griddles (see *piadina*, page 325), but usually it is produced exactly like bread. It is leavened, goes through one or two risings, and is baked in an oven.

There are many delicious versions of *focaccia*. The simplest, and one of the most satisfying, is studded with coarse salt. Sometimes it may contain bits of bacon, crackling, or sausage meat; it can be topped with onions or scented with rosemary or sage.

Focaccia is most enjoyable on its own, as a snack. It has been the delight and mid-morning sustenance for millions of Italian schoolchildren. I remember, when I was a young girl, stopping every morning on the way to school to buy a square of just-turned-out, warm *focaccia*, which the baker's wife would hand to me loosely wrapped in a piece of brown paper. I stowed it in my satchel, and at recess, light-headed from my meagre Italian breakfast, I devoured it in quick, large bites. How good it was, marvellously chewy and crackling with salt.

You can also serve *focaccia* at table as bread, or as an appetiser. It is ideal for picnics. If you let it rise slowly overnight, in a cool place, you can bake it for breakfast or brunch, and have it while it is still piping hot and at its best.

Focaccia con le cipolle

FLAT BREAD WITH ONION TOPPING

Makes one 350-mm (14-inch) round focaccia

About 400 g (14 oz) plain flour
30 g (1 oz) fresh yeast or 1 packet active dry yeast, dissolved in 8 tablespoons lukewarm water
7 tablespoons olive oil
4 tablespoons water
2 teaspoons table salt
1 medium onion, sliced very thin
Coarse sea salt or kosher salt
A baking stone or enough quarry tiles to line the oven rack

1 Knead 200 g (7 oz) flour and all the dissolved yeast for 8 to 10 minutes. Shape the kneaded dough into a ball.

2 Lightly dust the inside of a bowl with flour, and put the dough into the bowl. Wring out a wet tea-towel until it is just damp, fold it in two, and cover the bowl with it. Place the dough in a moderately warm (23° to 27°C/75° to 80°F) and draught-free corner of the kitchen, and let it rise for about 3 hours, until it has doubled in bulk.

3 Place the ball of dough on a work surface and knead it with the remaining 200 g (7 oz) flour, plus 4 tablespoons olive oil, 4 tablespoons water, and 2 teaspoons table salt. Knead it thoroughly for at least 8 minutes, until the newly added flour has been completely incorporated, and the ball of dough is smooth and elastic.

4 Place it again in a lightly floured bowl, cover with a dampened tea-towel, and let it rise in the same warm, cozy corner as before for another 3 hours, or until it has doubled in bulk.

5 Place the baking stone or tiles in the oven, on the uppermost rack, and at least 30 minutes before you are ready to bake turn on the oven to a 200°C/400°F/Mark 6 setting.

6 While the oven is warming up, soak the sliced onion in two or three changes of cold water, then drain and pat dry thoroughly in kitchen paper.

7 Place the dough on a floured paddle or sheet of cardboard, and roll it out into a disc about 350 mm (14 inches) in diameter. It should be around 7 mm ($\frac{1}{4}$ inch) thick. If you like your *focaccia* thicker and chewier, roll it out into a slightly smaller disc.

8 Roughen the surface of the dough by poking it here and there with your fingertips. Spread the onions over it pressing them lightly into the dough. Pour the remaining 3 tablespoons olive oil over the onions. Sprinkle with a very little coarse salt, and slide the *focaccia* from the paddle onto the preheated baking stone or tiles.

9 Bake for 15 minutes if it is no more than 6 mm ($\frac{1}{4}$ inch) thick. If you've rolled it out a bit thicker, cook for 5 to 10 minutes longer. Serve while still warm, if possible. If you must serve it cold, keep it at room temperature – do not refrigerate.

Note The kneading in steps 1 and 3 can be done in the food processor, and the dough worked over briefly by hand afterwards.

Focaccia col sale

PLAIN FLAT BREAD WITH SALT

Use all the ingredients in the preceding recipe for onion *focaccia*, with the following exceptions: omit the onions, and reduce the olive oil to 5 tablespoons. Use 1 tablespoon coarse salt, preferably sea salt.

Makes one 270-mm (11-inch) round focaccia

1 Knead 200 g (7 oz) flour and all the dissolved yeast for 8 to 10 minutes. Shape the dough into a ball, put it in a lightly floured bowl, cover with a damp cloth, and let it rise for about 3 hours, until it has doubled in bulk.

2 Knead the dough again, adding the remaining 200 g (7 oz) flour, 4 tablespoons olive oil, 4 tablespoons water, and 2 teaspoons table salt. Knead it thoroughly until all the added ingredients have been smoothly incorporated into the dough. If kneading by hand, it should take at least 8 minutes. However, both the first and second time, the kneading can be done in the food processor, and, if desired, finished briefly by hand.

3 Place the dough in the floured bowl again, cover with a damp cloth, and let it rise for about 3 hours more, or until doubled in bulk.

4 Place the baking stone or tiles in the oven, on the uppermost rack, and turn on the oven to 200°C/400°F/Mark 6 at least 30 minutes before you are ready to bake the *focaccia*.

5 Place the dough on a floured paddle or sheet of cardboard, and roll it out into a disc about 270 to 300 mm (11 to 12 inches) in diameter. It should be at least 12 mm ($\frac{1}{2}$ inch) thick. Dimple the surface, poking it here and there with your fingertips. Sprinkle the tablespoon of coarse salt over it, then the remaining tablespoon of olive oil.

6 Slide the *focaccia* from the paddle onto the preheated stone or tiles, and bake for 20 to 22 minutes, until it becomes coloured a rich gold. It is best served while still warm, but it is also quite good at room temperature. Refrigeration is not recommended.

Focaccia con la salvia

FLAT BREAD WITH SAGE

This is one of the most delicious and fragrant of all *focacce*. It is a great favourite on the Italian Riviera. It mixes well with the herb-scented cuisine of the Genoese coast, where, not infrequently, it is served at table as bread.

It would be ideal to use only fresh sage here, but if it is not available, you can make do with dried whole leaves, preferably the ones sold attached to their branches.

Use all the ingredients in the recipe for onion *focaccia*, page 38, with the following exceptions: omit the onions, and reduce the olive oil to 5 tablespoons. Add 2 teaspoons dried whole sage leaves, crumbled, or 10 to 12 sage leaves, cut up.

Makes one 270-mm (11-inch) round focaccia

1 Kneed 200 g (7 oz) flour and all the dissolved yeast for 8 to 10 minutes. Shape the dough into a ball, put it in a lightly floured bowl, cover with a damp cloth, and let it rise for about 3 hours, until it has doubled in bulk.

2 Knead the dough again, adding the remaining 200 g (7 oz) of flour, 4 tablespoons olive oil, 4 tablespoons water, 2 teaspoons table salt, and the sage. Make sure the sage is evenly distributed, not all bunched up in one spot. Knead thoroughly until all the newly added ingredients have been smoothly incorporated into the dough. If kneading by hand, it should take at least 8 minutes. Only the first kneading can be done in the food processor; the second, with the sage leaves, must be done by hand, otherwise the sage would become minced too fine. (This applies to the rosemary *focaccia* below, as well.)

3 Place the dough in the floured bowl again, cover with a damp cloth, and let it rise for 3 hours more, or until doubled in bulk.

4 Place the baking stone or tiles in the oven, on the uppermost rack, and turn on the oven to 200°C/400°F/Mark 6 at least 30 minutes before you are ready to bake the *focaccia*.

5 Place the dough on a floured paddle or sheet of cardboard, and roll it out to a thickness of 12 mm (½ inch), a circular sheet about 270 to 300 mm (11 to 12 inches) in diameter. Dimple the surface here and there with your fingertips, and trickle the remaining tablespoon of olive oil over it.

6 Slide the *focaccia* from the paddle onto the preheated stone or tiles, and bake for about 25 minutes, until it become coloured a rich gold. Transfer to a cooling rack, and serve lukewarm or at room temperature.

Focaccia al rosmarino

FLAT BREAD WITH ROSEMARY

Here is another lovely herb-flavoured *focaccia* that is delicious both as a snack and as a tasty country bread for the table. To make it, follow all the instructions for *focaccia* with sage (see preceding recipe), except that for the sage you will substitute 2 teaspoons dried rosemary leaves or 1½ teaspoons fresh rosemary, cut up.

Focaccia coi ciccioli

FLAT BACON BREAD

Ciccioli are cracklings or scratchings, the delicious crisp, brown residue of rendered pork fat. If they are not available, substitute, as I have here, crumbled well-browned bacon.

The dough for this *focaccia* is identical to that of *pane all'olio*. After the second rising, *ciccioli* and coarse salt are mixed into it.

Makes 1 focaccia

All the ingredients for *pane all'olio*, page 33, *reduced by half*
6 slices streaky green bacon
½ tablespoon kosher salt or coarse sea salt

1 Prepare the dough as for Italian Olive-Oil Bread, following the recipe on page 33, reducing all ingredients by half. Bring the dough to a complete second rising.

2 Place the baking stone or quarry tiles on the uppermost rack of the oven, and turn the thermostat to 230°C/450°F/Mark 7 to 8. The stone or tiles must warm up at least ½ hour before they are ready for baking.

3 Fry the bacon over medium heat, until it is very crisp. Transfer to kitchen paper to drain, and allow to cool completely.

4 When the bacon is cold, crumble it fine with your fingers.

5 Open up the dough on your work surface, and put in it the crumbled bacon and the salt. Close up the dough, and knead it until the bacon crumbs have been uniformly distributed.

6 Roll out the dough in either a square or round shape to a thickness of 12 mm (½ inch). Place it on a floured paddle or cardboard, and slide it onto the preheated baking stone or tiles.

7 Bake for 15 minutes, then turn the heat down to 190°C/375°F/Mark 5. Bake for an additional 10 to 15 minutes. The *focaccia* should nearly double in thickness, and become a light gold colour.

La crescentina bolognese

BOLOGNESE FLAT BREAD WITH BACON

This recipe for Bologna's traditional flat bread was given to me by Armando Simili, who operated, until his retirement, that city's most illustrious and popular bakery. Here, as in so many instances, the dough from the first rising is used as a 'sponge', that is, fresh flour is added to it. What is special about this recipe is that the dough is recharged with a new and larger dose of yeast. It is a method that produces a rich and finely textured bread. Studded with *pancetta*, it makes a substantial snack all by itself, but in Bologna it is often sliced in half and stuffed with tender *mortadella* or sweet Parma prosciutto.

The total rising time, in temperatures above 20°C/70°F, is approximately 5 hours.

20 g ($\frac{3}{4}$ oz) fresh yeast or $\frac{3}{4}$ packet dry yeast (about $1\frac{1}{2}$ teaspoons)
12 tablespoons lukewarm water
280 g (9 oz) plain flour
Unglazed quarry tiles or a baking stone, placed on the uppermost rack of the oven
110 g (4 oz) *pancetta* or green bacon, chopped fine
15 g ($\frac{1}{2}$ oz) lard
1 tablespoon olive oil
2 teaspoons salt

1 Dissolve 7 g ($\frac{1}{4}$ oz) fresh yeast or $\frac{1}{4}$ packet dry yeast in 4 tablespoons lukewarm water.

2 Pour 100 g ($3\frac{1}{2}$ oz) flour onto the work surface. Make a mound and form a hollow in the centre. Put the dissolved yeast in the hollow, and mix it thoroughly with the flour. Knead the dough for 10 minutes.

3 Dust the inside of a bowl with flour, put in the kneaded dough, and cover with a damp cloth. Set in a warm place and let it rise for 3 hours, or until doubled in bulk.

4 Dissolve 15 g ($\frac{1}{2}$ oz) fresh yeast or $\frac{1}{2}$ packet dry yeast in 8 tablespoons lukewarm water.

5 Pour the remaining flour onto the work surface, forming a mound. Make a hollow in the centre of the mound and put in the dissolved yeast, the chopped *pancetta* or bacon, the lard, olive oil, and salt. Mix all ingredients thoroughly with the flour.

6 Make a ring with the second mixture, and put into it the dough from the first rising. Close the ring, kneading it into the dough. Knead for 10 minutes, then put the dough into the bowl, and cover with a freshly dampened cloth. Set in the same warm place and allow to rise for 2 hours, or until doubled in bulk.

7 Place the baking stone or tiles in the oven and turn on the oven to 200°C/400°F/Mark 6 at least 30 minutes before you are ready to bake.

8 Roll out the dough to a thickness of just under 12 mm ($\frac{1}{2}$ inch). Give it a round or square shape, as you prefer. Place it on a floured board or paddle, and slip it from the board onto the baking stone or tiles in the preheated oven. Bake for 25 minutes. Transfer to a cooling rack when done. *Crescentina* may be eaten warm or cold.

Pizza

There exist a few things that are absolutely perfect, some of which Nature has bestowed on man, and others that man has produced all by himself. There is no way to improve the shape and function of the egg. Nor upon the taste of genuine Neapolitan pizza.

Neapolitan pizza is quite different from what is produced in the pizza shops that have become such a familiar part of English street life. It is different in the way it is baked, in the consistency and taste of the dough, in the flavour of the tomato topping.

Classic Neapolitan pizza is never baked in a pan. It must be cooked on a hot brick or stone surface. A pan traps the pizza in the oil with which it has been seasoned, and gives it a greasy, fried taste, rather than a crisp, clean, baked one.

The dough should be elastic, but not rubbery. Tender, but not spongy. It should have a faintly sour, yeasty taste. When cooked, it should be crisp on the outside and firm throughout. Except for the raised edges, pizza should never exceed a thickness of 9 mm ($\frac{3}{8}$ inch).

The tomatoes for the topping are simply tomatoes, not a sweetish sauce. Ideally, they should be plum tomatoes, and so fully and perfectly ripened that they can go into the oven raw, with no preliminary cooking. In practice, this rarely works out, unless you grow your own. Virtually all tomatoes available in shops and markets are so watery that they must be scalded with a little olive oil before they can go on the pizza.

When you cannot find acceptable fresh tomatoes, you can substitute tinned tomatoes, provided they are high-quality, imported Italian tomatoes of the San Marzano variety (see page 25).

PIZZA DOUGH

Makes one 250- to 275-mm (10- to 11-inch) pizza

200 g (7 oz) plain flour
1 teaspoon salt
1 tablespoon olive oil
15 g ($\frac{1}{2}$ oz) fresh yeast or $\frac{1}{2}$ packet dry yeast, dissolved in 8 tablespoons lukewarm water

Hand method

1 Pour the flour onto a work surface, shape it into a mound, and make a shallow hollow in the centre.

2 Put the salt, dissolved yeast, and olive oil in the hollow, and draw the sides of the mound together, combining the flour with all the other ingredients. Work with your hands until all the ingredients are amalgamated and form a ball of dough. Then knead for about 8 minutes.

Food-processor method

1 With metal blades inserted, put the flour and salt into the beaker. Start the processor, then slowly add the dissolved yeast and the olive oil. Continue processing until dough forms on the blades, either in a single ball or 2 or 3 smaller ones.

2 Remove the dough from the beaker, and knead it by hand for about 5 minutes.

The rising

Pizza dough goes through a single, fairly rapid rising; it doubles in volume in about 3 hours. The dough has a firm, yet elastic consistency, and faintly yeasty taste.

Put the kneaded dough in a lightly floured bowl. Wring out a wet tea-towel until it is just damp, fold it in two, and cover the bowl with it. Place the bowl in a warm, protected place, such as an unlit oven with a gas pilot.

It is ready to use when it has doubled in volume, in 3 hours or so. However, if you are not prepared then to bake the pizza, no harm will be done if you leave the dough in the bowl an extra hour or two.

Pizza margherita

PIZZA WITH TOMATOES, MOZZARELLA, OLIVE OIL, PARMESAN

The components of *pizza margherita* are tomatoes, mozzarella, olive oil and Parmesan cheese. In my recipe there is also oregano, because that is how my family likes it, but it is optional. This is probably the most universally popular of all toppings, but it is a fairly recent one, created late in the last century in honour of a pizza-loving queen of Italy named Margherita. The general procedure described here for assembling and baking pizza remains the same, no matter what ingredients you choose to put into your topping.

Makes one 250- to 275-mm (10- to 11-inch) pizza

Preparing the tomatoes

The best tomato flavour for pizza comes from fresh plum tomatoes. If they are true vine-ripened tomatoes, they can go into the topping raw. Just peel them, seed them, drain them, and cut them into strips. Unless the tomatoes come from your own garden, or from an exceptionally fortunate source of supply, it is necessary to scald them, as directed below.

450 g (1 lb) fresh ripe plum tomatoes
2 tablespoons olive oil
1 teaspoon salt

A food mill, fitted with the disc with smallest holes

1 Rinse the tomatoes in cold water, drain well, and cut them up into 4 or 5 pieces.

2 Put the cut-up tomatoes in a medium sauté pan, with the olive oil and salt. Cover, and turn on the heat to medium.

3 After 2 or 3 minutes, when the tomatoes have softened a bit, uncover the pan, and cook for 6 to 7 minutes more, stirring frequently.

4 Place the tomatoes in the food mill, but do not strain them just yet. Set the food mill over a bowl, and let any liquid from the tomatoes drip into the bowl for 5 minutes. Then discard the liquid, and strain the tomatoes into the bowl. Set aside to cool.

Note If you cannot find good, fresh plum tomatoes, use high-quality imported tinned Italian tomatoes. Substitute 350 g (12 oz) chopped, seeded, thoroughly drained tinned tomatoes for 1 pound fresh ones, and cook them as described above.

Preparing the mozzarella

The mozzarella available in Naples is made from buffalo's milk (a water buffalo, not the American bison), and it is wonderfully creamy. It melts beautifully when cooked, and it is tastier than cow's milk mozzarella. Much of the mozzarella available outside Italy is tougher, stringier when cooked and just about completely tasteless. In order to achieve results similar to those one gets with Neapolitan mozzarella, I have devised a treatment for it which is described below.

180 g (6 oz) whole-milk mozzarella
3 tablespoons olive oil

1 Grate the mozzarella on the large holes of a grater, or in the food processor, using the shredding disc.

2 Put the grated mozzarella into a bowl. Add the olive oil. Mix thoroughly, and steep for at least 1 hour before using.

You will find that in this recipe I have reversed the conventional order in which the topping is placed on the dough. The mozzarella is blanketed by the tomato, instead of the other way round. Again, this is to compensate for the plastic quality of factory mozzarella, and to keep it as creamy and as little rubbery as possible.

Assembling and baking the pizza

A baking stone or enough quarry tiles to line a rack of the oven
The pizza dough from page 44
180 g (6 oz) mozzarella, prepared as described above
450 g (1 lb) fresh ripe plum tomatoes, seeded, drained, and cut into strips or 350 g (12 oz) seeded and drained tinned Italian plum tomatoes, prepared as described on page 46
Salt
1 teaspoon oregano (optional)
1 tablespoon freshly grated Parmesan cheese

1 Place the baking stone or quarry tiles on the uppermost rack of the oven, and turn the thermostat to 235°C/450°F/Mark 8 at least 30 minutes before the pizza is ready for baking.

2 Roll out the pizza dough into a disc about 250 to 275 mm (10 to 11 inches) in diameter, which should work out to a thickness of around 6 mm ($\frac{1}{4}$ inch). Turn the dough over from time to time as you roll it out. This will keep it from shrinking back. Try not to roll past the edges. As you reach the desired diameter, use your fingertips to push some of the dough from the centre of the disc toward the edge, making the edges at least twice as thick as the rest of the disc.

3 Place the dough on a lightly floured wooden paddle or sheet of cardboard.

4 Spread the mozzarella evenly on the pizza dough. Then do the same with the tomatoes. Sprinkle with 2 or 3 pinches of salt, the oregano, and the Parmesan cheese.

5 Slide the pizza from the paddle onto the hot stone or tiles. Bake for 15 to 20 minutes, until the dough on the rim of the pizza has become coloured a rich gold with a few brown specks.

Note Do not cover the pizza with its topping until you are just ready to bake it, or the dough will become soggy. Remember that the stone or tiles must be heated for at least 30 minutes before they are ready to take the pizza.

Pizza alla marinara

PIZZA WITH GARLIC, TOMATOES, AND OLIVE OIL

There is no mozzarella in this most traditional of Neapolitan pizzas. At its best, with good tomatoes and fresh, sweet garlic, it has no rivals.

Makes one 250- to 275-mm (10- to 11-inch) pizza

The topping

680 g ($1\frac{1}{2}$ lb) fresh plum tomatoes or 450 g (1 lb) tinned Italian plum tomatoes, cut up, seeded, and thoroughly drained
5 tablespoons olive oil
Salt
4 medium cloves garlic, peeled and sliced very thin
2 teaspoons oregano

The pizza dough produced with the recipe on page 44
A baking stone or enough quarry tiles to line a rack of the oven

1 Prepare and cook the tomatoes with 3 tablespoons olive oil, as directed on page 46.

2 Preheat the baking stone or tiles in a 235°C/450°F/Mark 8 oven for at least 30 minutes.

3 Roll out the pizza dough as directed in the recipe on page 47 and place on a wooden paddle or sheet of cardboard. Top with the tomatoes, a sprinkling of salt, the garlic and oregano, and 2 tablespoons olive oil, spread evenly in a thin stream.

4 Slide the pizza onto the hot stone or tiles and bake for 15 to 20 minutes in the preheated oven, until the rim of the pizza forms a deep golden crust.

Pizza bianca alla romana

PIZZA WITH MOZZARELLA AND ANCHOVIES

Pizza can be made without tomatoes. In Naples it is called a *pizza bianca*. When anchovies are added, it is *pizza bianca alla romana*. Outside Naples, if you want pizza with anchovies, ask for *pizza alla napoletana*.

Makes one 250- to 275-mm (10- to 11-inch) pizza

The topping

350 g (12 oz) whole-milk mozzarella
5 tablespoons olive oil
4 flat anchovy fillets, cut up
60 g (2 oz) fresh basil leaves, torn into 2 or 3 small pieces
Salt
1 tablespoon freshly grated Parmesan cheese

The pizza dough produced with the recipe on page 44
A baking stone or enough quarry tiles to line a rack of the oven

1 Preheat the baking stone or tiles in a 235°C/450°F/Mark 8 oven for at least 30 minutes.

2 Grate the mozzarella as directed on page 47, and steep it for at least 1 hour in a bowl with 4 tablespoons olive oil.

3 Roll out the pizza dough as directed on page 47, and place on a floured wooden paddle or sheet of cardboard.

4 Mix the chopped anchovies with the mozzarella. Spread the mixture on the pizza. Sprinkle with the cut-up basil and grated Parmesan cheese. Taste the topping before adding what salt may be required. Pour 1 tablespoon oil on in a thin stream, spreading evenly over the topping.

5 Slide the pizza onto the hot stone or tiles and bake for 15 to 20 minutes in the preheated oven, until the rim of the pizza forms a deep golden crust.

Sfinciuni

STUFFED PIZZA, PALERMO STYLE

What pizza is to Naples, *sfinciuni* is to Palermo. Unlike pizza, *sfinciuni* is made of two layers of dough which completely enclose the stuffing, called *conza*. There are many different stuffings used, the most celebrated being one with meat created by the nuns of the monastery of San Vito. You will find the nuns' recipe here, along with the two other delectable stuffings, one with tomatoes, onions, and anchovies, and another with broccoli and ricotta.

I am indebted for these to my good friend Professor Tommaso D'Alba of Palermo, one of those rare scholars of cooking whose practical achievements in the kitchen are equal to their erudition. I have slightly adapted the original recipes to make use of ingredients, particularly the cheeses, more commonly available here.

The dough for *sfinciuni* is identical to that for pizza, except that it is rolled out very much thinner.

In each case makes 1 round sfinciuni about 250 to 275 mm (10 to 12 inches) in diameter

Sfinciuni di San Vito

SFINCIUNI WITH MEAT AND CHEESE STUFFING

The meat-and-cheese-stuffed *sfinciuni* of the nuns of San Vito recall somewhat the meat-filled *beorek* of Middle Eastern cooking. Not a surprising kinship, when one takes into account the unerasable marks that Arab domination has left upon Sicily's culture.

Substitutions have had to be made for the cheeses of the original version – Palermo's wonderful *primo sale* and fresh *caciocavallo*. I have used a combination of fontina and ricotta to achieve a similar balance of freshness and savouriness. I think it works, but there is no reason why you should not experiment with combinations of your own devising, if you have other ideas.

The stuffing

3 tablespoons olive oil for the stuffing, plus 1 additional tablespoon later for the *sfinciuni*
1 medium onion, sliced very thin
220 g (8 oz) ground lean beef
Salt
Freshly ground black pepper
8 tablespoons dry white wine
45 g (1½ oz) unsmoked ham, chopped rather coarse, or 30 g (1¼ oz) chopped mild salami (not spiced, garlicky, or smoked)
75 g (2¼ oz) fontina cheese diced very fine
50 g (1¾ oz) ricotta
2 tablespoons plain breadcrumbs, lightly toasted

The pizza dough produced from the recipe on page 44.
A baking stone or enough quarry tiles to line a rack of the oven

1 Put 3 tablespoons olive oil and the sliced onion in a sauté pan, and turn on the heat to medium high.

2 When the onion turns a deep, dark gold, add the ground beef, salt, and pepper. Crumble the meat with a fork, and cook it, stirring frequently, until it loses completely its raw red colour.

3 Add the wine, turn the heat down a little bit, and continue cooking until all the liquid has boiled away. Transfer to a bowl, and allow to cool completely.

4 Turn on the oven to 200°C/400°F/Mark 6, with the baking stone or tiles in place on the uppermost rack.

5 Add the ham or salami, the fontina, and the ricotta to the bowl. Mix thoroughly with a fork until all the ingredients have become smoothly amalgamated.

6 Divide the dough in half and place one half on a lightly floured paddle or sheet of cardboard. Roll it out into a circular sheet about 250 to 300 mm (10 to 12 inches) in diameter.

7 On the bottom sheet of dough, sprinkle half the breadcrumbs and 1 teaspoon olive oil, stopping about 12 mm (½ inch) short of the edge. Over this, spread the stuffing, again stopping short of the edge. Top with the remaining breadcrumbs and olive oil.

8 On a pastry board or other work surface, roll out the remaining half of the dough into a circular sheet large enough to cover the first. Place over the stuffing, covering the other sheet. Pinch the two edges together to form a tight seal.

9 Brush the top with a pastry brush moistened in water.

10 Slide the *sfinciuni* from the paddle onto the preheated baking stone or tiles. Bake for 25 minutes. Allow to rest for at least 30 to 40 minutes before cutting into pie-shaped wedges and serving. This long rest is required to allow the flavours of the smoking-hot meat stuffing to settle and develop.

Sfinciuni con la conza di pomodoro e cipolla

SFINCIUNI WITH TOMATO, ONION, AND ANCHOVY STUFFING

The stuffing

450 g (1 lb) fresh, ripe plum tomatoes or 350 g (12 oz) tinned Italian plum tomatoes, seeded, chopped, and thoroughly drained
225 g (8 oz) onion, sliced very thin
8 tablespoons olive oil
Salt
Freshly ground black pepper
6 flat anchovy fillets, chopped very fine
1 teaspoon oregano
30 g (1 oz) plain breadcrumbs, lightly toasted

The pizza dough produced with the recipe on page 44.
A baking stone or enough quarry tiles to line a rack of the oven

1 If using fresh tomatoes, bring about 3 litres (5½ pints) water to the boil, then put in tomatoes. Drain after 3 to 4 minutes. As soon as the tomatoes are cool enough to handle, peel them, open them, scoop out the seeds, and cut them into lengthwise strips no more than 12 mm (½ inch) wide. Set aside. (If using tinned tomatoes, begin with Step 2.)

2 Put the onion and 4 tablespoons olive oil on a medium sauté pan, and turn on the heat to medium. Cook the onion until it turns a light gold.

3 Add the tomatoes, salt, 2 or 3 grindings of pepper, and turn up the heat to medium high. Cook, stirring from time to time, until the oil and tomatoes separate, about 7 minutes.

4 Add the chopped anchovies, stir well, and turn off the heat.

5 Add the oregano, stir well, and set aside to cool completely.

6 Preheat the baking stone or the tiles on the uppermost rack of the oven for at least 30 minutes, the thermostat set at 200 °C/400°F/Mark 6.

7 Roll out the dough for the *sfinciuni* following the directions on page 51. Sprinkle the sheet with 2 tablespoons toasted breadcrumbs.

8 Spread the tomato and onion stuffing over the breadcrumbs, covering the dough but stopping just a little short of the edge. Sprinkle the remaining breadcrumbs over the tomatoes and onions, and over them pour the remaining 4 tablespoons olive oil in a thin stream, spreading it evenly.

9 Cover and seal the *sfinciuni* with the upper sheet of dough, following the directions in the basic recipe, page 51.

10 Brush the top of the *sfinciuni* with a pastry brush lightly moistened with water.

11 Slide the *sfinciuni* from the paddle onto the hot stone or tiles. Bake for 20 minutes, or until the dough has turned a pale gold.

12 Cut into serving portions, and allow to settle for a few minutes before eating.

Note When the *sfinciuni* is stuffed and sealed, place it immediately in the oven, otherwise the stuffing will make the dough soggy.

Sfinciuni con la conza di broccoli e ricotta

SFINCIUNI WITH BROCCOLI AND RICOTTA STUFFING

The stuffing

450 g (1 lb) broccoli
Salt
2 teaspoons chopped garlic
4 tablespoons olive oil for cooking plus 2 tablespoons for seasoning
2 tablespoons plain breadcrumbs, lightly toasted
150 g (5 oz) ricotta

The pizza dough produced from the recipe on page 44.
A baking stone or enough quarry tiles to line a rack of the oven

1 Cut 12 mm ($\frac{1}{2}$ inch) off the tough butt end of the broccoli stalks. Pare away the dark green skin on the stalks and the larger stems.

2 Bring about 3 litres ($5\frac{1}{4}$ pints) salted water to the boil, and put in the broccoli. Cook for about 5 to 7 minutes after the water returns to the boil, depending on the thickness and freshness of the broccoli. It should be quite firm and crunchy, because it will undergo additional cooking later.

3 Drain the broccoli, and chop into pieces no bigger than 25 mm (1 inch).

4 Put the garlic and 4 tablespoons oil in a sauté pan, and turn on the heat to medium. Sauté the garlic until it turns gold.

5 Add the chopped broccoli, and sprinkle liberally with salt. Cook for about 5 minutes, stirring frequently. Set aside to cool.

6 Turn on the oven to 200°C/400°F/Mark 6, with the baking stone or tiles in place on the uppermost rack.

7 Roll out the dough for the *sfinciuni*, following the directions on page 51.

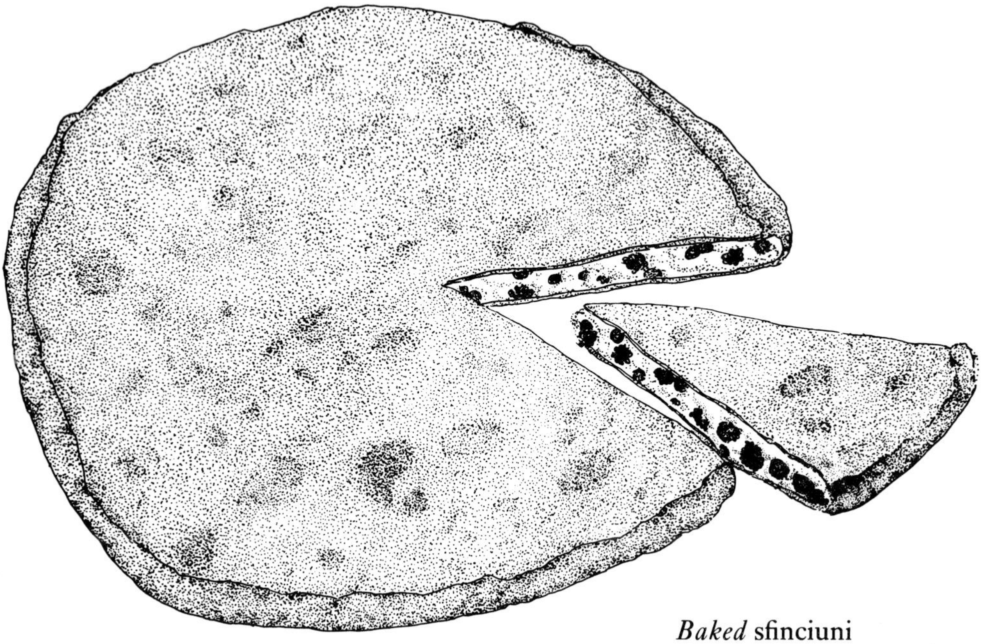

Baked sfinciuni

8 On the bottom sheet of the dough sprinkle half the breadcrumbs, then spread the ricotta over the breadcrumbs. Cover the ricotta with the cooled sautéed broccoli, and sprinkle with the remaining breadcrumbs. Pour the 2 tablespoons olive oil over the stuffing.

9 Cover and seal the *sfinciuni* as directed in step 8, page 51. Brush the top with a pastry brush moistened with water.

10 Slide the *sfinciuni* onto the hot stone or tiles. Bake for 25 minutes, then cut into individual portions, and allow to rest for at least 10 minutes before serving.

La piadina romagnola

STONE-GRIDDLE FLAT BREAD FROM ROMAGNA

This is one of the most typical products of Romagna, a generous, open-hearted land that lies in north-central Italy, between soft rounded hills and the quiet shores of the Adriatic. A *piadina* is a thin, flat cake, originally cooked on a terracotta slab over hot coals. It was the daily bread of Romagna's peasants. In their primitive kitchens there were no ovens in which to make any other kind of bread, and it was unthinkable to travel miles of frozen, muddy, or dust-choked dirt roads for shop-baked bread.

Peasant women in Romagna still make *piadina*. They make it on street corners for town folk and summer visitors who have discovered how delicious it is with a slice of sweet prosciutto, or grilled sausages, or heaped with sautéed, garlicky field greens.

It has become very chic from spring through to autumn, in Emilia-Romagna, to dine in nostalgically rustic style at some restored farmhouse surrounded by wheat fields or orchards. On such occasions, the fist things to appear on the bare wood table are plates piled with wedges of *piadina* and thick slices of hand-out home-made salami or *coppa*. There is an earthy, homespun quality to *piadina* and its accompaniments that loosens all reserve, comforting the palate with flavours out of a simpler, sturdier past.

Piadina is firmer and chewier than bread, but it is not brittle or hard like crackers or Scandinavian flat breads. It goes well with country ham, with coarse-grained salami, with pan-fried sausages, and it is at its best with the Sautéed Greens on page 325.

Makes 5 to 7 cakes, depending on their thinness, sufficient for six servings

45 g (1½ oz) lard (lard is the shortening that works best in this recipe, but if you must find a substitute, use 6 tablespoons olive oil)
550 g (1 lb 3 oz) plain flour
6 tablespoons milk
2 teaspoons salt
½ teaspoon bicarbonate of soda
8 tablespoons lukewarm water
A 300-mm (12-inch) stone griddle or a heavy cast-iron frying pan

Note The terracotta slab, called a *testo*, on which *piadina* is traditionally cooked is not available here, and it is fast becoming extinct even in Italy. A satisfactory, even if not ideal, substitute is heavy black cast iron. In using it, you must heat it up gradually until it becomes very hot, but not fiery. It must be hot enough to cook the *piadina* quickly, but without burning it. To make sure you are cooking at the right temperature, count to six when you put on your first *piadina*, then lift it and examine the side cooking next to the pan. If it is blackened, you must turn down the heat. If it has just a scattering of small black spots, you are doing well.

1 Liquefy the lard by heating it gently in a small saucepan until it is completely melted. Be careful not to overheat it. (If you are using olive oil it does not need to be warmed up.)

2 Pour the flour onto a work surface, and shape it into a mound. Make a hollow in the centre of the mound, and put in the melted lard and all the other ingredients. Draw the sides of the mound together, combining everything, and knead steadily for about 10 minutes until you have a smooth, tender, and elastic ball of dough.

3 Cut the ball into uniform pieces each the size of an extra-large egg. Roll out each piece into a very thin disc about 1 to 2 mm ($\frac{1}{16}$ inch) thick.

4 Over medium heat, warm up the stone slab or iron frying pan until it is hot enough to make a drop of water skip. Place one of the discs of dough on it. Cook without moving it for 10 seconds, then turn it over with a spatula, and let it cook on the other side for 10 seconds, again without moving it. At this point, prick the *piadina* here and there with a fork, and rotate it frequently, so that it doesn't stay in one spot long enough to be scorched. Flip it over from time to time to cook it evenly on both sides.

5 The *piadina* is done in 3 to 4 minutes. It will have a dull, parched, white surface lightly mottled with a few, scattered burn marks. Remove it from the griddle, cut it into four wedges, and prop these up somewhere, standing them on their one curved edge, letting air circulate around them while you cook another *piadina*. As each one is done, cut it into wedges and stand them up before proceeding to cook the next *piadina*.

Serve as promptly as possible after cooking, preferably while still warm.

Consum

STONE-GRIDDLE PASTIES

Consum are half-moon-shaped pasties made of dough nearly identical to that of *piadina* (page 55) and stuffed with a mixture of sautéed greens. They are cooked, like *piadina*, on an earthenware or soapstone griddle, or they can be fried. In Romagna they are often accompanied by liberal draughts of Sangiovese, a local dry red wine, sturdy and generous, usually consumed within a year of the vintage, when its flavour is fresh and grapy.

Consum are one of the most venerable products of Romagna's kitchens. They probably existed even before the kitchens did. To trace the origin of the unleavened dough, the stuffing of field greens, the scorching stone, we must turn back the leaves of man's story practically to his beginnings as a creature cooking for pleasure. And vigorous, earthy, soul-satisfying pleasure is what they still bring us.

For six

The stuffing

The stuffing is identical to the Sautéed Greens for *piadina*. For this recipe, use 1·35 kg (3 lb) raw greens in the following proportions: 900 g (2 lb) 'sweet' greens, such as Swiss chard, spinach, or Savoy cabbage, and 450 g (1 lb) 'bitter' greens such as *cime di rape* (turnip tops), chicory, or dandelion. For the preparation of the greens, and the cooking directions, see page 325.

The dough

260 g (8½ oz) flour
45 g (1½ oz) lard, partly melted in a pan, then softened completely at room temperature (lard gives the best results, but olive oil may be substituted)
¼ teaspoon bicarbonate of soda
1 teaspoon salt
8 tablespoons lukewarm water
A 300-mm (12-inch) soapstone griddle or a heavy cast-iron frying pan (see note on page 56)

1 Pour the flour onto a work surface and make a mound. Form a hollow in the centre of the mound, and put in the softened lard, the bicarbonate of soda, the salt, and the water. Draw the sides of the mound together, and knead steadily for 8 to 10 minutes.

2 Cut off a piece of dough the size of an egg, and roll it out into a circle 150 to 180 mm (6 to 7 inches) in diameter, about 3 mm (⅛ inch) thick or less.

Consum *cooking on soapstone*

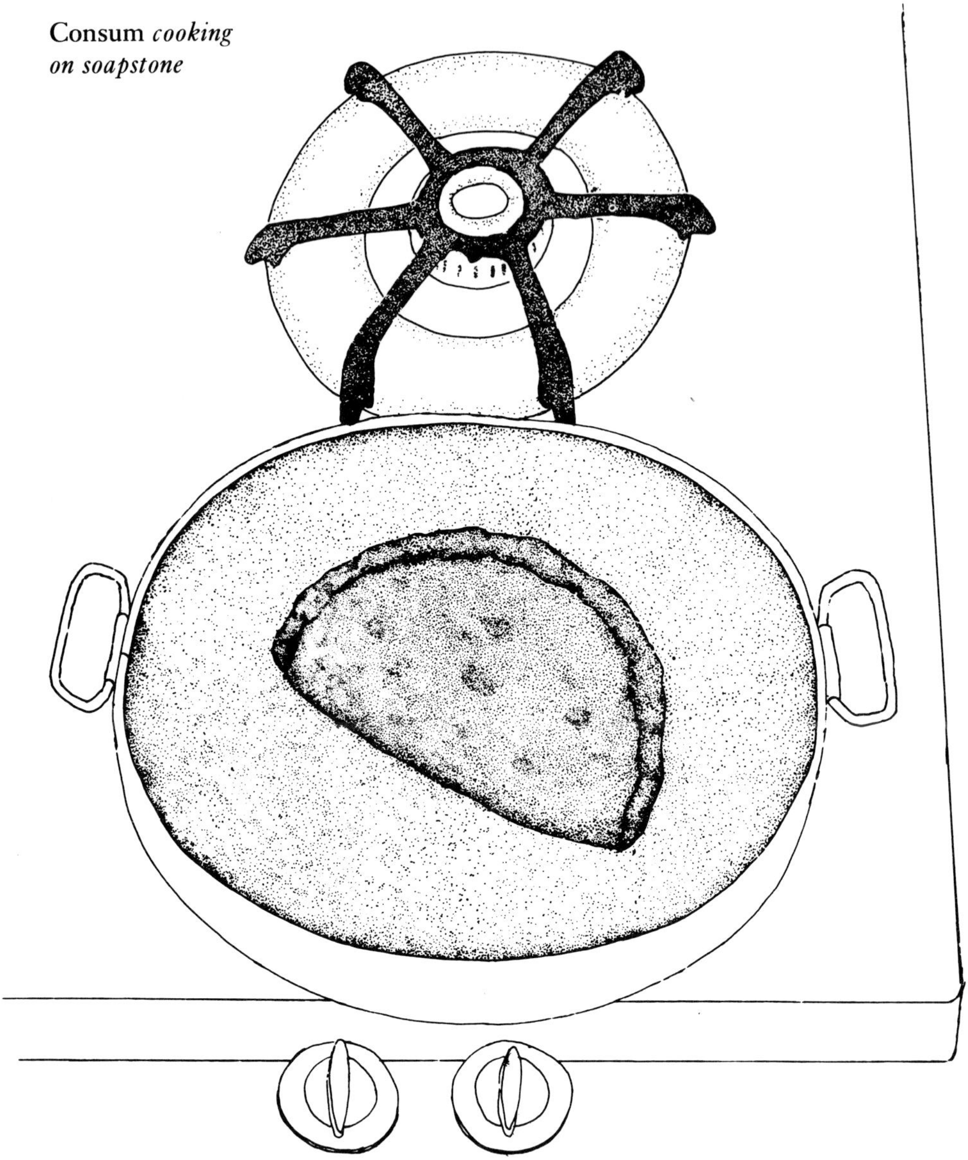

3 Over one half of the circle spread a 12-mm ($\frac{1}{2}$-inch)-thick layer of sautéed greens, drained of their cooking oil. Fold over the other half of the circle, and seal the edges tight, pressing them with your thumb or a pastry crimper.

4 Preheat the stone griddle over medium heat, or gradually heat up the iron frying pan until it is hot but not fiery. The frying pan needs more regulation of heat from time to time, because it does not maintain as steady a level of heat as the stone. Both the stone and frying pan are ready when they are hot enough to make a drop of water skip.

5 Put in 2 or 3 pasties at a time, depending on their size. Cook them altogether 4 or 5 minutes, turning them over frequently and standing them on edge for a brief time, holding them with tongs. They are done when the dough becomes dull and parched and lightly mottled where it has been charred here and there.

6 Serve at once.

Note The dough can be rolled out through a pasta machine, setting the rollers to obtain a thickness of no more than 3 mm ($\frac{1}{8}$ inch). The pasties can then be cut into rectangular or triangular shapes. It's not indispensable that they be half-moons. And they need not all be exactly the same size. What is important is that the thickness of the dough and of the vegetable stuffing be constant.

FRIED CONSUM

Consum are also extraordinarily good when fried. They are then sometimes called *cassoni.* When making them for frying the only adjustment you must make in the recipe is to reduce the melted lard in the dough to 20 g ($1\frac{1}{4}$ oz). They are tastiest when fried in hot lard, but if you wish, you can substitute vegetable oil.

Focaccette fritte

CHEESE-FILLED PASTA FRITTERS

This is finger food, like pizza, and a speciality of the Riviera, where it is very popular. When you drive down the coast road south of Genova, you often see signs reading *Focaccia* or *Focaccette* hung out by small *trattorie.* If you have not the time, inclination, or ready cash for a full-scale meal, or are accompanied by children, a plateful of *focaccette* is a satisfying answer to the call of hunger.

The charm of *focaccette* lies in the contrast of the tart, fresh, melting cheese filling and the crisply fried envelope of dough. There is no exact equivalent here to the fresh cheeses available in Italy. I have used my formula, as in other recipes of this book, which combines fontina for flavour and consistency, and ricotta for freshness. You can experiment with combinations of your own, or look for inspiration to Evan Jones's *The Book of Cheese* (Macmillan, 1980).

When you take your first bite of a *focaccetta*, use caution. The cheese oozes out quickly, and it may be scalding.

Makes enough fritters for four to five

The dough

130 g (4½ oz) plain flour
1 tablespoon olive oil
½ teaspoon salt
5 tablespoons water

The filling

45 g (1½ oz) Italian fontina cheese, or other semi-soft, savoury cheese, chopped fine
100 g (3½ oz) ricotta
1 egg white
Enough vegetable oil to come almost 12 mm (½ inch) up the sides of the frying pan
2 tablespoons freshly grated Parmesan cheese
salt
Freshly ground black pepper

1 Onto a pastry board or other work surface pour the flour and shape it into a mound. Press down the centre of the mound to form a cup-shaped hollow. Into this hollow put the olive oil, salt, and water, and bring the sides of the mound together toward the centre, thoroughly mixing all the ingredients.

2 Knead for 5 to 6 minutes, then form the dough into a ball and put it aside to rest between two soup plates. Let it rest for about 2 hours.

3 Prepare the filling, mixing the three cheeses in a bowl, and add a pinch of salt and one or two grindings of pepper.

4 When the dough has rested approximately 2 hours, flatten it into a thin sheet with a rolling-pin. As you begin to roll it out, you may find it offers some resistance and tries to shrink back. After a short while, however, it loosens up and opens out quite easily. If you prefer, you can run it through a pasta machine instead of using the rolling-pin. It should not be paper thin, so stop at the next-to-last thinning setting of the machine.

5 Cut the sheet of dough into rectangles about 90 to 120 mm ($3\frac{1}{4}$ to 4 inches) wide and 150 to 180 mm (6 to 7 inches) long. Spread a thin layer of the cheese mixture, about 2 teaspoons or so, over half of each rectangle. Fold the other half over, pinching the edges together. Dip a fingertip in the egg white, and run it over the edges to help seal them tight and keep them from opening while frying.

6 As you finish filling and sealing each fritter, lay it on a clean tea-towel. If you are not ready to fry them immediately, turn them from time to time to keep the side next to the towel from sticking. Do not overlap the fritters or pile them one on top of the other.

7 Put the oil into the frying pan, and turn the heat on to high. When the oil is very hot, slip in as many fritters as will fit loosely. Fry them to a golden colour on one side, then turn them and do the other side. Often the fritters will puff up, and even when you turn them some patches along the edges will jut out above the oil level. In this case, tip them over with a long-handled wooden spoon or a spatula until they are all more or less evenly fried.

8 Transfer to kitchen paper to drain, and serve while still hot.

I ripieni fritti

FRIED STUFFED PASTIES

These savoury pasties look like large triangular ravioli. They are very easy to do and, for those who like to experiment, lend themselves to a great variety of stuffings.

One of the most delicious fillings combines strips of raw tomato, anchovies and capers. Another way to stuff them is with cheese and parsley. Nearly any combination of cheeses can be successful as long as it is neither too bland nor too sharp. This is in fact a marvellous, quick way to transform leftover cheese into appetising titbits, or into a very satisfying snack.

One you've tried the basic versions and see how they work, you can devise your own stuffings. You might like to try bits of fried aubergine and roasted peppers in the stuffing. Or *funghi trifolati*, mushrooms sautéed in garlic and oil. Or whatever your taste and imagination may suggest.

Tomato stuffing for 20 pasties

100 g (3½ oz) raw, ripe, but firm tomato, peeled, seeded, and cut into strips about 12 mm (½ inch) wide and 37 mm (1½ inches) long
2 tablespoons whole small capers or chopped large ones
10 flat anchovy fillets, cut in two

Cheese stuffing for 20 pasties

2 tablespoons chopped parsley
90 g (3 oz) mild cheese } cut into very thin strips, or slivers,
60 g (2 oz) savoury cheese } crumbled, or grated

(Suggested cheese combinations are mozzarella and Parmesan; ricotta and Gorgonzola; smoked mozzarella and Fontina; Gruyère and Taleggio.)

Note Whether you use a tomato or a cheese stuffing, keep all components separate, using individual small bowls or saucers.

The dough for 20 pasties

200 g (7 oz) plain flour
½ teaspoon salt
½ teaspoon baking powder
1 tablespoon olive oil
6 tablespoons lukewarm water

To fry the pasties

Enough vegetable oil to come at least 12 mm (½ inch) up the side of a deep frying pan or sauté pan

1 Pour the flour onto a work surface and shape it into a mound. Make a deep hollow in the centre of the mound and put into it the salt, baking powder, olive oil, and lukewarm water. Draw the sides of the mound together, and knead for 8 to 10 minutes, until you have a smooth, elastic ball of dough.

2 Roll out the dough to a thickness of about 2 mm ($\frac{1}{16}$ inch). It should not be paper thin. You can use a pasta machine to do this. If using the Bialetti electric pasta machine, the correct final setting is 4. Do not make the dough any thinner.

3 Trim the pasta along the edges so that it has a fairly regular rectangular shape. Briefly knead the trimmings together to form a small ball of dough and roll it out or feed it through the pasta machine. Trim this last sheet of pasta so it also has a rectangular shape.

4 Cut the pasta into squares whose sides are 75 mm (3 inches) long or less. It doesn't matter if they are not all identical. Take a little bit of each of the components of the stuffing, and place in the centre of each square.

To make the stuffing come out evenly distributed at the end, carefully judge by eye the amount you need for each pasty. Fold the squares over on the diagonal, forming triangles. Seal the edges securely tight with your fingertips or with a pastry crimper. You must stuff the dough and seal it as soon as it is done, or it will dry out. When dry, the edges become very difficult to seal. If you find you have a little difficulty in sealing them, moisten the edges lightly with a little water. As you close each pasty, place it on a cloth or kitchen paper until you are ready to fry them. Do not lay them one over the other, or they may stick together.

5 Put the oil in the frying pan, and turn on the heat to high. When the oil is very hot, slip in the pasties. Do not crowd them. When they are fried to a nice golden colour on one side, turn them and do the other side. You will find they will puff up while they cook. When both sides are done, transfer them to kitchen paper to drain. Serve while still hot, but not quite scalding.

ANTIPASTI

Pisci d'ovu

EGG FRITTERS

Little spoonfuls of batter are dropped into hot oil and in a twinkling swell into soft, tiny, weightless puffs. That is all there is to these dreamlike Sicilian fritters. Biting into them is like biting into air that has through some enchantment been made palpable and savoury.

Pisci d'ovu means egg fish, so named because they are fried as one would fry whitebait or other miniature fish. They could well be served as part of a mixed fish fry, or of any *fritto misto* (see Mixed Fried Meats, Vegetables, Cheese, etc., *The Classic Italian Cookbook*, page 283). They also make the most civilised and delightful of appetisers, served with a glass of white wine.

For at least six

4 eggs
2 tablespoons freshly grated Parmesan cheese
½ small clove garlic, peeled and chopped fine
60 g (2 oz) dry, plain breadcrumbs
Salt
Freshly ground black pepper
Enough vegetable oil to come 25 mm (1 inch) up the sides of the pan

1 Break all the eggs into a bowl, and beat them lightly.

2 Add all the other ingredients (except the oil) to the bowl. Mix thoroughly.

3 Put the oil in a medium-sized frying pan, and turn on the heat to medium high.

4 When the oil is very hot (a test dribble of batter should stiffen and instantly float to the surface), put in the batter, a teaspoonful at a time; do not crowd the pan.

5 When the fritters have puffed up, turn them until they have formed a nice golden crust all over, then transfer to kitchen paper to drain, or to a cooling rack set on a dish. Serve at once, when the entire batch is done.

Cappelle di funghi ripiene

BAKED STUFFED MUSHROOM CAPS

Mushroom caps are nature's own *vol-au-vents*. They beg to be stuffed with good things. There is a fine assortment of them in this filling – *pancetta*, anchovy, garlic, egg, parsley, and marjoram.

A key ingredient – not mentioned above – is dried wild mushrooms. As in many other preparations in this book, their presence serves to transform the neutral flavour of cultivated mushrooms into the dense, rich one of boletus.

Stuffed mushrooms are more filling than most appetisers, and could easily replace a pasta course, when followed by any meat dish that does not contain mushrooms. They could also be served before stuffed crêpes, page 287, or any of the *frittate* on pages 288–98, for an informal but satisfying lunch.

For four to six

- 20 g (¾ oz) dried wild mushrooms
- 30 g (1 oz), or slightly more, crumb (the fresh, soft, crustless part of the bread)
- 4 tablespoons milk
- 450 g (1 lb) fresh mushrooms with firm, good-size caps
- 110 g (4 oz) *pancetta* or, if absolutely unavailable, green bacon
- 4 flat anchovy fillets
- 3 or 4 basil leaves
- 1 small clove garlic or ½ a large one, peeled and chopped fine
- 1 egg
- 3 tablespoons parsley, chopped fine
- ⅛ teaspoon marjoram
- Salt
- Freshly ground black pepper
- 6 tablespoons olive oil
- 60 g (2 oz) dry, plain breadcrumbs

1 Put the dried mushrooms in 450 ml (¾ pint) of lukewarm water, and let them soak in it for at least 30 minutes.

2 Put the crumb and milk in a bowl or deep dish and set aside to soak.

3 Wash the fresh mushrooms rapidly in cold running water, and dry them thoroughly, without bruising them, with a soft tea-towel. Gently detach the stems without breaking the caps.

4 Line a wire strainer with a sheet of kitchen paper, and place it over a small saucepan. Filter through the strainer and into the saucepan the water in which the dried mushrooms have been soaking. Rince the dried mushrooms thoroughly in cold water, then add them to the liquid in the saucepan. Cook, uncovered, over lively heat until all the liquid has boiled away.

5 Preheat the oven to 200°C/400°F/Mark 6.

6 Chop the cooked wild mushrooms, the fresh mushroom stems, the *pancetta* or bacon, the anchovy fillets, the basil leaves, all very fine. If you

have a food processor, drop the ingredients into the bowl and chop them all together.

7 Put all the chopped ingredients into a mixing bowl, including the chopped garlic. With your hand, gently squeeze the crumb until it stops dripping, and add it to the bowl. Break the egg into the bowl. Add the parsley, marjoram, salt, and pepper, and thoroughly mix all the contents of the bowl until they are well integrated into a smooth, uniform mixture. Taste and check for salt and pepper.

8 Turn the mushroom caps bottoms up, and stuff them with the mixture from the bowl. Put enough stuffing in each cap to make a small rounded mound. Sprinkle the mounds with dry breadcrumbs.

9 Choose a baking tin that will hold all the mushroom caps side by side in a single layer. Smear the bottom and sides of the pan with some of the olive oil.

10 Put the mushrooms into the pan, stuffing facing up. Criss-cross with a thin stream of olive oil, very lightly daubing the stuffing. Place the pan in the uppermost level of the oven, and bake for 30 minutes, or until the mounds of stuffing have formed a light crust. Allow to settle for several minutes after removing from the oven before serving.

Canestrelli trifolati

SAUTÉED SCALLOPS WITH GARLIC AND PARSLEY

There are two stages in the preparation of this dish, both very brief.

First, the scallops are sautéed in olive oil and garlic. Then they are mixed with parsley, capers, cut-up roasted peppers, put into scallop shells or flameproof dishes, topped with breadcrumbs, and run under a grill for a few seconds.

The success of the dish lies in taking care not to overcook the scallops and in the quality of the scallops themselves. Italian *canestrelli* are tinier than the smallest scallops sold here, and very sweet. Deep-sea scallops have a stronger flavour and chewier texture, but are good when fresh.

You may decide that this is too delicious a dish to consign to the limbo of appetisers. In larger quantities it will stand on its own as a fully fledged fish course.

For four

225 g (8 oz) fresh scallops, preferably tiny, or larger scallops cut into 3 or 4 pieces
2 tablespoons olive oil
1 clove garlic, peeled and chopped fine
Salt
Freshly ground black pepper
1 tablespoon parsley, chopped fine
1 tablespoon chopped capers
2 tablespoons chopped roasted peppers, preferably freshly home-roasted
1½ tablespoons fine, dry, plain breadcrumbs
4 scallop shells or small, shallow gratin dishes

1 Wash the scallops thoroughly in cold water, drain, and pat dry with a towelling kitchen cloth.

2 Put the olive oil and garlic in a small saucepan and sauté the garlic over medium heat until it turns a pale gold.

3 Put in the scallops, salt, several liberal grindings of pepper, and turn up the heat. Cook at lively heat, stirring frequently, for no more than 5 minutes.

4 Turn off the heat, add the parsley, capers, peppers, 1 tablespoon breadcrumbs, and mix thoroughly. Parcel out the contents of the pan into 4 scallop shells, or small flameproof gratin dishes. Sprinkle with the remaining ½ tablespoon breadcrumbs.

5 Run the shells or dishes under a hot grill for about a minute, or no more than necessary to brown the tops of the scallops very lightly. Serve at once.

Sarde in carpione

FRIED MARINATED SARDINES

In the Veneto they call it *in saor*, in Lombardy *in carpione*, in Sicily *a scapece*. These are methods used from north to south for cooking fish and preserving it for consumption up to several days later. The basic procedure is the same. The fish is fried and put aside; the frying oil is then reheated and flavoured with vinegar, onions or garlic and other vegetables, and herbs. It is poured over the fish, which is then left to marinate for a day or more. The dish is served at room temperature.

This practice dates back to the time when there was an abundance of fish and no refrigeration. Now that the situation is very nearly reversed, people don't do it very often, except in some restaurants. It makes a most appetising dish when it precedes any well-flavoured fish course. This version with sardines is particularly savoury, but if you cannot find fresh sardines, try the recipe with any other small fish that fry well, including any kind of fillets.

For four

4 large fresh sardines, about 250 mm (10 inches) long, or 6 to 8 smaller ones
6 tablespoons vegetable oil
75 g ($2\frac{1}{2}$ oz) plain flour, spread on a dish
Salt
Freshly ground black pepper
1 medium onion sliced very thin
6 tablespoons good wine vinegar
4 whole bayleaves

1 Scale and gut the fish, cut off the heads and central back fins. Wash them well in cold water, and dry most thoroughly with kitchen paper.

2 Heat up the oil in a frying pan over medium-high heat. While the oil is warming up, dredge the fish on both sides in the flour. As soon as the oil is quite hot, put in the fish.

3 Fry at lively heat for about 2 minutes on each side, or less if the fish is very small, until both sides of the fish have a nice brown crust. Add 2 or 3 pinches of salt, and a grinding or two of pepper.

4 With a slotted spoon or spatula transfer the sardines to a shallow serving dish, just large enough to contain them in a single layer, without overlapping. They would look most attractive in an earthenware dish. Do not remove the oil from the pan.

5 Put the sliced onions into the pan where the fish were fried. Turn on the heat to medium low, and cook gently, stirring once in a while, until the onion is tender but not coloured.

6 Add the vinegar, turn up the heat, stir rapidly, and let it bubble for 20 to 30 seconds. Pour all the contents of the pan over the fish. Put the bayleaves on top.

7 Cover the dish, and let the fish steep in the marinade for at least 12 hours. Turn the fish over once or twice. If you are going to eat the dish the following day, it does not need to be refrigerated. It will keep for several days in the refrigerator, but be sure to return it to room temperature at least 1 or 2 hours before serving.

La carne cruda come a Canelli

CHOPPED RAW STEAK, FROM CANELLI

This dish comes from the same Piedmont slopes that produce the *moscato* grape, from which the fine semi-sweet sparkling Asti wine is made.

The meat is steeped for 2 to 3 hours in a mixture containing lemon juice; this 'cooks' it, so to speak, and causes it to lose its raw red colour. In order to brighten up its appearance, and to balance its softness with something crunchy, it is served with tiny cucumber pickles, or that assortment of mixed pickled Italian vegetables called *giardiniera* (small jars of it imported from Italy are widely available), and olives. It makes a very tasty appetiser, quite different from tartar steak, and often pleasing even to those who are usually squeamish about raw meat. It can also be served on its own, as a light lunch, followed by salad and fruit.

For four

225 g (8 oz) lean rump steak
½ clove garlic, peeled
1 heaped tablespoon anchovy paste
Freshly ground black pepper
3 tablespoons lemon juice, freshly squeezed
3 tablespoons olive oil

For decoration: Cornichons (smalled pickled cucumbers) or assorted pickled Italian vegetables (*giardiniera*), and green or black olives

1 Chop the meat very fine, together with the garlic, running it twice through a meat grinder, or spinning it in the food processor, until it is ground fine, but not to a mush.

2 Put the meat in a small bowl. Add the anchovy paste, pepper, lemon juice, and olive oil. Mix thoroughly and allow to stand at room temperature for 2 to 3 hours.

3 Pour out any liquid that may have run off from the meat. Taste and check for pepper; the anchovy paste should have supplied all the salt necessary. Place the meat in a serving dish, decorating it with olives and any of the pickles listed at the beginning of the recipe.

Note Never prepare this more than 4 to 6 hours in advance, or the meat will absorb too much anchovy flavour and taste disagreeably sharp.

Arrosticini all' abruzzese

SKEWERED MARINATED LAMB MORSELS

This is a dish I was served at the start of one of the day-long country feasts my friend Angelo De Victoriis-Medori gives each year at his beautiful estate in Abruzzi, between Pescara and Teramo. It is a skewer of lamb, borrowed from the simple cooking of the shepherds of Abruzzi.

The lamb is cut into very small, bite-sized cubes, and marinated for 2 hours or more. Then it is skewered and grilled.

In Abruzzi this is done over a wood fire. While it can be done in a grill at home, it is a perfect dish for a barbecue, or for the fireplace grill. The tiny bitefuls of meat cook very rapidly, all crusty on the outside and tasty within.

They are an appropriate introduction to any meal in which the pasta and meat courses have a homespun, farm-country character, or they can be served before a *frittata* or *pizza rustica*, page 284, or *pizza di scarola*, page 281.

For four. (If you plan to serve this as the principal meat course, increase the quantities, calculating those given here as sufficient for two.)

225 g (½ lb) boned shoulder of lamb
2 tablespoons olive oil
Salt
Freshly ground black pepper
½ teaspoon marjoram
1 clove garlic, crushed
10 to 12 small skewers

1 Dice the meat into cubes about 18 mm (¾ inch) thick. Do not discard the fat, but try to leave some lean meat attached to each bit of fat you cut.

2 Put the meat in a bowl, add the oil, 1 or 2 large pinches of salt, a liberal grinding of pepper, the marjoram, and crushed garlic. Mix well, coating the meat thoroughly, and let the lamb steep in its marinade for at least 2 hours at room temperature, or several hours if refrigerated. Turn the meat from time to time.

3 If refrigerated, take the meat out ½ hour before cooking. Turn it thoroughly once again, and place all the pieces of lamb on the skewers.

4 Preheat the grill for 15 minutes, and place the skewers on the rack in the position closest to the source of heat. (If barbecuing, do it over very hot coals.) Cook for 3 to 4 minutes on one side, then turn the skewers and cook for 2 to 3 minutes on the other, until the meat forms a fine crackling crust on all sides. Serve at once.

Insalata di spaghetti

COLD SPAGHETTI SALAD WITH ANCHOVIES AND OLIVES

When cooks, like archaeologists, turn up something new, it is less by accident than because they know it's there. Once, when dining with Japanese friends, I was served a dish of ice-cold noodles with seaweed. It was delicious. Up to then I had always been convinced that eating cold pasta was an unnatural act, but at that moment I knew there had to be dishes with cold pasta that would be very good. And, indeed, I looked and I found.

This simple seasoning for cold *spaghetti* – olives, anchovies, and parsley – is as good as any I have tried. You can embroider or alter the basic version to suit your taste. You might add to it raw sweet peppers, peeled and sliced matchstick thin. Or try it with capers and cold fried aubergine, rubbed with garlic. Or with bits of boiled lobster, shrimp, or scallops seasoned with olive oil, lemon juice, parsley, and a little hot red pepper.

It is most important not to overcook the pasta because cold, soft pasta really doesn't work. And it would be preferable to use the best imported Italian pasta, for its superior, firm consistency.

Although this is a 'salad', it would not fit as such into an Italian meal, where salad is served after the second course. It could be an appetiser, or a light lunch, or a most successful party dish, as part of a buffet.

For four to six

450 g (1 lb) *spaghettini* (thin *spaghetti*)
4 tablespoons olive oil, plus 1 additional tablespoon for the final seasoning
12 black olives (Greek)
10 to 12 flat anchovy fillets
2 tablespoons parsley, chopped very fine

1 Cook the pasta in 3 to 4 litres (5¼ to 7 pints) salted rapidly boiling water. Do not overcook it. It should be firm to the bite, *al dente*.

2 When done, drain the pasta thoroughly, and transfer it to a bowl. Toss it at once with 4 tablespoons olive oil. If not well coated with oil, the *spaghetti* strands will stick to each other and become gummy. Set aside to cool completely.

3 Pit the olives. Slice half the olives into thin, 6-mm (¼-inch) sections; chop the rest into a fine pulp.

4 Cut or chop the anchovies into small bits. Do not chop them so fine as to make a paste of them; you should have tiny but firm individual pieces of anchovy in the dish.

5 Put all the olives and anchovies into the bowl with the *spaghetti*, and

toss well. Allow to rest for 30 minutes, long enough for the pasta to soak up the flavours of the seasoning.

6 Just before serving, add the chopped parsley and the tablespoon of olive oil. Toss, and serve.

Party suggestion Cook the pasta, coat it with olive oil, and let it cool, but do not add any other seasoning. Prepare different seasonings, as suggested in the introductory remarks, and serve them on the side, in separate small bowls. Guests will then be able to choose the seasoning that is most appealing to them, and toss their own *spaghetti* salad.

FIRST COURSES

I Primi

THE MENU SUGGESTIONS

AT the end of each of the recipes that follow – except for salads and desserts – there are menu-planning suggestions. They indicate how to choose a second course to follow a pasta or soup, or – vice versa – what first course to consider when you have decided on the meat or fish course, and also what vegetable accompaniments might be most compatible. These suggestions are based on the normal structure of an everyday Italian meal, as it is served in Italian homes.

Of course, there are as many ways to enjoy Italian food as there are shifts in mood and breaks in rhythm in our lives. A dish of *spaghetti* or a *frittata* or a dish of fried shrimps may be all we have time for or desire.

Such an approach can be compared to looking at a painting and responding to only one of its parts: to the landscape in the background, to the curve of a hand, to the treatment of light and colour.

Although the different courses of an Italian meal can be savoured independently, they are, in fact, related elements of a larger composition. Only when they have all been fitted back into place can one relish, with fully consummated pleasure, the unique creation that is the Italian art of eating.

In an Italian meal there is a first course – soup, pasta, or rice; a second course – meat or fish; and a side course of vegetables. Salad follows, and when at home, fresh fruit usually takes the place of dessert.

The first course is virtually never served with the second. The rare exceptions to this are *risotto*, when it is served, Milanese style, with *ossobuco*, and *polenta*, which in the Veneto is served with game, sausages, or other meat. (A soup course may sometimes precede *polenta*.)

Pasta is never at any time served with the meat course, and those Italian restaurants that do this expose their lack of authenticity.

However abundant all this may sound, it does not lead to overeating. Italian portions are very small, no butter is ever put on the table, and there are no heavy desserts at the end. It is a sequence of courses that does lead to variety, vivacity, and naturally balanced nutrition.

Nor does one have to take days to prepare a traditional Italian meal. There are recipes in this book that can be prepared from scratch in minutes and whole menus that can be done in under half an hour. And they are just as delicious and satisfying as more elaborate, time-consuming meals.

The menu suggestions are designed to guide, not to impose. They suggest a few of the many possible combinations. What the others may be let your taste decide. All the descriptions that introduce each recipe, defining its character and, where possible in words, describing its taste, should be of help in the making of your plans.

Zuppa di calamari e carciofi

SQUID AND GLOBE ARTICHOKE SOUP

In the kitchens of the Italian Riviera, any dish that does not make use of vegetables is considered an opportunity lost. Although this is a seafaring province, its cooking is the story of a love affair with the products of gardens, orchards, and woods. Where else would one make soup with squid and artichokes?

Here the squid is first stewed in a bath of olive oil and wine, scented with parsley and garlic. When the squid is tender, very thin slices of globe artichoke are added. When these are cooked, the soup is done. And a lovely, light soup it is, as fresh as it is beautiful, mingling pearly white rings and mossy slivers, the gifts of the deep and of the sun.

For four

450 g (1 lb) squid, preferably small ones
8 tablespoons dry white wine
8 tablespoons olive oil
1½ cloves garlic, peeled and chopped fine
3 tablespoons chopped parsley
Salt
Freshly ground black pepper
1 large or 2 medium globe artichokes
½ lemon
4 slices good crusty white bread
1 clove garlic, peeled and crushed

1 Clean the squid as directed on pages 191–2. Cut the sacs into very narrow rings, less than 6 mm ($\frac{1}{4}$ inch) thick. Separate the larger tentacle clusters in two, and cut in half all tentacles that are longer than 25 mm (1 inch).

2 Put the squid rings and tentacles into a large saucepan or a small soup pot. Add the wine, olive oil, garlic, parsley, a pinch of salt, and a grinding of pepper. If there is not sufficient liquid to cover by at least 35 mm ($1\frac{1}{2}$ inches), add as much water as necessary. Turn on the heat to medium. When the liquid begins to simmer, cover, and turn the heat down to medium low.

3 Cook for 40 minutes or more, until the squid is tender when pricked with a fork. Whenever the level of the liquid is less than 35 mm ($1\frac{1}{2}$ inches) above that of the squid, add more water.

4 While the squid is cooking, clean the globe artichokes as described on page 151. Cut them into the thinnest possible slices, leaving the stems on where possible. Put the sliced artichokes into a bowl, with enough cold water to cover, and add the juice of $\frac{1}{2}$ lemon.

5 When the squid is tender, drain the sliced artichokes, and rinse them in cold water; then add them to the pot. Add water, if there is not enough liquid to cover by 50 mm (2 inches). Add a pinch of salt, a grinding of pepper, stir well, and cover the pot. Cook until the artichoke is tender, about 15 minutes, perhaps more, perhaps less, depending on the artichoke. Taste and check the seasoning.

6 Toast the bread, or brown it under the grill. Rub all the slices lightly on one side with the crushed garlic clove. Place the bread in individual soup plates, pour the soup over it, and serve at once.

MENU SUGGESTIONS

Follow this soup with a delicate fish course, such as *Pesce tra i due piatti* or an exuberant one such as *Salmone a la stimpirata*, *Umido di gamberi al pomodoro piccante*, *Tonno in agrodolci alla Trapanese*, or *Il pesce in brodetto*.

Zuppa di piselli e vongole

PEA AND CLAM SOUP

In my native Emilia-Romagna we make a great use of fresh peas in soups. They are usually fairly thin soups in which peas are sometimes combined with chicken livers or with *manfrigul*, the barleylike home-made pasta (page 142), or, as in this recipe, with tender, small clams. Good peas always make a sweet and gentle soup. And they are especially good with clams, as long as these are not the monstrously large, rubbery ones.

Speaking of clams, I've always been mystified by those recipes that instruct you to discard any clams that don't open while cooking. I was born in a fishing town and all but weaned on clams, but I have never known anyone to do this. When clams are clamped shut they are alive. The most reluctant ones to loosen their hold and open up are the most vigorously alive of all. When eating them raw on the half shell, does anyone know which clams would not have opened in the pot? The only clams I ever discard are those that are already open before I start cooking. If it is going to ease your mind to throw out the good, tenacious clams, do. But what a waste.

In this recipe you will find that some of the pea pods are used along with the peas. Pods are not only perfectly edible, but they are very sweet and make the peas with which they are cooked taste younger and fresher than they actually are. This is an optional step, and if you find peeling pods too bothersome, you may want to omit it. If you are using frozen peas, the question does not even arise.

For six

3 dozen clams, the smaller the better
1·35 kg (3 lb) fresh peas (unshelled weight) or 680 g ($1\frac{1}{2}$ lb) frozen *petits pois*, thawed
6 tablespoons olive oil
1 small onion, chopped
2 cloves garlic, peeled and chopped
2 tablespoons chopped parsley
150 g (5 oz) tinned Italian plum tomatoes, cut up, with their juice
Salt
Freshly ground black pepper
Crostini (croûtons)

1 Fill the sink or a large basin with cold water, and put in the clams. After 5 minutes, drain the sink, and refill with fresh cold water. Scrub the clams vigorously with a stiff, coarse brush or by rubbing one against the other. After thoroughly scrubbing the clams, drain the sink and refill with cold water. Repeat the entire operation two or three times, scrubbing the

clams, draining, refilling, until you see not too much sand settling to the bottom of the sink or basin.

2 Discard any open clams that do not clamp shut again at the touch. Put the rest in a large pot, cover tightly, and turn on the heat to high. Move the clams around with a long-handled spoon, from time to time, bringing up to the top the clams from the bottom. As soon as the clams start to open, transfer them with tongs or a slotted spoon to a large dish or bowl. Some clams open up almost immediately; others take longer (see introductory remarks above). It is not necessary for the shells to swing open wide; a crack will do. When the last recalcitrant clams have given up, turn off the heat, always leaving the pot covered.

3 Detach the clam meat from the shells. Dip each clam in the juices in the pot to rinse off any remaining grains of sand; dip them in and out, without stirring them in the liquid.

4 Cut up each clam into 2 or 3 pieces, depending on its size, and set them aside in a clean bowl.

5 Pour any juices in the dish or bowl to which you originally transferred the clams back into the pot; then strain all the juices through a sieve lined with a sheet of kitchen paper. Pour just enough of the filtered juices over the clams to keep them moist, and reserve the rest.

6 Shell the peas, and set them aside.

7 Choose a handful of the crispest, healthiest, least blemished pods, and discard the rest. The inside of the pod is lined with a thin, filmlike skin that must be removed. Hold a half pod with one hand, its inside facing you; snap off one end of the pod, and pull down, stripping away the inside skin. If you don't manage to get the entire skin, don't fuss too much with it. Keep the skinless portion of the pod, cutting away and discarding the rest. Wash all the peas and pods in cold water, drain, and set aside.

8 Choose a sauté pan large enough to hold all the peas later with a couple of inches to spare. Put in the oil and chopped onion, and turn on the heat to medium. Cook briefly until the onion is translucent.

9 Add the garlic. Cook, stirring from time to time, until the garlic and onion turn a deep gold.

10 Add the chopped parsley, stir once or twice, then add the cut-up tomatoes with their juice. Cook for 10 minutes, stirring occasionally. Add salt and freshly ground pepper to taste.

11 Put in the peas and their pods. Add the filtered clam juice, and enough water, if necessary, to cover the peas by at least 25 mm (1 inch). Put on a cover, and cook at a gentle simmer until the peas are tender, 10 minutes or more, depending on their freshness. If using thawed frozen peas, cook for only a minute or two. Taste and check the salt.

12 Add the cut-up clams with their remaining juice. Heat them no

longer than the few seconds necessary to warm them through, or they will become tough. Ladle at once into soup bowls, and serve with croûtons.

MENU SUGGESTIONS

This is a light preliminary that can lead to any fish course. Try following it with *Orate al limone e maggiorana*, *Bocconcini di pesce spada fritto*, *Pesce spada al salmoriglio*, or *Pesce turchino al forno con le patate*.

Spinaci e riso in brodo

SPINACH AND RICE SOUP

This is one of those comforting country soups of humble origins that for me always hold an insuperable advantage over the puréed, suppressed textures of more sophisticated creamed soups.

It is simple but requires good ingredients: fresh spinach and real home-made broth.

The leaf spinach is very briefly blanched in its own moisture, and sautéed with butter and onions, before going into the soup.

The same procedure can be followed with chopped escarole (see *The Classic Italian Cookbook*, page 55).

For a more robust alternative, instead of using butter and onions, sauté the spinach in 3 tablespoons olive oil and 2 teaspoons chopped garlic. Serve with a sprinkling of grated Parmesan or *grana*.

For four to six

450 g (1 lb) fresh spinach
Salt
45 g (1½ oz) butter
½ medium onion, chopped
560 ml (1 pint) good home-made broth (page 18) or 2 bouillon cubes dissolved in the same quantity of water
The liquid shed by the cooked spinach
60 g (2 oz) Italian Arborio rice or 100 g (3½ oz) long grain rice
Freshly grated Parmesan cheese for the table

1 If part of the root is still attached to the stems of the spinach, cut it off and discard it, thus separating each spinach cluster into individual leaves. Do not pull off the leaves from the stems, because both leaf and stem go into this soup.

2 Soak the spinach in a basin of cold water, dunking it several times with your hands. Lift out the spinach, and pour out the water from the basin together with the soil and grit that have settled to the bottom. Refill with fresh water, and repeat the above operation, soaking the spinach and changing the water several times until you find that no more soil is settling at the bottom of the basin.

3 Cook the spinach in a covered pan, over medium heat, with a large pinch of salt and no more water than clings to the leaves. Do not cook too long, just 2 or 3 minutes after the liquid they shed comes to the boil.

4 Scoop up the cooked spinach with a wire strainer or large slotted spoon. Do not discard any of the liquid in the pan. Gently squeeze the spinach with your hands, as soon as it is cool enough to handle, letting all the liquid it sheds run into the pan. Set the squeezed spinach aside, and reserve the liquid.

5 Put the butter and chopped onion into a frying pan, and turn on the heat to medium high. When the onion becomes a light gold colour, add the spinach. Sauté at lively heat for a few minutes, stirring.

6 Transfer all the contents of the frying pan to a soup pot. Add all the broth and 250 ml (scant $\frac{1}{2}$ pint) of the reserved spinach liquid. Bring to the boil, add the rice, and cover the pot. Cook at a steady, moderate boil, stirring from time to time, until the rice is done. It should be tender but firm to the bite, after approximately 25 minutes' cooking time. Taste and check salt.

7 The soup should have some density but still be fairly runny on the spoon. If you find, while it is cooking, that it is becoming too thick, add more of the reserved spinach liquid. In the event that you run out, add water. Be careful not to make the soup too thin.

MENU SUGGESTIONS

Follow with something satisfying, down to earth: *Bistecchine dimanzo alla cacciatora*, *Farsumauru – il braciolone*, *Nodini di vitello con sughetto di acciughe*, *Salsicce col vino rosso e i funghi secchi*. It could also be a suitable preliminary to *pizza rustica*.

Zuppa dei poveri con la rucola

ARUGOLA AND POTATO SOUP

This is called a 'poor man's soup' because its bulk comes from potatoes and stale bread, and its flavour from arugola, often known as rocket (*rucola* in Italian). Arugola grew wild and free in the fields, and the women of the poor used to gather an apronful of it in an hour. Whatever else the Italian poor may have lacked, it was not good sense about food. It is demonstrated here. Nothing could be simpler or much better.

The quantities of potato, bread, and water are to be taken as suggestions. To me they are well balanced. But, if you want the soup thicker, you can put in more bread and/or potatoes, and if you want it thinner, a little less of those and a little more water.

For four

4 medium potatoes, peeled and diced
700 ml ($1\frac{1}{4}$ pints) water
60 g (2 oz) arugola leaves
Salt
100 g ($3\frac{1}{2}$ oz) cut-up stale Italian or French bread
Freshly ground black pepper
4 tablespoons green, fruity olive oil

1 Put the potatoes and water into a pot, and bring to the boil.

2 Wash the arugola in numerous changes of cold water, until you are sure it is completely free of sand.

3 After about 10 to 15 minutes, when the potatoes are half cooked, put in the arugola and 2 large pinches of salt. Cover the pot.

4 Cook for 15 to 20 minutes at medium heat, then turn off the heat. Put in the bread, and cover the pot. Leave to stand for about 10 minutes.

5 Add a liberal grinding of pepper and the olive oil. Stir well, then taste and check seasoning. Serve immediately.

MENU SUGGESTIONS

Follow this soup with a meat course that shares its simple country character. Any pork dish would be a good choice, such as *Costolette di maiale alla modenese*, or *Costicine di maiale ai ferri*, or *Salsicce col cavolo nero*. Other suggestions: *Il bollito rifatto alla moda di papi*, *Frittata con le cipolle*, *Pollo in umido col cavolo nero*.

Minestrina di broccoli e manfrigul

BROCCOLI AND HOME-MADE BARLEY SOUP

Mathematicians sometimes use the word 'elegant' to describe the grace and felicity with which the elements of a mathematical proposition connect. It may seem far-fetched to borrow the term and apply it to this most humble soup. But I believe it fits. It is certainly not elegant in the sense that it is fancy. It is elegant in the way the different properties of its meagre ingredients are explored, developed, and exquisitely related. The procedure is simple, and nothing is wasted; there are no loose ends.

The blanched broccoli is sautéed with garlic in olive oil. The florets are kept aside, but the stalks are puréed together with their oil, and added to the broth and the egg barley. The density of the soup is thinned out with some of the water in which the broccoli was blanched. When the pasta is done, the florets are dropped in, and the soup is done. The tenderness of the florets, the firmness of the pasta, the savouriness of the good broth enriched with oil, and the faintly garlicky puréed stalks, all fall nimbly into place. If there is a better word than 'elegant' for how it is done, I can't think of it.

For six

680 g ($1\frac{1}{2}$ lb) broccoli
6 tablespoons olive oil
$1\frac{1}{2}$ cloves garlic, peeled and chopped
Salt
450 ml ($\frac{3}{4}$ pint) home-made meat broth, see page 18
150 g (5 oz) *manfrigul*, home-made egg barley, page 142
1 tablespoon chopped parsley
Freshly grated Parmesan cheese for the table

1 Detach the broccoli florets from the stalks. Cut off about 12 mm ($\frac{1}{2}$ inch) from the tough butt end of the stalks. Peel away the dark green skin on the stalks and larger stems. Split the thickest stalks in two, lengthwise. Rinse all the stalks and florets in cold water.

2 Bring about 3 litres (5 pints) water to the boil. Add 2 tablespoons salt, and put in the broccoli stalks. Two minutes after the water returns to the boil, put in the florets. If they float, dunk them below the surface from time to time, to keep them green. Cook 1 more minute after the water again returns to the boil, then retrieve the broccoli with a colander or slotted spoon. Do not discard the water.

3 Choose a sauté pan large enough to accommodate later all the stalks and florets in a single layer. Put in the oil and garlic, and turn on the heat to medium high. Sauté the garlic until it becomes a light gold colour.

4 Add all the broccoli with a couple of large pinches of salt, turn up the heat, and cook, stirring frequently, for 2 to 3 minutes.

5 Transfer the florets with a slotted spoon to a plate, and reserve for later.

6 Put the stalks, the oil from the pan, and 1 tablespoon of the water in which they were blanched into the container of a blender, and purée. If using the food processor, put in the stalks first, run the steel blades for a moment, then add the oil and water, and finish puréeing.

7 Put the puréed stalks and the broth into a soup pot, and bring to the boil. Add the 'barley'. Stir and cook at a moderate boil until the pasta is tender but firm. It should take about 10 minutes, or more, depending on the thickness and freshness of the pasta. The consistency of the soup tends to become too dense as it cooks, so thin it out with some of the water reserved after blanching the broccoli. Do not make it too runny, however.

8 While the pasta is cooking, separate the floret clusters into single bite-sized pieces. As soon as the pasta is done, put in the florets and the chopped parsley. Stir, and taste and check salt. Serve promptly, with a bowl of freshly grated Parmesan cheese.

MENU SUGGESTIONS

Follow with something savoury: *Scaloppine piccanti*, *Bocconcini di vitello ai sapori e funghi*, *Spezzato d'agnello con peperone e prosciutto*, *Salsicce col cavolo nero*, *Salsicce col vino rosso e i funghi secchi*.

For a light supper, follow with *Frittata con le patatine fritte* or any *frittata* in my first book, *The Classic Italian Cookbook* (pages 272–82).

Zuppa di riso col cavolo stufato

RICE AND SMOTHERED CABBAGE SOUP

Soups are where good leftovers go when they are reborn. This one is the happy reincarnation of the Smothered Green Cabbage from Venice on page 311. Here we use the entire amount of cabbage produced by that recipe because we are starting from scrach, and the cabbage is so good one can never have too much of it. But, if you were actually making the soup with only the leavings of that recipe, you would fill it out the way a good Venetian cook does – with a few smothered onions, some diced potatoes, a little extra rice.

Like *risi e bisi*, the Venetian rice and pea soup (*The Classic Italian Cookbook*, page 53), this one is fairly thick, but it is not a *risotto*. It should be runny enough to require a spoon. A light home-made broth would be best here, but you can start it off, if necessary, with bouillon dissolved in water. If you need additional liquid during the cooking, switch to water, because adding anything but home-made broth would make the flavour too sharp.

For four to six

The smothered cabbage produced with the recipe on page 311 (It may be made 2 or 3 days ahead of time.)
700 ml ($1\frac{1}{4}$ pints) home-made broth (page 18) or $1\frac{1}{2}$ bouillon cubes dissolved in the same quantity of water
120 g ($4\frac{1}{4}$ oz) rice, preferably Italian Arborio rice
30 g (1 oz) freshly grated Parmesan cheese
Salt
Freshly ground black pepper

1 Put the cabbage and broth into a soup pot. Turn on the heat to medium.

2 When the broth comes to the boil, add the rice. Cook uncovered, at a slow boil, stirring from time to time. The soup is ready when the rice is done. It should be cooked *al dente*, tender but firm to the bite, about 15 to 20 minutes. If you find that the soup is becoming too thick while the rice is cooking, add more home-made broth, or water, as required. At the end, the consistency of the soup should be rather dense.

3 When the rice is done, add the butter and the grated cheese, and stir well. Taste, and add what salt and pepper may be needed. Serve medium hot, giving the soup just a few minutes' rest after it finishes cooking.

MENU SUGGESTIONS

A great variety of meat courses can follow this, but avoid those that have too much onion. Onion is sweet and would be a monotonous echo of the sweetness of the cabbage. Suggestions: *Farsumauru – il braciolone*, *Spiedini all'uccelletto*, *Costolette di maiale ai due vini*, *Arrosto di maiale ubriaco*, *Pollo in tegame al limone*.

Zuppa di riso e cavolo rapa

RICE AND KOHLRABI SOUP

The Italian name for kohlrabi, *cavolo rapa*, is a good description of its flavour and appearance. It looks like a miniature cabbage (*cavolo*) on the outside, and it is solid like a turnip (*rapa*) inside. It is, in fact, a cabbage with a tart turnip taste. Kohlrabi can be blanched and sautéed or gratinéed, but I like it best in soups, where it is indeed very, very good.

There are two parts to this soup, prepared separately and combined at the end. One part is the kohlrabi and vegetable soup, the other is rice cooked pilaf style, as it is sometimes done in Piedmont. Either part or both can be cooked a day or two in advance, and put with the other to be reheated just before serving.

For four to six

The soup

60 g (2 oz) butter
2 medium onions, chopped very fine
1½ cloves garlic, peeled and chopped very fine
2 kohlrabi heads, peeled and sliced very thin
1 medium carrot, sliced very thin
1 medium potato, peeled
900 ml (1½ pints) home-made broth (page 18) – broth made with bouillon is definitely not recommended in this soup
Salt
Freshly ground black pepper

1 Put the butter, onion, and garlic in a soup pot, and turn on the heat to medium. Cook briefly, until the onion is just wilted.

2 Add the sliced kohlrabi and carrot, and cook for about a minute, turning them in the hot butter.

3 Add the potato, the broth, salt, and one or two grindings of pepper. Stir well, and cover the pot. Turn the heat down low, and cook for 1½ hours at a very gentle simmer.

The rice

15 g (½ oz) butter
½ small onion, chopped
50 g (1¾ oz) rice
Salt

1 Preheat oven to 200°C/400°F/Mark 6.

2 Choose a medium-sized casserole with a tight-fitting cover. Put in the butter and onion, and turn on the heat to medium.

3 When the onion becomes a light gold colour, put in the rice. Stir it for a few moments, coating it well with butter. Add 200 ml (generous ¼ pint) water, a couple of pinches of salt, and stir well.

4 Cover tightly; if not sure of a tight fit, press a sheet of aluminium foil over the pot before covering it. Place in the uppermost level of the preheated oven, and cook for 17 minutes exactly. When done, remove at once, uncover, and stir the rice with a wooden spoon.

The combined rice and kohlrabi soup

The soup and the rice, cooked as directed above
450 ml (¾ pint) home-made broth (page 18)
40 g (1½ oz) freshly grated Parmesan cheese
1 tablespoon chopped parsley
Salt
Freshly ground black pepper

1 Add the 450 ml (¾ pint) broth to the kohlrabi soup. If the soup has been prepared much in advance, reheat it, bringing it to a gentle simmer, but do not boil it.

2 Remove the potato from the pot and mash it through a food mill or potato ricer, or even mash it with a fork. Put it back into the soup.

3 Add the rice to the soup, stirring it well. If the rice was prepared in advance and is cold, let it reheat for a minute or so in the simmering soup.

4 Add the grated cheese. Stir, and taste and check seasoning. Add the parsley and turn off the heat. Serve promptly.

Note If you are preparing the kohlrabi soup and the rice ahead of time, do not combine them until ready to serve.

MENU SUGGESTIONS

Any meat dish with a country taste, especially a stew, would be a good second course. Try *Stufatino di manzo con i piselli*, *Stufatino di agnello con l'aceto* or any of the pork chops on pages 240–3.

Zuppa primavera

SPRING VEGETABLES SOUP

This is fresher and lighter than the more familiar varieties of Italian vegetable soup. It doesn't have, nor does it seek, the complex resonance of flavours that a *minestrone* achieves through long cooking of an extensive assortment of ingredients. It is a cheery, sweet-tasting mixture of globe artichokes and peas, added to a base of potatoes, slow-cooked with olive oil and garlic.

Although 'seasonal' is no longer a term one can confidently use with precision, this is what we would once have called a seasonal soup, a hearty welcome to the products of spring.

For four to six

3 medium globe artichokes
1 tablespoon lemon juice
6 tablespoons olive oil
3 to 4 cloves garlic, peeled and chopped fine
450 g (1 lb) boiling potatoes, peeled, rinsed, and cut into 6-mm ($\frac{1}{4}$-inch) slices
Salt
Freshly ground black pepper
450 g (1 lb) fresh peas (unshelled weight) or 150 g (5 oz) frozen peas, thawed
3 tablespoons parsley chopped very fine
Toasted crusty bread, lightly rubbed with garlic, 1 slice per serving (*optional*)

1 Trim the tough green tops of the leaves from the globe artichokes, cut them in half, and remove the choke and inner prickly leaves. (For a more detailed explanation of how to clean artichokes, see page 151.)

2 Cut the trimmed artichokes into the thinnest possible lengthwise slices, put them in a bowl with enough water to cover and add the lemon juice.

3 Put the olive oil and garlic into a soup pot, and turn on the heat to medium high. When the garlic turns a pale gold, add the sliced potatoes. Lower the heat to medium, cover the pot, and cook for about 10 minutes.

4 Drain the artichoke slices, and rinse them clean of their acidulated water. Put the artichokes into the pot. Add salt and a few liberal grindings of pepper. Cook, stirring the artichokes, letting them absorb some of the savoury flavours in the pot, for 3 to 4 minutes. Then add enough water to cover, turn the heat down to medium low, and cover the pot. Cook the artichokes until very tender when prodded with a fork – about 30 minutes or so, depending on their freshness and youth.

5 Add the thawed peas, and cook for another 10 minutes. If you are using fresh peas, put them in before the artichokes and the salt. Add enough water to cover them, and cook for 20 minutes. Then add the artichokes, and proceed as directed above.

(**Note** The soup may be cooked in advance, up to this point, then reheated gently when you are ready for it.)

6 Just before serving, put in the parsley, stir once or twice, and remove from heat. Ladle into soup plates, over the optional slice of toasted bread. Serve promptly.

MENU SUGGESTIONS

Zuppa primavera can precede either a fish or a meat dish. The fish could be *Pesce da taglio in salsa*, *Bocconcini di pesce spada fritto*, *Gamberi ai ferri come le cannocchie*. An appropriate meat course would be *Scaloppine ammantate*, *Messicani di vitello*, *Costolette di maiale ai due vini*, *Costicine di maiale ai ferri* or *Pollo in fricassea alla marchigiana*.

Minestrone alla novarese

NOVARA'S GREAT VEGETABLE SOUP

This spectacularly hearty minestrone from one of Italy's northernmost regions has at least two lives. It is, first of all, a magnificent, deeply satisfying vegetable soup. But it is also the base for one of the most robust of all *risotti*, *la paniscia* (page 97).

If you are using it principally to make *paniscia*, there will be some soup left over, because only part of it is needed for the *risotto*. The leftover soup can be kept in the refrigerator for a few days, and expanded with pasta and broth to make yet another, and slightly lighter, version.

All the ingredients that go into this *minestrone* are usually available, except for the cranberry beans. These are a variety of kidney beans, veined with pale pink markings, possessing a fine-textured flesh and tender skin. If not available, substitute tinned *cannellini*, white kidney beans. But if you should see the real thing, consider them an inducement to collect the rest of the ingredients, and make this good soup.

Like most vegetable soups, this one improves when made ahead of time and reheated a day or two later.

For four to six

6 tablespoons vegetable oil
15 g ($\frac{1}{2}$ oz) butter
2 medium onions, sliced very thin
110 g (4 oz) pork rind, cut into strips 12 mm ($\frac{1}{2}$ inch) long and 6 mm ($\frac{1}{4}$ inch) wide
1 carrot, peeled, washed, and diced
1 large stick of celery, washed and diced
2 medium courgettes, washed (see instructions on page 160) and diced
90 g (3 oz) shredded red cabbage
450 g (1 lb) fresh cranberry beans (unshelled weight) or 225 g (8 oz) tinned *cannellini*, drained
3 tinned Italian plum tomatoes, chopped, with their juice
Salt
Freshly ground black pepper
450 ml ($\frac{3}{4}$ pint) home-made broth (page 18) or 1 bouillon cube dissolved in the same quantity of water
Freshly grated Parmesan cheese for the table

1 Put the oil, butter, sliced onion, and pork rind into a soup pot. Turn on the heat to medium; cook, stirring from time to time, until the onion becomes a deep gold.

2 Add all the diced vegetables, the shredded cabbage, and the shelled fresh beans. (If you are using tinned beans, do not put them in at this time.) Stir well for a minute or two, coating the vegetables as thoroughly as possible with the hot fat.

3 Add the chopped tomatoes with their juice, a tiny amount of salt, and several liberal grindings of pepper. Stir again, and add all the broth. If there is not enough to cover all the vegetables by 25 mm (1 inch), add water, as much as needed.

4 Cover the pot, turn the heat down very low, and cook at a very lazy simmer for at least 2 hours. If you are using tinned beans, add them to the soup about 15 minutes before you turn off the heat. The consistency at the end should be rather thick. Taste and check seasoning.

If serving as a soup, allow it to rest a few minutes in the soup plates. Serve with a bowl of freshly grated Parmesan cheese.

If using in *paniscia*, proceed to page 97.

MENU SUGGESTIONS

This should lead to a solid meat course in which there are no vegetables. Any roast, such as *Arrosto di maiale ubriaco*, *Anatra arrosto* or *Arrosto di agnello pasquale col vino bianco* (from *The Classic Italian Cookbook*, page 235). Other suggestions: *Ossobuchi in bianco* or grilled steak.

Zuppa di lattughe ripiene

STUFFED LETTUCE SOUP

For cooks of the Riviera, Easter is the time for roast baby lamb and stuffed lettuce soup. In traditional versions of this soup, the hearts of small, tender lettuce heads are scooped out and replaced with a filling that contains herbs, cheese, and a blend of delicately flavoured meats, among which are chicken, veal, calves' brains and sweetbreads. In Rapallo I have had a simpler version, without brains or sweetbreads, that I like just as well.

Breast of chicken, veal, celery, and carrots are sautéed in butter and combined in a fine, minced mixture with ricotta, Parmesan, marjoram, parsley, and egg yolk. Instead of stuffing the whole head of lettuce, individual leaves are blanched, then rolled up with the stuffing, much like stuffed cabbage. They are cooked and served in broth, over a slice of bread toasted or browned in butter.

For four to six

210 g (8 oz) veal, all solid meat
1 whole chicken breast, boned and skinned
60 g (2 oz) butter
Salt
Freshly ground black pepper
½ small onion, chopped
1 tablespoon celery, chopped very fine
1 tablespoon carrot, chopped very fine
20 g (¾ oz) ricotta
50 g (1¾ oz) freshly grated Parmesan cheese plus a small amount to sprinkle on soup
1 teaspoon fresh marjoram or ¾ teaspoon dried
1 tablespoon chopped parsley
1 egg yolk
3 heads round lettuce
700 to 900 ml (1¼ to 1½ pint) good home-made meat broth (see page 18)
For each serving: 1 slice of bread toasted or browned in butter

1 Cut up the veal and the skinned, boned chicken breast into pieces about 25 mm (1 inch) square.

2 Put all the butter in a large sauté pan (about 300 mm/12 inches), and turn on the heat to medium.

3 When the butter foam begins to subside, put in the veal and a little salt and pepper. Cook and turn the veal until it is nicely browned on all sides. Transfer the pieces to a plate, using a slotted spoon or spatula.

4 Put in the cut-up chicken, add salt and pepper, and cook it very briefly, just until it loses its raw shine. Transfer it to the plate where the veal is.

5 Put the chopped onion into the pan, and, always at medium heat, cook

until it turns a pale gold. Add the celery and carrot, and cook for a few minutes, stirring from time to time, until the vegetables are tender. Transfer all the contents of the pan to a bowl.

6 Chop the veal and chicken very fine, with a knife or in the food processor. Add them to the bowl.

7 Put the ricotta, Parmesan, marjoram, parsley, and egg yolk into the bowl. Mix well, until all the ingredients are thoroughly amalgamated. Taste and check seasoning.

8 Discard any of the bruised or blemished outer leaves of the lettuce. Pull off all the others, except for the small ones at the heart, which can be saved for a salad. Be careful not to rip them. Wash the leaves one by one under cold running water. Handle gently, so as not to tear them.

9 Bring 5 litres (1 gallon) of water to the boil, add 1 tablespoon salt, then put in 3 or 4 lettuce leaves. Retrieve them after 5 or 6 seconds, using a colander spoon or wire skimmer.

10 Lay the leaves flat on a board or other work surface. Cut away any part of the central rib that is not tender. On each leaf, place about 1 tablespoon stuffing pressed into a narrow sausage shape. Roll up the leaf, completely wrapping the stuffing. Gently squeeze each stuffed leaf in your hand to keep it securely wrapped, and set it aside.

11 Blanch another 3 or 4 leaves, and stuff them as instructed above. When you get to the smaller leaves, you can use 2 overlapping leaves to make one roll.

12 When all the leaves have been blanched and stuffed, place them side by side in a soup pot or large saucepan. Pack them tightly, leaving no space between them, and make as many layers as necessary. Choose a dinner plate or pot cover small enough to slip into the pan, and rest it upon the topmost layer of stuffed lettuce. This is to keep them put while they are cooking.

13 Pour in enough broth to cover the plate or pot cover by about 25 mm (1 inch). Cover the soup pot, bring the broth to a gentle simmer, and cook for 30 minutes from the time it starts to simmer.

14 At the same time, in a separate small saucepan, put in the rest of the broth – there should be at least 350 ml ($\frac{2}{3}$ pint) – cover, and turn on the heat to low.

15 When the stuffed lettuce is done, transfer it to soup plates over the slices of toasted or browned bread. Handle with care to keep the rolls from unwrapping. Pour over the lettuce any of the remaining broth in which it cooked, and the hot broth from the other pan. Sprinkle a little grated Parmesan cheese on top, and serve at once.

MENU SUGGESTIONS

Follow with *Punta di vitello arrosto*, *Agnello in fricassea*, *Arrosto di agnello pasquale col vino bianco* (from my first book, page 235), *Pollo al limone* or *Pollo arrosto in tegame*.

Passatelli di carne in brodo

MEAT-DUMPLING SOUP

There are two versions of *passatelli*, one with eggs, cheese, and breadcrumbs, and another in which the same ingredients are enriched by the addition of veal or beef tenderloin, and beef marrow or butter. The recipe for the meatless, lighter version is in *The Classic Italian Cookbook*, page 60. Here is the more substantial, but equally fine version with meat.

In Emilia-Romagna *passatelli* are made by pressing the mixture through the holes of a simple tool, a perforated, curved disc with handles. A food mill can be substituted.

Meat *passatelli* are usually served in a rich, beautiful capon broth. If you have no capon broth, use any good home-made broth of chicken, meat, or both.

For six

150 g (5 oz) beef fillet
30 g (1 oz) beef marrow or 30 g (1 oz) butter
40 g (1½ oz) freshly grated Parmesan cheese
¼ teaspoon salt
¼ teaspoon grated nutmeg
1 egg
60 g (2 oz) fine, dry, breadcrumbs
1·15 litres (2 pints) home-made broth

1 Remove any skin or membrane from the beef fillet, and cut the meat into 12-mm (½-inch) pieces.

2 Put the meat and marrow (or butter) into a food processor fitted with steel blades, or into a blender. Process or blend to a soft, almost creamy consistency.

3 Put the meat into a bowl, and add the Parmesan, salt, nutmeg, egg, and breadcrumbs. Mix thoroughly, and shape into a ball.

4 Bring the broth to the boil in a soup pot.

5 Fit your food mill with the disc that has the largest holes, and pass the *passatelli* mixture through the mill directly into the boiling broth.

6 Cook at a lively boil for not much more than 1 minute. Turn off the heat, and let the *passatelli* rest for 3 to 4 minutes before serving.

MENU SUGGESTIONS

This soup can precede a fine roast such as *Punta di vitello arrosto* or a lusty country dish such as *Salsicce col cavolo nero*. Also try following it with *Rotolo di vitello con spinaci*, *Agnello in fricassea*, *Costolette di maiale con i funghi*.

RICE AND RISOTTO

Riso con la verza

RICE WITH SAVOY CABBAGE

In this most satisfying dish, Savoy cabbage sautéed with garlic provides the flavour. A pure boiled white rice is the simple vehicle that carries it. And the fine tangles of melted mozzarella are what hold it all together.

For four to six

- 1 head Savoy cabbage, approximately 680 g ($1\frac{1}{2}$ lb)
- 6 tablespoons olive oil
- 6 cloves garlic, peeled and chopped fine
- Salt
- Freshly ground black pepper
- 300 g ($10\frac{1}{2}$ oz) rice, preferably Italian Arborio rice
- 225 g (8 oz) mozzarella cheese, very coarsely grated
- 50 g ($1\frac{3}{4}$ oz) freshly grated Parmesan cheese
- 2 tablespoons parsley, chopped fine

1 Pull off and discard one or two of the dark-green outer leaves of the

cabbage, and trim away the bottom end of the stem if it is bruised or discoloured. Cut the cabbage in four, and rinse it in cold water.

2 Bring 3 to 4 litres (5 to 6½ pints) water to the boil. When the water is boiling, put in the cabbage, and set the cover on the pot slightly askew. Cook for about 20 minutes, or until the cabbage feels tender when prodded with a fork. When tender, drain well and allow the cabbage to cool a little. When it is no longer too hot to handle, chop it all up into pieces not much bigger than 12 mm (½ inch).

3 Choose a sauté pan broad enough to contain the cabbage later without crowding it or piling it high. Put in the olive oil and garlic, and sauté over medium heat until the garlic becomes a light gold colour.

4 Add the chopped cabbage, turning it in the oil so it becomes well coated. Add salt and pepper, taking into account that this will be the principal seasoning of the dish, and allowing also for the sweetness of the cabbage.

5 Turn the heat up to medium high, and sauté the cabbage for about 10 minutes, turning it frequently. Turn off the heat.

6 Bring 3 litres (5 pints) water to the boil, using, if you like, the same pot in which you cooked the cabbage. When the water comes to the boil, add 1 tablespoon salt, and put in the rice, stirring it with a wooden spoon. Cover and cook at a steady but not too lively boil until the rice is tender but *al dente*, firm to the bite (about 15 to 20 minutes). Stir the rice with a wooden spoon from time to time while it is cooking.

7 Drain the rice and put it in a warm serving bowl. Add the grated mozzarella, the cabbage together with all the olive oil from the pan, the Parmesan cheese, and the chopped parsley. Mix quickly and thoroughly. Serve piping hot.

MENU SUGGESTIONS

The rice is compatible with any meat dish you like, but the Savoy cabbage in it makes it obvious you should avoid any that also contain cabbage. The second course can be as light and elegant as *Ossobuchi in bianco* or *Pollo al limone*, or something very hearty such as *Costicine di maiale alla trevigiana*.

Risotto col sedano

RISOTTO WITH CELERY

The lively herbal fragrance of celery is most delightful to work with in cooking. One can use it as part of a chorus of flavours in more complex productions, or let it sing out alone, clear and fresh, against the simple white background of a *risotto*.

The leaves are used here to strengthen the aroma. The celery is put into the *risotto* in two batches, at different times: the first batch with the leaves, at the beginning, to give the rice time to absorb as much celery flavour as possible; the second batch at the midway point, giving the vegetable time enough to cook, while retaining some of its crunchy texture.

For four

1·15 litres (2 pints) home-made broth, page 18, or 3 bouillon cubes dissolved in the same quantity of warm water
1 medium chopped onion
2 tablespoons vegetable oil
60 g (2 oz) butter
200 g (7 oz) celery sticks, diced fine
1 tablespoon chopped celery leaves, pulled from the heart
Salt
300 g (10½ oz) Italian Arborio rice
30 g (1 oz) freshly grated Parmesan cheese
1 tablespoon chopped parsley

1 Put the broth in a saucepan, and bring it to a barely perceptible simmer.

2 Choose a heavy-bottomed flameproof casserole, and put in the chopped onion, all the oil, and half the butter. Turn on the heat to medium high, and sauté the onion until it turns a golden brown.

3 Add half the diced celery and all the chopped celery leaves, and a pinch of salt. Cook, stirring frequently, for about 3 minutes.

4 Add the rice, stirring it well for a minute or less, coating it thoroughly with the butter and oil in the pot. Add 8 tablespoons of the simmering broth. Stir constantly, with a wooden spoon, loosening the rice from the sides and bottom of the casserole. When the broth has completely evaporated, add another 8 tablespoons. Never cease stirring, and add broth, 8 tablespoons at a time, the moment all the broth in the pot has boiled away.

5 After the rice has cooked for 10 to 12 minutes, add the remaining diced celery. Continue to stir and to add small quantities of broth whenever there is no more liquid in the pot. The rice is done when it is tender and cooked through, but firm to the bite. It should take altogether about 35 minutes. As long as the rice is cooked, you are not required to use up all the broth

you started out with. But if the rice is still underdone, and you run out of broth, continue the cooking with warm water. Bear in mind that at the end there should be no more liquid in the *risotto* pot; therefore, in the last minutes of cooking, reduce the amount of liquid you put in each time, so there will not be any to boil away after the rice is done.

6 As soon as the rice is done, add the remaining butter and all the grated cheese. Stir rapidly, and taste and check salt. Turn off the heat, and stir in the chopped parsley. Serve promptly.

MENU SUGGESTIONS

Follow with dishes that are lightly and elegantly flavoured. Good choices might be *Filetto al barolo*, *Spalla di vitello brasata*, *Punta di vitello arrosto*, *Pollo in tegame al limone*.

Risotto primavera

RISOTTO WITH SPRING VEGETABLES

In the last few years there has been a vogue in Italian restaurants for pasta and *risotto* dishes poetically called *primavera*. This simply means the sauce is a collection of various seasonal spring vegetables; it is something Italian cooks have been doing in one form or another for a long time.

Here the fresh vegetables are added in separate batches. The first batch goes in sufficiently early to extract vegetable flavour for the *risotto*. The later batches do not cook long enough to alter the vegetables' texture and freshness. A piquant herbal accent at the end is contributed by a sprinkling of raw parsley.

Lightness is the essential character of this *risotto*. The leaden taste of tinned broth would become oppressive here. Plain water would be preferable. The only broth I can recommend in the list of ingredients is the good home-made variety.

For four

1·15 litres (2 pints) home-made broth, page 18
$\frac{1}{2}$ small onion, chopped
60 g (2 oz) butter
1 tablespoon vegetable oil
$\frac{1}{2}$ small carrot, diced fine

½ stick celery, diced fine
220 g (8 oz) Italian Arborio rice
60 g (2 oz) shelled fresh peas or frozen peas, thawed
1 medium courgette, scrubbed and cleaned (see page 160) and diced fine
Salt
1 large, firm, ripe tomato (preferably plum), peeled, seeded, and diced
30 g (1 oz) freshly grated Parmesan cheese
1 tablespoon parsley, chopped not too fine

1 Bring the broth to a barely perceptible simmer.

2 Choose a heavy-bottomed flameproof casserole, and put in the chopped onion, 40 g (1½ oz) butter, and the oil. Turn on the heat to medium high, sautéing the onion until it becomes a deep golden brown.

3 Add *half* the diced carrot and celery to the pot. Stir them for 2 or 3 minutes, sprinkle with salt, then add the rice and the fresh peas. (Frozen peas would go in later.)

4 Stir the rice, thoroughly coating it with the hot fat in the pot, for less than a minute. Add 8 tablespoons of the simmering broth. Stir constantly, with a wooden spoon, loosening the rice from the sides and bottom of the casserole. When the broth has completely evaporated, add another 8 tablespoons. Never cease stirring, and add broth, 8 tablespoons at a time, the moment all the broth in the pot has evaporated.

5 When the rice has been cooking for about 15 minutes, add the remaining carrot, celery, and half the courgette. Always continue to stir, and add simmering broth when needed.

6 After another 10 minutes, when the rice has cooked altogether for 25 minutes, add the remaining courgette, the diced tomato, and the thawed frozen peas, if you are using them. Continue to cook, stirring, and adding small quantities of broth whenever there is no more liquid in the pot. The rice is done when it is tender and cooked through, but firm to the bite. It should take altogether about 35 minutes, counting from the time you put in the first 8 tablespoons of broth. When done there should be no more liquid in the pot; therefore, regulate the quantity of broth you add in the last few minutes of cooking. If you have to boil away broth after the rice is cooked, it will become too soft.

7 When the rice is done, stir in the remaining butter, and all the grated cheese. Turn off the heat, and taste and check salt. Serve immediately, either directly from the casserole, or from a warm serving dish. Sprinkle with the chopped parsley before serving.

MENU SUGGESTIONS

Almost any meat dish can follow, except those that are cooked with an assortment of vegetables. An interesting choice could be *Agnello in fricassea*, *Costolette di maiale ai due vini* or *Piccata di fegato di vitello al limone*.

La paniscia novarese

RISOTTO COOKED WITH VEGETABLES AND RED WINE

No one who conceived such a dish as *paniscia* thought small. This is no light, tripping springtime *risotto* for feeble appetites. It is a bountiful merger of two lusty dishes: a *risotto* cooked with red wine and a generously endowed minestrone. It is the fitting product of Novara, in Piedmont, a region whose expansive cooking is matched by Italy's biggest red wines.

La paniscia is a *risotto* to which a soup is added – the vegetable soup from Novara, page 87. Another special ingredient is Novara's own soft salami, *salam d'la duja*. A substitute for it can be a good-quality, tender salami that is not highly spiced or garlicky. Also important is the wine with which it is cooked. If possible, use a good Piedmontese wine, a Gattinara, Spanna, or Barolo. If not possible, then try a California Barbera. Failing this, any good-quality, dry, full-bodied red wine will do.

For four

6 tablespoons vegetable oil
½ small onion, chopped
30 g (1 oz) tender, mild salami, chopped fine
200 g (7 oz) Italian Arborio rice
350 ml (scant ⅔ pint) dry red wine
450 ml (¾ pint) *minestrone alla novarese* (see recipe on page 88)
Salt
Freshly ground black pepper
Freshly grated Parmesan cheese for the table

1 Put the oil, chopped onion, and salami into a heavy casserole. Turn on the heat to medium high. Sauté the onion and salami, stirring from time to time, until the onion becomes a deep gold colour.

2 Add the rice, and turn it quickly several times with a wooden spoon, until it is well coated with oil.

3 Add 8 tablespoons wine, and stir constantly. Do not let the rice stick to the sides or bottom of the pan. When all the wine has evaporated, and the rice is quite dry, add another 8 tablespoons wine. Never stop stirring

and loosening the rice from the sides and bottom of the pan. When the wine has completely evaporated again, add the remaining 8 tablespoons. Continue to stir. When the wine has evaporated, add 8 tablespoons warm water. And stir continuously.

4 When the rice has cooked for about 15 minutes, add the minestrone, mixing it thoroughly with the rice. Continue adding 8 tablespoons warm water at a time, whenever all the liquid in the pot has evaporated. And, of course, continue stirring. The rice is done when it is tender but still firm. Altogether, calculate about 30 to 35 minutes' cooking time at moderately high heat. When the rice is nearly done, you must carefully regulate the rate at which you add water. If you add too much too late, you will find the rice is done and there is too much liquid in the pot. This *risotto* should have a minimum amount of liquid at the end, enough for it to possess the 'flowing' consistency Italians call *all'onda*. A few minutes before it is done, taste and check salt and pepper. In Novara they like it rather peppery. Allow to rest a few minutes before serving. Serve, with a bowl of freshly grated cheese.

MENU SUGGESTIONS

You want something substantial and earthy to follow this: *Arrosto di maiale ubriaco*, *Costicine di maiale alla trevigiana*, *Rognoncini di agnello saltati con cipolla*; or something with a fresh taste such as *Pollo in tegame al limone*. Avoid braised or stewed meats that already have vegetables with them.

FACTORY-MADE PASTA

How to cook it Pasta can be one of the easiest dishes in the world to prepare. It is also one of the easiest to ruin. More often than not it is indeed ruined, or at least flawed. The suggestions below are the key to making good pasta.

— For 450 grams or 1 lb of pasta use a minimum of 4 litres (7 pints) of water. Never use less than 3 litres ($5\frac{1}{4}$ pints), even for a small amount of pasta. Calculate at least 1 more litre ($1\frac{3}{4}$ pints) of water for each additional 225 g ($\frac{1}{2}$ lb). Do not attempt to cook more than 900 g (2 lb) of pasta at the

same time in the one pot. It is difficult to stir, to drain well, and to season quickly and thoroughly.
— Bring the water to a rapid boil.
— For every 450 grams (1 lb) of pasta, put in 1½ to 2 tablespoons salt, depending on the saltiness of the sauce that will be used later.
— Wait for a moment for the water to return to a rolling boil, then drop in the pasta.
— Make sure all the pasta is covered by water. *Spaghetti* or other long strands of stiff factory-made pasta may have to be bent – but not broken – to force them below the surface. Stir from time to time, while the pasta is cooking.
— After about 4 minutes taste to see whether the pasta is done. Don't go by the clock or a manufacturer's directions on the box or packet. Bear in mind that fresh, home-made pasta cooks in a fraction of the time it takes for macaroni pasta. It should be drained the moment it is cooked through but still firm to the bite.
——Pasta must be cooked *al dente*, tender but *firm*. Pasta that is soft and squishy is no more agreeable than tough, stringy chicken, soggy salad greens, or unripe, mouth-puckering fruit.
— The instant pasta is drained, it should be transferred to a warm bowl or dish, and tossed with sauce. This is a critical moment. If the pasta is not quickly coated with sauce, it will stick together and turn into a disastrous, gummy mass.
— Serve it at once, unless it is to be eaten cold, as in *Insalata di spaghetti*, page 71, or cooked again, as in *Frittata di spaghetti*, page 291.

Spaghettini coi canestrelli

THIN SPAGHETTI WITH SCALLOPS

Seafood, of any kind, makes wonderful sauce for pasta. Of all the recipes I've tried, up and down Italy's long coasts, there is none I have found more delectable than this. And none so lightning quick to prepare.

The scallops are cut up very small, to the size of *canestrelli*, the miniature Italian scallops (see comments on scallops on page 66). They are sautéed in olive oil, garlic, parsley, and hot pepper. That is the sauce. When it is tossed with the pasta, toasted breadcrumbs are added.

For six

450 g (1 lb) fresh bay or deep-sea scallops
9 tablespoons olive oil
3 cloves garlic, peeled and chopped fine
2 tablespoons chopped parsley
$\frac{1}{4}$ teaspoon or more chopped hot red pepper (see note in recipe), dried or fresh
Salt
680 g ($1\frac{1}{2}$ lb) thin *spaghetti* or 450 g (1 lb) if using high-quality Italian *spaghettini*
60 g (2 oz) plain breadcrumbs, lightly toasted in the oven

1 Rinse the scallops in cold water, pat dry thoroughly with a tea-towel, and cut up into pieces about 18 mm ($\frac{3}{8}$ inch) thick.

2 Put the oil and the chopped garlic in a saucepan, and sauté over medium heat until the garlic turns a light gold colour.

3 Add the parsley and hot pepper, stirring once or twice. (**Note** It is difficult to tell in advance just how hot the pepper is going to be. Put in $\frac{1}{4}$ teaspoon at this point. When you taste the sauce a little later on you can add more if you think it needs it.)

4 Add the scallops and one or two large pinches of salt. Turn the heat on to high and cook for about 1 minute, stirring a few times, until the scallops turn a flat white. Turn off the heat.

5 Cook the pasta in 4 to 5 litres (7 to $8\frac{3}{4}$ pints) of salted boiling water until it is *al dente*, or firm to the bite. Bear in mind that thin *spaghetti* cook very quickly. When the pasta is nearly done, turn on the heat under the saucepan containing the scallops to high. Stir rapidly and taste, adding salt and hot pepper if needed. If you see the scallops throwing off some liquid, do not attempt to boil it away. You would toughen the scallops and lose a very tasty part of the sauce. Do not heat the sauce for more than 30 or 40 seconds altogether.

6 Drain the pasta the moment it is done, tossing it vigorously in the colander to shake away all the water. Transfer to a warm serving bowl, mix in the scallop sauce and the toasted breadcrumbs, and serve at once. No grated cheese is required here.

MENU SUGGESTIONS

This dish may precede virtually any fish course. An excellent choice to follow it would be *Pesce spada al salmoriglio*. It can also be followed by more delicate dishes such as *Branzino alla rivierasca coi carciofi*, *Il pesce coi finocchi freschi* or *Pesce tra i due piatti*, but since the scallop sauce is rather peppery, it may leave the palate somewhat less responsive to them.

Pasta con le sarde alla palermitana

PASTA WITH SARDINES FROM PALERMO

One of the most fascinating aspects of food is how its character reflects that of the land where it is produced. What we see in that glorious miscellany that is the city of Palermo, we find in its dishes: strongly contrasting elements collide, settle, and are ultimately reconciled.

A perfect illustration is *pasta con le sarde*, one of the ornaments of Palermo's cooking. This brilliantly conceived dish brings together the pungencies of sardines and anchovies, the nectar of raisins, the fragrance of saffron and mountain fennel, and disciplines them into perfectly balanced, appetite-arousing harmonies.

There are substantial problems in this country with some of the key ingredients. The Atlantic sardine is not that of the Tyrrhenian Sea. Our raisins are fleshy and sugary compared with the lean, lentil-size, fruity ones of Sicily. And the wild, intense mountain fennel of Palermo just does not exist here. But some acceptable compromises can be made to produce satisfactory *pasta con la sarde* which duplicates the spirit, even if not every nuance of flavour, of the original.

If you cannot find fresh sardines, you can substitute frozen or tinned sardines, although this results in a little loss of zest. Raisins must be soaked in several changes of water to drain them of their excessive sweetness. And, instead of wild fennel, use the leafy tops of domestic fennel.

The best pasta to use is the thick *spaghetti* with a hole, called '*u pirciatu*' in Palermo, and sold here as *perciatelli* or *bucatini*.

As one might expect, there are many different and vehemently sustained points of view on the 'true' version of *pasta con le sarde*. The recipe given here is adapted from one I saw prepared in the home of friends in Bagheria, an ancient town not far from Palermo. It was the finest *pasta con le sarde* and one of the most perfect dishes of pasta I have ever had.

For four to six

450 g (1 lb) fresh sardines or frozen sardines, thawed, or 200 g (7 oz) tinned boneless sardines packed in olive oil, drained
50 g ($1\frac{3}{4}$ oz) fennel leaf tops or 40 g ($1\frac{1}{2}$ oz) wild fennel
Salt
8 tablespoons very good, fruity olive oil
$\frac{1}{2}$ small onion, chopped
4 flat anchovy fillets, chopped
35 g ($1\frac{1}{2}$ oz) *pinoli* (pine nuts)
1 tablespoon sultanas, soaked 15 minutes in several changes of cold water, drained, and chopped
$1\frac{1}{2}$ tablespoons tomato purée and $\frac{2}{3}$ packet (or a good pinch) powdered saffron, or $\frac{1}{2}$ teaspoon crumbled saffron threads, dissolved in 225 ml (scant $\frac{1}{2}$ pint) water
Freshly ground black pepper
450 g (1 lb) *bucatini* or *perciatelli*
60 g (2 oz) plain breadcrumbs, lightly toasted in the oven

How to prepare the fresh sardines for cooking

Snap off the head of a sardine, pulling away with it most of the intestines.

Snap off head

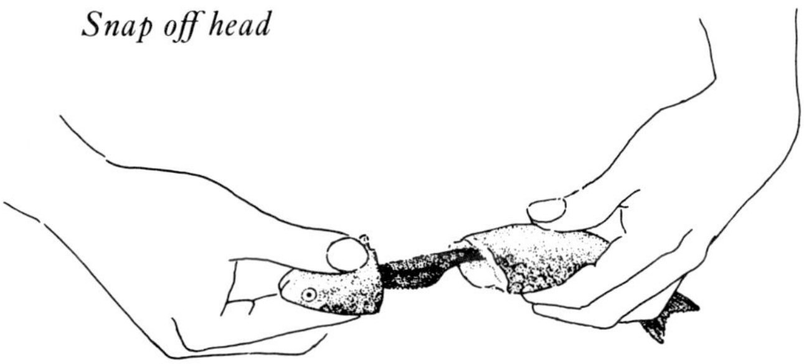

Work spine loose from flesh

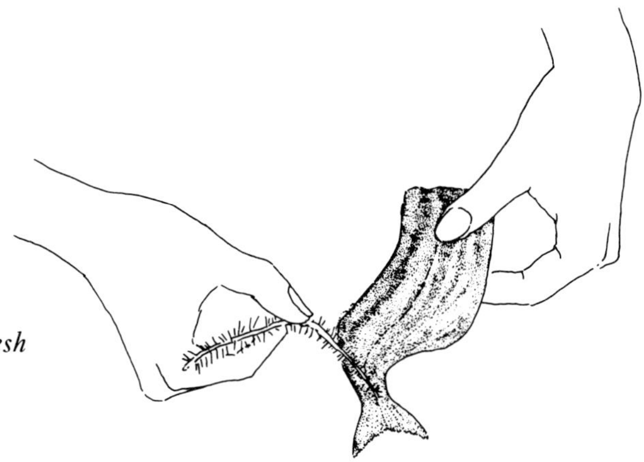

Pull off the centre back fin and the bones attached to it by tearing it from the tail end toward the head.

Hold the sardine with one hand, slip the thumbnail of the other hand into the belly cavity, and run it against the spine all the way to the tail. This will open up the sardine completely flat. The spine will now be exposed. Slip the nails of your thumb and forefinger under the spine, working the spine loose from the flesh. Lift the spine, loosening it from the entire body, but without snapping it. Pull it toward the tail, pulling the tail sharply away with it.

Wash the boned sardines under cold running water, rinsing away any remaining part of the intestines or loose bones.

Lay the sardines flat on a cutting board, and prop up one end of the board to let the fish drain.

(All this may appear to be intolerably laborious, but after the second or third sardine, when you have got the feel of it, it really goes very fast.)

1 Wash the fennel tops or the wild fennel in cold water. Bring 4 to 5 litres (7 to 8¾ pints) water to the boil in a large pot, add salt, then put in the washed greens. Cook for 10 minutes with the pot partly covered. Turn off the heat and remove the greens with a slotted spoon, but do not discard the water in the pot. Set it aside; it will serve later for cooking the pasta.

2 Gently squeeze the moisture out of the greens and then chop them.

3 Choose a sauté pan large enough to contain later all the ingredients except the pasta. Put in the olive oil, chopped onion, and chopped anchovies. Turn on the heat to medium. Stir occasionally, mashing the anchovies with a wooden spoon.

4 When the onion becomes translucent, put in the chopped fennel greens. Cook for about 5 to 6 minutes.

5 Clear some space in the pan by pushing to one side, with your spoon, the ingredients already in it. Into this clearing put as many sardines as will fit flat down. Sauté them briefly on one side, turn them and sauté the other side, no more than a few seconds for each side. Then push them toward the other ingredients in the pan, and make room for more sardines. (If you are using tinned sardines, omit this step, and refer to the special note below.)

6 When all the sardines have been cooked, put in the *pinoli*, the chopped raisins, and the water in which you have dissolved the saffron and tomato purée. Add salt and pepper. Cook at medium heat until the water in the pan has bubbled away completely. Turn off the heat.

7 Bring to the boil the water in which the fennel greens were cooked. Put in the pasta. When cooked *al dente*, tender but firm to the bite, drain, and put into a warm serving bowl. Shortly before this moment, when the pasta is not quite yet cooked, start warming up the sardine sauce in the pan over medium-low heat. As soon as the pasta is in the serving bowl,

pour the sauce over it. Toss thoroughly. Add the toasted breadcrumbs, and toss again. Allow to rest just a few minutes before serving.

Note The flavour of tinned sardines is rather dim; so, if using these, in order not to eclipse the sauce altogether, they should be added to the sauce at the end, after the saffron and tomato purée. When you come to the point in step 6 where the water has evaporated, put in the tinned sardines. Turn them for a few seconds in the sauce, then turn off the heat.

MENU SUGGESTIONS

There are two ways of following up this pasta: match its intensity of flavour with an equally vigorous dish, or seek relief in something simpler and restrained. For the first alternative you could have *Tonno in agrodolce alla trapanese*, *Cicala al salmoriglio* or, as long as you have sardines available, *Saraghine alla brace*. For the second, try *Cotolette alla palermitana*, *Costolettine di agnello fritte* (from my first book, page 230), or *Frittata con le cipolle*.

Spaghetti al sugo di pesce

SPAGHETTI WITH FISH-HEAD SAUCE

For some unaccountable reason most people assume that a fish's head, while it may originally have been important to the fish, is of negligible interest as food. Quite the contrary is true. There is no part of the fish that is as sweet-tasting and flavourful as those delectable morsels that are concealed in the head. Any fish soup in which the heads are used is infinitely the better for it. And this *spaghetti* sauce, made exclusively with heads, is one of the tastiest and most appealing of all the wonderful pasta sauces based on fish. There is so much flavour in a fish head that a few will go a long way, and practically every fishmonger but the most rapacious will let you have all the heads you need for next to nothing.

For eight

12 tablespoons olive oil
1 small onion, chopped
3 cloves garlic, peeled and chopped
4 tablespoons chopped parsley
680 to 900 g (1½ to 2 lb) assorted fish heads, from such fish as sea bass, red snapper, sea bream, etc. Wash the heads in cold water.
6 tablespoons dry white wine
300 g (10½ oz) tinned Italian plum tomatoes, cut up, with their juice
Salt
Freshly ground black pepper
900 g (2 lb) *spaghetti*
40 g (1½ oz) butter

1 Choose a saucepan that can later contain all the heads without overlapping. Put in the oil and the onion, and sauté the onion over medium heat until it is translucent.

2 Add the garlic and sauté until it becomes lightly coloured.

3 Add half the chopped parsley (2 tablespoons), stir once or twice, then add the fish heads.

4 Turn the heads once, coating them well, then add the wine and turn up the heat to high. When the wine has bubbled away for about 30 seconds, add the cut-up tomatoes with their juice, and turn the heat back down to medium.

5 Add salt and pepper, and cook for 15 to 20 minutes, depending on the size of the heads, turning them from time to time.

6 Remove the heads from the pan. With a small spoon scoop out all the bits of meat you find in the heads – under the cheeks, next to the neck, and so on. Put the meat aside in a small dish.

7 Remove all the larger bones and discard. Take a food mill fitted with a disc with very small holes, and pass what remains of the heads through it into the saucepan.

8 Turn the heat on to medium low, and cook at a very gentle simmer for about 30 minutes, stirring from time to time, until the sauce thickens to a dense, creamy consistency. Add the bits of meat that had been set aside, and cook for 5 more minutes, stirring the sauce a few times. Turn off the heat.

9 Cook the *spaghetti* in abundant salted water until done *al dente*, very firm to the bite. Drain, transfer to a heated serving bowl, toss with the sauce, mixing in the remaining 2 tablespoons chopped parsley and the butter. Serve at once.

MENU SUGGESTIONS

To balance the savouriness of the fish-head sauce, follow with a fish course that is neither too bland nor too exuberant. Good choices would be *Branzine alla rivierasca coi carciofi*, *Orate al limone e maggiorana*, *Bocconcini di pesce spada fritto* or *Gamberi dorati*.

Spaghetti alla carbonara

SPAGHETTI WITH RAW EGGS AND ITALIAN BACON

While there are innumerable minor variations in the way people make this celebrated Roman dish, there are really only two substantially different schools of thought. One maintains that *pancetta*, a mild, cured, unsmoked Italian bacon, is the only correct bacon to use. The other school insists on the smoked variety. Both are good, and both are popular in Italy, but the version I prefer is the one with *pancetta*. The flavour of smoke is not usually associated with Italian food; certainly hardly ever outside Alto Adige, a German-speaking region in the North that was once part of Austria. In this dish, I find that smoked bacon adds a sharpness that wearies the palate after the first mouthfuls. Try it both ways, and decide for yourself. If you want to use *pancetta*, but cannot find it, you can substitute green bacon quite successfully.

For four to five

225 g (8 oz) *pancetta* cut in a single slice 12 mm ($\frac{1}{2}$ inch) thick, or an equal amount of smoked bacon (see remarks above)
2 tablespoons olive oil
15 g butter
4 cloves of garlic, peeled and lightly crushed
4 tablespoons dry white wine
Salt
450 g (1 lb) *spaghetti*
3 eggs
25 g ($\frac{3}{4}$ oz) freshly grated *pecorino romano* cheese
60 g (2 oz) freshly grated Parmesan cheese
Freshly ground black pepper
2 tablespoons parsley, chopped fine

1 Cut the *pancetta* or bacon into strips a little less than 6 mm ($\frac{1}{4}$ inch) wide.

2 Put the oil, butter, and crushed garlic into a saucepan or small sauté pan, and turn on the heat to medium high. When the garlic turns a deep gold, remove and discard it.

3 Put the *pancetta* or bacon into the pan, and sauté until it begins to be crisp at the edges.

4 Add the wine, and let it boil away for a minute or two; then turn off the heat.

5 Bring 4 to 5 litres (7 to $8\frac{3}{4}$ pints) water to the boil. Add 2 to 3 tablespoons salt, and when the water returns to the boil, put in the *spaghetti*.

6 Take the bowl from which you'll be serving the *spaghetti* later, and into it break the 3 eggs. Beat them lightly, then mix into them both grated cheeses, a liberal grinding of pepper, and the parsley.

7 When the *spaghetti* is tender but firm to the bite, drain it, and put it into the serving bowl with the egg-and-cheese mixture. Toss rapidly and thoroughly until it is well coated.

8 Reheat the *pancetta* or bacon quickly over high heat, then pour the entire contents of the pan over the *spaghetti*. Toss again thoroughly, and serve immediately.

MENU SUGGESTIONS

Follow with a simple, savoury, not too fussy meat course. Try *Brasato di manzo con le cipolle*, *Cotolette alla palermitana*, *Ossobuchi in bianco*, *Punta di vitello arrosto*, *Stufatino di agnello con l'aceto*, or *Pollo in umido col cavolo nero*.

Spaghetti col sugo di cipolle

SPAGHETTI WITH SMOTHERED ONIONS

If onions were to be wiped out by some botanical calamity, it would undo much of Italian cooking. The sweet savouriness of cooked onion gently supports the structure of flavours upon which rest countless roasts, stews, sauces, and vegetable dishes. And in this simple and delicious *spaghetti* sauce it is given the opportunity to come forward and triumph on its own.

The onion is cooked slowly for at least $\frac{3}{4}$ hour, until it is meltingly soft and sweet. Then it is browned to sharpen its flavour with a livelier, keener edge. The sauce is completed with a little white wine and parsley. When the *spaghetti* is cooked, it is tossed briefly in the pan with the sauce.

The recipe calls for a combination of lard and olive oil. If you object to lard, you may substitute more olive oil.

For four to six

25 g ($\frac{3}{4}$ oz) lard and 5 tablespoons olive oil or, if not using lard, 6 tablespoons olive oil
680 g ($1\frac{1}{2}$ lb) onions, sliced very thin
Salt
Freshly ground black pepper
8 tablespoons dry white wine
2 tablespoons chopped parsley
450 g (1 lb) *spaghetti*
30 g (1 oz) freshly grated Parmesan cheese

1 Put the lard, olive oil, and onions into a large sauté pan. Cover the pan and turn on the heat very low. Cook for at least 45 minutes.

2 Uncover the pan, raise the heat to medium high, and cook the onion until it becomes a dark, deep gold colour. Do not be alarmed if upon uncovering the pan you find that the onions have thrown off a great deal of liquid. It sometimes happens, but the liquid will have evaporated by the time the onions are well browned.

3 Add a liberal amount of salt and pepper. Bear in mind that onions are quite sweet, and need an adequate amount of seasoning.

4 Add the wine, raise the heat to high, and stir until the wine has bubbled away.

5 Add the parsley, stir rapidly once or twice, and turn off the heat.

6 Cook the *spaghetti* in 4 to 5 litres (7 to $8\frac{3}{4}$ pints) boiling salted water. Regularly taste the pasta for readiness. When nearly done, turn on the heat under the pan with the onions to medium low. When the pasta is done – it should be quite firm to the bite – drain it at once, and transfer it to the sauté pan. Turn up the heat under the pan to medium high, and toss the *spaghetti* with the sauce for about half a minute.

7 Transfer to a warm serving bowl, add the grated cheese, toss thoroughly, and serve at once.

MENU SUGGESTIONS

I like to follow the sweet taste of onion in this *spaghetti* with a sharp and lively second course. For example: *Umido di gamberi al pomodoro piccante*, *Scaloppine piccante*, *Nodini di vitello con sughetto di acciughe*, *Spiedini all'uccelletto*, *Stufatini di agnello con l'aceto* or *Costicine di maiale alla trevigiana*.

Spaghetti alla siciliana

SPAGHETTI WITH AUBERGINES AND RICOTTA

Nowhere as in Sicily does an aubergine fulfil the promise of its voluptuous purple curves with deliciously gentle, honeyed flesh. Elsewhere, and in northern countries in particular, this vegetable is often touched with traces of bitterness that turn anticipation into disappointment. In this recipe, after steeping it at length in salt to draw off its harsh liquid, it is rinsed in cold water. This step purges the aubergine of most of its lingering sharpness and lets its sweeter, milder self emerge. The original Sicilian dish, with its perfectly ripened vegetables and tingling, fresh cheeses, is immensely satisfying. If you choose your ingredients carefully, the following version lets you come remarkably close. Look for aubergines that are firm, not spongy to the touch, with a slick, glossy, unpocked skin.

For six

1 medium to large aubergine, about 680 g ($1\frac{1}{2}$ lb)
Salt
Enough vegetable oil to come 12 mm ($\frac{1}{2}$ inch) up the sides of the pan
6 tablespoons olive oil
1 medium onion, sliced very thin
2 cloves garlic, peeled and chopped
400 g (14 oz) tinned Italian plum tomatoes, drained and cut into thin strips, without their juice
Freshly ground black pepper
450 g (1 lb) *spaghetti*
3 tablespoons grated mild *romano pecorino* cheese
30 g (1 oz) fresh ricotta
8 to 10 fresh basil leaves **or**, if out of season, 2 tablespoons chopped parsley
Freshly grated Parmesan cheese for the table

1 Peel the aubergine, cutting off and discarding its green cap.

2 Cut it into cubes 37 mm ($1\frac{1}{2}$ inches) thick. Put the cubes in a pasta colander, and sprinkle them liberally with salt. Set the colander in the sink or a basin, and let the aubergine sit for at least 1 hour.

3 Scoop up a few of the aubergine cubes with your hands, and rinse them in cold running water. Wrap them in a tea-towel, and twist it to squeeze all the moisture you can out of them. Then lay them out on a clean, dry towel. Proceed in this manner until you've rinsed and wrung out all the aubergine cubes.

4 Put the vegetable oil into a large frying pan, and turn on the heat to medium high. When the oil is quite hot, slip in as many of the aubergine pieces as will fit loosely in the pan. If they don't all fit in at one time, fry

them in two or more batches, until all the pieces are done. When the aubergine is tender, transfer it with a slotted spoon to kitchen paper to drain.

5 Pour off the vegetable oil from the pan. (Do not discard it. When it cools off, filter it through kitchen paper into a glass jar, and save it for the next time you'll be frying aubergine.)

6 Add the olive oil to the pan, along with the sliced onion. Cook over medium-high heat until the onion becomes a light gold colour. Add the chopped garlic, and cook for just a few seconds, stirring as you cook.

7 Add the strips of tomatoes, turn the heat up to high, and cook for 8 to 10 minutes, stirring frequently.

8 Add the aubergine, turn the heat down to medium, and cook for a minute or two, mixing it with the other ingredients. Taste and check salt, and add a grinding of pepper.

9 Cook the *spaghetti* in 4 to 5 litres (7 to 8¾ pints) boiling, lightly salted water. When tender, but very firm to the bite, drain, and transfer to a warm serving bowl.

10 Stir in the aubergine sauce, the grated *romano*, the ricotta, and the basil or parsley. Before adding the *romano*, taste the *spaghetti* with a bit of sauce. If it tastes a little on the salty side, hold back about 1 tablespoonful of the cheese.

11 Serve immediately, with a bowl of grated Parmesan cheese.

MENU SUGGESTIONS

Almost any dish that is uncomplicated, and obviously, does not contain aubergines. It would be good before *Gamberi dorati*, *Bistecchine di manzo alla cacciatora*, *Cotolette alla palermitana*, *Scaloppine piccanti* or *Nodini di vitello con sughetto di acciughe*.

Spaghetti alla nursina

SPAGHETTI WITH BLACK TRUFFLES FROM NORCIA

This dish should be reserved just for lovers. Some pleasures are too keen to be shared with a crowd. And, in this case, too expensive. *Spaghetti alla nursina* comes from the black-truffle country of central Italy, and it requires a prodigal amount of truffles, enough to wrap each pasta strand with a coat of thick, voluptuous black. With the price of truffles nearly catching up to that of gold, it is an extravagant dish indeed. But it is also extravagantly good.

It can be produced at any time of the year using preserved truffles. In this case you should buy only the ones in glass jars, so you can be sure of obtaining selected large, unblemished 'tubers'. But to achieve the finest results you need fresh truffles, which are available during the winter months in a few specialist food shops. Good fresh truffles must be firm, not spongy, and possessed of a subtle but distinct aroma.

The other critical ingredient in the sauce is the olive oil. The thin, tasteless oils from the supermarket are a waste of time. If you have become seriously interested in good Italian cooking, you should find a source for green, fruity oil that tastes of olives. It is the only kind to use.

Moreover, for a dish that requires such a formidable investment of materials, you should not settle for any pasta but a high-quality durum-wheat imported Italian pasta.

For two

75 to 90 g ($2\frac{1}{2}$ to 3 oz) black truffles, preferably fresh
3 tablespoons high-quality green, fruity olive oil
1 clove garlic, peeled and crushed
1 flat anchovy fillet, chopped very fine
Salt
180 g (6 oz) imported Italian *spaghettini* (thin *spaghetti*)

1 If using fresh truffles, clean them with a stiff brush, rinse them briefly, and pat thoroughly dry. If using preserved truffles, drain them and pat them dry. Do not discard the liquid; save it to add to a roast or a meat sauce.

2 Grate the truffles to a very fine-grained consistency, using the smallest holes of a flat-sided grater. If you have a good mortar and pestle, chop them up and grind them to a pulp in the mortar.

3 Put the truffles into a small earthenware saucepan. If you do not have earthenware, use enamelled cast iron. Add the olive oil, trickling it in a little at a time, and stirring thoroughly.

4 Turn on the heat to low, and add the garlic and the chopped anchovy. Stir with a wooden spoon for about 10 minutes, mashing the anchovy until it is almost completely dissolved into a paste. Keep the heat low, and do not let the oil bubble. If the oil becomes too hot, move the pan away from the heat for a few moments. Add salt to taste, stir once or twice, and remove from heat.

5 Cook the pasta in 3 to 4 litres ($5\frac{1}{4}$ to 7 pints) salted boiling water. Bear in mind that thin *spaghetti* cooks rather quickly. As soon as it is cooked *al dente*, tender but firm to the bite, drain it quickly, and transfer to a warm bowl.

6 Remove the garlic from the truffle sauce, and pour all the contents of the pan over the *spaghetti*. Toss thoroughly, and serve at once.

MENU SUGGESTIONS

Spaghetti with truffles is a momentous start for any meal. It should be followed by something very simple or equally rich. I might choose *Filetto al barolo*, *Punta di vitello arrosto*, *Arrosto di agnello al ginepro* (from my first book, page 236), *Pollo al limone* or *Anatra arrosto*.

Maccheroncini alla saffi

SMALL MACARONI WITH ASPARAGUS, CREAM, AND HAM

History has at times a quirky way of perpetuating great men's names. The doings of Aurelio Saffi, a governor of the nineteenth-century Republic of Rome, will interest only those who specialise in the more fleeting episodes of Italy's past. But the exquisite dish upon which he bestowed his regard and his name should endure as long as there are lovers of asparagus, and cream, and pasta.

In this recipe, the asparagus is given a preliminary boil, long enough to make it tender, brief enough to leave it firm. It is then combined with sautéed strips of ham and double cream, and that is the sauce.

The original version, as it is prepared at Bazzano's Ristorante della Rocca, calls for prosciutto. I use boiled ham instead, because it is less sharp and salty, and does not intrude upon the delicacy of the dish. If you like, try it both ways, and decide which suits you better.

For four to six

680 g ($1\frac{1}{2}$ lb) fresh asparagus
Salt
450 g (1 lb) *maccheroncini*, *penne*, or other smooth, short tubular pasta
180 g (6 oz) boiled unsmoked ham, cut into long strips 6 mm ($\frac{1}{4}$-inch) wide
30 g (1 oz) butter
225 ml (scant $\frac{1}{2}$ pint) double cream
Freshly grated Parmesan cheese

1 Cut 25 mm (1 inch) or more off the butt end of each asparagus, until you reach the moist, tender part of the stalk. Pare away the tough green skin from the whole lower half of the stalk to a depth of about 1 to 2 mm ($\frac{1}{16}$ inch). Remove any small leaves sprouting below the tip of the spear. Wash all the asparagus in cold water.

2 Choose a pan long or broad enough to accommodate later all the asparagus lying flat. Put in 50 mm (2 inches) water and 1 tablespoon salt. Turn on the heat to medium high. When the water boils, slip in the asparagus and cover the pan. Cook for 4 to 8 minutes after the water returns to the boil, depending on the freshness and thickness of the asparagus. It should be cooked until tender but still firm.

3 Drain the asparagus. When cool enough to handle, cut off the spear tips at their base, and cut the rest of the stalks into lengths of about 18 mm ($\frac{3}{4}$ inch). Discard any parts of the stalks that are still woody and tough. Set aside all the rest for later.

4 Brings 4 to 5 litres (7 to 8$\frac{3}{4}$ pints) water to the boil, add salt, and when the water resumes boiling, put in the pasta.

5 Put the ham and half the butter into a small sauté pan. Cook gently over medium-low heat for 2 to 3 minutes. Do not crisp the ham.

6 Wipe dry the pan in which you cooked the asparagus. Put in the remaining butter, and turn on the heat to medium. As soon as the butter is completely melted, but before it begins to foam, put in the cut-up asparagus. Turn up the heat to high, and cook for about 30 to 40 seconds, long enough to turn all the asparagus in the butter.

7 Add the ham to the asparagus, put in the cream, and turn on the heat to medium high. Stir constantly for about 30 seconds, or until the cream thickens. Turn off the heat. Taste and check salt.

8 When the pasta is cooked *al dente*, tender but firm to the bite, drain it well, and transfer it to a warm serving bowl. Add the asparagus and all the contents of the pan. Toss thoroughly, mixing in 60 g (2 oz) grated cheese. Serve at once, with an additional bowl of grated cheese.

MENU SUGGESTIONS

Because the macaroni is delicate in flavour, but rich and creamy, follow with something simple and elegant: *Filetto al barolo*, *Ossobuchi in bianco*, *Nodini di vitello alla salvia* (from my first book, page 229), *Piccata di fegato di vitello al limone* or *Il pollo ripieno*.

Maccheroncini coi piselli e i peperoni

SMALL MACARONI WITH PEAS AND PEPPERS

Peas, prosciutto, and cream make one of the loveliest, best-known sauces for pasta. This version includes diced roasted sweet red peppers.

You need very meaty bright red peppers here, for both textural and visual interest. Do not roast them more than is required to loosen their skin, because you want their flesh to stay firm. The roasted peppers that come in jars would not be satisfactory, because they are too flabby.

For four to six

3 medium red peppers
A brown paper bag
1 single slice of *prosciutto*, about 180 g (6 oz), cut 12 mm ($\frac{1}{2}$ inch) thick or slightly less. (Westphalian ham or, if desperate, green lean bacon may be substituted.)
60 g (2 oz) butter
100 g ($3\frac{1}{2}$ oz) frozen petits pois, thawed
225 ml (scant $\frac{1}{2}$ pint) double cream
Salt
Freshly ground black pepper
450 g (1 lb) small tubular macaroni
100 g ($3\frac{1}{2}$ oz) freshly grated Parmesan cheese

1 Roast the peppers under a hot grill, or resting over the flames of a gas burner, turning them to every side, until all the skin is charred and blistered. They do not need to cook through because they must remain crunchy. Put them in the paper bag, folding it two or three times at the opening to seal it. Set aside.

2 Dice the slice of prosciutto very fine. Set aside.

3 When the peppers have cooled off a bit (they should be lukewarm) remove them from the paper bag and peel them with your fingers. It doesn't matter if a patch of skin here and there remains attached to the pepper. Cut them open removing all the seeds and pulpy inner core. Pat them dry with kitchen paper and cut them into squares of about 6 mm ($\frac{1}{4}$ inch).

4 Put the butter and diced prosciutto into a sauté pan and cook for a few seconds over medium heat.

5 Add the thawed peas, stir, and cook for an additional minute.

6 Add the cut-up peppers, stirring them for a few seconds.

7 Add the cream, salt and a liberal amount of ground pepper. (Bear in mind when adding the salt that ham may be quite salty. It would be prudent to salt lightly at first, then taste and add what salt may be needed later.) Turn up the heat and cook, stirring constantly, until the cream thickens. Turn off the heat and set aside.

8 Boil the pasta in the customary manner, in abundant salted water, until it is done, tender but firm to the bite. A half minute or so before the pasta is done, warm up the sauce. Drain the pasta, toss with the sauce in a warm serving bowl, mixing in the grated cheese. Serve immediately.

Note This is one of those rare occasions on which a frozen vegetable can be preferred to the fresh variety. Choice frozen *petits pois* are so tender, sweet, and thin-skinned that they are perfect for this sauce. Only very young, just picked peas would be as good, and if you are lucky enough to get them, enjoy them on their own, as in *Pisellini alla fiorentina* in my first book (page 328).

MENU SUGGESTIONS

The creamy sauce of vegetables and prosciutto makes it desirable to choose a very simple meat course to follow. For example, *Ossobuchi in bianco*, *Punta di vitello arrosto*, *Piccata di fegato di vitello al limone* or *Pollo al limone*.

Maccheroncini alla boscaiola

FORESTER'S SMALL MACARONI WITH MUSHROOMS

It's because of the mushrooms that this is called 'forester's' macaroni. If you want to intensify the woody flavour of the sauce, follow the procedure for adding dried imported wild mushrooms, as directed below.

This is one of those pastas that is *saltata in padella*. This means it is given a brief finishing turn in the pan with the sauce, which induces the pasta to absorb an extra measure of flavour.

For four

30 g (1 oz) dried imported boletus mushrooms (*optional*)
360 g (12 oz) fresh mushrooms
6 tablespoons vegetable oil
2 cloves garlic, peeled and crushed
45 g ($1\frac{3}{4}$ oz) cooked ham, cut into very narrow strips about 3 mm ($\frac{1}{8}$ inch) wide
2 tablespoons chopped parsley
Salt

Freshly ground black pepper
225 g (8 oz) tinned Italian plum tomatoes, chopped very fine, with their juice
450 g (1 lb) *maccheroncini*, *penne*, *ziti*, or other short, tubular pasta
35 g ($1\frac{1}{4}$ oz) freshly grated Parmesan cheese, plus additional cheese for the table

1 (Proceed to step 3 if not using wild mushrooms.) Soak the dried mushrooms in a small bowl in 450 ml ($\frac{3}{4}$ pint) lukewarm water for at least 30 minutes. When they have finished soaking, lift them out carefully, without stirring the water. Rinse them several times in cold water. Chop them fine, and set aside.

2 Filter the water in which the mushrooms have soaked through a wire strainer lined with kitchen paper. Reserve for later.

3 Wash the fresh mushrooms rapidly under cold running water. Wipe them thoroughly dry with a soft towel. Cut the mushrooms into very thin lengthwise slices, without detaching the caps from the stems.

4 Put the oil and crushed garlic cloves in a large sauté pan, and turn on the heat to medium high.

5 When the garlic turns a deep golden brown, remove it. Add the fine ham strips, stir once or twice, then add the reconstituted wild mushrooms and their filtered water. (If you are not using wild mushrooms, proceed immediately to step 6.) Cook at lively heat until all the mushroom liquid has evaporated.

6 Add the fresh mushrooms, the chopped parsley, salt, and a few grindings of pepper. Stir constantly for about 30 seconds, then add the tomatoes and their juice. Stir well, turn the heat down to low, and cover the pan.

7 Bring 4 to 5 litres (7 to $8\frac{3}{4}$ pints) water to the boil, add salt, and when the water returns to the boil, put in the pasta. Cook until done *al dente*, tender but firm to the bite.

8 Drain the pasta well, and put it in the pan where the sauce has been cooking. Raise the heat to medium, and turn the pasta thoroughly in the sauce, uncovered, for about 20 seconds.

9 Transfer to a warm serving bowl, and mix in the grated cheese. Serve at once, with an additional bowl of grated cheese.

MENU SUGGESTIONS

Apart from avoiding those that contain mushrooms, try to direct your choice towards a meat course on the savoury, earthy side. Examples: *Brasato di manzo con sedano e cipolle*, *Costolette di vitello profumate all'aglio e rosmarino*, *Rotolo di vitello con spinaci*, *Agnello in fricassea* and *Arrosto di maiale ubriaco*.

Penne con spinaci e ricotta

PENNE WITH RICOTTA AND SPINACH SAUCE

When I tasted this in Palermo, there was something about it that strongly reminded me of home, although I was having it for the first time. A second forkful, and I understood. The sautéed spinach and ricotta that coated the pasta was very much like the stuffing we make in Romagna for *tortelloni.* Here it was turned inside out and had become a sauce. What a beautiful idea. If only we had thought of it first!

For four to six

900 g (2 lb) fresh spinach or 200 g (7 oz) frozen leaf spinach, thawed
110 g (4 oz) butter
Salt
450 g (1 lb) *penne* or other short tubular macaroni
100 g ($3\frac{1}{2}$ oz) fresh whole-milk ricotta
50 g ($1\frac{3}{4}$ oz) freshly grated Parmesan cheese

1 (If you are using frozen spinach, allow it to thaw, then begin at step 4.) Pull the spinach leaves from the stems, discarding all the stems. Soak the spinach in a basin of cold water, dunking it with your hands several times. Lift out the spinach, and pour out the water along with the grit that will have settled at the bottom. Fill again with fresh water, and repeat the whole operation with several changes of water until you see that there is no more grit settling at the bottom of the basin.

2 Cook the spinach in a covered pan over medium heat with a pinch of salt and no more water than is still clinging to the leaves. Cook until tender, about 10 minutes or more, depending on how young and fresh the spinach is.

3 Drain well, and as soon as the spinach is cool enough to handle, press as much of the remaining liquid from it as you can, but do not squeeze it too tightly.

4 Chop the spinach rather fine, and set aside.

5 Choose a frying pan or sauté pan that can contain all the spinach later without overcrowding. Put in 60 g (2 oz) butter, and turn the heat on to medium high. When the butter is melted, add the spinach and a liberal 2 or 3 pinches of salt. (Bear in mind that this, along with the ricotta, will be the principal component of the sauce. The ricotta has no salt, so the spinach must be adequately seasoned.) Sauté the spinach for 2 minutes or so, turning it frequently, then turn off the heat.

6 Cook the pasta in 4 to 5 litres (7 to $8\frac{3}{4}$ pints) salted boiling water until

tender but *al dente*, firm to the bite. Drain into a pasta colander, giving several vigorous up-and-down shakes to drain the pasta thoroughly.

7 Transfer the pasta to a warm serving bowl, adding all the spinach from the pan, the ricotta, the remaining butter, and all the grated cheese. Mix thoroughly and serve at once.

MENU SUGGESTIONS

The ricotta and spinach make this a fresh and light course. You can maintain the same spirit in the second course, choosing something delicate like *Pesce tra i due piatti* or *Pollo al limone*. Or you can let it lead you to the stepped-up flavours of *Spiedini all'uccelletto*, *Bocconcini di vitello ai sapori e funghi*, *Arrosto di maiale ubriaco*, *Salsicce col vino rosso e i funghi secchi*, *Pollo in fricassea alla marchigiana*.

Penne col sugo di cavolfiore

PENNE WITH CAULIFLOWER, GARLIC AND OIL

One of the basic mother sauces for pasta is *aglio e olio*, garlic and oil. From it has been spawned a multitudinous brood of sauces wherein we find most varieties of vegetables. An example is this one, featuring cauliflower.

In this family of sauces additional flavourings such as parsley, hot pepper, and anchovies may be used, although not all need be present. They are almost invariably *sughi in bianco*, 'white' sauces – that is, without tomato. They are supposed to be served without grated cheese, and that is how I prefer them. But one may do as one pleases, and choose to have either *pecorino* or Parmesan cheese, depending upon whether one wants the sauce more or less sharp.

For four to six

1 head cauliflower [about 680 g (1½ lb)]
8 tablespoons olive oil
2 large cloves garlic, peeled and chopped fine
6 flat anchovy fillets, chopped
¼ teaspoon chopped hot red pepper
Salt
450 g (1 lb) *penne* or other macaroni
2 tablespoons chopped parsley

1 Strip the cauliflower of all its leaves except for a few of the very tender inner ones. Rinse it in cold water, and cut it in two.

2 Bring 4 to 5 litres (7 to $8\frac{3}{4}$ pints) water to the boil, then put in the cauliflower. Cook until tender, but compact – about 25 to 30 minutes. Test it with a fork to know when it is done. Drain and set aside.

3 Put the oil, garlic, and chopped anchovies into a medium-sized sauté pan. Turn on the heat to medium, and sauté until the garlic becomes a golden brown colour. Stir from time to time with a wooden spoon, mashing the anchovies with it.

4 Put in the boiled cauliflower, and break it up quickly with a fork, crumbling it into pieces no bigger than a peanut. Turn it thoroughly in the oil, mashing part of it to a pulp.

5 Add the hot pepper and a liberal amount of salt. Turn up the heat, and cook for a few minutes more, stirring frequently. Then turn off the heat.

6 Bring 4 to 5 litres (7 to $8\frac{3}{4}$ pints) water to the boil, add a liberal amount of salt, and as soon as the water returns to the boil, put in the pasta. When cooked *al dente*, tender but firm to the bite, drain it well and transfer it to a warm serving bowl.

7 Very briefly reheat the cauliflower, and pour all the contents of the pan over the pasta. Toss thoroughly. Add the chopped parsley. Toss again, and serve at once.

MENU SUGGESTIONS

After this earthy cauliflower sauce do not bring on a second course whose flavour is either too shy or too sharp. Nice combinations could be with *Spalla di vitello brasata*, *Spiedini all'uccelletto*, *Stufatino di agnello con l'aceto* or *Costolette di maiale alla modenese*.

Conchiglie con bacon, piselli e ricotta

PASTA SHELLS WITH BACON, PEAS, AND RICOTTA

I am not usually fond of bacon in Italian dishes, but in this sauce for pasta its smoky bite is pleasingly tempered by the sweetness of the peas and ricotta. The sauce takes so little time to prepare you could start it at the same time you put on the water for the pasta; the whole dish can then be done in under 15 minutes. That is, unless you are using fresh peas. These must be cooked before they go into the sauce, and that will take several minutes more. The actual time depends on the youth and freshness of the peas. Although pasta shells are recommended, any pasta shape, that will catch bits of the sauce, such as *fusilli*, will do. An excellent choice would be home-made *orecchiette* (see *The Classic Italian Cookbook*, page 148).

For four to six

110 g (4 oz) lean bacon
150 g (5 oz) frozen *petits pois*, thawed, or 450 g (1 lb) fresh peas (unshelled weight)
Salt
110 g (4 oz) ricotta
450 g (1 lb) *conchiglie* (pasta shells) or other pasta (see remarks above)
15 g ($\frac{1}{2}$ oz) butter
35 g ($1\frac{1}{4}$ oz) freshly grated Parmesan cheese
Freshly ground black pepper

1 Cut the bacon into narrow strips. Put it into a small sauté pan or saucepan, and turn on the heat to medium. Cook the bacon until it becomes very lightly browned, and the fat melts. Do not let it become as crispy as you might if you were having it for breakfast. Pour off from the pan all but 2 tablespoons fat.

2 Put the thawed peas into the pan. Cook them for a minute or so, stirring them, so they absorb some of the bacon flavour. (If you are using fresh peas, shell them, and cook them in a small amount of boiling water for 5 to 10 minutes, depending on their freshness and size. Then add them to the bacon, cooking them another minute or two.) Turn off the heat.

3 Bring 4 to 5 litres (7 to $8\frac{3}{4}$ pints) water to the boil, add salt, and when the water has returned to the boil put in the pasta.

4 Put the ricotta into the bowl from which the pasta will be served, and crumble it with a fork. Add the butter.

5 When the pasta is tender but firm to the bite, drain it well, and put it into the serving bowl. Toss two or three times with the ricotta.

6 Rapidly heat up the bacon and peas, and pour the entire contents of the pan over the pasta. Toss thoroughly. Add the grated cheese, 1 or 2 grindings of pepper, toss once more, and serve at once.

MENU SUGGESTIONS

Except for avoiding those dishes that have cream or mozzarella, any meat course can follow. Especially agreeable choices might be *Bistecchine di manzo alla cacciatora*, *Messicani di vitello*, *Stufatino di maiale alla boscaiola*, *Costicine di maiale ai ferri* or *Rognoncini di agnello saltati con cipolla*.

Rigatoni alla napoletana coi peperoni freschi

RIGATONI FROM NAPLES WITH ROASTED SWEET PEPPERS

Those to whom Southern Italian pasta means tomato sauce laid on with a trowel may be dismayed to find, in this quintessentially Neapolitan dish, not a fleck of tomato. There is even more butter than there is olive oil. The Southern Italian way with pasta sauces, contrary to what some forgetful sons and daughters of the South have perpetrated away from those shores, can be exceptionally lighthanded. In fact, I think our Northern Italian sauces can be heavier sometimes than those of our unjustly maligned cousins from Naples and Sicily.

The star of this dish is the fresh sweet pepper. It must be ripe and meaty. It would be most desirable and attractive to have a combination of red and yellow peppers, but red peppers alone would do, provided they are the large sweet ones. Green peppers are not suitable because they do not have a ripe enough flavour for this recipe.

Fresh basil is also a must. Some people may be tempted to supplant it with parsley, but it is in no way an acceptable substitute.

For four

5 fresh, glossy, and meaty sweet red peppers
3 tablespoons olive oil
4 whole cloves garlic, peeled

Salt
450 g (1 lb) *rigatoni* or *ziti* or other stubby tubular pasta
60 g (2 oz) butter
15 small or 20 large fresh basil leaves
75 g ($2\frac{1}{2}$ oz) freshly grated Parmesan cheese

1 Wash the peppers in cold water. Cut them along their deep folds into lengthwise sections. Scoop out and discard their seeds and pulpy core.

2 Peel away the skin of the peppers, using a swivel-action peeler and a light touch. Cut the peppers into lengthwise strips about 12 mm ($\frac{1}{2}$ inch) broad, then shorten the strips by cutting them in half.

3 Choose a sauté pan large enough to contain all the peppers without crowding. Put in the olive oil and the garlic, and turn on the heat to medium high. Sauté the garlic until it turns light brown; then remove it and discard it.

4 Put the peppers into the pan, and cook them at lively heat for 15 minutes or so. They should become tender but not mushy and shapeless. When nearly done, salt them liberally. They must be well seasoned or the pasta will be insipid. Turn off the heat when done.

5 Bring 4 to 5 litres (7 to $8\frac{3}{4}$ pints) water to the boil, add salt, and when the water returns to the boil, put in the pasta.

6 While the pasta is cooking, melt the butter slowly over low heat – make sure it doesn't cook.

7 Rinse the basil leaves in cold water, and pat them dry gently with a soft tea-towel or kitchen paper; do not bruise them. Tear large leaves into smaller pieces with your hands.

8 When the pasta is cooked *al dente*, tender but firm to the bite, drain it thoroughly, and put it in a warm serving bowl. Add the peppers and all the oil from the pan, the melted butter, the basil, the grated cheese, and toss thoroughly. Serve at once.

MENU SUGGESTIONS

Any meat course that does not contain peppers and is not aggressively seasoned can follow this. For example: *Ossobuchi in bianco*, *Arrosto di maiale ubriaco*, *Piccata di fegato di vitello al limone*, *Pollo al limone* or *Anatra arrosto*.

La sfoglia

HOME-MADE EGG PASTA

The basic dough for home-made pasta consists of eggs and flour. Nothing else. No salt. No water. No olive oil. Salt adds nothing to the dough, since it is always present in the sauce. Water dilutes its flavour and consistency. Oil adds slickness, flawing its texture. Using just eggs and flour is the way pasta is made in Emilia-Romagna, and it sets the standard by which all other pasta in Italy is judged.

PASTA EQUIPMENT

To make pasta by hand, you will need a work table and a rolling-pin. (You can also make pasta by machine – see page 134.)

The best surface for working on pasta is wood. A large butcher's block is what I use. Formica is also quite satisfactory. The least desirable material is marble, which appears to inhibit the dough, making it unyielding and inelastic.

If you have a wooden table, make sure the side near you is not sharply angular at the edge. It should be smoothly rounded, or it will cut a sheet of pasta hanging over it. Sand down a sharp edge, blunting it and rounding it.

Formica tops are usually no problem because the moulding that finishes the edge is rounded.

A depth of 600 mm (24 inches) is sufficient for the top. But the longer it is, the more comfortable it is to work on. One metre (3 feet) is adequate, but closer to 1·5 metres (4½ feet) would be better.

The pasta pin is narrower and longer than other rolling-pins. Its traditional measurements are 37 mm (1½ inches) in diameter and 820 mm (32 inches) long. You will probably not find it in any shop, but you can easily have one cut for you from a length of hardwood curtain-pole at a good timber merchant.

The thickness can vary from 37 to 50 mm (1½ to 2 inches). Sand the edges to make them perfectly smooth.

Before using a new wooden rolling-pin, wash it with soap and water, and rinse well. Dry thoroughly with a soft cloth: allow it to dry further in a moderately warm room. Then dampen a cloth with some tasteless vegetable oil, and rub it over the entire surface of the pin. It should be an extremely light coating. When the oil has seeped into the wood, rub the pin with flour.

Repeat this procedure every dozen times the pin is used.

Store the rolling-pin hanging free, to keep it from warping. Screw an eye hook into one end, and suspend the pin from a hook set into any wall, or inside a cabinet or cupboard.

Notes on flour The flour used for home-made pasta in Italy is called *doppio zero* – double zero, '00'. It is a soft-wheat flour, moderately high in gluten. (Hard-wheat flour is used almost exclusively for factory-made macaroni pasta.) There are a few exceptions; for example, home-made *tonnarelli* from Abruzzi (page 143) is made with durum flour, and *pizzoccheri*, from Valtellina (page 165), is made with a large proportion of buckwheat flour.

There is no exact equivalent for '00' flour outside Italy. The closest might be unbleached flour, but the kind available in this country is not satisfactory.

In Bologna, the standard ratio of flour to eggs works out to 100 g (3½ oz) to 1 egg, but I have been gradually revising this proportion, in batch after batch of pasta. I have found that it is possible, in fact desirable, to work with little more than half the amount of flour used in Bologna. It produces a far more yielding and easily stretching dough than the old proportions. The exact amount of flour will always depend, of course, upon the size and flour-absorbing capacity of the eggs. As your skills and speed develop, work with as much flour, and as tough a dough, as you can handle. The firmer the dough is, the better the pasta. But don't risk frustration by getting ahead of yourself.

Note for beginners You will find it easier to start with the *pasta verde* (spinach and egg pasta dough), page 126.

Pasta all' uovo

YELLOW EGG PASTA DOUGH

About 130 g (4½ oz) plain flour
2 large eggs, brought to room temperature

(If making dough for stuffed pasta, such as *tortellini*, add 1 tablespoon milk. It will make the pasta easier to seal.)

Makes approximately 350 g (12 oz) fresh pasta, when rolled out and cut

1 Pour out the flour onto the work surface, shape it into a mound, and scoop out a deep hollow in the centre of the mound.

2 Break the eggs into the hollow. (Add the milk, if making dough for stuffed pasta.) Beat the eggs lightly with a fork, for 1 or 2 minutes. Draw some of the flour down over the eggs. Mix the flour with the eggs, a little at a time, until they are no longer runny. Draw the sides of the mound together, and work the mixture of flour and eggs with your fingertips and the palms of your hands, until it is a well amalgamated paste. If it is still exceptionally moist, work in a little additional flour. But don't overdo it.

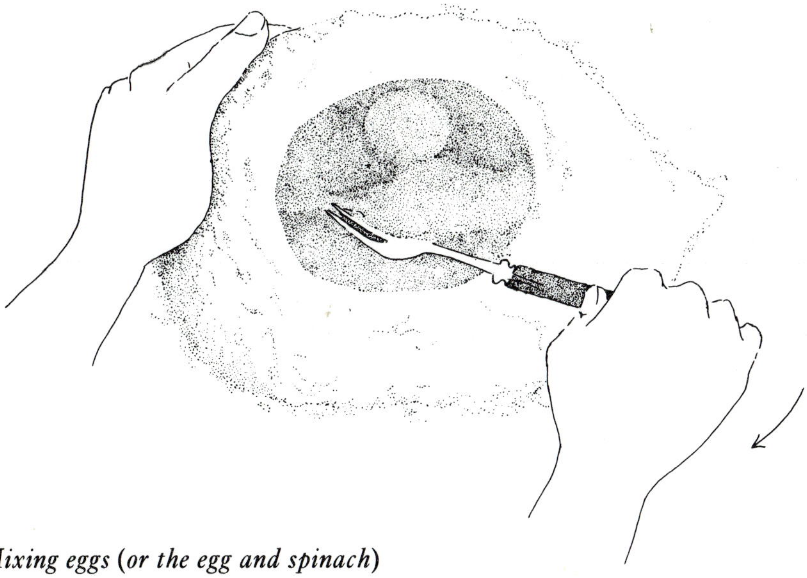

Mixing eggs (or the egg and spinach)

3 Put the egg and flour mass aside for a moment, while you scrape off all bits of caked flour and crumbs from the work surface. Wash your hands and dry them. Return the mass to the work surface, and begin kneading it. Push against it with the heel of your palm, fold it in half, turn it, press again hard, and continue folding, turning, and kneading for at least 8 minutes.

Do not skimp on the kneading time. Many of the problems that arise when stretching pasta can be traced to insufficiently kneaded dough. Even when making pasta by machine, the dough should be kneaded by hand. (**Note** While the processor does a marvellous job of kneading bread dough, pizza, or flaky pastry, it fails to deliver an equally satisfactory pasta dough. For well-structured pasta there is no substitute for hand kneading.)

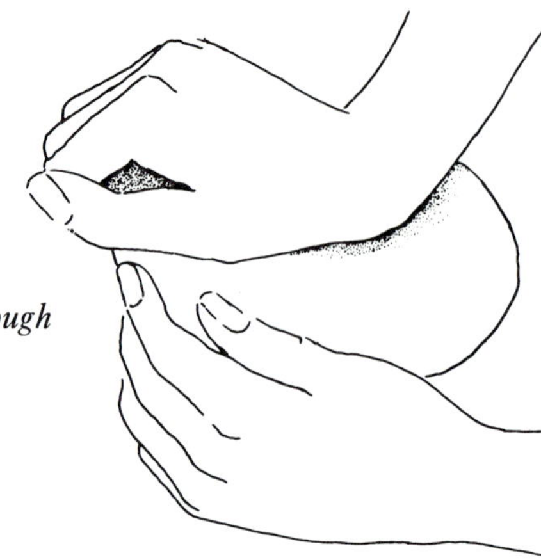

Kneading dough

4 If you are not sure that you have put in enough flour, push a finger into the ball of dough as far as its centre. When drawing it out, the finger should feel somewhat sticky, but not moist. Moistness means a little more flour should be worked in.

5 Wrap the dough in clingfilm, and let it rest for 15 minutes or as long as 2 or 3 hours. This will help relax the gluten and make the dough easier to stretch.

6 When you unwrap the dough, it will seem much damper than it did originally. Do not add any more flour to it at this point. Lightly dust your hands with flour, and knead the dough for 1 minute.

7 Roll out and stretch the dough as directed on pages 127–34.

Pasta verde

SPINACH AND EGG PASTA DOUGH

All those beginning to make pasta by hand should start with spinach dough. One of the main problems that must be overcome in rolling out pasta by hand is to get it stretched and thin enough before it dries and cracks. Spinach dough is perfect for one's first attempts because it is moister and more tender than yellow dough, and will not dry out so quickly. It gives the beginner a more encouraging start in acquiring the necessary hand skills that can then be applied to all pasta.

Makes approximately 300 g (10 oz) fresh spinach pasta, when rolled out and cut

140 g (5 oz) frozen leaf spinach, thawed
¼ teaspoon salt
About 110 g (4 oz) plain flour
1 large egg, brought to room temperature

1 Put the thawed spinach and the salt into a small pan, cover, and turn on the heat to medium. Cook for about 5 minutes after the moisture in the pan begins to simmer. Drain.

2 When the spinach is cool enough to handle, squeeze it firmly with your hands (or wrap it in muslin, and then squeeze) until all the liquid has run off.

3 Chop the spinach very fine. Use a knife, not a processor or blender, which bring out liquid and make the spinach too soggy.

4 Pour the flour onto a work surface, shape it into a mound, and scoop out a deep hollow in the centre.

5 Break the egg into the hollow. Take enough spinach to form a ball about 25 mm (1 inch) in diameter, and put it in with the egg.

6 Mix the egg and spinach, beating them with a fork until they are well amalgamated, see illustration, page 125. Draw enough flour over them to combine with them and make a paste. Then push the sides of the mound together, and work the flour into the spinach-and-egg combination until it has absorbed as much flour as it is able to, and you have a compact, but not overdry mass.

7 Set the mass aside. Scrape the work surface clean of all crumbs and caked flour. Wash and dry your hands. Return the mass of dough to the worktop, and knead, following the instructions in the recipe for yellow dough, on pages 124–6, steps 3, 4 and 5.

8 Roll out and stretch the dough as directed on pages 127–34.

ROLLING OUT PASTA
THE TWO METHODS, BY HAND AND BY MACHINE

There are two approaches to home-made egg pasta. One is to consider it simply as an ingredient that one must include in the composition of a dish, in the same way that one makes use of good olive oil, or tomatoes, or veal. The other is to think of it as the product of a craft, which like those of other hand crafts, has certain unique properties that machines cannot duplicate.

If it is merely an ingredient, one can settle for the machine-made variety, which can be quite good if the machine is used correctly. I shall discuss pasta-machine technique a little further on. But first I shall take up the *craft* of hand-made pasta.

If there were no significant difference between pasta made by hand and that made by machine, it would be pointless to pursue the subject. There is a difference, a decidedly important one. It is in the texture.

Pasta rolled out by hand with a wooden rolling-pin is stretched. Pasta squeezed through the rollers of a machine is compressed – a slick, compact, uniform, almost waxy sheet of dough. Stretched pasta is porous and gossamer. It has the fine-grained, irregular texture of skin. An enlargement of its surface would show minute peaks and valleys, microscopic hollows, wherein sauces can be harboured and absorbed more completely than by machine pasta. In the mouth, hand-made pasta has a flavour and a liveliness of texture that are inimitable. It is not a matter of taste but of perception. In my classes, where students have the opportunity to taste, side by side, skilfully hand-made pasta and the machine variety, the difference has always shown up, without a single exception, as obvious and startling to everyone.

If this is the pasta you want to make, you must be prepared to do more than follow a recipe. You must learn a craft. Fortunately, it is not a forbiddingly difficult thing to do. Children do it. But, like any other craft, you cannot expect to master it at the first go.

Your first attempts at making pasta may not produce anything edible. You must be willing, in the course of developing the skill, to waste a dozen eggs, perhaps, and a pound or two of flour. Begin on a day when you are not pressed for time, when you feel relaxed, and when you have something else ready for dinner. Once the first awkward experiments are behind you, you'll begin to get the motion and the timing. If you persevere, you will make perfect pasta without even thinking about it, as so many of my students have learned to do.

Defined in one sentence, the craft of hand-made pasta consists in the transformation of a lump of well-kneaded egg and flour dough into a large, paper-thin, circular sheet. It is accomplished by stretching the dough in a precise series of movements, using a long, narrow rolling-pin.

Although I have described the technique of hand-made pasta before, in *The Classic Italian Cookbook*, here I have expanded and completely revised the instructions, taking into account the questions and experiences of students and readers gathered in the years since. Take your time in reading through the instructions, and note particularly the comments at the end on the problems you may encounter and their solutions.

Even before you pick up a rolling-pin try to visualise what you will be doing. These movements are like a ballet of the hands, and they should be learned as a dancer learns a part. Before your hands take over, the logic and sequence of their actions should unfold clearly in the mind.

(**Note** The measurements given in the instructions that follow are based on the quantity of kneaded dough produced using the basic recipe on page 124.)

The first movement When the ball of dough – kneaded as directed on page 125 – is ready, place it in the centre of the work table, but within comfortable reach. Flatten it a bit by pounding it two or three times smartly with the palm of the hand.

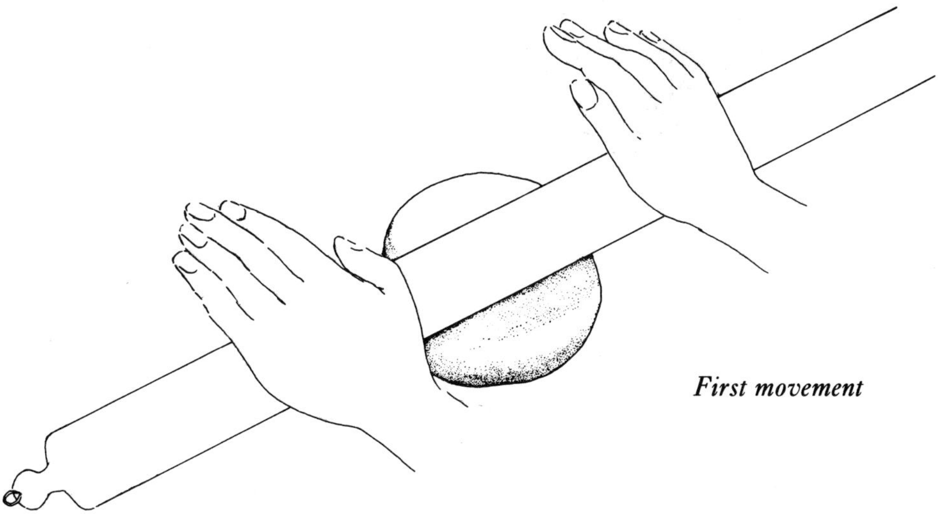

First movement

Place the rolling-pin across the flattened ball, about one-third of the way in toward its centre. The pin must be parallel to your side of the table.

Begin to open out the ball of dough by pushing the pin forcefully forward, letting it roll lightly backward to the starting point, and pushing it forward again. Do this a few times, rapidly. Do not roll the pin over or past the edge of the dough.

Turn the dough a full quarter turn, and repeat the above procedure.

Continue to turn the gradually flattening disc of dough a full quarter turn at first, then gradually less, but always in the same direction. If you are doing it correctly, the dough will spread into an evenly flattened, regular circular shape. When it has been opened up to a diameter of about 200 to 220 mm (8 to 9 inches), proceed to the next movement.

The second movement Here one begins to *stretch* the dough. Hold the near edge of the dough down with one hand. Place the rolling-pin at the opposite, far edge of the dough, laying the pin parallel to your side of the table. One hand will work the pin, while the other will act as a stop, holding still the edge of the dough nearest you.

Curl the far edge of the dough around the pin. Begin to roll the pin toward you, taking up as much dough as is needed to fit snugly under the pin. Hold the near edge of the dough steady with your other hand. After rolling the pin toward you, use the heel of your palm to force it back. Do

Second movement

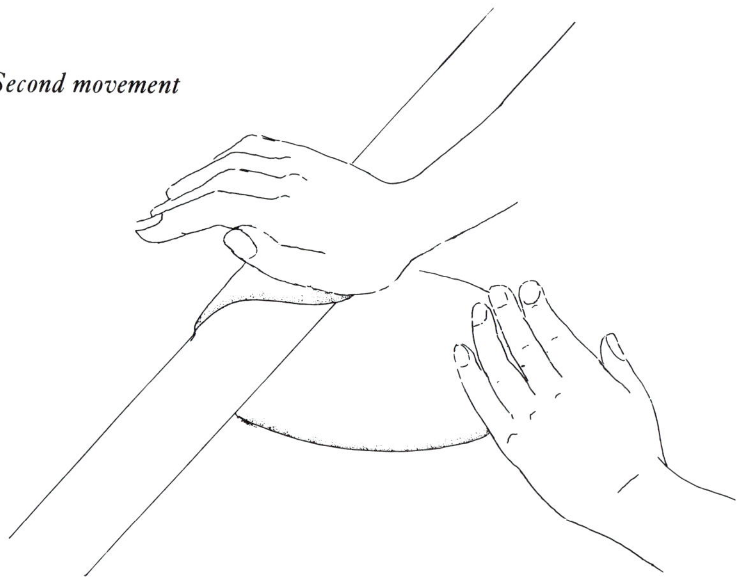

not *roll* it back, but *push*, making the sheet of dough taut between your two hands, and stretching it. This should be done very rapidly, in a continuous and fluid motion. Do not put any downward pressure into the movement. Do not let your hand rest longer than 2 or 3 seconds against the dough, or it will stick.

Keep rolling the pin towards you, stopping, stretching the dough, then rolling up more dough, until you have taken up all the dough. Then rotate the pin a full half turn – 180° – so that it points towards you, and unfurl the sheet of dough, opening it up flat.

Repeat the rolling and stretching movement described above, until the dough is once again completely wrapped around the pin. Turn the pin round again, unwrap the dough, and repeat the procedure once more.

Continue until the sheet of dough has been stretched to a diameter of about 300 mm (12 inches). Proceed immediately to the next movement.

The third movement Now comes the big step, where the sheet of dough is stretched to nearly double its diameter – depending upon how thin you need it – and finally becomes pasta. All the skill and mastery of the craft lies in the rhythmic and weightless execution of this movement.

You have the circle of dough lying flat on the table before you. Place the rolling-pin at its far end, laying it parallel to your side of the table. Curl the end of the dough around the centre of the pin, and roll the pin towards you, taking up with it about 100 mm (4 inches) of the sheet of dough. Place the heels of both your palms lightly over the centre of the pin, and roll the pin away from you, and back towards you, without rolling up any more dough than the first 100 mm (4 inches). *At the same time*, repeatedly move

Third movement

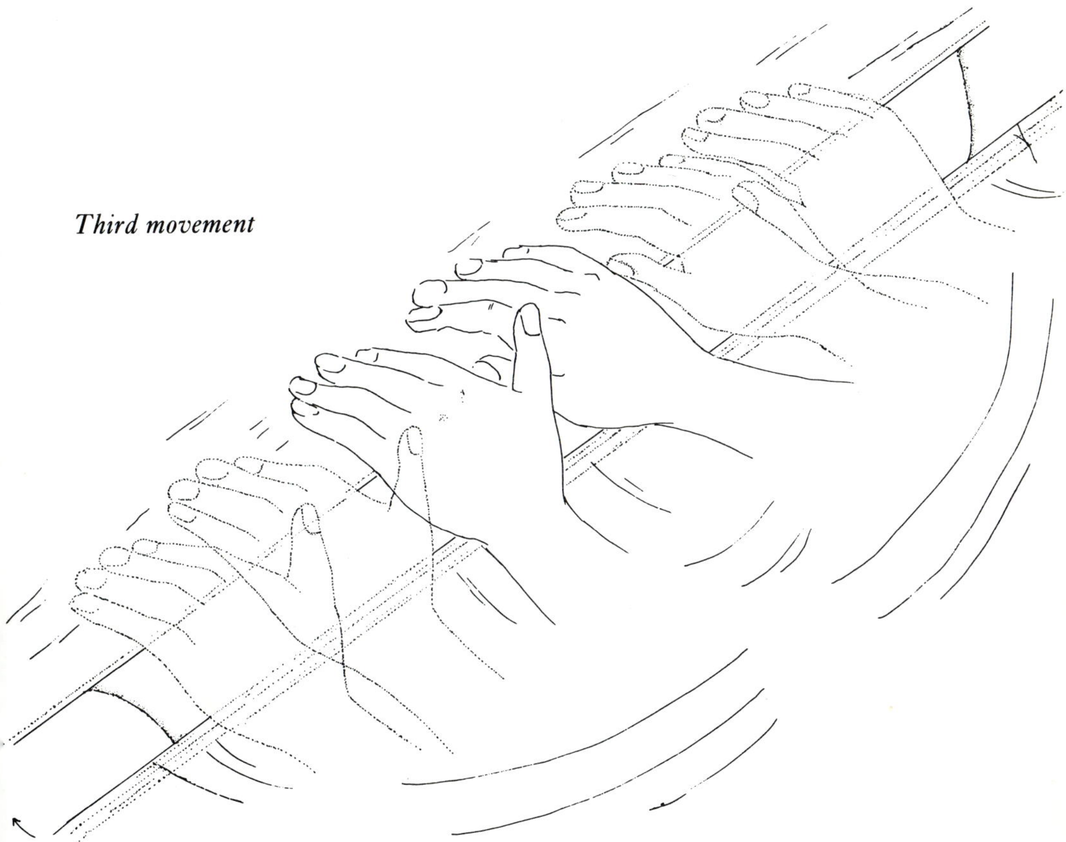

your hands away from each other towards the ends of the pin, and quickly back together at the centre of the pin.

As your hands move away from the centre, let the heels of your palms brush against the surface of the dough, dragging it, pulling it, stretching it towards the ends of the pin. At the same time, roll the pin toward you. Bear in mind that the pressure in this motion goes sideways, not downwards. If you bear down on the dough, it will stick, not stretch.

When the hands move back together towards the centre, they should glide in an upward-directed arc, barely skimming the dough. You want to drag the dough outwards, towards the ends of the pin, but not back again towards the centre. As your hands return to the centre of the pin, roll it forward, away from you.

The hands should be flitting out and back very rapidly. Only the heels of the palms may touch the dough, applying pull, not weight. And all this while you must also be rolling the pin forward and back.

Take up another few inches of dough with the pin, and repeat the same sideways stretching motions, always rocking the pin back and forth.

When you have taken up all but the last couple of inches of dough, turn the pin round towards you, and unfurl the dough, opening it up flat on the table. Start again at the far end, repeating the whole procedure described above.

As the sheet of dough becomes larger, let it hang over the side of the table near you when you open it up. It will act as a counterweight, and contribute to the stretching action. But do not lean against it: you might break it. Of course, as you keep taking up dough on the pin, you will let the sheet of dough slide back gradually onto the table.

When you have finished stretching the dough, open it up flat on the table again, and use the rolling-pin on it to flatten any creases, and to even off the edges. This entire stretching movement must be executed very quickly, in 10 minutes or less for a standard amount of pasta.

Suggestions and observations

— Thinning out pasta is a race against time. Dough can be stretched only as long as it is soft and pliable, but its pliancy is short-lived. The moment the dough begins to dry, it refuses to give and starts to crack. Speed is one of the principal factors in making successful pasta. You must work on developing it from the very beginning.

— Do not roll out pasta while the oven is turned on, or near a hot radiator. Heat will accelerate the drying-out process.

— Work with the dough within easy reach of your arms. You will have better control of your movements.

— Before you start working with dough, it might be helpful to try

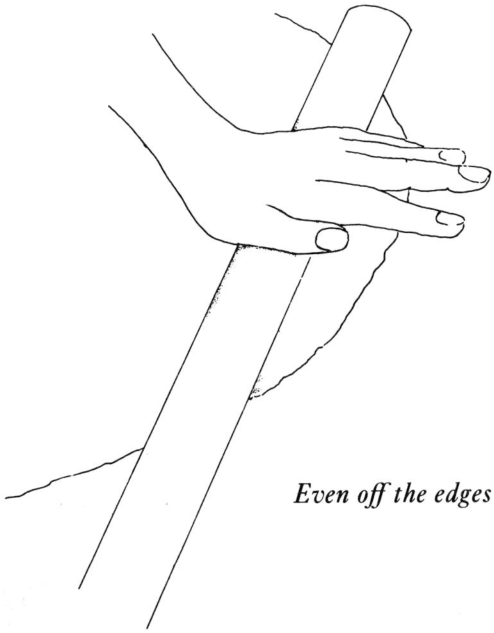

Even off the edges

out the stretching movements using a circular sheet of oilcloth or nonstick plastic.

Problems, their causes and possible solutions

— There are holes in the pasta. This is something that happens to everyone, sometimes even to experts. It is usually not serious. Patch the dough, narrowly overlapping the edges of the tear. Seal with slightly moistened fingertips, if necessary. Flatten and smooth over with the rolling-pin, and resume working the pasta.

— There are tiny cracks at the edges. This means the dough began to dry faster than you were able to stretch it. Or you thinned out the edges of the sheet more than the centre. If, as a whole, the dough is thin enough, the pasta is still usable.

— The dough breaks and falls apart. Either you are not working it fast enough, and letting it dry out, or you may have kneaded it too dry originally, that is, with too much flour. Or it may be a combination of both. In either case it is fatal. Start again with a fresh batch of flour and eggs, and take special care in kneading, keeping the dough tender and elastic.

— You cannot seem to get the pasta thin enough. Basically this is a question of practice and perseverance. Reread the instructions on the stretching movements, and work on speeding up your motions. There may also be technical causes. You may not have kneaded the dough long enough or thoroughly enough. You may have kneaded it too dry. You may not have given it sufficient time to rest. Or you may be working in an exceedingly dry and hot kitchen.

— The dough keeps sticking to itself or to the rolling-pin. You may be putting downward pressure into your movements. Concentrate on pulling sideways on the dough, not pressing down on it. It may also be that you are kneading the dough too soft, with not enough flour. In this case, although it is not orthodox, try adding more flour, spreading it uniformly over the sheet of dough.

— The pasta is too thick for noodles or *lasagne*, but otherwise it looks too good to throw away. Cut it into small squares, or *maltagliati*, page 386, and use it in soup. If very thick, allow additional time for cooking.

NOTE ON THE PASTA MACHINE

The operating principle of the pasta machine is that of a wringer on a wash bucket. There are two cylindrical rollers through which pasta is squeezed. The space between the rollers can be opened wide for kneading dough, and it can be narrowed gradually until a thin band of pasta is extruded.

I have concluded, after comparing many different batches, that kneading the dough by machine contributes substantially to the slick and inferior quality of machine-made pasta. I strongly urge those who will be using the machine to invest the 8 or 10 minutes required for kneading dough by hand. It is well worthwhile.

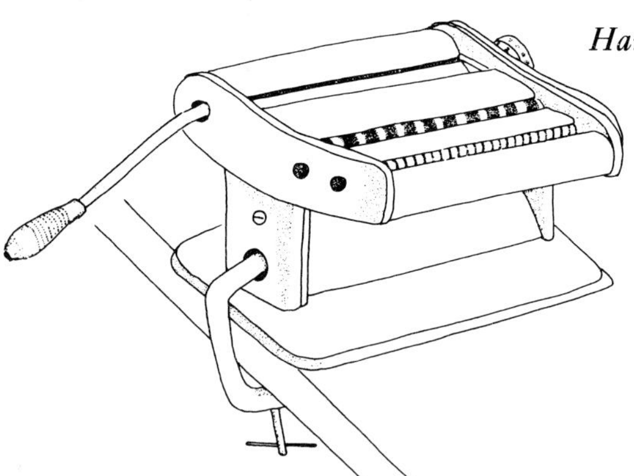

Hand-cranked pasta machine

Additional cutters for the electric machine to the right

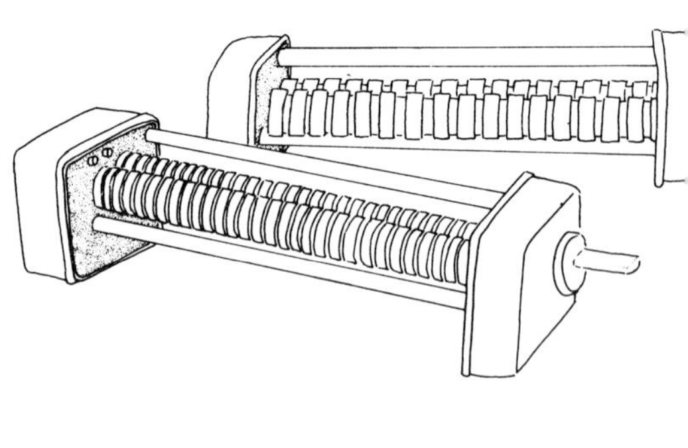

There are two types of pasta machine for home use. One, made by various manufacturers, is hand cranked. The other, made by Bialetti, is electrically driven. The electric machine has a maddeningly noisy motor that must have been designed by a motorcycle enthusiast, but it does make better pasta than the hand-cranked model.

There are two reasons for this. The first is speed. The electric machine is dazzlingly fast, and the speed at which dough is flattened is closely related to quality in the consistency of pasta. The second reason is the material of which the rollers are made. The hand-cranked machine has smooth, polished steel rollers that produce the slithery surface characteristics of machine-made pasta. The electric model has textured nylon rollers that turn out pasta with a surface not quite so slick, almost resembling hand-rolled pasta.

Unfortunately, the electric pasta machine is much more expensive. Although it makes unquestionably finer pasta, it is up to you to decide whether the difference is worth the higher price.

HOW TO USE THE PASTA MACHINE

1 Knead the dough as directed on pages 127–34, for yellow pasta or for spinach pasta. It is not necessary to let it rest.

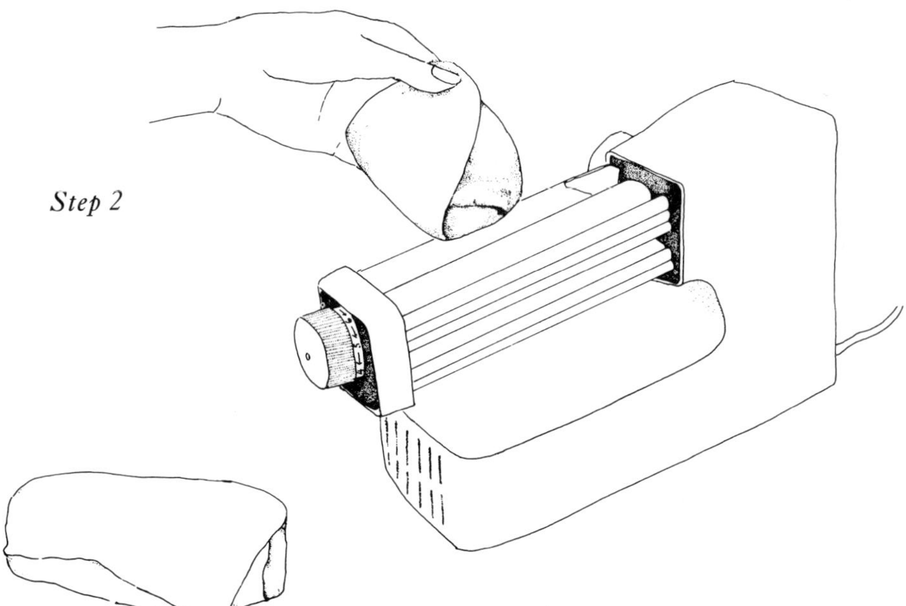

Step 2

2 If using a dough made with 2 eggs, divide it into four parts, or more if it is a larger amount of dough. Flatten each piece, pressing it with the palm of your hand. Set the rollers at their maximum opening. Run the dough through three or four times, folding it and turning it each time you feed it through the rollers.

3 Close the opening one notch, and run the dough through once. Keep closing the opening one notch at a time, and feed the gradually thinning pasta ribbon through the rollers once each time. Stop when you have reached the desired thinness.

For noodles and *lasagne* it should be about 1 mm ($\frac{1}{32}$ inch). For *fettuccine*, slightly thicker. For stuffed pasta, the thinner the better. When you find the thickness of pasta that suits you best, note the notch at which it was produced, so that from then on you can always duplicate it.

Pasta machines provide two sets of cutters, one broad, the other narrow. The broader one is for noodles. The other will turn out a very thin noodle, suitable for soup, or for *tonnarelli* (pages 143–5).

For *lasagne* or stuffed pasta, cut the dough by hand into the required shape and size.

Note The electric pasta machine has two speeds: very fast, and faster. At

Step 3

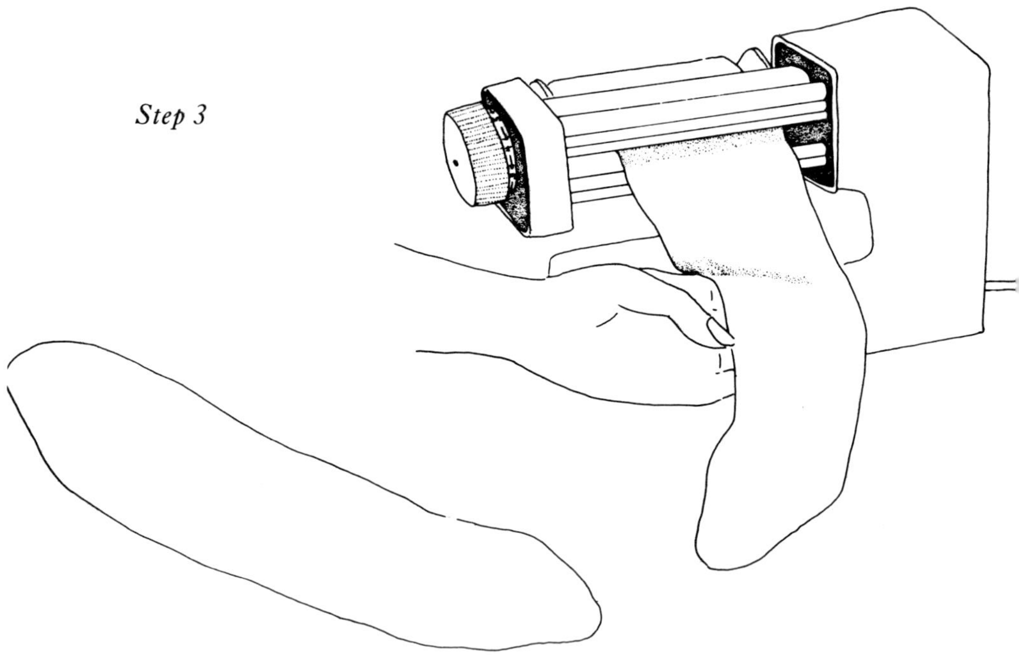

the faster speed, if you are doing a lot of pasta, the motor may overheat, and the pasta comes through so fast you have to be very nimble in dealing with it. The slower speed is quick enough for me, and a little quieter to boot.

There is a little metal ledge that supports the dough as it is fed through the rollers. Once these begin to take up the dough, do not hold on to the dough at the feeding end. Even if it begins to twist, it will straighten itself out, if you let it rest on the ledge. But do take up the band of dough as it emerges from the rollers, to keep it from falling into folds.

CUTTING THE DOUGH

When pasta dough has been rolled out, either by hand or by machine, to the desired thinness, you must cut it into the shape you need.

It is possible to turn out an infinite number of shapes, some of them very intricate; and we could devote pages to discussing the special tools or hand skills required to produce them. But all we have to consider for our needs here are two broad categories of pasta shapes: flat noodle pasta – such as *fettuccine*, *tagliatelle*, *tagliolini*, *lasagne*, etc, and stuffed pasta – such as *tortellini* and *ravioli*.

To make *tortellini*, or any such pasta shape that encloses a stuffing, the dough must be cut and stuffed as soon as it is made, while it is still soft and sticky. Its softness and stickiness are necessary to produce a tight seal, without which the stuffing would spill out while cooking.

On the other hand, for flat pasta you must allow the dough a little time to dry and lose its stickiness, to prevent the strands of *fettuccine*, or whatever kind of noodle you are cutting, from sticking to each other.

Cutting fettuccine

With dough rolled out by machine

Lay the bands of dough out on a table or worktop, over a soft cloth. Do not overlap the dough. Machine dough tends to dry out faster than hand-rolled dough, so the pasta may be ready for cutting in as little as 5 or 10 minutes, depending on the temperature of the kitchen. The dough should be soft and pliant, otherwise it will break when cut. But it should not be so moist that it will stick easily to itself. When you feel it is ready, feed it through the broad cutters on your pasta machine. If using an electric machine, refer to the special note on feeding and retrieving the dough on page 136. Separate the cut noodles, and spread them out to dry for about 5 minutes on a tea-towel laid out on the worktop. From then on, they are ready for cooking whenever you are ready.

With dough rolled out by hand

Spread a dry towel on a table or worktop. Lay the sheet of dough flat over the towel. Let one third of the sheet hang over the edge of the table or worktop. After about 10 minutes, turn the sheet so that another part of it hangs over the edge. Turn it again after another 10 minutes, letting the last third hang over the edge. Total drying time depends on the softness of the dough and the temperature of the room. The dough should lose enough of its moistness so that it will not stick to itself when folded and cut, but it must not dry out too much or it will become brittle and break. When the surface of the pasta begins to have a leathery look, it is ready to fold and cut.

Roll up the dough on the rolling-pin, remove the towel from the worktop, and unroll the dough from the pin, laying it out flat on the worktop.

Pick up the edge of the sheet of dough furthest from you, and fold it towards you loosely, taking up about 75 mm (3 inches). Fold it again, and again, until the whole sheet of dough has been folded into a long, flat, rectangular roll, about 75 mm (3 inches) wide.

Take a cleaver or other broad-bladed knife. Place one hand on the roll of dough, near the end, drawing your fingertips part of the way back under your knuckles. Hold the knife with the other hand, placing its edge crossways to the roll, and resting the flat part of the blade against your knuckles. Cut the pasta to the width desired. For *fettuccine*, it should be between 6 and 3 mm ($\frac{1}{4}$ and $\frac{1}{8}$ inch). After each cut, slide the hand holding the roll back a trifle, and let the knife follow, always leaning the flat part of the blade against your knuckles. Never lift the cutting edge above your knuckles. It should skim along the surface of the dough, stopping and cutting through at regular intervals. Concentrate on cutting the noodles all the same width.

When the whole roll has been cut, unfold the *fettuccine* and spread them out to dry for about 5 minutes on a clean tea-towel. They will then be ready for cooking.

Fresh pasta can be cooked immediately, in which case it takes just seconds to be done. Or it can be left to dry completely, and then stored for weeks in a cupboard, just like *spaghetti*. If drying *fettuccine* for future use, take a few strands at a time and curl them into nest shapes. Handle with care when dry, because they will be very brittle. Dry pasta will take a little longer to cook than fresh. To cook it, always gather it up in a towel, and let the pasta slide off the towel and into the pot.

Using the same cutting method, you can cut pasta into hair-thin *tagliolini* or *capelli d'angelo* for soup. For other flat pasta cuts, see *The Classic Italian Cookbook*, pages 103–105. For *lasagne* and *pappardelle*, follow the directions in the specific recipes in this book.

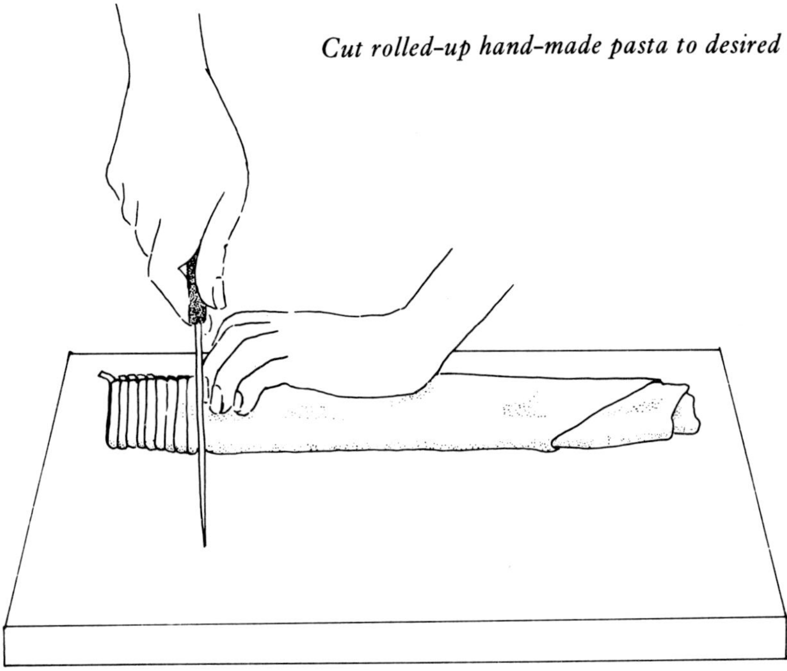

Cut rolled-up hand-made pasta to desired width

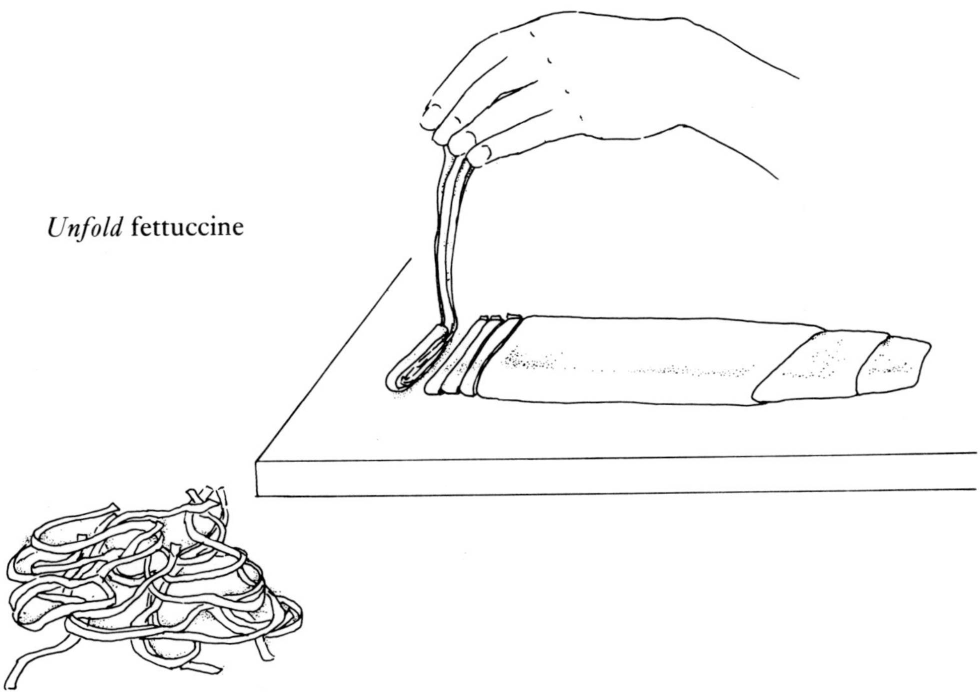

Unfold fettuccine

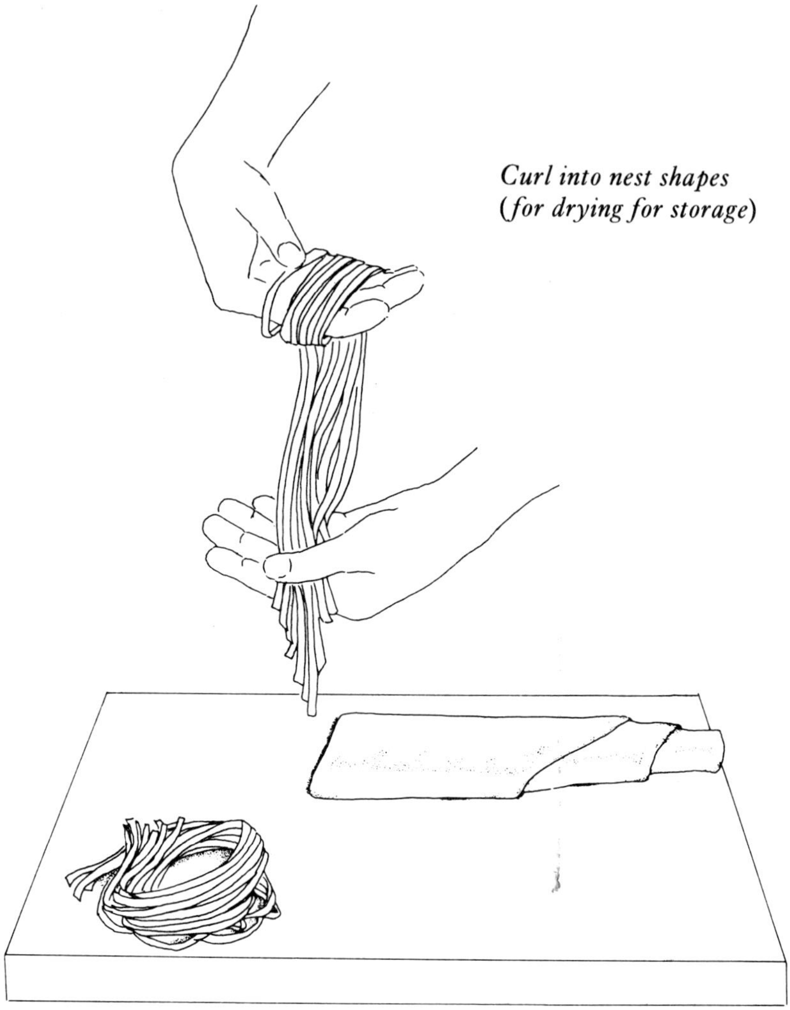

Curl into nest shapes (for drying for storage)

Tortellini/Cappelletti

Tortellini are small, peaked, hat-shaped dumplings from Bologna, into which one can put a variety of stuffings. A virtually identical shape is called *cappelletti* in Romagna, a few miles east of Bologna. The dough for *tortellini*, or for any other stuffed pasta you may want to make, must be freshly rolled out and still moist and very soft, otherwise it will not seal tightly.

If you are using machine dough, cut and stuff only one band of dough at a time. Keep the others under film wrap so that they do not dry out. If you are using hand-rolled dough, trim one edge of the sheet so that it is perfectly straight. (Save the trimmings and cut them later into soup squares.) Cut off a rectangular strip of dough from the sheet, making your cut parallel to the straight edge. The strip should be as wide as the size of *tortellini* called for in the recipe – usually 30 to 37 mm ($1\frac{1}{4}$ to $1\frac{1}{2}$ inches). Move the remaining sheet of dough aside, and cover it with film wrap to keep it from drying.

Cut the band of machine dough or the strip of hand-rolled dough into the size squares required by the recipe. Put about $\frac{1}{4}$ teaspoon of filling in the centre of each square. Fold the square diagonally across, forming a triangle. The upper edges should stop about 3 mm ($\frac{1}{8}$ inch) short of meeting the lower edges. Press down firmly all along the edges to seal them tightly.

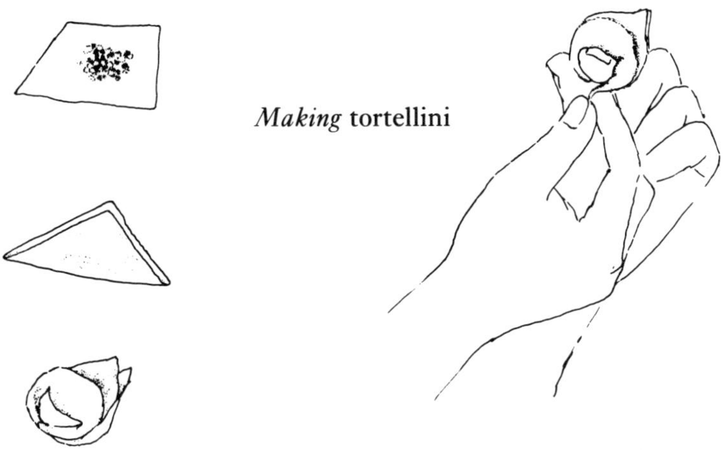

Making tortellini

With your left hand, pick up one end of the long side of the triangle, and with your right hand pick up the other end, holding it between your thumb and middle finger. With the index finger of the right hand push the tip of the triangle down, folding it towards you. Then, as you bring both ends together, forming a ring, slip the tip of your right index finger in the centre of the ring. Let the two ends overlap slightly, and press them firmly together between thumb and index finger. Slip the dumpling off your finger, and set it down on a dry, clean towel.

Proceed until all the pasta has been cut, stuffed, and shaped into *tortellini*. Lay all the *tortellini* in rows on the towel, making sure there is a little space between them, or they will stick to each other. If you are not ready to cook the *tortellini* as soon as they are done, turn them from time to time so that they will dry evenly.

When ready to cook them, pick them up in the towel, pulling the ends of the towel together. As you bring the towel over the pot, loosen one end, and let the *tortellini* slide into the boiling water.

Note Before making any *tortellini*, it might be a good idea to cut some paper into several squares 37 by 37 mm ($1\frac{1}{2}$ by $1\frac{1}{2}$ inches), and practise on them, instead of on your precious dough.

Manfrigul

EGG BARLEY

Manfrigul is home-made pasta chopped into small nuggets for use in soups. Something very similar is made in Central Europe, and I have seen it also in shops, where it is sold as egg barley. In Italy it is native to the Romagna section of Emilia-Romagna. The ingredients are the same simple ones that go into Romagna's superlative home-made pasta – eggs and flour. Nothing else. Originally it was produced by rubbing a ball of firm pasta dough against a wooden grater. The graters have gone the way of many wonderful old kitchen tools and today the job is done with a knife. One can even use the food processor.

Once made, *manfrigul* can be stored in a cupboard in a glass jar, and kept for months. It is marvellous in a vegetable soup or a bean soup where you would use pasta or rice. And it is also good on its own, in a home-made consommé, served with a little grated cheese. Its distinguishing feature is a robust, inimitable chewiness that imparts character and textural contrast to soup.

If you are wondering why you need bother to make it at home when there are so many kinds of soup pasta available at the delicatessen or grocer, the answer is that *manfrigul* is much better – and it does not take all that much bother, even if you do not have a food processor.

Makes about 100 g ($3\frac{1}{2}$ oz) manfrigul *if chopped by hand, or 75 g ($2\frac{1}{2}$ oz) if done in the food processor*

200 g (7 oz) plain flour

2 eggs

1 Pour the flour onto a worktop and shape it into a mound. Make a deep hollow in the centre of the mound, and break into it the 2 eggs. Beat the eggs lightly with a fork. Bring the sides of the mound together, and knead thoroughly for 8 to 10 minutes until you have a firm compact mass of dough. Shape the dough into a flattened ball about 50 mm (2 inches) high. (**Note** Although the kneading process can be done by the steel blades of the food processor, it is recommended that you do it by hand, as with other forms of pasta. Should you decide to use the processor, knead the dough by hand afterwards, in any case, for at least 1 minute.)

2 Cut the ball of dough into the thinnest possible slices, and spread them on a towel. Turn them from time to time. They must dry enough to lose their stickiness, but not be so dry as to become brittle. Depending on the temperature of the kitchen, it should take about 20 to 30 minutes. Cut one of the slices after a while, to see if it is ready. When the dough is no longer sticky, transfer it to a chopping board, and dice it very fine with a sharp knife. The individual nuggets should be no more than 3 mm ($\frac{1}{8}$ inch) thick. (**Note** This chopping step can be done in the food processor, using the steel blades. Turn the processor on and off several times, to ensure fairly even chopping. When done, part of the dough will have become pulverised, and must be discarded. Empty the processor bowl into a fine strainer, and shake the fine, pulverised dough away.)

3 If you intend to store the *manfrigul* for future use, spread it on a towel and let it dry out thoroughly. It will take about 12 hours, so it would be practical to leave it out overnight. If you are going to use the pasta the same day, this step is not required. When cooking *manfrigul*, bear in mind that, in spite of its minute size, it is rather tough and will take a little while to become tender.

Tonnarelli

SQUARE HOME-MADE NOODLES

Tonnarelli are as broad as they are thick, which earns them the description of square noodles. They are much firmer than *fettuccine* and other home-made noodles because they are made with hard-wheat flour. In Abruzzi, where they originated, they are called *maccheroni alla chitarra*, because there they are cut on the taut steel strings of a guitar-like flat instrument. They can be duplicated perfectly using the pasta machine.

Tonnarelli are chewier than other home-made pasta, yet finer than commercial pasta. They provide a delightful change from *fettuccine* and *spaghetti*. They go well with just about any sauce but I particularly recommend that you try *tonnarelli* with rosemary sauce, page 164, mushroom sauce, page 162, and the peppery seafood sauce with scallops on page 128. They would also marry well with a Bolognese meat sauce (see *The Classic Italian Cookbook*, page 109).

Yield: Approximately 450 g (1 lb) tonnarelli

240 g ($8\frac{1}{2}$ oz) hard-wheat (durum) flour
3 large eggs

A pasta machine

1 Pour the flour onto a work surface, shape it into a mound, and scoop out a deep hollow in the centre.

2 Break the eggs into the hollow. Beat them lightly with a fork. Draw enough flour over the eggs to combine with them into a moist paste.

3 Bring the rest of the flour over the paste, and work with your fingers and palms until it is thoroughly incorporated. Put the mass to one side.

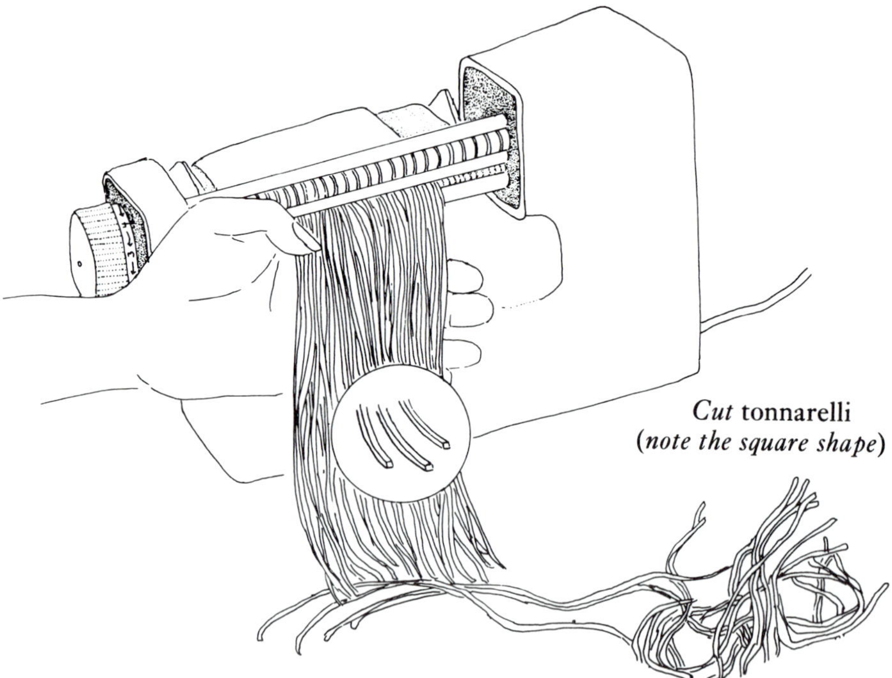

Cut tonnarelli
(*note the square shape*)

4 Scrape the work surface clean of crumbs and caked flour. Wash and dry your hands. Take the mass of dough and knead it for 8 to 10 minutes. (Refer to the detailed kneading directions on page 127.) It is not necessary to wrap the dough after kneading and let it rest.

5 Thin out the dough on the pasta machine, following the instructions on page 136. Do not thin it as much as you would for noodles. It should be between 3 and $1\frac{1}{2}$ mm ($\frac{1}{8}$ and $\frac{1}{16}$ inch) thick. If you are using the electric pasta machine, the setting is $3\frac{1}{2}$. On hand-turned models it will vary. The pasta should be exactly as thick as the width of the groove in the narrow noodle cutter on the machine.

6 When the bands of pasta are dry enough for cutting, after about 20 minutes, depending on the heat and humidity in the room, run them through the noodle-cutting cylinders. Make sure it is the narrower one in the machine, or the separate cutter for narrow noodles, if you are using the electric machine.

Tortellini verdi

GREEN TORTELLINI WITH PROSCIUTTO AND CREAM SAUCE

There are many ways of producing coloured pasta, but the only one that has a gastronomic reason for it, that can be justified by its appeal to taste as well as to sight, is where spinach is used to make green pasta. Spinach pasta is more tender than egg pasta, and while the spinach does not produce a substantial change in flavour, its presence imparts a faint but nonetheless perceptible and very pleasing mossy aftertaste.

Spinach pasta can be cut into all the basic home-made pasta shapes (see *The Classic Italian Cookbook*, page 108, and, for green *lasagne*, page 122, or green *fettuccine*, page 124). Here it is used to make beautiful, festive green-clad *tortellini*, for a dish that tastes as spectacularly good as it looks.

The stuffing for the *tortellini* consists of sautéed chopped pork and veal combined with *mortadella*, egg yolk, ricotta, and Parmesan. It is very lightly spiced with a hint of nutmeg. The sauce is a very simple and lovely one of diced prosciutto and cream, just savoury enough to enhance, but not compete with, the harmonious mix of textures and flavours in the *tortellini*.

For four to six (approximately 130 tortellini)

The stuffing

110 g (4 oz) lean pork
110 g (4 oz) lean veal
15 g (½ oz) butter
Salt
Freshly ground black pepper
60 g (2 oz) *mortadella*, chopped very fine
100 g (3½ oz) ricotta
35 g (1¼ oz) freshly grated Parmesan cheese
1 egg yolk
¼ teaspoon grated nutmeg

The pasta

Salt
50 g (1¾ oz) frozen leaf spinach, thawed, or 180 g (6 oz) fresh spinach
200 g (7 oz) plain flour
2 large eggs

The sauce

110 g (4 oz) prosciutto, sliced approximately 6 mm (¼ inch) thick, or if prosciutto is not available, plain boiled ham is an acceptable, although not wholly satisfactory, substitute
45 g (1½ oz) butter
8 tablespoons double cream

To cook the tortellini

4 to 5 litres (7 to 8¾ pints) water
1 tablespoon olive oil
Salt

1 Cut the pork and veal into thin pieces about 25 mm (1 inch) square. Keep the two meats separate.

2 Put the butter and the pork into a small frying pan, and turn on the heat to medium low. Brown the meat, turning it frequently, for 5 to 6 minutes.

3 Add the veal, and brown it on both sides, cooking it for about 2 minutes. Add salt and pepper.

4 Remove the meat from the pan, and chop it very fine. (If using the food processor, you can chop all the cooked meat, and the *mortadella* too, all at the same time. Process fine, but not to a pulp.)

5 Put the chopped meat and *mortadella* into a bowl, add the ricotta, the grated cheese, the egg yolk, and the nutmeg. Mix and combine all the ingredients thoroughly. Taste and check salt and pepper.

6 Prepare the spinach pasta. If rolling it out by hand, follow the instructions on pages 127–34. If doing it in the pasta machine, see page 134. Also refer to page 126 for special directions on spinach pasta.

7 Cut the pasta and stuff it as directed in the basic recipe for *tortellini*, page 140.

8 Dice the prosciutto or ham very fine, then put it in a saucepan with the butter, and turn on the heat to medium. Lightly brown the prosciutto for a couple of minutes, turning it from time to time.

9 Add the double cream, and cook it down, reducing it by at least one third. Turn off the heat.

10 Put the tablespoon of olive oil and 4 to 5 litres (7 to $8\frac{3}{4}$ pints) water into a large saucepan. Bring the water to a rolling boil, add about 2 tablespoons salt, then drop in all the *tortellini*. Cook until tender but *al dente*, firm to the bite. If the *tortellini* are fresh, they should be done in about 5 minutes. If they have been made a day in advance, the pasta will be dry and will take quite a bit longer. As soon as they are done, drain thoroughly, and transfer to a warm serving dish.

11 Quickly heat up the sauce, pour it over the *tortellini*, and serve at once, with a bowl of grated Parmesan cheese. If you acquire a feel for how long it takes pasta to cook, you can do the prosciutto sauce while the *tortellini* are cooking, and thereby avoid reheating it later.

Note You can make the *tortellini* up to a day before they are to be cooked. Spread them on dry towels, and make sure they do not touch each other while the pasta is still soft, or they will stick. Turn them from time to time until they are thoroughly dry on all sides. There is no need to refrigerate them, provided they are kept at normal room temperature.

MENU SUGGESTIONS

This can be a meal for a holiday or a special occasion. In choosing a meat course to follow the *tortellini*, look for a dish that will match it in importance and high spirits, but uncomplicated in flavour. The pale, delicate *Pollo al limone* would be lovely. Another good choice would be *Punta di vitello arrosto* or *Anatra arrosto*. Also any of the veal *scaloppine* or veal chop dishes in this book or in my first book, as long as you avoid those with cream.

Cappelletti di pesce col sugo di gamberetti

CAPPELLETTI WITH FISH STUFFING AND SHRIMP SAUCE

This is one of those rare pasta-and-fish dishes where the fish is inside the pasta as well as in the sauce. They are seldom found in cookbooks, and very few cooks I have talked to know how to make them. The two regions where they stuff pasta with fish are the Italian Riviera and the Adriatic coast of Romagna. This recipe is one I have devised after tasting versions from both coasts, and combines, I think, the most appealing features of the two styles of cooking. The stuffing owes more to the Riviera, while the pasta and the sauce bear the stamp of Emilia Romagna.

The stuffing is smooth and light, with few ingredients, carefully balanced. The fish is sea bass, whose firm and sweet-tasting flesh makes it not too dissimilar from the Mediterranean *branzino*. It is boiled in the traditional Italian manner, with vegetables and a little vinegar. When cooked, it is combined with egg yolks, Parmesan cheese, marjoram, and nutmeg.

An extraordinary pale pink shrimp sauce goes with these *cappelletti*. It is velvety in texture, spirited in flavour, and plays a lively counterpoint to the understated elegance of the pasta stuffing. The shrimps are first cooked in a sauce of olive oil, garlic, tomato purée and white wine. They are then blended, and the sauce is thickened with cream. This sauce can also be a splendid accompaniment to *fettucine*, *spaghetti* or *tonnarelli*.

For six (approximately 140 cappelletti)

The stuffing

1 small onion, peeled
1 100- to 125-mm (4- to 5-inch) piece of celery stick, rinsed in cold water
1 medium carrot, peeled
350 g (12 oz) sea bass, preferably in a single slice
2 tablespoons wine vinegar
Salt
2 egg yolks
20 g ($\frac{3}{4}$ oz) freshly grated Parmesan cheese
$\frac{1}{8}$ teaspoon marjoram
$\frac{1}{4}$ teaspoon grated nutmeg
Freshly ground black pepper

The pasta

3 large eggs
1 tablespoon milk
210 g ($7\frac{1}{4}$ oz) flour

The sauce

6 tablespoons olive oil
2 cloves garlic, peeled and crushed
1½ tablespoons tomato purée, dissolved in 8 tablespoons dry white wine
110 g (4 oz) medium-sized shrimps, preferably fresh, shelled, deveined and rinsed in cold water
Salt
Freshly ground black pepper
225 ml (scant ½ pint) double cream
2 tablespoons parsley, chopped very fine

1 Put the fish in a pan, add enough water to cover it, then remove the fish. Put in the onion, celery and carrot, and bring to a fast boil.

2 Add the fish, the vinegar and some salt. When the water returns to the boil, turn the heat down to reduce the boil to a slow but steady bubbling. Cover the pan. Cook for about 10 to 12 minutes, depending on the thickness of the fish.

3 Using a slotted spoon or spatula, transfer the fish to a dish. Remove the skin, any gelatinous matter and the centre bone, and carefully pick out all the small bones you may find. Do not worry about breaking up the fish because you will have to do so anyway for the stuffing.

4 Put the fish into a bowl, and mash it with a fork. Add the egg yolks, grated cheese, marjoram, nutmeg and black pepper. Mix all the ingredients thoroughly with a fork, until they are smoothly amalgamated. Taste and check salt. In adding the pepper, use a light hand, because you do not want the stuffing to have too strong a bite.

5 Prepare the pasta dough, following the basic directions on pages 124–6. When rolling out the dough, see pages 127–34 for the hand method, or page 134 for the machine method.

6 Cut the sheet of dough (or strips of dough, if rolled out by machine) into squares with 37 mm (1½-inch) sides. Dot each square with about ½ teaspoon stuffing, then fold it, seal it, and twist it into a *cappelletti* shape, as directed on pages 140–1.

7 Spread the *cappelletti* on towels, leaving tiny spaces between them to prevent them sticking to each other.

To make the sauce

1 Put the olive oil and the crushed cloves of garlic into a saucepan, turn on the heat to medium, and cook the garlic until a rich brown.

2 Add the dissolved tomato purée and wine, pouring it into the pan quickly and all at once. If you dribble it in you may be spattered with hot oil. Cook for about 10 minutes, stirring from time to time.

3 Add the cleaned shrimps, with a liberal amount of salt and pepper. Turn up the heat to medium high, and cook the shrimps for 2 to 3 minutes, turning them from time to time. Turn off the heat.

4 Using a slotted spoon or spatula, remove the shrimps from the pan. Also remove and discard the garlic, but leave everything else in the pan. Put the shrimps into a blender or a food processor fitted with steel blades, and purée them.

5 Return the puréed shrimps to the pan containing the rest of the sauce. Add the cream. Turn on the heat to medium, and cook for about 1 minute, stirring constantly, until the cream thickens. Taste and check salt and pepper. Add the chopped parsley, stir once or twice, and turn off the heat.

To cook the pasta

4 litres (7 pints) boiling water
1½ tablespoons salt
1 tablespoon olive oil

1 Bring the water to the boil, and put in the salt and olive oil.

2 Gather up all the *cappelletti* with a towel, and drop them into the pot. Cook them until they are *al dente*, firm to the bite. If the pasta is still fresh and moist, it should not take more than a minute.

3 Gently warm the sauce while the pasta is cooking.

4 Drain the pasta as soon as it is done, transfer to a warm serving dish, and toss thoroughly with the sauce. Serve at once.

Note This dish should be cooked at the time you are going to serve it. The *cappelletti*, however, may be prepared in advance, but always within the same day that you are going to cook them. The sauce may be prepared several hours ahead of time, up to the point when the cream is to be put in. Put in only half the cream and none of the parsley. At the time you are ready to use the sauce, put in the rest of the cream, cook it briefly until it thickens, then add the parsley and turn off the heat.

MENU SUGGESTIONS

If you follow these *cappelletti* with *Branzino alla rivierasca coi carciofi* you will have put together a memorable menu for serious fish devotees. Another good choice for the second course is *Il pesce coi finocchi freschi*. Any fried or grilled fish is also suitable. Avoid fish cooked in piquant or tomato sauces.

Le lasagne coi carciofi

LASAGNE WITH GLOBE ARTICHOKES

Lasagne, as they are understood in Emilia-Romagna, are made only with home-made egg pasta. And the light, precious texture of the pasta is never buried by a haphazard pile-up of ingredients. The pasta, in *lasagne*, becomes a dainty mounting for the tasteful display of either a fully integrated filling or a single ingredient. The classic example is *lasagne* with meat sauce (see *The Classic Italian Cookbook*, page 122). Another is the version with mushrooms (see next recipe). Yet another is this finely wrought *lasagne* with artichokes.

For six to eight

4 to 5 medium globe artichokes
½ lemon
Salt
110 g (4 oz) butter
Béchamel sauce (page 16) of medium density, made with 450 ml (¾ pint) milk, 60 g (2 oz) butter, 50 g (1¾ oz) plain flour, ¼ teaspoon salt

For the pasta dough:
3 large eggs
210 g (7¼ oz) plain flour
An ovenproof *lasagne* dish
75 g (2½ oz) freshly grated Parmesan cheese

1 Bend back the outer leaves of the globe artichokes until they snap off easily, not too far from the base. Continue to pull off and discard these tough outer leaves until you expose a central cone of leaves pale at the base and darker green at the tip. Slice off at least 50 mm (2 inches) from the top, eliminating all the green part, which is too tough to be edible. With a paring knife, trim away all the dark green part of the artichoke's bottom. Rub with half a lemon to keep the artichoke from turning black. Cut each artichoke in four parts, lengthways. Remove at the base the soft, curling leaves with prickly tips, and cut away the fuzzy 'choke' beneath them. Rub all the newly cut parts with lemon. Then slice the artichoke quarters lengthways into the thinnest slices possible and sprinkle a few drops of lemon juice over them.

2 Put the sliced artichokes into a 250- to 275-mm (10- to 11-inch) sauté pan with a large pinch of salt or two 60 g (2 oz) butter and enough water to cover, then turn on the heat to medium. Cook at a simmer until all the water has evaporated and the artichokes have become lightly browned. If at this point the artichokes are not quite tender, add a little water and continue cooking. When done, pour all the contents of the pan into a bowl, and set aside.

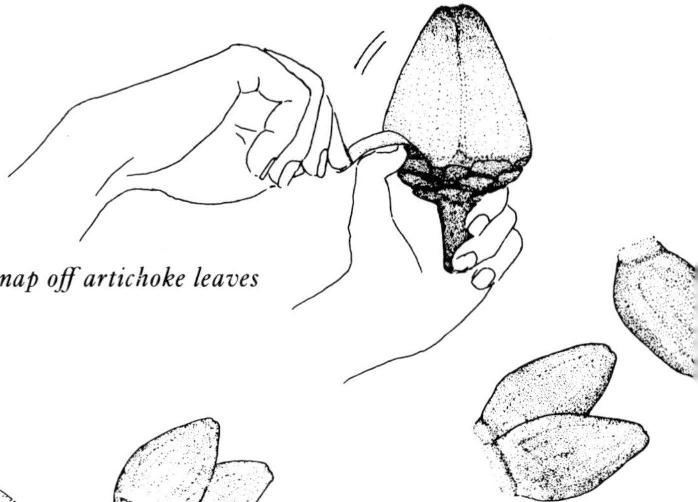

Snap off artichoke leaves

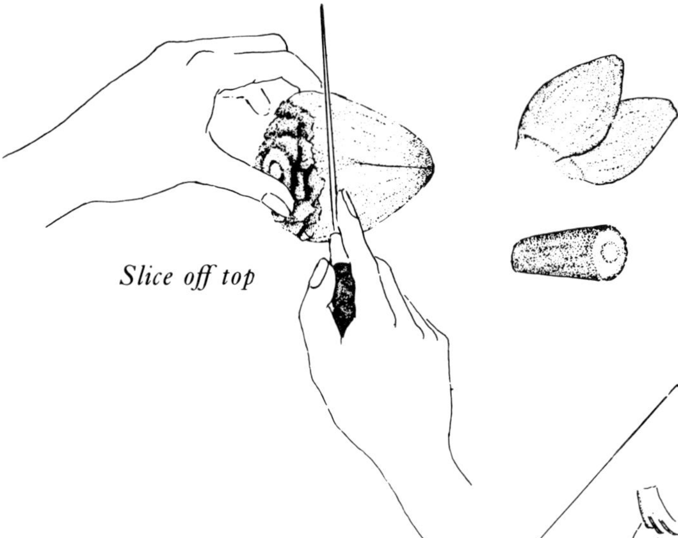

Slice off top

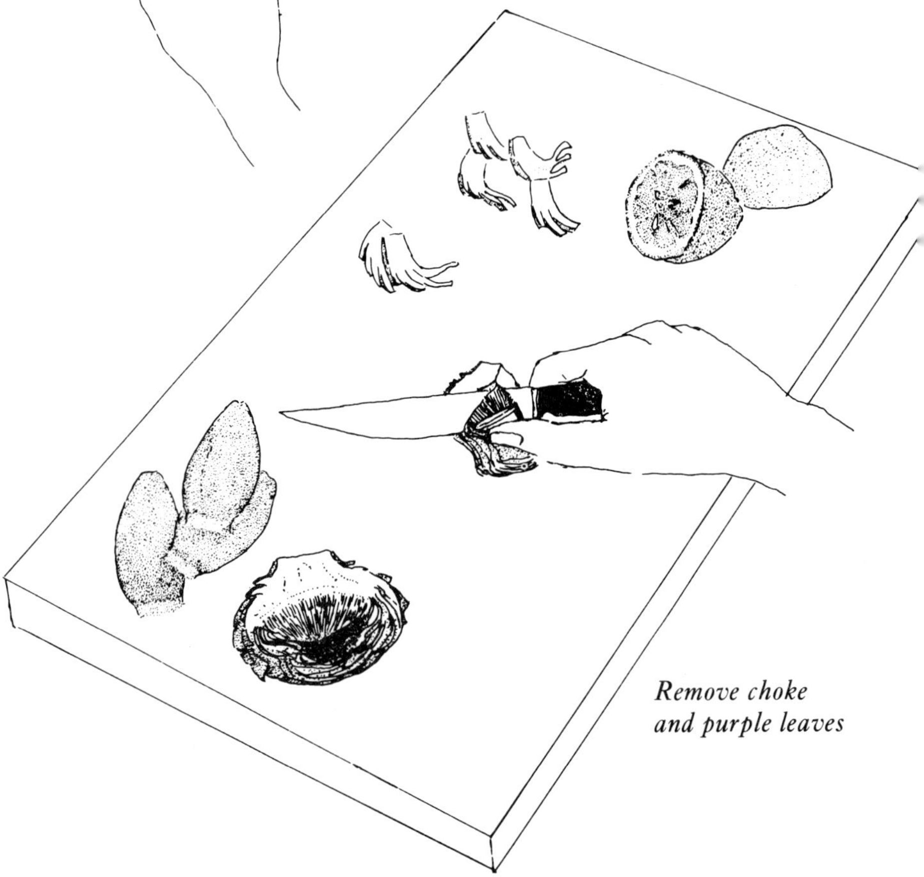

Remove choke and purple leaves

3 Make the béchamel sauce. When it is the density of a rather thick sour cream, combine it with the artichokes in the bowl, reserving just 4 or 5 tablespoons of it, which you will set aside.

4 Roll out the pasta by hand or machine, as directed on pages 127–34 and 134, until it is as thin as you can make it. Cut it into strips about 115 mm ($4\frac{1}{2}$ inches) wide and 250 mm (10 inches) long. If you are making the pasta by machine, leave the strips as wide as they come from the rollers, cutting them into 250-mm (10-inch) lengths.

5 Set a bowl of cold water near the oven and lay some clean, dry towels flat on a worktop. Bring 4 litres (7 pints) water to a rapid boil, add 1 tablespoon salt, and put in two or three pasta strips. Cook the pasta very briefly, just a few seconds after the water returns to the boil. Retrieve it with a slotted spatula or colander scoop, plunge it into the bowl of cold water, then take the pasta strips one by one and rinse, rubbing them under cold running water. Squeeze each strip gently, then lay it out flat on one of the towels to dry. Cook all the pasta in this fashion, no more than two or three strips at a time, and when it is all laid out on the towel, pat it completely dry with another towel.

(**Note** All this washing and wringing and drying of pasta is tedious indeed, but it is necessary, and if you understand why you must do it, the procedure may seem less irksome. You first dip the pasta in cold water to stop the cooking instantly. This is important because of *lasagne* are not kept very firm at this stage they will become horribly mushy later on when they are baked. And you must rinse off their surface starch before laying them out to dry or they will become glued to the towel and tear apart when you are ready to pick them up.)

6 Preheat the oven to 200°C/400°F/Mark 6.

7 Thickly smear the bottom of the *lasagne* dish with butter. Line the bottom of the dish with a single layer of pasta. Cut the strips of pasta to fit the dish, overlapping them very slightly, no more than 6 mm ($\frac{1}{4}$ inch).

8 Over the pasta spread a thin, even coating of the artichoke and béchamel mixture. Add a few tiny dots of butter, and a light sprinkling of grated Parmesan cheese.

9 Cover this with another single layer of pasta, again cutting the strips to fit, and making as few and as narrow overlaps as possible. Continue to alternate layers of pasta with coatings of béchamel and artichoke, always dotting with butter and sprinkling with cheese before adding a new layer of pasta. You should end up with a maximum of six layers of paper-thin pasta.

10 Over the topmost layer of pasta spread the 4 or 5 tablespoons of béchamel you set aside earlier. Dot with butter, sprinkle with the remaining Parmesan, and place the dish on the uppermost rack of the oven.

11 Bake for 10 to 15 minutes, until a light, golden crust forms on top. If

after 10 minutes you see that no crust is beginning to form, raise the oven temperature another 20° to 30°C (50° to 75°F) for the next 5 minutes.

12 After removing the dish from the oven, allow the *lasagne* to settle for at least 10 minutes before serving. Serve directly from the dish, and try serving small portions at first. You will find when you come back for a second helping, the *lasagne* that have rested longer in the dish taste even better.

MENU SUGGESTIONS

The same suggestions made for the *lasagne* recipe below are valid here. Additional meat courses that can be recommended are *Costolette di maiale coi i funghi*, or *Stufatino di maiale alla boscaiola*.

Le lasagne coi funghi e prosciutto

LASAGNE WITH MUSHROOMS AND HAM

In Bologna we make this version of *lasagne* throughout the winter, when the mushroom hunters fill the vegetable markets with freshly picked wild boletus mushrooms (*funghi porcini*). Here, as elsewhere in the book, I have used a combination of fresh cultivated mushrooms and reconstituted dried wild mushrooms, which recaptures much of the woody flavour of the fresh boletus.

For six

40 g (1½ oz) imported dried boletus mushrooms
680 g (1½ lb) fresh, firm cultivated mushrooms
4 tablespoons vegetable oil
90 g (3 oz) butter
½ small onion, chopped very fine
75 g (2½ oz) tinned Italian plum tomatoes, drained and chopped
2 tablespoons chopped parsley
Salt
Freshly ground black pepper
130 g to 170 g (4½ to 5½ oz) plain flour
2 large eggs
Béchamel sauce (page 16), made with 450 ml (¾ pint) milk, 60 g (2 oz) butter, 50 g (1¼ oz) plain flour, ¼ teaspoon salt
350 g (12 oz) unsmoked ham, cut into thin strips
60 g (2 oz) freshly grated Parmesan cheese, plus additional bowl for the table
A ovenproof *lasagne* dish

1 Soak the dried mushrooms for at least 30 minutes in a small bowl with 450 ml ($\frac{3}{4}$ pint) lukewarm water. After soaking, lift them out carefully without stirring up the water in the bowl, and rinse them in several changes of water to rid them of any remaining grit. Chop them into large pieces, and set aside.

2 Filter the water in which the mushrooms have soaked through a wire strainer lined with kitchen paper. Reserve for later.

3 Rinse the fresh mushrooms rapidly under cold running water. Drain well, and wipe thoroughly dry with a soft towel or kitchen paper. Cut them into thin lengthways slices, without detaching the caps.

4 Choose a sauté pan that will be large enough to contain all the fresh mushrooms without crowding. Put in the oil, 60 g (2 oz) butter and the chopped onion, and sauté over medium heat.

5 When the onion becomes translucent, put in the reconstituted wild mushrooms, the filtered water in which they soaked, the chopped tomatoes and the parsley. Stir well, and cover the pan, with the cover slightly askew. Turn the heat down to medium low.

6 When the liquid in the pan has evaporated, put in the sliced fresh mushrooms, and raise the heat to high. Add salt and a grinding of pepper. Cook uncovered, always at lively heat, stirring frequently, for 7 to 8 minutes until all the liquid thrown off by the fresh mushrooms has evaporated. Turn off the heat, and taste and check seasoning. Set on one side.

7 Prepare the pasta dough, using either the hand method (pages 127–34) or the machine (page 134). Cut it into *lasagne* strips, and parboil these, following the directions in steps 4 and 5 of *Le lasagne coi carciofi*, page 151.

8 Preheat the oven to 200°C/400°F/Mark 6.

9 Make the béchamel sauce. Keep it warm by leaving it in the upper half of a double boiler, with the heat turned on very low. Do not worry if a film forms on the top; just stir it before using it later. Any tiny lumps that may form will dissolve while the *lasagne* are baking.

10 Thickly smear the bottom of the *lasagne* dish with butter. Line the bottom of the dish with a single layer of pasta. Cut the strips of pasta to fit the pan; overlap them slightly, but no more than 6 mm ($\frac{1}{4}$ inch).

11 Spread a thinly distributed layer of mushrooms over the pasta; it is not necessary to cover every square inch of pasta with mushrooms. Cover the mushrooms very thinly with béchamel sauce. Scatter a few strips of sliced ham on top, then sprinkle with a little Parmesan cheese. Cover with another layer of pasta, and repeat the sequence of mushrooms, béchamel, ham and cheese. Continue building up the layers of pasta and filling until you reach a maximum of six layers of pasta. Over the topmost layer of pasta, spread a little béchamel, sprinkle with some cheese, and dot with the remaining butter.

12 Place the pan in the uppermost level of the preheated oven. Bake for 10 to 15 minutes, until a light golden crust forms on top. If after 10 minutes there is no crust beginning to form, raise the oven temperature another 20° to 30°C (50° to 75°F) for the next 5 minutes.

13 After removing the *lasagne* from the oven, allow them to rest for at least 10 minutes before serving. Serve directly from the dish with a bowl of freshly grated cheese.

MENU SUGGESTIONS

This is a beautiful dish for a dinner where you want to pull out all the stops. Follow with *Filetto al barolo*, *Scaloppine al marsala arricchite*, *Ossobuchi in bianco*, *Spalla di vitello brasata* or *Il pollo ripieno*. My own favourite meat course to follow this is *Anatra arrosto*. You would then go on to a salad with mixed greens, such as *arugola*, round and lamb's lettuce, and conclude with *Il mandarino farcito*.

Le piccagge col pesto di ricotta

LASAGNE WITH RICOTTA PESTO

Some years ago, when my husband and I spent a summer in a small town near Genoa on the Italian Riviera, one of our favourite dishes in the local *trattorie* was a *lasagne*-like pasta seasoned with a very light pesto. It was called *Piccagge al pesto*. *Piccagge*, in Genoese dialect, we learned, means napkins or small tea-cloths; in culinary usage it is applied both to *lasagne* and, sometimes, to noodles.

Piccagge are cut smaller than conventional *lasagne*, and they are not baked in a pan. They are boiled, like conventional noodle pasta, and seasoned on the serving dish.

The pesto is not quite as sharp as traditional pesto because it contains ricotta. This is a step neither forward nor backward in the evolution of the sauce. It is simply another way of doing it, for those occasions when a lighter pesto is desired. For a more complete discussion of pesto, see *The Classic Italian Cookbook*, page 118. This pesto is also very good with *gnocchi*, thin *spaghetti*, or standard egg noodles.

The pasta made on the Riviera has a third to a quarter the proportion of eggs used in Emilia-Romagna. And water is added to supplant the missing eggs. In the recipe below, although it is in every other detail authentically Genoese, I have substituted the pasta of my own native Romagna, which, many of my Genoese friends concur, is a better-tasting pasta than theirs.

For six

The pesto

100 g (3½ oz) fresh basil leaves
8 tablespoons olive oil
35 g (1¼ oz) pine nuts
60 g (2 oz) freshly grated Parmesan cheese
15 g (½ oz) freshly grated *pecorino romano* cheese
2 cloves garlic, lightly crushed, peeled, and cut into 4 or 5 pieces
1 teaspoon salt
30 g (1 oz) ricotta
30 g (1 oz) butter, softened at room temperature

(**Note** If in your freezer you have some pesto base that contains no cheese, thaw it and add the cheeses and butter called for in this recipe.)

The pasta

2 large eggs
About 130 g (4½ oz) plain flour

1 Put the basil, olive oil, pine nuts, garlic and salt into the food processor, fitted with steel blades, or into a blender, and process or blend at high speed. (If you have a choice, use the processor. It will produce a better, less homogenised texture.) It may be necessary to stop the machine after the first few seconds and scrape down with a spatula any of the mixture clinging to the sides of the bowl.

2 Transfer to a mixing bowl. Add the Parmesan, *pecorino* and ricotta. Mix thoroughly, using a wooden spoon. Add the softened butter, and mix again, until all the ingredients have been smoothly amalgamated.

3 Knead the eggs and flour for 8 to 10 minutes, following the special directions for pasta on page 127.

4 Roll out the pasta dough, using either the rolling-pin method described on pages 127–34, or the machine method on page 134. Roll it out as thin as possible.

5 Cut the sheet of pasta or the machine-made bands into rectangular strips about 87 mm (3½ inches) wide and 125 mm (5 inches) long.

6 Bring 4 to 5 litres (7 to 8¾ pints) water to the boil; add 2 tablespoons salt and 1 tablespoon olive oil. As the water returns to a fast boil, put in half the pasta. (It is not advisable to put it all in at once, because the strips may stick to each other.) As soon as it is cooked *al dente*, firm to the bite, scoop it out with a colander spoon or large skimmer, and place on a warm dish.

7 Take a spoonful of hot water from the pasta pot and mix it into the pesto. Spread half the pesto over the cooked pasta.

8 Drop in the remaining pasta; when it is cooked *al dente*, drain it and place it over the other pasta on the dish. Spread the remaining pesto over it and serve at once.

Note If cooking the pasta when it is freshly made, it cooks so quickly that the first batch will not have time to get cold while the other is cooking. However, if you are making the pasta in advance and letting it dry, you should cook it simultaneously, in two separate pots, because dried pasta takes longer to cook, and if you do just one batch at a time, the first will get cold while it waits for the other to be done.

MENU SUGGESTIONS

Pesto is always an appropriate beginning for a fish menu. Good choices for the second course would be *Pesce turchino al forno con le patate*, *Pesce da taglio in salsa*, *Orate al limone e maggiorana*, *Gamberi ai ferri come le cannocchie*. Particularly nice would be *Calamari ripieni coi funghi secchi*. The second course could also be a meat dish. Any of the meat courses in this book would go well, but especially suitable would be *Bocconcini di vitello ai sapori e funghi*, *Spezzato d'agnello con peperone e prosciutto* or *Costolette di maiale con i funghi*.

Le pappardelle del Cantunzein

YELLOW AND GREEN BROAD NOODLES WITH SWEET PEPPERS AND SAUCE

This lovely dish is one of the most perfect summer pastas ever devised. It is the creation of an incomparable restaurateur and old friend, Evio Battellani, grand keeper of the flame at Bologna's sanctuary of pasta, Al Cantunzein.

Here we have both yellow and green spinach pasta, cut into short, broad noodles, *pappardelle*. The principal ornament of the sauce is sweet red pepper, cooked in olive oil, with sautéed onion. Also present are a touch of tomato, very briefly cooked, and a few nuggets of browned sausage. If you see some on your market stalls or at the greengrocer's, you could add the stunning yellow peppers Signor Battellani uses alongside the red. They are meaty, sweet, and look ravishing in the plate, but even without yellow peppers this dish can be an absolute success. The important thing to remember is to use red rather than green peppers, because they are sweeter, and to choose them only at their peak, when they are firm, thickly fleshed, and a bright, glowing red.

For six to eight

The pasta

Yellow egg pasta, made with 2 eggs and about 130 g (4½ oz) plain flour (see basic recipe, page 124). Follow the directions on pages 127–34 if rolling it by hand, or page 134 if doing it in the pasta machine. When rolled out, cut the sheet or the machine-made bands of pasta into strips 30 mm (1¼ inches) wide and 100 to 125 mm (4 to 5 inches) long.

Spinach pasta, made with 1 egg, 100 to 130 g (3½ to 4½ oz) flour, and a tiny fistful of cooked spinach (see the basic recipe for spinach pasta on page 126). If rolling out by hand, see the directions on pages 127–34, if by machine, see page 134. Cut the pasta into the same size strips as the yellow pasta above.

The sauce

3 large, meaty, fresh red (and yellow) peppers
5 tablespoons olive oil
¾ small onion, chopped very fine
Salt
Freshly ground black pepper
225 g (8 oz) fresh ripe tomatoes, peeled, seeded, and cut up, or 1½ tablespoons tomato purée, dissolved in 6 tablespoons water
225 g (8 oz) sausages, cut into 12 mm (½-inch) pieces
30 g (1 oz) butter
30 g (1 oz) freshly grated Parmesan cheese, plus additional bowl for the table

1 Quarter the peppers, discard the seeds and core, and peel them, using a swivel-action peeler. Cut them into more or less square pieces, 25 mm (1 inch) long on a side.

2 Put 3 tablespoons olive oil and the onion in a frying pan or sauté pan, and turn the heat to medium high.

3 When the onion turns pale gold, add the peppers, and cook them, turning them from time to time for 7 to 8 minutes. Add salt and pepper and stir well.

4 In another pan, put the remaining 2 tablespoons olive oil, the tomatoes or the dissolved tomato purée, and a little salt, and cook over medium heat for about 10 minutes.

5 Add the peppers, and let the peppers and tomatoes cook together for about 1 minute, turning them frequently.

6 In another pan, put the cut-up sausage and 4 tablespoons water. Turn on the heat to medium. When the water has completely evaporated, continue cooking the sausage until it is lightly browned all over.

7 Add the sausage, and no more than 2 tablespoons of the fat it has thrown off while cooking, to the peppers and tomatoes. Cook together over medium heat for about 30 seconds, mixing well the contents of the pan.

8 Bring 3 to 4 litres ($5\frac{1}{4}$ to 7 pints) water to the boil. Add 1 or 2 tablespoons salt. When the water is bubbling fast again, put in the yellow pasta. In just a few moments, long enough to stir the pasta, add the spinach pasta. When cooked *al dente*, firm to the bite, drain and transfer to a warm bowl. If the pasta is freshly made, it will be ready just a few seconds after the water returns to the boil.

9 Add the sauce, which should have been gently reheated while the pasta was cooking. Toss thoroughly, add the butter and grated Parmesan, toss again, and serve at once. Serve with a bowl of freshly grated cheese.

MENU SUGGESTIONS

The happiest choice for a meat course to follow would be a roast, such as *Punto di vitello arrosto*, *Arrosto di maiale ubriaco* or *Arrosto di agnello pasquale col vino bianco* (from my first book, page 235). Any veal with simple, understated seasoning would also be a good choice.

Fettuccine con le zucchine fritte

FETTUCCINE WITH FRIED COURGETTES

A 'sauce' for pasta may be simply any ingredient for whose flavour and texture the pasta acts as a foil. Here it is courgettes, cut into matchsticks and fried very crisp and brown. It is a terrific combination, especially with tender, fresh home-made pasta. A lovely touch is the fresh basil tossed in at the end.

For four

680 g ($1\frac{1}{2}$ lb) courgettes, preferably young and small
A pasta colander
Salt
10 to 12 fresh basic leaves, or fewer, if very large
90 g (3 oz) butter
60 g (2 oz) plain flour
Enough vegetable oil to come at least 6 mm ($\frac{1}{4}$ inch) up the sides of the frying pan
3 cloves garlic, peeled
Home-made *fettuccine* (see pages 137–40), made with 2 large eggs and about 130 g ($4\frac{1}{2}$ oz) plain flour
50 g ($1\frac{3}{4}$ oz) freshly grated Parmesan cheese

1 Soak the courgettes for 10 minutes in a basin of cold water. Then scrub them with your hands under cold running water until the skin feels clean and smooth. If they are mature, and the skin is not fresh and taut, it may be necessary to pare away the first thin layer of skin to be sure you have eliminated all trace of grit.

2 Cut off and discard both ends of the courgettes, then cut the courgettes into sticks about 65 mm ($2\frac{1}{2}$ inches) long and not much more than 6 mm ($\frac{1}{4}$ inch) thick.

3 Put the courgette sticks into the pasta colander and sprinkle very liberally with salt. Toss them two to three times to distribute the salt evenly, set the colander over a deep bowl, and let it stand for at least 2 hours, and possibly longer. Check the bowl occasionally, and if the liquid that collects in it comes up high enough to seep into the colander, empty the bowl.

4 When you feel the courgettes have drained long enough, remove them from the colander and pat them thoroughly dry with kitchen paper. Rinse and dry the colander for later use.

5 Heat 4 litres (7 pints) water over medium heat. It should come to the boil and be ready for the cooking of the pasta about the time you have finished frying the courgettes (step 9).

6 Rinse and pat dry the basil leaves. Tear each leaf into two or three pieces, and set aside.

7 Put the butter in the upper part of a double boiler. Keep the water in the lower half of the pot at a gentle, steady simmer: the butter should melt and stay hot.

8 Put the courgette sticks in the dry colander. Set a large plate or bowl under the colander. Dust the courgettes with the flour, shaking the colander until they are evenly coated, and any excess flour has passed through the colander.

9 Heat the oil and garlic in a 228- or 250-mm (9- or 10-inch) frying pan over high heat. When the oil is quite hot, put in as many courgette sticks as will fit loosely in a single layer. Check the garlic, and as soon as it begins to

turn brown remove it. Turn the courgettes to brown them on all sides, then transfer them to kitchen paper to drain.

10 Bring the water for the pasta to the boil when you are about to finish frying the last batch of courgettes. When the water is boiling, put in 1 to 2 tablespoons salt, and drop in the *fettuccine*. If you are using thin, fresh home-made pasta, it will cook very quickly, in less than a minute after the water returns to the boil. If you are using dried pasta, take into account the extra cooking time it takes, and begin cooking it a little earlier, otherwise the courgettes will be cold by the time the pasta is done.

11 When the pasta is *al dente*, tender but firm to the bite, drain it, and put it on a warm serving dish. Pour the melted butter over it, add the fried courgettes, the basil leaves and the grated cheese. Toss thoroughly and serve at once.

MENU SUGGESTIONS

Virtually any meat course would go well with this. An interesting group to choose from would include *Brasato di manzo con le cipolle*, *Cartoccio di scaloppine con asparagi*, *Stufatino di agnello con l'aceto* and any of the pork chops on pages 240–4.

Tonnarelli con i funghi

SQUARE NOODLES WITH MUSHROOM SAUCE

This sauce is one of the many delicious things you can produce when you combine dried wild mushrooms with freshly cultivated ones. It comes astonishingly close to the taste of the wild mushroom sauce served with *risotto* or pasta that everyone in Italy looks forward to so eagerly when the boletus is in season.

In this recipe the mushrooms are shredded very fine and cooked in butter rather than in the traditional olive oil. Butter makes the sauce creamier and sweeter, and that is the way it is often done in the North when served with *risotto*, I happen to like this sauce very much with pasta, in particular with *tonnarelli*, the square home-made egg noodle, but it is also quite good with *spaghetti*.

For four to six

10 g ($\frac{1}{3}$ oz) imported dried boletus mushrooms
450 g (1 lb) fresh, firm mushrooms
1 small onion, chopped
10 g (4 oz) butter
Salt
Freshly ground black pepper
Tonnarelli made with 3 eggs and 240 g ($8\frac{1}{2}$ oz) hard-wheat (durum) flour, as directed on page 143, or 450 g (1 lb) *spaghetti*
3 tablespoons parsley chopped fine
50 g ($1\frac{3}{4}$ oz) freshly grated Parmesan cheese, plus additional bowl for the table

1 Soak the dried mushrooms in 225 ml (scant $\frac{1}{2}$ pint) lukewarm water for at least 30 minutes.

2 Gently remove the mushrooms without stirring up the water, and rinse them repeatedly under cold running water. Chop them very fine, and set aside.

3 Filter through kitchen paper the water in which the mushrooms have soaked. Set aside.

4 Rapidly rinse the fresh mushrooms in cold running water, and dry with a towel. Shred very fine. You can do the shredding in the food processor, using the disc with the grating and shredding holes.

5 Put the onion and half the butter into a sauté pan over medium heat. When the onion turns a rich gold, add the reconstituted dried mushrooms and their filtered water. Cook until the water boils away completely.

6 Add the shredded fresh mushrooms, salt and pepper, and cover the pan. Cook for 25 to 30 minutes. This may seem a lot longer than you would ordinarily cook mushrooms, but it is necessary in order to concentrate their flavour and help them acquire that elusive boletus taste. If at the end of this time there is some liquid in the pan, uncover, and boil the liquid away over higher heat. Then turn off the heat.

7 Cook the pasta in 3 to 4 litres ($5\frac{1}{4}$ to 7 pints) salted boiling water. Drain when it is done *al dente*, firm to the bite. Toss immediately with the mushroom sauce, the rest of the butter, the parsley and the Parmesan. Serve with a bowl of freshly grated cheese.

MENU SUGGESTIONS

As long as it does not contain mushrooms, any meat course can follow these *tonnarelli*. I like them with *Filetto al barolo*, *Scaloppine ammantate*, *Costolette di vitello profumate all'aglio e rosmarino*, *Rotolo di vitello con spinaci*, *Costolette di maiale ai due vini* or *Arrosto di maiale all'alloro* (from my first book, page 241).

Tonnarelli col rosmarino

SQUARE NOODLES WITH BUTTER AND ROSEMARY

In Italy pasta is sometimes dressed with the leftover juices and little bits of meat from a roast. We call it pasta *col tocco d'arrosto*, 'with a touch of the roast'. The sauce in this recipe is an imitation 'touch of the roast', because it is made without the roast. But its savouriness comes from similar elements – browned garlic and rosemary and a shadowy meat presence, courtesy of a bouillon cube. I find it, in fact, fresher and more fragrant. It is one of the most rapid sauces for pasta you can prepare. If you start it at the same time that you put on the water for the pasta, it will be ready before the pasta is cooked. It is perfect in conjunction with *tonnarelli*, home-made square egg noodles, but it can be excellent with *spaghetti* or *fettuccine*.

For four to six

Salt
Tonnarelli, made with 3 large eggs and 240 g ($8\frac{1}{2}$ oz) hard-wheat (durum) flour (see page 143), or home-made *fettuccine* (see pages 137–40), made with 3 large eggs and 225 g (8 oz) plain flour, or 450 g (1 lb) *spaghetti*
110 g (4 oz) butter
3 large or 4 medium garlic cloves, peeled and crushed
3 sprigs fresh rosemary, about 75 mm (3 inches) long, or 2 teaspoons dried leaves
1 bouillon cube, mashed
30 g (1 oz) freshly grated Parmesan cheese, plus additional bowl for the table

1 Bring 3 to 4 litres ($5\frac{1}{4}$ to 7 pints) water to the boil, add 3 heaped tablespoons salt, and when the water resumes boiling, put in the pasta.

2 While the water is coming to the boil, prepare the sauce. Cut up the butter, and cook it in a small saucepan, together with the garlic and rosemary, over medium heat for 4 to 5 minutes, stirring frequently.

3 Add the crushed bouillon cube. Stir, and cook until the bouillon cube has completely dissolved. Turn off the heat, because the sauce is done.

4 When the pasta is tender but firm to the bite, drain, and put it in a warm serving bowl. Add the sauce, pouring it through a fine wire strainer. Toss thoroughly.

5 Add the grated cheese, and toss again. Serve at once, with a bowl of additional grated cheese.

MENU SUGGESTIONS

Whether or not you would like to follow this with a roast where there is rosemary is up to you. It could be considered a theme with variations. But it might be more varied for the palate to choose something else, such as *Brasato di manzo con le cipolle*, *Stufatino di manzo con i piselli*, *Scaloppine ammantate* or any of the lamb dishes on pages 236–7.

I pizzoccheri

BUCKWHEAT NOODLES WITH SWISS CHARD AND POTATOES

Pizzoccheri is a speciality of the sunny valley of Valtellina, backed up against and sheltered by the Alpine masses that stand between it and Switzerland. From its immaculate vineyards, perched on precipitous, terraced slopes, come big, velvety wines that are the most congenial accompaniment to its earthy cooking. Sitting down to a dish piled high with *pizzoccheri* and several bottles of Sassella is part of the agreeable ritual with which visitors to Valtellina are welcomed.

Pizzoccheri are beautiful brown-grey, broad, short noodles. They are cooked with potatoes and a vegetable, such as Swiss chard or Savoy cabbage, tossed with the soft local cheese and garlic-scented butter, and then put briefly into the oven. In place of Valtellina's good cheese, which is not available here, one can use fontina, which comes from another of Italy's Alpine valleys, the Val d'Aosta. It is a perfect substitute.

The startling colour of the pasta comes from the buckwheat flour which is its principal constituent. Buckwheat, called *grano saraceno* in Italy (Saracen wheat) because it arrived from Asia Minor, grows well in hilly, cool country. An excellent grey polenta is made from it. Those familiar with Central European cooking know the hulled kernels of buckwheat, called kasha. Buckwheat is very soft, and in order to knead it into workable dough it is necessary to add approximately 1 part wheat flour to 2 parts buckwheat. Otherwise this is made just like other pasta, but, being softer, it is a bit easier to handle.

For four to six

The pasta

200 g (7 oz) buckwheat flour
75 g ($2\frac{1}{2}$ oz) plain flour
2 large eggs
$\frac{1}{2}$ teaspoon salt
1 tablespoon milk
1 tablespoon water

1 Pour the two kinds of flour onto a work surface, and mix them well. Shape the flour into a mound, making a deep hollow in the centre. Put the eggs, salt, milk and water into the hollow, and draw the sides of the mound over them. Knead for about 10 minutes, until you have a smooth, compact ball of dough. If you find the mixture too soft to knead, add a large pinch or two of plain flour.

2 Put the ball of dough between two soup plates, and let it rest for 15 to 20 minutes.

3 Roll out the dough as you would other pasta, using either the rolling-pin method (see pages 127–34), or the pasta machine (page 134). Do not roll it out too thin. It should be a bit thicker than conventional egg noodles – about $1\frac{1}{2}$ mm ($\frac{1}{16}$inch) thick.

4 Lay the sheet of paste or the machine-made bands on a table to dry for 2 or more minutes, depending on the temperature and humidity of the room. The dough should be dry enough not to stick to itself when folded and cut, but not so brittle that it will crack.

5 Loosely fold the dough into a flat roll, as you would for cutting noodles (refer to page 139). Cut the rolled-up dough into 25-mm (1-inch) wide strips, and cut each strip diagonally in the middle. This will give you diamond-shaped noodles, 25 mm (1 inch) wide and about 75 to 87 mm (3 to $3\frac{1}{2}$ inches) long. Some may be slightly longer or shorter, but it does not matter much. Unfold the noodles, and spread out on a towel.

200 to 250 g (7 to 8 oz) Swiss chard stalks (all green tops removed), cut into pieces about 50 to 70 mm (2 to 3 inches) long, and approximately 12 mm ($\frac{1}{2}$ inch) wide
2 tablespoons salt
150 g (5 oz) potatoes, preferably new, cut into slices 6 mm ($\frac{1}{4}$ inch) thick
100 g ($3\frac{1}{2}$ oz) butter
4 large cloves garlic, peeled and lightly crushed
A 300- to 500-mm (12- to 14-inch) ovenproof dish
Buckwheat noodles (see above)
110 g (4 oz) Italian fontina cheese, cut into thin slivers
60 g (2 oz) freshly grated Parmesan cheese

1 Preheat oven to 200°C/400°F/Mark 6.

2 Wash the Swiss chard thoroughly in cold water.

3 Bring about 4 litres (7 pints) water to the boil, add 2 tablespoons salt, and as it returns to the boil put in the Swiss chard.

4 After the Swiss chard has cooked for about 10 minutes, put in the sliced potatoes.

5 While the potatoes are cooking, sauté 90 g (3 oz) butter and the garlic in a small pan over medium heat. When the garlic turns a light nut brown, remove and discard it, and turn off the heat.

6 Lightly smear the baking dish with the remaining butter.

7 When the potatoes and the Swiss chard stalks are done – test them both with a fork – drop the pasta into the same pot. Cook the pasta until it is very firm to the bite, *molto al dente*. If the pasta was freshly made it will take just a few seconds. Drain immediately, and transfer the pasta, Swiss chard and potatoes to the baking dish.

8 Add the garlic-flavoured butter, and toss thoroughly.

9 Add the fontina and the Parmesan, mixing them into the pasta and vegetables.

10 Level off the contents of the dish, and place it on the topmost level of the preheated oven. Remove after 5 minutes, and allow to settle for 2 to 3 minutes before serving.

Note Savoy cabbage can be used instead of Swiss chard, following the same procedure, but I find the chard gives it a fresher flavour.

MENU SUGGESTIONS

Pizzoccheri is quite substantial, as those who have read the recipe will already have concluded. It should be followed by a meat course sturdy enough to bear comparison with it, yet without a complicated taste. *Brasato di manzo con le cipolle*, *Ossobuchi in bianco*, *Arrosto di maiale ubriaco*, *Arrosto di maiale al latte* (from my first book, page 240) or *Pollo in tegame al limone* are all good choices.

SECOND COURSES

I Secondi

Branzino alla rivierasca coi carciofi

BAKED SEA BASS WITH GLOBE ARTICHOKES, FROM THE RIVIERA

This unusual combination of fish and globe artichokes comes from the Riviera, a balmy garden of a land, where herbs and vegetables inspire the making of every dish but dessert.

The artichokes are sliced very thin and baked with the fish, together with lemon juice and rosemary. There is not much to do except to assemble it all, slip it into the oven, and wait to enjoy the delectable results.

You must be careful to trim the artichoke leaves well down, so that only the tender parts are left. Any tough, unchewable bits from the top of the leaves would interfere with the pleasure one gets from eating fish and artichoke together.

For four

4 medium globe artichokes
½ lemon
8 tablespoons olive oil
3 tablespoons lemon juice
Salt
Freshly ground black pepper
900 g (2 lb) sea bass, cleaned and scaled, but with head and tail on, and rinsed in cold water (see note below)
1 teaspoon rosemary leaves

1 Preheat oven to 220°C/425°F/Mark 7.

2 Clean the artichokes and slice them as directed on page 151.

3 Mix the olive oil, lemon juice, salt and pepper in a small bowl and set aside.

4 Pat dry the fish with kitchen paper, and place it in a rectangular baking dish just large enough to contain it.

5 Add the sliced artichokes and the oil-and-lemon-juice mixture, and sprinkle the rosemary over the fish. Turn the artichoke slices so they are all coated with juice, and stuff some of the artichokes into the fish's cavity. Baste the fish with the juice and place it in the upper third of the preheated oven.

6 After 20 minutes' cooking, baste the fish and stir the artichokes.

7 Bake for another 15 to 20 minutes, then transfer the fish to a warm serving dish. This has to be done very carefully, otherwise the fish will break up. The best way is probably to lift it with two spatulas, one in each hand. Spread the artichokes over the fish, pour over it all the juices from the baking dish and serve immediately.

Note A small whole sea bass is sometimes difficult to find. You may have to settle for a single slice of equivalent weight cut from a larger fish. In this case divide the slice into two fillets and remove the bone. Put the artichokes and all the flavourings in the baking dish, and cook in the preheated oven for 20 minutes. Then place the fillets skin side down in the baking dish. Cook for 15 minutes, basting the fish after 7 to 8 minutes as directed in the recipe.

MENU SUGGESTIONS

Any first course with a fresh, sweet flavour can precede this: *Spaghetti col sugo di cipolle* or *Le piccagge col pesto di ricotta*. No vegetable dish is required. Follow with a salad of tender greens, or tomatoes with fresh basil, or *Insalata di arancia*.

Il pesce coi finocchi freschi

SEA BASS WITH FRESH FENNEL

When it comes to joining unexpected ingredients, Sicilians are the most successful and brilliant matchmakers in Italy. The combination of fresh fennel and fish does not occur anywhere on the mainland, to my knowledge. The fennel is first slowly cooked in oil until it becomes very tender and sweet and loses all the bite of its aniseed flavour. The fish is then sautéed alongside it.

In Sicily, I had this dish made with *dentice*, a member of the bream family. I find the sea bream here sometimes has a less delicate flavour than its Mediterranean kin, and sea bass seems to me the most successful choice, but you can try the bream and experiment, if you like, with other firm-fleshed light-flavoured fish.

For four

2 large fennel bulbs
8 tablespoons olive oil
Salt
Freshly ground black pepper
2 whole small sea bass, about 500 g (1 lb 2 oz) each, scaled, gutted, but with heads and tails left on, and rinsed in cold water

1 Cut off and discard the tops of the fennel down to the bulbs. Trim away any bruised, discoloured parts from the bulbs. Cut the bulbs into very thin lengthways slices less than 12 mm ($\frac{1}{2}$ inch) thick. Rinse thoroughly in cold water.

2 Choose a sauté pan that can contain the two fish comfortably. Put in the olive oil and the sliced fennel and 8 tablespoons water. Cover, and cook over medium heat for 30 minutes or longer, until the fennel has completely wilted and become very tender. Turn it from time to time. If the fennel is still rather tough after the first 20 minutes, add 4 tablespoons water.

3 When the fennel is tender, uncover the pan, sprinkle liberally with salt, and turn up the heat. Boil away any liquid remaining in the pan, and cook, turning the fennel frequently, until it turns a rich deep gold. Season with 2 or 3 grindings of pepper, turn the heat down to medium, and push the fennel to one side of the pan, making enough room for the fish.

4 Put the fish into the pan, season it with salt and pepper, and baste with some of the olive oil from the pan. Cover, and cook for 7 to 8 minutes. Then gently turn the fish over on to its other side, baste again with olive oil, and cover. Cook another 5 to 6 minutes.

5 The fish may be served whole with the fennel slices on top. Even better would be to fillet the fish, which is not difficult to do with sea bass. Arrange the fillets on a serving dish, and cover them with all the fennel and oil from the pan.

MENU SUGGESTIONS

A lively preamble to this sweet-tasting sea bass would be *Insalata di spaghetti*. A more substantial, but just as compatible choice is *Cappelletti di pesce col sugo di gamberetti*, or you might try the cool, fresh *Polpettone di tonno e spinaci*. No vegetables are necessary, but a crisp green salad is, after the fish.

Pesce turchino al forno con le patate

BAKED MACKEREL WITH POTATOES, GENOESE STYLE

There is a marvellous group of dishes in the repertoire of Genoese cooking in which the leading rôle is taken each time by a different player, but the supporting cast always stays the same. The regulars are potatoes, garlic, oil and parsley; the star may be fish, shrimps, tiny octopuses, meat or fresh wild mushrooms.

In the original version of this particular recipe one finds the fresh native anchovies of the Riviera. In their place I use mackerel, which is a perfectly successful substitute. It works so well, in fact, that even some of my students who were not before particularly fond of mackerel have now made this one of their favourite dishes.

The recipe consists of two basic steps. First, the potatoes are partially cooked with garlic, oil and parsley. Secondly, the fish is added, and cooks together with the potatoes until both are done. It all takes place in the oven.

Although the dish works well with mackerel, which take on some sweetness from the potatoes, the method suits most firm-fleshed fish, so feel free to experiment.

For six

680 g (1½ lb) boiling potatoes
A 400 by 250 mm (16 by 10 inch) ovenproof dish, preferably enamelled cast iron
12 tablespoons olive oil
3 cloves garlic, peeled and chopped
50 g (1¾ oz) chopped parsley
Salt
Freshly ground black pepper
900 g (2 lb) mackerel fillets, with the skin on, or other firm-fleshed fish

1 Preheat oven to 230°C/450°F/Mark 8.

2 Peel the potatoes, and cut them into very thin slices. If they are too thick, they may not be quite done at the end. Wash them in cold water, then pat them thoroughly dry with kitchen paper.

3 Into the baking dish put all the potatoes, half the olive oil, half the garlic, half the parsley and a liberal amount of salt and freshly ground pepper. Mix everything thoroughly, then spread the potato slices evenly over the bottom of the dish.

4 Place the dish in the upper third of the preheated oven. Bake until the potatoes are about half cooked, for approximately 12 to 15 minutes.

5 Remove the dish from the oven, and place the fish fillets, skin side down, over the potatoes. Mix the remaining oil, garlic and parsley in a small bowl, and pour the mixture over the exposed surface of the fish, basting it well. Sprinkle with a generous amount of salt and pepper. Return the dish to the oven.

6 After 10 minutes, remove from the oven. With a spoon, scoop up some of the oil in the dish and baste the fish and potatoes with it. Loosen those potatoes that have become browned and stuck to the sides of the dish, moving them away. Push into their place some of the slices that are not so brown. Return the dish to the oven and bake for 5 more minutes.

Serve piping hot, with all the juices from the dish, scraping loose all those potatoes stuck to the dish. These are the most delectable bits, so save them for yourself or for your favourite guest.

MENU SUGGESTIONS

A well-rounded menu could start with *Canestrelli trifolati* as an appetiser, follow with *Le piccagge col pesto di ricotta*, and then the mackerel. A much simpler meal would have *Zuppa di piselli e vongole* as the first course. If you feel like a substantial salad, the *Insalata di lattuga e gorgonzola* can follow the fish. A sweeter, more refreshing choice would be *Rape rosse al forno.*

Il pesce in brodetto

A SINGLE FISH COOKED FISH-SOUP STYLE

This is an ingenious way for two to four people to enjoy the spirited taste of fish soup without having to cook the customary large assortment of fish. All you need is one good fish, of almost any kind – sea bass, bream, red snapper, mullet, halibut or swordfish fillets or steaks; or even plaice. This preparation is one of the rare ones, I find, that can make plaice interesting.

The procedure is the same as that for a full-scale fish soup (see *The Classic Italian Cookbook*, page 200), except that here there are no fish heads to strain into the broth. The result is a lighter, less complex flavour than that of fish soup, but every bit as gratifying.

For four. (*This is also an excellent recipe for two; use a smaller fish, and halve the other ingredients. See Halving or Doubling Recipes, page 13.*)

8 tablespoons olive oil
1 small onion, chopped
1 large clove garlic, peeled and chopped
2 tablespoons chopped parsley
8 tablespoons dry white wine
200 g (7 oz) Italian plum tomatoes, chopped, with their juice
A 1·1 to 1·35 kg ($2\frac{1}{2}$ to 3 lb) whole fish, scaled, gutted and rinsed in cold water, or 680 g ($1\frac{1}{2}$ lb) fish fillets or steaks
Salt
Freshly ground black pepper

1 Choose a sauté pan that will be able to contain the whole fish comfortably, or all the fish pieces in a single layer. Put in the olive oil and the onion, and sauté over medium heat until the onion is translucent.

2 Add the garlic, and sauté until it turns light gold.

3 Add the parsley, stir once or twice, then add the white wine.

4 When the wine has been bubbling for a few moments, add the chopped tomatoes with their juice. Cook, uncovered, for 6 or 7 minutes, stirring from time to time.

5 Put in the whole fish or the fish pieces in a single layer. Sprinkle with several liberal pinches of salt and 2 or 3 grindings of pepper. Cover the pan, and turn down the heat to medium low.

6 When the fish has cooked for 5 to 10 minutes (the shorter time is for the pieces, the longer for the whole fish, depending also on their thickness), turn it, and re-cover the pan. Cook another 5 to 10 minutes, then serve at once, with the onions and juices from the pan.

MENU SUGGESTIONS

This is a savoury dish that should be preceded by something that tastes fresh and uncomplicated, such as *Zuppa di calamari e carciofi* or *Carciofini gratinati*. Follow the fish with *Le patate in insalata*, raw *Finocchio in pinzimonio* or a mixture of any greens.

Pesce da taglio in salsa

HALIBUT WITH WHITE WINE AND ANCHOVY SAUCE

Halibut and other fish steaks can be terribly dull, but not when they are prepared this way.

The fish is floured and fried, then you prepare a sauce for it, with olive oil, chopped onion, anchovies, parsley and white wine, cooked just long enough to brown the onions, dissolve the anchovies, and boil down the wine. The fish is briefly reheated with the sauce, then it is all ready, and tastes very good.

For four

900 g (2 lb) halibut cut into slices 25 mm (1 inch) thick
12 tablespoons olive oil
Salt
90 g (3 oz) plain flour, spread on a dish or wax paper
3 medium onions, chopped very fine
1 or 2 flat anchovy fillets, coarsely cut up
3 tablespoons chopped parsley
12 tablespoons dry white wine
Freshly ground black pepper

1 Wash the fish in cold water, and pat it thoroughly dry. Do not tear or remove the skin that circles it.

2 Choose a frying pan or sauté pan broad enough to contain all the fish without any overlapping. Heat up half the olive oil over medium heat.

3 Sprinkle the fish slices with salt, and dredge them in the flour on both sides. When the oil is quite hot slip them into the pan, and cook them for 5 minutes on each side. Turn off the heat, and draw off most of the oil from the pan.

4 Put the remaining olive oil and the chopped onion into a small saucepan, and cook over medium heat until the onion colours lightly.

5 Add the cut-up anchovy fillets, the chopped parsley and a pinch of salt. Cook, stirring frequently, mashing the anchovies with a wooden spoon until they dissolve.

6 Add the white wine and boil it until half of it has evaporated.

7 Pour all the contents of the saucepan over the fish in the frying pan. Add a few grindings of pepper. Over medium heat baste the fish for a couple of minutes, letting it draw in the flavours of the sauce.

8 With two spatulas or one broad one gently transfer the fish to a warm serving dish, taking care that the slices do not break up. Pour all the sauce from the pan over them, and serve at once.

MENU SUGGESTIONS

Take into account the savouriness of the anchovy sauce here when choosing the first course; it could be *Zuppa primavera*, *Le piccagge col pesto di ricotta*, *Frittata con le cipolle*, *Frittata di spaghetti*. Accompany the fish with *Dadini di patate arrosto* (from my first book, page 332), or any fried potatoes, or follow with *Le patate in insalata*.

Orate al limone e maggiorana

PAN-ROASTED SEA BREAM WITH MARJORAM AND LEMON

This is a savoury treatment for small to medium firm-fleshed fish, to be served whole. Sea bass and sea bream are both suitable.

The fish is cooked in butter, together with marjoram and garlic. It is lightly browned at first, then the lemon juice and seasoning are added, and it continues cooking, covered, under the slow-cooking method I call pan-roasting. Note that the garlic goes in at the same time as the fish, to give it a less conspicuous presence, in accord with the lightness and reticent fragrance of the dish.

For four

4 small sea bream, about 360 g (12 oz) each, cleaned and scaled, but with heads and tails on
75 g (2½ oz) butter
140 g (4¾ oz) plain flour, spread on a dish
3 cloves garlic, peeled and slightly crushed
1 teaspoon fresh or ½ teaspoon dried marjoram
Salt
Freshly ground black pepper
1 tablespoon lemon juice
Lemon wedges

1 Rinse the cleaned fish, inside and out, in cold water, dry thoroughly with kitchen paper and set aside.

2 Choose a frying pan or sauté pan deep enough and large enough to contain the fish loosely, without overlapping. Melt the butter over medium-high heat.

3 As the butter foam begins to subside, dredge the fish lightly in the flour on both sides, and put it into the pan, together with the garlic and marjoram. The butter should be very hot, and the heat high, but be careful that it is not so high that it will burn the fish.

4 Brown the fish for about 2 minutes on each side. Add a liberal sprinkling of salt, some pepper and the lemon juice, and cover the pan. Turn the heat down to medium, and cook for 10 to 12 minutes, turning the fish once more half way through the cooking time.

5 Transfer the fish to a warm serving dish. Lift it carefully, with a spatula in each hand perhaps, to make sure it does not break apart. Pour the cooking juices from the pan over the fish and serve immediately, with lemon wedges.

MENU SUGGESTIONS

There are no problems in choosing a first course, because so many things will go well. It can be a light soup, a fish pasta or appetiser, a vegetable pie. Examples: *Zuppa di piselli e vongole*, *Spaghetti al sugo di pesce*, *Le piccagge col pesto di ricotta*, *Risotto con le vongole* (from my first book, page 164), *Polpettone di tonno e spinaci, Torta di carciofi* or *Frittata di spaghetti*. You could get along without a vegetable accompaniment, but *Fiori di broccoli fritti* would go well, or *Crocchette di patate alla romagnola*. Follow with a salad of baked beetroots or beetroot tops, or of simple greens.

Bocconcini di pesce spada fritto

FRIED SWORDFISH MORSELS

The fine, sweet flesh of swordfish has just one drawback: it easily becomes dry in cooking. Sicilians, who have the finest swordfish in the world, also have some of the most successful methods for cooking it so that it does not lose any of its precious juices. This recipe demonstrates one of them.

The fish is soaked for about 1 hour in a light marinade of olive oil and lemon juice, then it is fried. The cooking goes very fast because the fish is cut into thin, bite-sized pieces. It ends up coming out of the pan about as moist and tender as it was when it first came out of the sea.

For four

900 g (2 lb) fresh swordfish, cut into slices about 18 mm ($\frac{3}{4}$ inch) thick
Salt
Freshly ground black pepper
8 tablespoons olive oil
3 tablespoons parsley, chopped fine
4 tablespoons lemon juice
2 eggs
Enough vegetable oil to come 6 mm ($\frac{1}{4}$ inch) up the sides of the pan
140 g (4$\frac{3}{4}$ oz) plain flour, spread on a plate
Lemon wedges

1 Cut the swordfish slices into pieces about 50 by 75 mm (2 by 3 inches). It does not matter at all if some pieces are irregular.

2 Into a bowl or deep dish put a liberal amount of salt and freshly ground pepper, the olive oil, the chopped parsley, and the lemon juice. Beat the mixture lightly with a fork to amalgamate the ingredients. Put in the swordfish pieces, turning them two or three times in the marinade. Let the fish marinate for at least 1 hour but no more than 2 hours at room temperature. Turn it from time to time.

3 Remove the fish from the marinade, and pat it thoroughly dry with kitchen paper.

4 Break the eggs into a deep dish, and beat them with a fork just until the yolks and whites combine.

5 Pour the vegetable oil into a frying pan, and turn on the heat to high.

6 While the oil heats up, dip a few pieces of fish into the beaten eggs. Pick up one of the pieces, let the excess egg flow back into the dish, and dredge both sides of the fish in the flour. Holding the piece of fish at one end with your fingertips, dip one corner into the pan. If the oil around it bubbles, it is hot enough; slip the whole piece in. Dredge more egg-coated pieces of fish in flour, and slip them into the pan. Do not crowd the pan.

7 When the fish has formed a nice light crust on one side, turn it. When both sides have a light golden crust, transfer the fish to kitchen paper, or to a cooling rack set on a dish, to drain. As space opens up in the pan, put in more fish, until it is all done. Sprinkle lightly with salt, and serve at once, with lemon wedges.

MENU SUGGESTIONS

The first course can be *Zuppa primavera*, *Zuppa di piselli e vongole*, *Spaghetti al sugo di pesce* or *Cappelletti di pesce col sugo di gamberetti*. The fried swordfish can be agreeably accompanied by a variety of vegetables, such as *Topinambur fritti*, *Insalatina tenera con la pancetta*, *Funghi fritti alla moda dei porcini*, *Patate con le acciughe* or *Crocchette di patate alla romagnola*. A nice salad afterwards would be sliced tomatoes with fresh basil, seasoned with olive oil, salt, and lemon juice.

Pesce spada al salmoriglio

SWORDFISH WITH SALMORIGLIO SAUCE

Salmoriglio consists of olive oil, lemon juice, oregano, salt and pepper, lightly beaten together; it is brushed over thin fish steaks after they have been grilled.

In Sicily, the fish is almost invariably the fine, juicy swordfish from Messina. Occasionally it may be tuna. But you could use any firm-fleshed fish – halibut or turbot, for example – that can be sliced into thin steaks. There can be no simpler way to sauce a fish than with this clear, silken wash, wherein are dissolved the cool zest of lemon and oregano's sultry fragrance. There is certainly none more enticing to the nose and palate.

For four

1 tablespoon salt
2 tablespoons freshly squeezed lemon juice
1 teaspoon oregano
4 tablespoons olive oil
Freshly ground black pepper
900 g (2 lb) swordfish steaks, sliced no more than 12 mm ($\frac{1}{2}$ inch) thick

1 Preheat the grill 20 to 30 minutes before you are ready to cook.

2 Put the salt and lemon juice into a bowl and beat with a fork until the salt has dissolved.

3 Add the oregano, and mix it in with two or three turns of the fork.

4 Trickle in the olive oil, drop by drop, beating it in with the fork until it is well blended with the lemon juice.

5 Add a few grindings of pepper, and stir it to distribute it evenly.

6 Place the fish under the grill, as close as possible to the source of heat. It must grill quickly, at very high heat. Cook it about 1 to $1\frac{1}{2}$ minutes on one side, then turn it and cook it for another $1\frac{1}{2}$ minutes on the other. It does not need to become brown on the surface.

7 Transfer the fish to a large warm dish. Pour the *salmoriglio* sauce over

the fish, moistening it thoroughly. Serve at once, spooning a little sauce from the dish over the fish as it is transferred to individual plates.

Note This is a perfect dish for outdoor cooking, over charcoal. Make sure the coals are hot, and that the grill is positioned very close to the fire. Whether cooking this in the home or at a barbecue, do not prepare the *salmoriglio* sauce long in advance – it will lose the freshness that is its most precious characteristic.

MENU SUGGESTIONS

For a first course serve *Spaghettini coi canestrelli* or *Penne con spinaci e ricotta*, or *Rigatoni alla napoletana coi peperoni freschi*.

Vegetable accompaniments could be *Topinambur fritti*, *Fiori di broccoli fritti* or any fried potatoes. Follow with a salad of greens or mixed raw vegetables or *Insalata di arancia*.

Pesce (o carne) tra i due piatti

STEAMED FISH (OR VEAL) BETWEEN TWO PLATES

Every cuisine has in its repertoire dishes to coddle delicate stomachs or to nourish the diet cultists. It is characteristic of the Italian approach that an occasion for producing something that is very good for us is turned into an opportunity for making something that is also very good to eat. This method of steaming a delicate slice of fish or veal is as kind with our palate as it is with our infirmities.

This recipe closely follows a traditional procedure employed in countless Italian homes. No steamer is required. A large dinner plate rests on the rim of a sauté pan where some water is boiling. The fish or veal is put on the plate with a little olive oil and salt, and covered tightly. You would find most Italian cooks using a second dinner plate, turned upside down, as a cover. To me, it seems much more practical to use a saucepan lid. There is no danger of its sliding off, and it provides a tighter seal. Unlike other steaming methods, here the food cooks in the steam from its own vaporised juices. The understated yet lovely result can be likened to what happens when one photographs a snowy landscape with colour film. The austerity of the subject is tempered by an endearing softness and warmth.

Swordfish is particularly good prepared in this manner, but halibut is excellent too, and there is no reason for not trying other firm-fleshed lean fish. It is also a most delicate way to cook veal, using the same cut as for veal *scaloppine*, only sliced a little thicker.

For four

A large, possibly ovenproof, dinner plate
3 tablespoons olive oil
Salt
Freshly ground black pepper
2 tablespoons chopped parsley
680 g ($1\frac{1}{2}$ lb) swordfish or other firm-fleshed fish, cut into slices 6 mm ($\frac{1}{4}$ inch) thick
3 tablespoons small cucumber pickles, preferably *cornichons*, chopped not too fine
Lemon wedges

1 Choose a sauté pan slightly narrower than the dinner plate. Put in enough water to come 37 mm ($1\frac{1}{2}$ inches) up the sides, and turn on the heat to medium.

2 When lots of little bubbles form around the edge, cover the pan with the dinner plate. Put the fish on the plate, in a single layer if possible, but in no more than two partly overlapping layers.

3 Add the olive oil, salt, and a grinding of pepper. Cover tightly, using a lid that fits snugly over the plate.

4 Cook for 3 minutes or so on one side, then turn the slices over and cook for 2 to 3 minutes longer. Cook an additional minute per side if there are two layers. Replace the lid after turning the fish.

5 Transfer the fish to individual plates or to a warm serving dish. Pour over it both the liquid and creamy cooking juices from the plate. Sprinkle with parsley and chopped pickles, and serve at once, with lemon wedges.

Note The same procedure can be applied, without any changes, to cooking veal.

MENU SUGGESTIONS

The amiable, gentle flavour of this steamed dish follows well upon that of virtually any first course. If you are doing it with fish, a good choice for the first course would be *Spaghettini coi canestrelli* or *Penne con spinaci e ricotta*. If instead you are steaming veal, you could precede it with *Risotto primavera*, *Risotto alla parmigiana* (*The Classic Italian Cookbook*, page 155), *Spaghetti alla siciliana* or *Fettuccine con zucchini fritte*.

In either case, whether it is fish or veal, the most agreeable vegetable accompaniment would be any of the fried vegetables from this book or *The Classic Italian Cookbook*.

Salmone a la stimpirata

STIMPIRATA SALMON

Stimpirata is the particularly tasty way they have of cooking swordfish in Syracuse in Sicily. While working with the recipe, I thought it would be interesting to see if it could be adapted to other varieties of fish, especially those that are more common here than in Sicily. I have done it with salmon, and though it is undoubtedly a most unorthodox and irreverent way to handle the noblest of all fishes, it works well, I think, and that is all the justification any cook needs.

Thin floured fish steaks are fried very briefly in olive oil, and set aside. Chopped onions are lightly browned in the same oil, chopped celery is added and cooked until tender, and a small handful of capers is thrown in. Then the fish is returned to the pan together with some vinegar, and cooked until the vinegar evaporates.

The result, in this particular recipe, is salmon robed in flavours of unaccustomed earthiness and audacity. If you like to experiment, there is no reason why this method should not be successful with other firm-fleshed fish, such as bass or turbot, if it is cut into thin slices.

For four to six

12 tablespoons olive oil
900 g (2 lb) salmon (or turbot, or other fish; see remarks above), skinned, boned, and cut into thin steaks, 12 mm (½ inch) thick
90 g (3 oz) plain flour, spread on a plate
Salt
Freshly ground black pepper
½ small onion, chopped very fine
60 g (2 oz) celery, chopped fine
2 tablespoons capers, drained and chopped
4 tablespoons good-quality wine vinegar

1 Heat the oil into a medium-sized frying pan or sauté pan over medium-high heat.

2 When the oil is quite hot, dredge the fish steaks on both sides in the flour, and slip them into the pan. Do not fill the pan with more fish than will fit in a single uncrowded layer. Cook the fish briefly, about 1 minute on each side, then transfer them to a dish, using a slotted spoon or spatula. Sprinkle with salt and pepper.

3 Put the chopped onion into the pan, and reduce the heat to medium. Cook the onion, stirring frequently, until it turns pale gold.

4 Add the chopped celery, and cook for a few minutes, stirring from time to time, until it is tender.

5 Add the chopped capers, and cook for about ½ minute, stirring steadily.

6 Return the fish to the pan (it no longer has to fit in one layer). Pour all the vinegar over it, and cook for 2 minutes or so, until the vinegar has evaporated. Turn the fish over carefully once or twice, so it becomes well coated with the flavoured sauce. Transfer to a warm dish, using a slotted spoon or spatula, and serve at once.

MENU SUGGESTIONS

My own preference for a first course here would be *Zuppa di calamari e carciofi*. Other interesting combinations are *Pasta con le sarde alla palermitana*, *Penne con spinaci e ricotta*, *Pizza di scarola*, *Frittata con le cipolle* or *Frittata di spaghetti*. No vegetables. Just a fresh salad of mixed greens to follow, or *Insalata di arancia*.

Tonno in agrodolce alla Trapanese

SWEET AND SOUR TUNA STEAKS, TRAPANI STYLE

There is no part of the tuna that does not have gastronomic value. It can be cured, dried, made into a dozen different kinds of sausages, or cooked in ways too infinite to number. It is the pork of the sea. In this remarkably delicious dish, it tastes, in fact, more like pork than fish.

These tuna steaks are first sautéed, then given a brief and scalding bath in a mixture of vinegar, wine, and a little sugar. It is all done quickly, or the tuna would dry out. Despite the name, the taste is neither sickly sweet nor bitingly sour. The sweetness and sourness never break through alone, but flow together into a smooth and altogether luscious blend.

For six

- 1·1 kg (2½ lb) fresh tuna, cut into steaks no thicker than 18 mm (¾ inch), and about 125 mm (5 inches) long
- 6 onions sliced very thin
- 8 tablespoons olive oil
- Salt
- 110 g (4 oz) plain flour, spread on a plate
- Freshly ground black pepper
- 2 tablespoons granulated sugar
- 4 tablespoons good-quality wine vinegar
- 6 tablespoons dry white wine
- 2 tablespoons chopped parsley

1 Remove the skin round the tuna steaks. Rinse them in cold water, and dry thoroughly with kitchen paper.

2 Choose a sauté pan large enough to contain all the fish steaks later in a single layer. Put in the sliced onion, the olive oil, 1 or 2 pinches of salt, and turn the heat to medium low. Cook until the onion has wilted, then raise the heat to medium, and continue cooking, stirring from time to time, until the onion turns a rich golden brown.

3 Push all the onion to one end of the pan. Dredge the fish steaks on both sides in the flour, and put them into the pan. Raise the heat to medium high. Cook them for 3 minutes, then turn them over. Add salt, pepper, sugar, vinegar and wine, raise the heat to high, and cover the pan.

4 After 2 or 3 minutes, uncover, add the parsley, and turn the steaks once or twice. Transfer the fish to a warm serving dish.

5 If there should be runny cooking juices in the pan, boil them away, while scraping loose, with a wooden spoon, any cooking residue stuck to the bottom. If there is no liquid in the pan, add 2 tablespoons water and boil it away, while loosening the cooking residue. Pour all the contents of the pan over the tuna, and serve at once.

MENU SUGGESTIONS

My choice for the first course would be *Spaghettini coi canestrelli*. Other possibilities are *Zuppa di calamari e carciofi*, *Pasta con le sarde alla palermitana*, *Frittata con le patatine fritte* or *Canestrelli trifolati*.

Some nice, crisp salad greens to follow, including, if possible, some arugola.

Saraghine alla brace

GRILLED SARDINES

There are some smells that have the power to summon intact a whole period of one's life. For some it may be the scent of a particular flower, or of smouldering autumn leaves, or of someone's favourite perfume. For me it is the odour of sardines roasting over a slow charcoal fire. Wherever I am, it sharply brings back my early girlhood, and an image of my father's mother in never-changing long black dress and black kerchief, bending over a wobbly grill set on bricks in our yard, waving at the embers with a fan of rooster-tail feathers.

In our dialect we call these fish *saraghine*. They are not quite either sardines or anchovies, but taste deliciously of both. They are so plentiful and cheap they are considered poor people's fare. It must be one of Providence's special ways of rewarding the poor, I think, because there is hardly anything that comes from the sea that tastes so good.

Eating them requires a special technique, not difficult to master. As a little girl I learned whilst watching the fishermen of my town as they cooked and ate their *saraghine*, grilling them right on the cobblestone dock by their boats, after returning from a night's fishing. You pick up the fish with your fingers, holding it by the head and the tail, and, pursing your lips around it, you suck and pull away one whole fillet. You then turn it round, and with the same method you take the other fillet. All that is left is the head, tail and bones. It beats fancy linen and silver and any sole in white sauce.

The sardines and anchovies that are found in fish markets and fishmongers here are not quite *saraghine*, of course, but they can be excellent, and you should not pass up an opportunity to try them in this way. They are best by far over charcoal, which should not be fiery hot, but they turn out well in an ordinary grill. If you have one of those hinged double grills that sandwich around the fish, it will make it much easier to turn them over.

For four to six

900 g (2 lb) fresh sardines, preferably small ones, or anchovies
Salt
Freshly ground black pepper
4 tablespoons olive oil
Lemon wedges (optional)

1 Gut the sardines, gently scooping out the insides with the tip of your thumb, running it from the base of the head towards the tail.

2 Wash the belly cavity thoroughly under running water, then lay the sardines slightly overlapping on a dish. Prop up the dish to allow the sardines to drain for a few minutes.

3 Dry the fish thoroughly with kitchen paper, and lay them on a dry dish. Add several pinches of salt, a few liberal grindings of pepper, and all the olive oil. Let them steep in the marinade for 20 minutes, turning them over once or twice.

4 Put them in a single layer on a grill over glowing coals, or under an ordinary hot grill. They should be no more than 50 or 75 mm (2 or 3 inches) away from the source of heat. After 2 to 3 minutes, turn them over, and cook for another 2 minutes or so. (It is much simpler to turn them if you use a hinged double grill.)

5 Serve at once. Wedges of lemon should be available for those who want them, but grilled sardines are usually eaten without lemon.

MENU SUGGESTIONS

Whilst you have the fresh sardines, you might as well make a meal of it, and start with *Pasta con le sarde alla palermitana*. In my town, where the Sicilian pasta with sardines had never been heard of, we would start with some *Piadina romagnola* and *Erbette saltate*; or *Consum*. This would make an authentic meal *alla romagnola*; you could close your eyes and think you were in one of the towns in a Fellini film.

Gamberi dorati

SHRIMPS FRIED IN LEAVENED BATTER

There are many frying batters, suited to different purposes. One of my favourites is the simple flour-and-water batter for courgettes (*The Classic Italian Cookbook*, page 337), which produces a thin, almost eggshell-like crust of unsurpassed crispness. Another is this golden batter for shrimps, which many cooks in Sicily use. It contains yeast, which has a similar, but more complete, effect than beer has in other batters. It swells into a light, fluffy, crisp coating, within which the shrimps remain marvellously tender and moist.

I like to skewer each shrimp with a toothpick. It is not absolutely necessary, but there are several reasons why it is a good idea. If the shrimps are small it keeps them from coming together as they fry, forming lumps of two or three in the pan; it helps them maintain a regular and attractive shape; and it is very convenient to hold on to one end of the toothpick when dipping the shrimp in batter. But you must not forget to warn your guests or family to remove the toothpick before the first greedy bite!

For four

450 g (1 lb) small-to-medium-sized shrimps
Toothpicks
2 eggs
Salt
10 g ($\frac{1}{3}$ oz) fresh yeast or $\frac{1}{2}$ packet dry yeast, dissolved in
225 ml (scant $\frac{1}{2}$ pint) lukewarm water
110 g (4 oz) plain flour
Enough vegetable oil to come at least 6 mm ($\frac{1}{4}$ inch) up the sides of the pan
Lemon wedges

1 Shell and devein the shrimps. Wash them in cold water, and pat them thoroughly dry with kitchen paper.

2 Bend each shrimp, following its natural curve, so that the head and tail meet, and skewer it with a toothpick. If the shrimps are tiny enough, string two on each toothpick.

3 Break both eggs into a bowl, add 2 teaspoons salt, and beat them well with a fork. Add the dissolved yeast, and, while beating steadily with the fork, add the flour, shaking it through a sieve.

4 Heat the oil in a frying pan over high heat. The oil will be hot enough for frying when a drop of the batter dropped into it stiffens and instantly comes to the surface.

5 Dip the shrimps into the batter, allowing the excess batter to flow back into the bowl, and slip them into the hot oil. Do not crowd the pan. As soon as they have formed a rich golden crust on one side, turn them over. When both sides have formed a crust, transfer the shrimps with a slotted spatula to kitchen paper to drain, or lay them on a cooling rack set on a dish. Stir the batter, and add more shrimps to the pan as space is created for them, until they are all done.

6 Sprinkle with salt, and serve promptly, with lemon wedges.

MENU SUGGESTIONS

A good choice for the first course is *Spaghetti coi canestrelli*. Other possibilities: *Spaghetti alla siciliana* or *Spaghetti al sugo di pesce*. Serve with a fried vegetable accompaniment, such as *Topinambur fritti*, *Fiori di broccoli fritti* or *Finocchi fritti* (from my first book, page 324). Follow with *Insalata di arancia*.

Umido di gamberi al pomodoro piccante

SHRIMPS WITH TOMATOES AND HOT PEPPER

This is a good dish for those who like their shrimps with a little fresh and peppery tomato sauce.

The tomatoes are cooked only a short time, to protect their freshness, together with a lively seasoning of garlic and hot pepper. It all needs a light touch, or it can become ordinary. Do not overbrown the garlic, and use restraint with the hot pepper. Keep the shrimps tender and moist by cooking them for the very minimum time necessary. If you are lucky enough to be using tiny fresh shrimps, this could be as little as a minute.

For four to six

680 g ($1\frac{1}{2}$ lb) medium shrimps, in their shells
6 tablespoons olive oil
3 tablespoons onion, chopped
1 large clove garlic, chopped
$\frac{1}{8}$ teaspoon dried hot red pepper, chopped, or 1 small dried hot red pepper (*peperoncino*), cut in two
3 tablespoons chopped parsley, preferably Italian parsley
350 g (12 oz) tinned Italian plum tomatoes, coarsely chopped, with their juice
Salt

1 Shell and devein the shrimps. Wash them in several changes of cold water, until the water runs clear. Set them aside in a colander to drain.

2 Put the olive oil and the chopped onion into a sauté pan. Over medium-high heat cook the onion, stirring steadily, until it is translucent. Add the garlic and the hot pepper, and sauté until the garlic colours lightly.

3 Add the chopped parsley, stir once or twice, then add the chopped tomatoes with their juice. Sprinkle very liberally with salt, stir thoroughly, and turn the heat down to medium. Cook for about 20 minutes at a steady simmer, stirring from time to time.

4 Add the shrimps, mixing them well into the sauce, cover the pan, and cook for 2 to 3 minutes – less if the shrimps are very small and tender. Before turning off the heat, taste and check salt. If the sauce is too thin and runny, uncover the pan, raise the heat to high, and boil away the excess liquid for a few seconds.

MENU SUGGESTIONS

Choose a mild first course, such as *Zuppa di calamari e carciofi* or *Spaghetti col sugo di cipolle*. Follow with a green salad, or, from my first book, *Insalata di carote* (page 350) or *Insalata di spinaci e topinambur* (page 349).

Gamberi ai ferri come le cannocchie

GRILLED SHRIMPS CANNOCCHIE STYLE

These shrimps are grilled according to the method used by the fishermen of my town for cooking *cannocchie*, a local and delectably sweet-fleshed crustacean.

They are marinated in olive oil, salt, and a prodigal quantity of black pepper, then grilled rapidly over a hot and fast fire. How you cook them is only half the story, however. The full degree of pleasure you take from these shrimps depends on how you eat them. It is done this way: pick up the shrimp with your fingers, break open and loosen its shell, and curl your lips around it, sucking in the meat. In Romagna we say this is eating it *col bacio*, with a kiss. And it is a most savoury kiss, as you lick from the shell its coating of oil and pepper, spiked with flavour leached from the charred shell itself. There may be more elegant ways to eat shrimps, but none more enjoyable.

If you are travelling in Italy, you are unlikely to find *cannocchie* grilled like this in restaurants, but you will find them steamed, shelled, and served at room temperature with olive oil and lemon juice. They are a speciality of Emilia-Romagna. If your wanderings take you there (and if you are interested in food, where else would you go?) do not fail to try them. Ask for *Cannocchie lesse con olio e limone*. It is well worth your writing it down.

For six

680 g (1½ lb) medium-to-large shrimps, in their shells
Round wooden toothpicks
150 g (5 oz) dry, plain breadcrumbs
6 tablespoons olive oil
Salt
Freshly ground black pepper

1 Rinse the shrimps without shelling them, in cold water. Drain well and pat dry with kitchen paper.

2 Run a single toothpick into each shrimp along its entire length, placing it just under the shell. This is to straighten it and keep it from curling while cooking.

3 Put all the shrimps into a bowl, and add all the other ingredients. Be very liberal with both salt and pepper. Turn the shrimps to coat them thoroughly. Let them marinate at room temperature for at least ½ hour and as long as 2 hours. Turn them over occasionally.

4 Preheat the grill. Even better would be a charcoal grill, if you have a fireplace, or if you can cook outdoors.

5 Place the shrimps on the grill rack, or in one of those hinged two-sided grills. Cook very close to the source of heat, 2 minutes on one side and 1½ minutes on the other. Serve at once, with plenty of paper napkins for everyone (see introductory remarks above).

MENU SUGGESTIONS

The first course: *Zuppa primavera*, *Spaghettini coi canestrelli*, *Le piccagge col pesto di ricotta*, or *Risotto con le vongole* (from my first book, page 164). Follow with *Insalata di arancia* or *Rape rosse al forno*.

Cicala al Salmoriglio

GRILLED LOBSTER TAILS WITH SALMORIGLIO SAUCE

Frozen lobster tail does not enjoy the esteem of many food writers, and after the disagreeable things I myself have had to say about frozen foods, it may seem surprising to find a recipe for it here. The fact is that choice frozen lobster tail bought from a good fishmonger can be juicy, sweet, and quite delectable. No one need be ashamed of enjoying it.

A thick, meaty lobster tail is close in taste to the Mediterranean *cicala* – a dark brown squat crustacean with stumpy claws. In Sicily they cook *cicala* with a sauce of olive oil, lemon juice, and oregano. This is the same sauce that appears in the recipe for swordfish *al salmoriglio*, page 178. In the swordfish recipe the sauce is poured over the fish after it is cooked, while here the *salmoriglio* cooks together with the lobster. The result is a more penetrating flavour of lemon and oregano that broaches the insulating sweetness of the lobster flesh.

For four

900 g (2 lb) good-quality frozen lobster tails, thawed
45 g (1½ oz) fine, dry, plain breadcrumbs
6 tablespoons olive oil
4 tablespoons freshly squeezed lemon juice
1½ teaspoons oregano
Salt
Freshly ground black pepper

1 Preheat the grill 15 minutes in advance.

2 Remove the lobster meat from the shell, and cut it into slices about 37 mm ($1\frac{1}{2}$ inches) thick.

3 Choose a flameproof grilling pan in which the slices will fit in a single layer. Put in the sliced lobster, and sprinkle it with half the breadcrumbs.

4 Put the olive oil, lemon juice, oregano, salt, and several liberal grindings of pepper into a small bowl. Beat thoroughly with a fork. Spoon the contents of the bowl over the lobster, making sure that all pieces are evenly coated.

5 Place the pan in the grill about 125 to 150 mm (5 to 6 inches) from the flame. Cook for about 4 minutes, then turn the lobster slices over, sprinkle over them the rest of the breadcrumbs, and baste with some of the juices in the pan. Cook for $3\frac{1}{2}$ to 4 minutes more. Transfer the lobster and its cooking juices to a warm dish, and serve at once.

MENU SUGGESTIONS

As a first course serve *Rigatoni alla napoletana coi peperoni freschi*, or, from my first book, *Risotto con le vongole* (page 164). Follow the lobster with *Cime di rape rosse in insalata*, *Fagiolini verdi in insalata* (from my first book, page 355) or any salad greens.

Calamari ripieni coi funghi secchi

STUFFED SQUID WITH DRIED WILD MUSHROOMS

In the last few years, I have noticed, people increasingly have overcome their uneasiness about squid, discovering how delectable it can be and how much one can do with it. It can be fried, baked, braised, grilled or stewed. It can be sliced into tender, meaty rings, or stuffed like a sausage. Stuffing is undoubtedly one of the most savoury ways of preparing it. Once you have become familiar with the basic and simple procedure, you can go on to devise your own stuffings. There is a good basic recipe for stuffed squid in *The Classic Italian Cookbook*, page 197. The one below is very elegant, with dried wild mushrooms, white wine, and no tomatoes.

For four

25 g ($\frac{3}{4}$ oz) dried boletus mushrooms
4 large whole squid, about 125 mm (5 inches) long, excluding the tentacles
Salt
Freshly ground black pepper
50 g ($\frac{3}{4}$ oz) dry, plain breadcrumbs
1 large clove garlic, peeled and chopped
2 tablespoons chopped parsley
2 tablespoons olive oil for the stuffing, plus 6 tablespoons
A needle and heavy duty (but not trussing) cotton thread
8 tablespoons dry white wine

1 Soak the mushrooms at least 30 minutes in advance in a bowl with 450 ml ($\frac{3}{4}$ pint) warm water. Proceed to rinse them and to filter the water, as described on page 199.

2 After thoroughly rinsing the reconstituted mushrooms, as directed, chop them very fine. Put them into a small pan with the filtered water, and turn on the heat to medium high. Cook until all the liquid has boiled away.

3 To prepare the squid for cooking first separate the tentacles from the sac. Hold the sac in one hand, and with the other, firmly pull off the tentacles, together with the pulpy insides of the squid, to which they are attached. Cut the tentacles straight across above the eyes, and discard everything from the eyes down, squeezing out the small bony beak. Divide the tentacles into two clusters. Remove the thin bone from the sac, and thoroughly rinse out the inside of the sac, clearing it of anything it may contain. Peel off the sac's outer skin. It is easiest to do this under cold running water. Wash all the sacs and tentacles in several changes of cold water. Drain and pat thoroughly dry.

4 Chop the tentacles very fine.

5 Put into a bowl the mushrooms, tentacles, 1 teaspoon salt, several liberal grindings of pepper, the breadcrumbs, chopped garlic, parsley and 2 tablespoons olive oil. Mix, with a fork or a spatula, until all the ingredients have become thoroughly amalgamated.

6 Set aside 1 tablespoon of the mixture for later use, and divide the rest into four equal parts. Spoon the stuffing into each of the four squid sacs. Do not fill the sacs all the way to the top. Leave about one-quarter of the sac empty, because the squid will shrink while cooking; if packed too full, the sac will crack open. If you have any stuffing left over, add it to the tablespoon previously set aside.

7 Sew up the opening of each squid sac with a needle and cotton thread. Remember to put away the needle as soon as you have finished with it, or you may find it later in the dish.

8 Choose a sauté pan in which the stuffed squid will fit in a single layer, but quite snugly, bearing in mind that they will shrink while cooking. Put 6 tablespoons olive oil in the pan, and turn the heat to high.

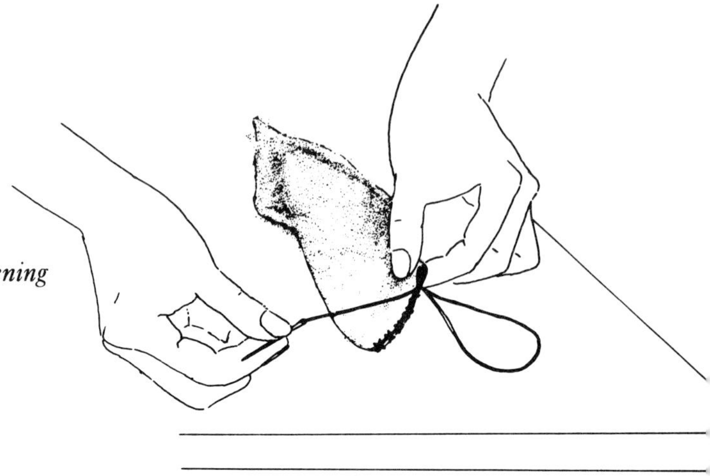

Sew up opening

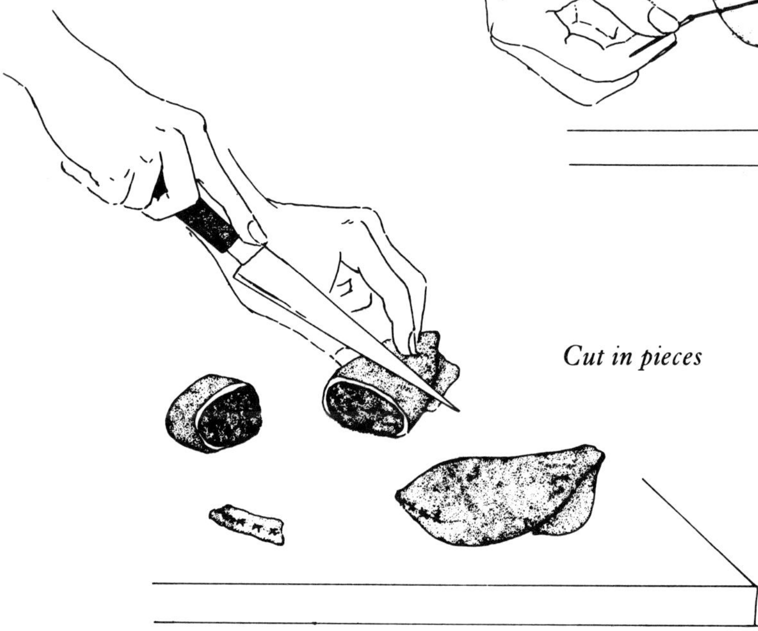

Cut in pieces

9 When the oil is very hot, put in the squid and brown them well on all sides. Add a tiny pinch of salt and a small grinding of pepper, the white wine, and the reserved unused stuffing. Turn the squid over once or twice, quickly, then reduce the heat to minimum and cover the pan.

10 Cook for 40 to 50 minutes, depending on the size of the squid, turning them from time to time. The squid are done if they feel tender when gently pricked with a fork.

11 Transfer the squid to a chopping board, and allow to rest for a few minutes. Then slice away a thin strip from the top of each, enough to dispose of the thread. Cut each sac into two shorter pieces and place them on a warm serving dish.

12 Add 1 or 2 tablespoons water to the pan, and boil it away over lively heat while scraping loose all the cooking residue from the bottom of the pan. Pour all the contents of the pan over the squid, together with any juices left on the chopping board. Serve at once.

MENU SUGGESTIONS

My first choice would be to precede it with *Le piccagge col pesto di ricotta*. Or serve other pasta, sauced with traditional basil pesto (see my first book, page 118). Other good choices are *Spaghetti al sugo di pesce* and *Rigatoni alla napolitana coi peperoni freschi*. Accompany with boiled new potatoes, and follow with a salad of mixed greens.

Totani e patate in tegame alla genovese

SQUID AND POTATOES, FROM GENOA

This is a delicious combination of squid and potatoes, from the Riviera. The squid are briefly sautéed in olive oil, garlic and parsley, and then cooked slowly with tomatoes and herbs. After a while one adds the sliced potatoes, and when these are done the dish is ready. The squid turn out exquisitely tender, and the potatoes very savoury, since they absorb most of the sauce. If you like more sauce and fewer potatoes, you can adjust the proportions to your taste.

Fresh marjoram, if available, should be the first choice of herb in this dish. It would be more authentically Genoese than if you used oregano. But herbs follow one's moods, and there are times when I find the swaggering southern accent of oregano quite seductive.

For six

900 g (2 lb) whole squid, cleaned as directed on page 191, or 680 g (1½ lb) ready-sliced squid
560 g (1¼ lb) boiling potatoes
5 tablespoons olive oil
2 large cloves garlic, peeled and chopped
1½ tablespoons chopped parsley
6 tablespoons dry white wine
Salt
225 g (8 oz) tinned Italian plum tomatoes, cut up, with their juice
¼ teaspoon chopped marjoram or oregano
Freshly ground black pepper

1 If starting with whole squid, after cleaning them as directed, slice the sacs into rings about 25 mm (1 inch) wide. Keep the tentacles whole, but divide them into two or three clusters if very large. Wash the squid, whether you have cut them up yourself or bought them ready-sliced, in several changes of cold water. Pat thoroughly dry with kitchen paper and reserve them on one side.

2 Peel the potatoes and cut them up roughly into pieces about 37 mm ($1\frac{1}{2}$ inches) thick. Set aside.

3 Put the oil, garlic and parsley into a sauté pan, and sauté over high heat until the garlic turns a rich golden brown.

4 Put in all the squid, turning them in the hot oil with a long-handled fork. As squid heats up it sometimes bursts spraying hot drops of oil in all directions, so do not hunch over the pan.

5 When the squid turn a dull, flat white, add the wine, and let it bubble away for a couple of minutes. Put in 2 or 3 large pinches of salt, the cut-up tomatoes with their juice and the marjoram or oregano. Stir well, cover the pan, lower the heat, and cook at a gentle simmer for 30 minutes.

6 Put in the potatoes, another pinch of salt, a few grindings of pepper, mix well all the contents of the pan, and cover. Cook at slow heat until the potatoes are tender, about 40 minutes. Taste and check for salt and pepper, and serve hot.

Note This dish can be prepared a day or two ahead of time and reheated gently, but it will lose some of its sweetness and freshness after refrigeration. If you must prepare it in advance, it would be best if it were done no earlier than the morning of the day that you plan to serve it.

MENU SUGGESTIONS

Precede with *Canestrelli trifolati*, *Insalata di spaghetti* or *Zuppa di piselli e vongole*. Follow with a salad of *Rape rosso al forno*, or a salad with a nice variety of greens.

Zuppa di frutti di mare

ALL-SHELLFISH FISH SOUP

This is an ideal dish for people who like fish soup but do not like fishbones. You can vary the proportions of the ingredients to suit your taste, without forgetting, however, that the charm of all fish soups is in variety. While it would be desirable to use only fresh seafood, you might have to settle for frozen shrimps and squid. But the clams and mussels must be absolutely choice and fresh, not tinned.

For six

900 g (2 lb) squid, cleaned as directed on page 191
2 dozen small clams
900 g (2 lb) mussels
12 tablespoons olive oil
1 small onion, chopped
3 to 4 cloves garlic, peeled and chopped
3 tablespoons chopped parsley
225 ml (scant ½ pint) dry white wine
350 g (12 oz) tinned Italian plum tomatoes, cut up, with their juice
450 g (1 lb) shrimps
Salt
Freshly ground pepper
Crusty good-quality bread

1 Cut the sacs of the cleaned squid into rings 12 mm (½ inch) wide, and reserve them for later, together with the tentacles.

2 Soak the clams in a basinful of cold water for several minutes. Empty out the water, refill the basin, and scrub the clams, either with a coarse brush or by rubbing one clam forcefully against another. When finished, drain and refill the basin, and scrub the clams again. Repeat the entire operation several times until the water runs perfectly clear. Set the clams aside in a bowl.

3 Clean the mussels, using the same procedure you used for the clams. In addition trim off with a sharp knife the wisps of beard that may protrude from the shells. Set the mussels aside in a bowl.

4 Put all the clams into a covered pot over high heat. As the clams open up, remove them and extract them from their shells. Leave just six clams in their shells, and reserve. Put the shelled clam meat into a small bowl.

5 Carefully filter all the clam juice in the pot through kitchen paper, then pour it into the bowl containing the shelled clam meat.

6 Repeat the same operation with the mussels. After the mussels have opened, set aside six nice, large mussels without shelling them. Shell the rest and add them to the bowl containing the clam meat. Filter the mussel juice, and put it into the same bowl.

7 Put the oil and the chopped onion into a deep saucepan, and sauté the onion over medium-high heat until translucent.

8 Add the chopped garlic. When the garlic has coloured lightly, add the chopped parsley. Stir rapidly once or twice, then add the wine. Allow the wine to boil for about 30 seconds, then add the cut-up tomatoes with their juice. Cook the tomatoes at a steady simmer for 10 minutes.

9 Add the squid, and the clam and mussel juice, leaving just enough in the bowl to cover the clams and mussels. Cover the pan, with the lid slightly askew, and cook at a gentle simmer for 45 minutes, or until the squid are very tender when pricked with a fork.

10 While the squid are cooking, shell, devein and wash the shrimps.

11 When the squid are done, season liberally with salt and pepper. Add the shrimps and cook for 3 to 4 minutes at high heat, stirring from time to time. Add all the remaining ingredients, the clam and mussel meat with their juice, and the unshelled clams and mussels. Cook for one more minute. Serve immediately, with plenty of good, crusty bread.

MENU SUGGESTIONS

Like all fish soups, this can be a substantial meal all by itself, especially if you sop up its juices with good bread. Should you want to expand it into a more varied meal, you can precede it with *Canestrelli trifolati*, cold, sliced *Polpettone di tonno e spinaci* or, from my first book, *Pomodori ripieni di tonno* (page 33).

It should definitely be followed by a salad: any green salad dressed with olive oil, salt and lemon juice, or *Insalata di arancia*.

La pearà

A PEPPERY SAUCE FOR BOILED MEATS

This is one of several sauces derived from a medieval sauce – the *peverata*. As the Venetian name suggests, its taste depends on a free hand with the pepper mill. The body of the sauce is formed by the slow swelling and massing of breadcrumbs as broth is added to them, little by little, while they cook in melted butter and bone marrow. Originally it was done in an earthenware pot sitting for hours on embers by the kitchen fireplace. The slower it cooks the better it is. For good results you should calculate about 45 minutes to 1 hour.

La pearà is an earthy, substantial creamy seasoning, perfectly suited to mixed boiled meats, such as beef, veal and chicken. Unlike most seasonings for boiled meat, this one should be served hot.

200 g (7 oz) beef marrow
25 g ($\frac{3}{4}$ oz) butter
3 tablespoons dry, plain breadcrumbs
450 ml ($\frac{3}{4}$ pint) home-made broth, page 18 (it is pointless to make this sauce with anything but good broth)
Salt
Freshly ground black pepper

1 Put the marrow and the butter into a small saucepan. A flameproof earthenware pot would be ideal because it maintains constant heat best of all, but an enamelled cast-iron pan will do very well. Over medium heat, stir frequently, mashing the marrow with a wooden spoon.

2 When the marrow and butter have melted and begun to foam, put in the breadcrumbs. Sauté the crumbs for a minute or two, turning them in the fat.

3 Add 6 tablespoons broth. Cook over slow heat, uncovered, stirring as the broth evaporates and the breadcrumbs thicken.

4 Add 2 or 3 pinches of salt, and a very liberal quantity of freshly ground black pepper.

5 Continue to add broth, little by little, letting it evaporate before adding more. Stir frequently, and keep the heat low. The final consistency should be creamy and thick, without lumps. Taste and check seasoning. If the sauce is too dense for your taste, thin it by cooking it briefly with some more broth. Serve hot over sliced boiled meat, or in a sauceboat.

La peverada di Treviso

A PEPPERY SAUCE FOR ROAST BIRDS

Here is another descendant of the medieval *peverata*, the sauce mentioned in the preceding recipe for *pearà*. The principal components are pork sausage and chicken livers, pounded or processed to a creamy consistency and cooked in olive oil with sautéed onion and white wine. Pickles and grated lemon peel contribute their tart, pointed notes to the chorus of flavours.

In other versions of this sauce, salami can be used instead of sausage, pickled hot green peppers instead of cucumber pickles, garlic instead of onion, vinegar can take the place of wine, or butter can be used rather than oil. You may experiment along any of those lines if you like, but take care not to spike the sauce with excessive sharpness.

Peverada is ideal served with roast feathered game, such as pheasant or guinea fowl. It will also go well with tamer roast birds, such as chicken or a small, young turkey. It is served hot, poured over the cut-up pieces or carved slices of the bird.

About six servings

110 g (4 oz) *luganega* sausage or other mild pork sausage
110 g (4 oz) chicken livers
30 g (1 oz) cucumber pickles in vinegar, preferably *cornichons*
6 tablespoons olive oil (or 4 tablespoons if the sausage is very fatty)
1 tablespoon onion, chopped very fine
½ teaspoon salt
Abundant freshly ground black pepper
1½ teaspoons grated lemon peel (taking care not to dig into the bitter white pith beneath the skin)
12 tablespoons dry white wine

1 Skin the sausage. Put the sausage meat, chicken livers and pickles into the food processor, fitted with steel blades, or into a blender. Process or blend to a thick, creamy consistency. If using the blender, take care not to overpurée the mixture.

2 Put the olive oil and onion into a small saucepan, and sauté over medium heat until the onion turns pale gold. Put in the sausage, liver, and pickle mixture, and stir thoroughly.

3 Add the salt and a liberal amount of pepper. Stir. Add the grated lemon, and continue stirring.

4 Add the wine, stir well once or twice, then turn the heat down to cook the sauce at a steady, but very gentle simmer. Cover the pan, and cook for 1 hour. Stir the sauce occasionally while it cooks.

5 Serve hot over roast pheasant, guinea fowl, quail, squab, chicken or turkey.

Note The sauce may be prepared a day or two ahead of time and reheated gently, but it has a better flavour when prepared the same day it will be used.

Bistecchine di manzo alla cacciatora

THIN STEAKS WITH WILD MUSHROOMS

Italy does not have many beef recipes, simply because it has never had much beef. But we can learn from Italian cooks how to make a little beef go a long way.

Here the steaks are cut quite thin, so they need very little cooking and are quick to absorb the flavours of the savoury mushroom and tomato sauce. A crusty piece of good Italian bread with which to mop up would be a fine and satisfying addition to the dish.

For four

20 to 30 g ($\frac{3}{4}$ to 1 oz) dried boletus mushrooms
5 tablespoons olive oil
1 small onion, sliced very fine
4 thin rump or rib steaks, less than 12 mm ($\frac{1}{2}$ inch) thick
75 g ($2\frac{1}{2}$ oz) plain flour, spread on a plate
Salt
Freshly ground black pepper
8 tablespoons dry red wine
110 g (4 oz) tinned Italian plum tomatoes, cut up, with their juice

1 Soak the mushrooms for at least 30 minutes in a small bowl with 350 ml ($\frac{2}{3}$ pint) lukewarm water. After soaking, lift them out carefully without stirring up the water in the bowl; rinse them in several changes of cold water to rid them of any lingering traces of grit. Cut them up into large pieces, and set aside.

2 Filter the water in which the mushrooms have soaked through a fine wire strainer lined with kitchen paper, and reserve.

3 Choose a sauté pan which will be able to contain the steaks later without overlapping. Put in the olive oil and onion, and sauté over medium heat until the onion is translucent.

4 Dredge the steaks on both sides in the flour, and put them in the pan. Raise the heat to high, and cook the meat very briefly, turning it just once. The onion will turn brown in the meantime, which is precisely what you want it to do. As soon as the meat is done, season it with salt and pepper, and transfer it to a warm (not hot) dish. Leave the onion and oil in the pan, and reduce the heat to medium.

5 Add the mushrooms and their filtered water to the pan. Cook, stirring from time to time, until the water has evaporated.

6 Add the wine, and turn up the heat again for a minute or so, while the wine bubbles away. Stir frequently.

7 Put in the tomatoes and their juice, and turn down the heat to low. Cook very slowly for 15 to 20 minutes, until the oil separates from the tomatoes. Stir occasionally. Add salt and pepper to taste.

8 Raise the heat to medium high, and return the steaks to the pan. Turn them once or twice, but do not reheat them for more than 20 or 30 seconds, or they will dry out. Serve immediately, pouring the entire contents of the pan over the steaks.

MENU SUGGESTIONS

Precede with *Spinaci e riso in brodo*, *Conchiglie con bacon, piselli e ricotta*, *Spaghetti alla siciliana* or, from my first book, *Riso filante con la mozzarella* (page 166). Accompany with *Fettine croccanti di melanzana*, *Crocchette di patate alla romagnola*, or, from my first book, *Broccoli all'aglio* (page 310).

Fettine di manzo farcite

STUFFED THIN STEAKS

These stuffed steaks are thin, coupled slices of beef, embracing a layer of cheese and a slice of ham. The completed dish is an impressive and luscious one, but putting it together is absolutely elementary. It cooks in no time, but be sure you are working with the cut of meat described in the recipe, sliced very thin.

While reading the instructions, you may wonder what will keep the unfastened meat jacket from flapping open while it cooks, and losing its stuffing. First, there is the coating of flour, egg, and breadcrumbs that sets as it is immersed in the hot cooking fat, and seals the edges. Second, there is the melting cheese inside clinging to the meat and pulling it together. Third, there has to be a little care exercised in the handling. If you are worried about it, you can clasp the two sides of the steak together with toothpicks. But it does not look quite so nice, because it bunches up the meat.

For four

450 g (1 lb) *braciole* steaks, sliced paper thin (see note below)
Salt
Freshly ground black pepper
180 g (6 oz) Italian fontina cheese, cut into thin slices
4 very thin slices prosciutto or other unsmoked ham
Enough vegetable oil to come 6 mm ($\frac{1}{4}$ inch) up the sides of the pan
75 g ($2\frac{1}{2}$ oz) plain flour, spread on a dish
1 egg, lightly beaten in a bowl with $\frac{1}{8}$ teaspoon nutmeg and a pinch of salt
90 g (3 oz) fine, dry, plain breadcrumbs, spread on a dish

Note *Braciole* steaks come from the centre cut of the top or bottom round. If they are taken from the broadest part, the slices will be quite long, about 250 to 300 mm (10 to 12 inches). In this case four slices are sufficient, which you will then cut in half into eight shorter ones. If the slices are much smaller to begin with, you will need eight of them, which you will leave whole. If they have not been sliced thinner than 6 mm ($\frac{1}{4}$ inch), flatten them with a meat pounder.

1 Pair off the *braciole* slices that are closest in size and shape, placing one slice above the other. If necessary, slightly trim the edges of each pair so that the slice above matches the one below as closely as possible, without large gaps or overlaps.

2 In between the slices of each *braciole* pair put salt, pepper, a layer of sliced fontina, and a slice of prosciutto or ham. Centre the fontina, so that it is not too close to the edges of the slice. Line up the upper half and lower half of each *braciole* pair so that the edges coincide. (Everything can be prepared in advance up to this point on the same day that you are going to cook it.)

3 Heat up the oil in the frying pan over high heat.

4 Dredge each pair of stuffed *braciole* in the flour, taking care that they do not come apart. Make sure that the edges are sealed all round with flour. Then dip them in the beaten egg, and dredge them in the breadcrumbs.

5 As soon as the oil is quite hot, slip the *braciole* into the pan. When they are nicely browned on one side, turn them over and cook until the other side is browned, but do not overcook. Place them on kitchen paper to drain, then transfer them to a warm serving dish and serve at once.

MENU SUGGESTIONS

Begin with *Risotto primavera*, *Riso con la verza*, *Spaghetti col sugo di cipolle* or *Rigatoni alla napoletana coi peperoni freschi*. Accompany with *Funghi fritta alla moda dei porcini*, *Carciofini gratinati*, *Carote con i capperi* or any of the fried vegetables in my first book.

Farsumauru – il braciolone

STUFFED BEEF BRACIOLE FROM SICILY

Here is a simplified version of a celebrated dish which appears in various editions, not only in Sicily but throughout the mainland. In Sicily it is a large slice of beef or veal *braciole* (hence the name *braciolone*), stuffed with a copious assortment of sausages, salami, various cheeses, and hard-boiled eggs. It is slowly pan-roasted in a little white wine and cooking fat.

One of the characteristics of Sicilian cooking is that almost every dish starts out with an idea as simple and severe as one of their Norman chapels, but can end as densely embellished as the most prodigally baroque of their cathedrals. I have opted for a restrained version, first, because I think it is quite good enough, and second, because I have never found any really satisfactory substitutes for the pork products and cheeses of Sicily. There is no reason why you should not experiment with the filling, following the suggestions of your imagination and good taste.

In nearly every recipe for *farsumauru*, the *braciole* is spread with a layer of filling and then rolled up like a swiss roll. I prefer the approach described below, where the *braciole* is sewn up to form a casing for the stuffing. When sliced it looks a little bit like *cotechino* or some other large cooked sausage, and the stuffing stays very tender and succulent.

The name *farsumauru*, which translates as 'false lean', seems to have puzzled most writers on Italian food, who think it must have something to do with Lent. The explanation I was given in Sicily seems more plausible – 'lean' because its wrapping is lean; 'false' because its stuffing is decidedly not.

For six

2 beef *braciole* (see note on page 000), cut 12 mm ($\frac{1}{2}$ inch) thick (i.e., twice the usual thickness), weighing about 560 g ($1\frac{1}{4}$ lb) altogether
A needle and lightweight cotton trussing string
360 g (12 oz) pork, not completely lean, minced once with its fat
1 clove garlic, peeled and chopped fine
2 tablespoons chopped parsley
1 egg
2 tablespoons freshly grated Parmesan cheese
Salt
Freshly ground black black pepper
30 g (1 oz) butter
2 tablespoons vegetable oil
60 g (2 oz) plain flour, spread on a plate
225 ml (scant $\frac{1}{2}$ pint) dry white wine

1 Place the 2 *braciole* one above the other, and stitch them together on

three sides, leaving one narrow side open, like a pillow case. (Put away the needle in a safe place, away from the cooking area.)

2 Put the minced pork, garlic, parsley, egg, grated cheese, salt and a couple of grindings of pepper into a bowl. Mix thoroughly with a fork.

3 Place the mixture inside the sewn-up *braciole*, distributing it evenly. Sew up the open end. It may look like a very floppy meat roll to you at this point, but it will tighten up and become compact while cooking. (Again, remember to put the needle safely away.)

4 Choose a sauté pan or a flameproof casserole, preferably oval in shape, where the meat will later be able to fit straight and snug. Put in the butter and oil, and turn on the heat to medium high.

5 Dredge the meat roll all over in the flour. When the butter foam in the pan begins to subside, put in the meat. Turn the roll, browning it well all over.

6 When the meat is well browed, sprinkle with salt and pepper, and add the wine. Let the wine bubble for about half a minute, then lower the heat to medium low, and cover the pan, with the lid set slightly askew.

7 Cook for 1½ hours, turning the meat occasionally. When done, there should be dense cooking juices at the bottom of the pan with fat floating on top of them. (If the juices are not very dense, uncover the pan, turn up the heat to high, and boil them down for a few seconds.)

8 Transfer the meat roll to a chopping board. Tip the pan, and remove about two-thirds of the floating fat, using a spoon or small ladle. Add a couple of tablespoons water, and over high heat scrape loose with a wooden spoon any cooking residue stuck to the bottom of the pan. Turn off the heat when you have a small quantity of dense sauce.

9 Cut the roll like a salami, into slices 12 mm (½ inch) thick. Use a very sharp slicing knife with a slim blade. This is one of those rare cases where the use of an electric knife is forgivable because it helps keep the slices compact. You can pick out the bits of string now, or leave it for people to do on their own plates.

10 Arrange the sliced *farsumauru* on a serving dish. Pour over it the sauce from the pan, and serve at once.

MENU SUGGESTIONS

Begin with *Riso con la verza*, *Penne col sugo di cavolfiore*, *Fettuccine con le zucchine fritte*, or, from my first book, *Spaghettini con le melanzane*. Accompany with *Asparagi e funghi passati al burro*, *Cipolline stufate col topinambur*, or *Carote con i capperi*.

Filetto al barolo

BEEF FILLET WITH RED WINE

The fillet has never been my favourite cut of beef. Perhaps it is because, when I was a child, the only occasions I had it were just after I had been ill, as a restorative. I find it a bland, boring cut, suited to those people who do not really care for the taste of meat, much as that yellow processed cheese in supermarkets must be for people who do not care for the taste of cheese.

In this recipe, however, fillet is magically transformed. It is not merely camouflaged in a sauce; it emerges with flavour and character that appear to be its very own. The reason for this is that the fillet is cooked from the start in the flavouring agents that form the sauce. It is very fast to do because the fillets must be cut rather thin. You have nothing to gain from having the meat cut in great thick chunks; you would end up with more meat, but with less flavour. An important part here is taken by the wine. The ideal wine to cook with would be a choice Barolo, Gattinara, or Barbaresco, but, if you cannot get hold of a big Piedmontese red, settle for a good Côte Rotie.

For four

1 tablespoon vegetable oil
45 g (1½ oz) butter
4 beef fillet steaks, cut 25 mm (1 inch) thick
90 g (3 oz) flour, spread on a plate
3 cloves garlic, peeled and crushed
Salt
Freshly ground black pepper
12 tablespoons big, fleshy red wine (see introductory remarks above)

1 Choose a sauté pan that can later contain the 4 fillets in a single layer. Put in the oil and butter, and turn on the heat to medium high.

2 Dredge the meat in the flour on both sides. As soon as the butter foam begins to subside, put in the fillet steaks and the crushed garlic. Cook very briefly, about 1½ minutes per side. Add salt and a liberal grinding of pepper.

3 Add about a third of the wine, letting it boil away rapidly at high heat. When it has evaporated, add half the remaining wine. Turn the fillet steaks from time to time. When the wine has evaporated again, put in all the remaining wine. By the time the last of the wine has evaporated, if you are cooking at fast enough heat, the steaks will be done, pink inside. Remove the garlic.

4 Transfer the steaks to a warm, not sizzling, dish.

5 Tip the pan and remove up to half the fat with a spoon or small ladle. There will be more fat in the pan if the steaks have been wrapped by the butcher with a strip of fat. Add 2 or 3 tablespoons warm water, and over

high heat scrape loose any cooking residue stuck to the bottom. Pour all the juices from the pan over the meat, and serve at once.

MENU SUGGESTIONS

A first course of *Spaghetti alla nursina*, either of the *lasagne* recipes on pages 151–4, *Maccheroncini alla saffi*, or, from my first book, *Risotto coi funghi secchi* (page 158). Accompany with *Carciofi e patate passati al forno*, *Cavolfiore gratinato con la balsamella*, or *Porri al burro e formaggio*. Avoid vegetable dishes that have a tomato sauce.

Stufatino di manzo con i piselli

BEEF STEW WITH RED WINE AND PEAS

One of the most gratifying things about stews is their resistance to elegant trappings and immunity from all food fads. They belong to that category of dishes that will never let down those whose only criterion for judging food is how good it tastes.

This is a stew that bridges the seasons, carrying its winter heartiness far enough into spring to welcome the arrival of the first peas. It has a fresh, clean taste, uncomplicated by herbs or any seasonings other than salt and pepper. To make it you need good red wine, olive oil, and a few vegetables. In examining the recipe you will notice that the vegetables are added at different stages: the onions first, because they must cook with the meat from the very beginning, suffusing it with sweetness; the carrots after a while, the celery later still, so as not to dampen its sprightly fragrance, and at the very last, the peas.

You can, of course, use frozen peas, if good fresh ones are not available, and it will still be a respectable stew, if you are willing to accept a somewhat foggy copy of the original.

For four to six

4 tablespoons vegetable oil
900 g (2 lb) boneless chuck steak, cut into 37- to 50-mm ($1\frac{1}{2}$- to 2-inch) stewing cubes
350 ml ($\frac{2}{3}$ pint) sturdy red wine, preferably Barbera
450 g (1 lb) small white onions
60 g (2 oz) butter

8 tablespoons olive oil
4 medium carrots
4 meaty celery sticks
680 g ($1\frac{1}{2}$ lb) fresh peas (unshelled weight) or 450 g (1 lb) frozen petits pois, thawed
Salt
Freshly ground black pepper

1 Put the vegetable oil into a small frying pan, and turn on the heat to medium high. When the oil is quite hot, put in the meat, a few pieces at a time, so as not to crowd the pan. Brown the meat to a dark colour on all sides. Transfer the browned pieces to a dish, and add more meat to the pan in successive batches, until all of it has been browned.

2 Pour the fat out of the pan. Put in 8 tablespoons wine, and turn the heat up high. Let the wine bubble for a few moments, while you scrape loose the browning residue from the bottom of the pan, then turn off the heat.

3 Peel the onions, and cut a cross into each of them at the root end.

4 Choose a flameproof casserole, with a tight-fitting cover, that will be able to hold all the ingredients of the recipe. Put in the browned meat, the onions, butter, olive oil, the wine, residue and juices from the pan where the meat was browned, and the remaining wine. Cover tightly, and turn on the heat very low.

5 Peel the carrots, rinse them in cold water, and trim them into sticks about 2 mm ($\frac{1}{2}$ inch) thick and 75 mm (3 inches) long. When the meat has cooked for about 15 minutes, add them to the casserole, turning them over with the other ingredients.

6 Cut the celery sticks into pieces about 75 mm (3 inches) long, and split these in half lengthways. Peel away or snap off any strings. Rinse them in cold water. Add them to the casserole when the meat has cooked for about 1 hour. Give all the contents of the casserole a thorough stirring.

7 Shell the peas, and put them in the casserole after the meat has cooked for 1 hour 45 minutes. If there is very little liquid left in the casserole, add 8 to 12 tablespoons water. After 15 minutes, add several pinches of salt, a few grindings of pepper, and stir the contents of the pot thoroughly. Continue cooking until the meat is tender when pricked with a fork. It should take a little over 2 hours from the time it started cooking, but the cooking time will depend on the quality of the meat.

8 If you are using frozen peas, add the thawed peas, without adding water, when the meat is already fairly tender. Let them cook just another 4 to 5 minutes. If the fresh peas you are using are exceptionally tiny and fresh, they also may need little or no water, and should be added several minutes later than larger, mealier peas, since they require less cooking time.

9 Taste and check salt and pepper before serving.

Note Like all stews, this one is excellent prepared a day or two in advance and gently reheated before serving.

MENU SUGGESTIONS

To begin: *Zuppa dei poveri con la rucola*, *Maccheroncini alla boscaiola* or *Tonnarelli col rosmarino*. It needs no vegetable accompaniment, but should be followed by a simple salad.

Brasato di manzo con le cipolle

BEEF BRAISED WITH ONIONS

What is remarkable about this roast is that it is cooked without the help of any liquid. All the moisture necessary to cook the meat rises from the ample bed of onions on which it rests. At first, as the onions wilt, the meat soaks in the abundant juices they throw off. Eventually all the liquid vanishes, the meat becomes tenderly impregnated with sweet onion flavour, and the onions themselves turn deliciously brown.

This recipe calls for larding the meat with *pancetta* or blanched green bacon. It is an important contribution to the flavour and tenderness. If you do not have a larding needle, it is very easy to push strips of *pancetta* into the meat by folding them over the end of a chopstick or similar blunt stick, or of a knife with a rounded tip on the blade. The best way to pierce the meat is to follow the direction of the grain.

For four to six

110 g (4 oz) *pancetta* in a single piece or 110 g (4 oz) green bacon
900 g (2 lb) boneless beef, preferably brisket
5 cloves
4 medium onions, sliced very thin
Salt
Freshly ground black pepper

1 Preheat the oven to 170°C/325°F/Mark 3.

2 If using *pancetta*, cut it into strips about 6 mm ($\frac{1}{4}$ inch) wide. If using bacon, cut each strip into three shorter pieces.

3 Lard the meat, using a larding needle or the method described in the introductory remarks above, with half the *pancetta* or bacon strips.

4 Insert the cloves at random into any five of the places where the meat was larded.

5 Choose a heavy casserole with a tight-fitting lid, just large enough to accommodate the meat snugly. Spread the sliced onions on the bottom of the pot, and over it the rest of the *pancetta* or bacon. Put in the meat, and season liberally with salt and freshly ground pepper. Cover tightly. If doubtful about the tightness of the fit, place a sheet of aluminium foil between the pot and the lid. Put the pot in the topmost level of the preheated oven.

6 Cook for 3½ to 4 hours, until the meat is very tender when pricked with a fork. Turn the meat after 30 minutes, and every 30 to 40 minutes thereafter. At first it may look dull and unattractive, but at the end of the cooking time, as the onions turn brown, the meat acquires a dark, rich colour.

7 When done, carve the meat on a chopping board, and lay the slices on a warm serving dish. Pour the juices left on the board and all the contents of the casserole over the meat, and serve at once.

MENU SUGGESTIONS

Start with *Spaghetti alla carbonara*, *Fettuccine con le zucchine fritte*, *Tonnarelli col rosmarino* or *I pizzoccheri*. No vegetable accompaniment is necessary, but it can be followed by *Insalata di borlotti e radicchio*, *Le patate in insalata* (unless you have started with buckwheat noodles), or any raw salad.

Brasato di manzo con sedano e cipolle

BEEF BRAISED WITH CELERY AND ONIONS

Mechanised agriculture arrived fairly late in Italy, and up to then (even now in some places) what ended up as beef for the table was frequently an animal retired from the farm's working force. Braising became a favourite method of handling the meat because it relaxed and made tender the tough muscle fibres and sweetened them with the fragrance of the fresh vegetables with which the meat was cooked. This remains one of the juiciest and tastiest ways there is to cook beef. And it is thrifty because you can use a less expensive grade and cut of meat. In this particular preparation, there are just two vegetables, celery and onions. The herbal aroma of celery with the sweet taste of onion gives this braised beef a most appealing freshness.

For six

4 or 5 large, meaty celery sticks
1 dozen small white onions
2 tablespoons vegetable oil
900 g (2 lb) boneless beef in one piece (chuck, topside or similar braising cut)
2 tablespoons olive oil
30 g (1 oz) butter
350 ml ($\frac{2}{3}$ pint) dry red wine
8 tablespoons home-made broth (page 18) or $\frac{1}{2}$ bouillon cube dissolved in 8 tablespoons water
Salt
Freshly ground black pepper

1 Strip the strings from the celery sticks by breaking off a small piece of stick and pulling it down, or using a vegetable peeler. Cut the sticks into pieces about 75 mm (3 inches) long, and rinse them in cold water.

2 Peel the onions, and cut a cross in the root end of each one. This is to allow them to cook more evenly.

3 Preheat the oven to 180°C/350°F/Mark 4.

4 Choose a frying pan just broad enough for the meat. Put in the vegetable oil, and turn on the heat to medium high. When the oil is very hot, put in the meat and brown it well on all sides, then turn off the heat.

5 Choose a flameproof casserole with a tight-fitting lid that is just large enough to contain the meat snugly. Put in the olive oil, butter, celery, onions, and the browned meat.

6 Tip the pan in which you browned the meat, and draw off all the fat with a spoon or small ladle. Put the red wine into the pan. Over high heat, for a few seconds scrape loose the browned residue stuck to the bottom of the pan. Then pour all the contents of the pan into the casserole containing the meat.

7 Add the broth to the casserole, with a generous sprinkling of salt and pepper.

8 Place the casserole, uncovered, over medium heat and bring the liquid in the pot to a simmer, turning the meat once or twice. Then cover tightly, and place the casserole in the uppermost level of the preheated oven.

9 Cook for 2 to $2\frac{1}{2}$ hours, until the meat is very tender when pricked with a fork.

10 Transfer the meat to a chopping board. If the juices in the casserole are thin and runny, boil them down over high heat until they are rather dense.

11 Carve the meat into thin slices. Transfer the slices to a warm dish, and pour over them all the contents of the casserole and any juices left on the chopping board. Serve at once.

Note The meat may be cooked through to the final stages even a day or two in advance. Do not slice it, however, until it has been reheated just before serving in a 140°C/275°F/Mark 1 oven for about 25 minutes. Allow the meat to come to room temperature before placing it in the oven.

MENU SUGGESTIONS

Begin with *Spaghetti alla carbonara*, *Conchiglie con bacon, piselli e ricotta*, *Maccheroncini alla boscaiola* or *Tonnarelli col rosmarino*. No vegetable accompaniment is necessary, but the beef can be followed by *Le patate in insalata* or any raw salad.

Il bollito rifatto alla moda di papi

GRILLED LEFTOVER BOILED BEEF

My father, like most men born and brought up on the land, had a gift for making a little go a long way. An example of his touch is this grilled sliced boiled beef. When I was growing up, beef was not as common as it is today on Italian tables. It was a rare and expensive treat, and we always fell on it greedily. Once there was a little more than was needed to go round, and father's way of resuscitating it the following day was so delicious that thereafter we always held ourselves back, hoping there would be leftovers. Whenever I make boiled beef for my family now, I deliberately make some extra so that they can have it again, my father's way.

For four

450 g (1 lb) cold boiled beef, all solid meat
3 tablespoons olive oil
Salt
Freshly ground black pepper
1 teaspoon rosemary leaves

1 Preheat grill.

2 Cut the beef across the grain into bite-sized slices about 6 mm ($\frac{1}{4}$ inch) thick. Spread them in a single layer, without overlapping, on a dish.

3 Pour the oil over the meat, and turn the beef so that it is well coated on both sides. Add 2 or 3 pinches of salt, a couple of grindings of pepper, and the rosemary. Turn the meat again to season it thoroughly.

4 Place the meat under a grill in the position closest to the source of heat.

5 After about 2 minutes, or when the surface of the meat becomes brown, turn the meat over and cook for another minute or so until it browns on the other side. Serve piping hot.

MENU SUGGESTIONS

To start: *Zuppa primavera*, *Penne col sugo di cavolfiore* or *Spaghetti 'ajo e ojo'* (from my first book, page 88). Accompany with *I topinambur al pomodoro*, *Sedano in umido*, *Erbette saltate per la piadina* or *Melanzane e peperoni fritti*.

Polpettine invernali con la verza

WINTER MEATBALLS WITH SAVOY CABBAGE

Meatballs and cabbage – if ever there were names to conjure with, they must be these. Forthright, unintimidating food, food to make one feel complete, filled to the brim with happiness and gratitude.

The meatballs are a tasty composition of meat, egg, Parmesan, onion, *pancetta*, and bread macerated in milk. First, they are breaded and fried. The cabbage is cooked until it is dissolvingly soft, a little tomato is added, and the meatballs are returned for a while to the pan, to soak up all the wonderful flavours. A rousing good dish, and make sure you have plenty of good bread to go with it.

For four to six

1 slice of good, solid white bread, without the crust
6 tablespoons milk
450 g (1 lb) minced chuck steak
60 g (2 oz) *pancetta*, chopped very fine
1 egg

Salt
Freshly ground black pepper
1 tablespoon chopped parsley
3 tablespoons freshly grated Parmesan cheese
2 tablespoons onion chopped fine
110 g (4 oz) fine, dry, plain breadcrumbs, spread on a plate
6 tablespoons vegetable oil
660 to 680 g ($1\frac{1}{4}$ to $1\frac{1}{2}$ lb) Savoy cabbage
2 tablespoons olive oil
2 large cloves garlic, peeled and chopped
150 g (5 oz) tinned Italian plum tomatoes, drained and cut up

1 Heat up the bread and milk in a small saucepan over low heat. When the bread has completely soaked up all the milk, mash it to a fine pulp with a fork. Turn off the heat, and set aside to cool.

2 Put the steak, *pancetta*, egg, salt, pepper, parsley, Parmesan, onion, and the bread-and-milk mush into a bowl. Mix all the ingredients thoroughly. Shape the mixture into meatballs about 25 to 37 mm (1 to $1\frac{1}{2}$ inches) across. Dredge the meatballs on both sides in the breadcrumbs.

3 Choose a sauté pan large enough to contain all the meatballs in a single layer. Put in the vegetable oil, and turn on the heat to medium high.

4 When the oil is quite hot, slip in the meatballs, and brown them nicely on all sides, turning them gently. When they are done, transfer them to a dish lined with kitchen paper, and turn off the heat. Do not empty the pan.

5 Discard any bruised or blemished cabbage leaves. Shred the rest of the cabbage into strips about 6 mm ($\frac{1}{4}$ inch) wide, and discard the core.

6 Into the pan where the meatballs were fried put the olive oil and the chopped garlic. Sauté the garlic over medium heat until it turns gold, then add all the shredded cabbage. Stir and turn it thoroughly. Cover the pan, and turn the heat down to minimum.

7 Cook the cabbage, turning it over from time to time, for 40 minutes to 1 hour, until it is very soft and is reduced to a third of its original bulk. Add a liberal amount of salt and pepper, bearing in mind that the cabbage is sweet and will take considerable seasoning. If in doubt, taste.

8 Raise the heat to medium and, with the pan uncovered, cook the cabbage, turning it from time to time, until it turns a light nut brown.

9 Add the chopped tomatoes, and cook for 10 minutes, stirring occasionally.

10 Return the fried meatballs to the pan, turning them well, cover the pan, and reduce the heat. Cook for 10 minutes over low heat, turning them two or three times. Serve piping hot.

Note The entire dish may be cooked in advance and refrigerated for a day or two. When reheating, it may be necessary to add 1 or 2 tablespoons water.

MENU SUGGESTIONS

Begin with *Minestrina di broccoli e manfrigul*, *Penne con spinaci e ricotta*, or, from my first book, *Zuppa di cannellini con aglio e prezzemolo* (page 67). Unless you have chosen the bean soup as a first course, follow with *Insalata di borlotti e radicchio*; otherwise, choose any mixed raw salad.

Scaloppine al marsala arricchite

VEAL SCALOPPINE WITH MARSALA AND CREAM

Marsala is a Sicilian dessert wine, which is used in the island's cooking sometimes to sauce sautéed pork chops, and, in many northern kitchens, with veal *scaloppine*. The following version is a departure from traditional recipes because in addition to the usual ingredients it uses cream. The cream softens some of the Marsala's impact while robbing it of none of its flavour, and turns this into a rather more gentle dish than it is in its standard edition. These *scaloppine* are perfectly accompanied by almost any vegetable, except those in a tomato sauce. Particularly fitting would be those vegetables sautéed with butter and cheese.

For four

2 tablespoons vegetable oil
45 g ($1\frac{1}{2}$ oz) butter
450 g (1 lb) thin veal *scaloppine* (see note below)
100 g ($3\frac{1}{2}$ oz) plain flour, spread on a dish
Salt
Freshly ground pepper
8 tablespoons dry Marsala
6 tablespoons double cream

1 Put the oil and butter into a large sauté pan or frying pan and heat them up over high heat.

2 As the butter foam begins to subside, dredge the *scaloppine*, one at a time and on both sides, in the flour and put them in the pan. Do not put in any more than will fit without overlapping.

3 Brown the *scaloppine* quickly on both sides. One minute or so for each side is quite sufficient if they are very thin, and if the cooking fat is hot

enough. Try to turn and brown the pieces of meat in the pan in the same order in which you put them in, so that all the *scaloppine* will be cooked evenly. When the *scaloppine* are done, transfer them to a dish large enough to hold them without overlapping. Use more than one dish, if necessary. As you take the *scaloppine* out of the pan, replace them with the raw *scaloppine* that remain, dredging them in flour just before putting them into the pan. When all the meat is done and has been transferred to the dish, turn off the heat under the pan, and season the meat with salt and pepper to taste.

4 Add the Marsala to the pan, turning the heat on again to high.

5 Scrape the cooking residue loose from the bottom of the pan, stir, and when you see the Marsala and fat separate, add the cream. Stir constantly over high heat until the cream is bound with the juices in the pan into a thick sauce.

6 Turn the heat down to medium, and put into the pan all the *scaloppine*, one at a time, turning each one over in the sauce. Turn off the heat as soon as the last of the *scaloppine* has been put into the pan.

7 Transfer the *scaloppine* to a warm serving dish, and pour over them all the sauce from the pan.

Note The very best *scaloppine* come from a single muscle in the hind leg called the top round. Whether you cut them yourself at home or the butcher does it for you, they should be cut by slicing the meat against the grain. If they are cut along the grain they will shrivel and curl while cooking. They can be as thick as 9 mm ($\frac{3}{8}$ inch) when cut; then they should be flattened with a meat-pounding tool or the flat side of a heavy cleaver. (See the remarks on cutting and pounding scaloppine on page 13.)

MENU SUGGESTIONS

A first course of *Maccheroncini alla saffi*, either of the two *lasagne* on pages 151–4, or, from my first book, *Risotto con gli asparagi* (page 162). Accompany with *Polpettone di fagiolini alla genovese*, *Fiori di broccoli fritti*, *Fettine croccanti di melanzana* or *Zucchine fritte con la pastella* (from *The Classic Italian Cookbook*, page 337).

Scaloppine piccanti

VEAL SCALOPPINE IN AN ANCHOVY AND CAPER SAUCE

Here is a piquant sauce for *scaloppine* that is handled with finesse. It is made with butter, diced ham, anchovies and capers, to which are added the cooking juices of the *scaloppine* deglazed with *grappa* or other brandy. It is thickened with cream, and spread over the sautéed *scaloppine*.

For four

110 g (4 oz) cooked (but not smoked) ham, cut in a slice (or slices) about 6 mm ($\frac{1}{4}$ inch) thick
75 g ($2\frac{1}{2}$ oz) butter
4 flat anchovy fillets, coarsely cut up
$1\frac{1}{2}$ tablespoons coarsely chopped capers (if packed in vinegar, rinse them in cold water)
2 tablespoons vegetable oil
75 g ($2\frac{1}{2}$ oz) plain flour, spread on a dinner plate or on wax paper
450 g (1 lb) veal *scaloppine*, sliced very thin and pounded flat
Salt
Freshly ground black pepper
3 tablespoons *grappa* or grape brandy
4 tablespoons double cream

1 Dice the ham very fine. Put it into a small saucepan with 30 g (1 oz) butter, and sauté it over medium heat for just a few seconds. Add the chopped anchovies and capers, and cook for a few more seconds, softening and mashing the anchovies with a wooden spoon until they dissolve into a paste. Turn off the heat.

2 In a large frying pan over medium-high heat put the oil and the remaining butter. When the butter foam begins to subside, dredge the *scaloppine* in the flour, one at a time and on both sides, and slip them into the frying pan. Do not put in any more than will fit very loosely in the pan. Brown them nicely on both sides, 1 minute or so for each side, then transfer them to a warm dish, seasoning them with salt and pepper.

3 When all the *scaloppine* are done, turn off the heat, and pour the *grappa* or brandy into the frying pan. Quickly scrape up the cooking residue with a spoon and pour everything into the saucepan containing the ham-and-anchovy mixture.

4 Turn on the heat under the saucepan to medium high, add the double cream and stir briefly until the cream thickens. Turn off the heat, and spread the hot sauce over the *scaloppine* on the dish. Serve without delay.

MENU SUGGESTIONS

Precede this with any rich, creamy dish of pasta where there are no sharp flavours, such as those of anchovies or capers. Good choices: *Spaghetti alla carbonara*, *Conchiglie con bacon, piselli e ricotta*, *Penne con spinaci e ricotta*, *Le pappardelle del Cantunzein.*

A sweet-tasting vegetable accompaniment is appropriate, such as *Asparagi e funghi passati al burro*, *Carciofini gratinati* or *Porri al burro e formaggio.*

Scaloppine ammantate

VEAL SCALOPPINE WITH MOZZARELLA

This is an appetising way to dress up *scaloppine*. Over already browned *scaloppine* a slice of mozzarella is placed and the cooking continued until it starts to melt. The *scaloppine* are served with their mozzarella blanket prettily stippled with the deglazed brown cooking juices from the pan.

For four to six

180 to 220 g (6 to 8 oz) Italian mozzarella
45 g ($1\frac{1}{2}$ oz) butter
2 tablespoons vegetable oil
680 g ($1\frac{1}{2}$ lb) *scaloppine*, sliced very thin and pounded flat
Salt
Freshly ground black pepper

1 Slice the mozzarella into 6-mm ($\frac{1}{4}$-inch) thick slices, making sure that you end up with as many slices of mozzarella as you have *scaloppine*. Set aside.

2 Choose a sauté pan large enough to contain all the *scaloppine* later in a single layer without overlapping. If they do not fit into a single pan, use two, and increase the quantity of butter by 15 g ($\frac{1}{2}$ oz) and the oil by 1 tablespoon, dividing the fat equally between the two pans. Heat up the butter and oil over high heat.

3 When the butter foam begins to subside, put in the *scaloppine*. Brown them quickly on both sides, about 1 minute on each side. Sprinkle with salt, and turn the heat down to medium.

4 Cover each *scaloppina* with a slice of mozzarella, and sprinkle with pepper. Cover the pan for a few seconds until the mozzarella begins to soften. Then carefully transfer the *scaloppine* to a warm serving dish, with the mozzarella-covered side facing up.

5 Add 1 or 2 tablespoons water to the pan, raise the heat to high and while the water boils away scrape loose the cooking residue. Pour the few drops of dark sauce that this produces over the *scaloppine*, and serve at once.

MENU SUGGESTIONS

To start: *Zuppa primavera*, *Fettuccine con le zucchine fritte* or *Tonnarelli con i funghi*. Accompany with *Insalatina tenera con la pancetta* or, if mushrooms have not already appeared in the first course, *Funghi fritti alla moda dei porcini*, or *Zucchine gratinate*.

Cartoccio di scaloppine con asparagi

VEAL SCALOPPINE AND ASPARAGUS IN FOIL

In all the vast repertoire of veal *scaloppine* dishes there is none lovelier than this, I think. It is a fresh and elegant union of sautéed *scaloppine* and slivers of asparagus, sealed by melted fontina cheese, and accompanied by a buttery Marsala sauce.

One of the problems of cooking thin slices of veal with cheese is that while one waits for the cheese to melt the meat may become tough. There is no danger of that in this preparation. The melting of the cheese takes place within the protective enclosure of a foil wrap, from which the veal's volatile tenderness cannot escape.

For four

225 g (8 oz) asparagus
60 g (2 oz) butter
3 tablespoons vegetable oil
450 g (1 lb) veal *scaloppine*, cut from the top round and pounded flat
90 g (3 oz) plain flour, spread on a plate
Heavy-duty aluminium foil
Salt
Freshly ground black pepper
180 g (6 oz) Italian fontina cheese
6 tablespoons dry Marsala wine

1 Trim, peel, rinse, and cook the asparagus as described in steps 1 and 2 on page 112. Do not overcook them; drain the asparagus when they are

still rather crunchy, and leave them whole (they are not to be cut until step 7).

2 Put 30 g (1 oz) butter and all the oil into a medium-sized sauté pan, and turn on the heat to high.

3 When the butter foam begins to subside, take as many *scaloppine* as will fit loosely in the pan, dredge them on both sides in the flour, shake off the excess flour, and slip them into the pan. Brown the *scaloppine* very briefly on both sides, about 1 minute altogether. Transfer the browned *scaloppine* to a dish, and add more *scaloppine* to the pan as space becomes available. Continue in this way until all the *scaloppine* are browned.

4 Preheat the oven to 200°C/400°F/Mark 6.

5 Choose a baking tin or oven dish that will be able to contain all the *scaloppine* in a single layer. Line it with a large enough sheet of heavy-duty aluminium foil to lap over the edge of the dish, taking care not to pierce it when folding it at the corners.

6 Lay the *scaloppine* in the dish in a single layer. Sprinkle with salt and pepper.

7 Cut the asparagus, slicing them diagonally into pieces no more than 12 mm ($\frac{1}{2}$ inch) thick. The length of the pieces is not important provided they are not any longer than the *scaloppine*.

8 Cover each of the *scaloppine* with a layer of cut asparagus. Sprinkle very lightly with salt.

9 Cut the fontina into thin slices, using either a cheese-slicing tool or a swivel-action vegetable peeler. It does not matter if the slices are irregular, they will all run together when the cheese melts. Cover each of the *scaloppine* with a layer of fontina slices.

10 Pour out all the fat from the pan in which the meat was browned. Put in the Marsala and any juices from the dish where the browned *scaloppine* rested. Over high heat scrape loose the cooking residue on the bottom of the pan, while reducing the Marsala to about 3 tablespoons.

11 Spoon a little of the sauce from the pan over each of the *scaloppine.* Dot all of them with the remaining butter.

12 Take a sheet of foil large enough to cover the dish and overlap it. Place it over the dish, fold together the edges of the two sheets of foil and make an airtight seal all around.

13 Slide the dish onto the uppermost rack of the preheated oven. Remove after 15 minutes, by which time the fontina should have melted.

14 Open the foil wrap. Start at the side furthest from you, taking care not to be stung by the outrushing steam. Gently transfer the *scaloppine* to a warm serving dish. Spoon the juices over them and serve at once.

Note This dish may be prepared a few hours in advance up to the point where it is ready to go into the oven. Do not refrigerate.

MENU SUGGESTIONS

For an elegant menu, *Tortellini verdi* would be an ideal choice. Other appropriate first courses: *Maccheroncini coi piselli e i peperoni*, *Fettuccine con le zucchine fritte*, or, from my first book, *Risotto alla parmigiana* (page 155). They do not need a vegetable accompaniment, but *Topinambur fritti* or *Funghi fritti alla moda dei porcini* would not be disagreeable.

Messicani di vitello

STUFFED VEAL ROLLS

Veal *scaloppine* may be very expensive, but there is no cut of meat that goes further. Here, with just 450 g (1 lb), you can serve at least four persons elegantly; if you preface the dish with a *risotto* or a little pasta, in the Italian manner, you could even serve six.

The *scaloppine* are stuffed with a tasty pork and cheese filling, very faintly spiked with a little nutmeg. They are first browned, then cooked in a small quantity of good broth. They are served with their own reduced pan juices, dark, dense, and delicious.

For four

20 g (⅔ oz) soft crumb (the crustless part of the bread), preferably from Italian or French bread
4 tablespoons milk
60 g (2 oz) unsmoked ham, chopped fine
60 g (2 oz) lean pork, chopped fine
1 egg
30 g (1 oz) freshly grated Parmesan cheese
Salt
Freshly ground black pepper
⅛ teaspoon grated nutmeg
450 g (1 lb) veal *scaloppine*, from the top round, pounded very flat
Round toothpicks
45 g (1½ oz) butter
1 tablespoon vegetable oil
75 g (2½ oz) plain flour, spread on a plate
6 tablespoons dry white wine
8 tablespoons home-made broth (page 18) or ½ bouillon cube, dissolved in water

1 Put the bread into a deep dish or a small bowl with the milk, and let it soak thoroughly. Transfer it to another dish, and mash it with a fork to a creamy consistency. Drain off all the excess milk.

2 In a small mixing bowl put the chopped ham, pork, egg, grated cheese, 2 or 3 pinches of salt, a grinding of pepper, the nutmeg, and the mashed bread crumb. With a fork, or with your hands, mix all ingredients thoroughly. Put the mixture on a chopping board or work top and divide it into as many parts as you have *scaloppine*. If some of the *scaloppine* are larger than others, divide the stuffing accordingly, into larger and smaller portions.

3 Lay the *scaloppine* flat on a dish or work surface. Coat each with a full portion of the pork-and-ham mixture, spreading it evenly. Roll the *scaloppine* up tightly, and fasten them with one or two toothpicks. Insert the toothpicks lengthways.

4 In a sauté pan large enough to contain the *rollatini* later in a single layer, heat the butter and oil over medium-high heat.

5 Dredge the rolled-up *scaloppine* in flour on all sides and put them in the pan as soon as the butter foam subsides.

6 Brown the meat well all over, then put in the wine. When the wine has bubbled away for a minute or so, sprinkle lightly with salt, put in the broth, and cover the pan. Turn down the heat to medium low, and cook at a gentle simmer for 25 to 30 minutes, until the *rollatini* are cooked all the way through.

7 Transfer the meat to a warm dish. If the juices are too thin and runny, turn up the heat. Boil down the juice until it is rather dense, while scraping loose any cooking residue from the bottom of the pan. If, on the other hand, the juices are too thick and stuck to the pan, add a tablespoon or two of water to the pan, turn up the heat, and scrape loose the residue with a wooden spoon.

Serve the *rollatini* immediately with all the cooking juices poured over them.

MENU SUGGESTIONS

Start off with *Riso con la verza*, *Spaghetti alla carbonara*, or *Penne con spinaci e ricotta*. Accompany with *Funghi stufati*, *Patate con le acciughe*, or *Zucchine trifolate con le cipolle*.

Cotolette alla palermitana

VEAL CUTLETS FROM PALERMO

Anywhere in the world but in Palermo, a breaded veal cutlet is fried. There it is grilled, and a marvellous difference it makes. The breadcrumb coating turns crackling crisp, like well-done toast, while the veal turns out remarkably tender and juicy.

You can make these cutlets with *scaloppine* or you can use rib chops. In either case the cutlet should not exceed 12 mm ($\frac{1}{2}$ inch) in thickness; otherwise, before it cooks through, the breadcrumbs will become too charred. If you are using rib chops with the bone in, have the butcher knock off the corner of the bone so that the meat can be pounded evenly to the desired thinness.

Usually a little rosemary is sprinkled over the coating, but if you prefer a lighter, less aromatic flavour, you can omit it.

For four

680 g ($1\frac{1}{2}$ lb) top round of veal, cut into slices 12 mm ($\frac{1}{2}$ inch) thick, or 4 veal rib chops, pounded until they are no more than 12 mm ($\frac{1}{2}$ inch) thick
2 tablespoons olive oil
180 g (6 oz) dry, plain breadcrumbs, spread on a plate
Salt
Freshly ground black pepper
2 teaspoons rosemary (optional)
1 lemon, cut into 4 wedges

1 Preheat the grill 15 minutes in advance of cooking, placing the rack as close as possible to the source of heat.

2 Rub both sides of all the cutlets with olive oil.

3 Turn the cutlets in the breadcrumbs, pressing the crumbs against the meat with the palm of your hand.

4 Lay the cutlets on a dish, without overlapping them. Sprinkle with salt, pepper, and the optional rosemary leaves.

5 Place the meat on the rack under the grill, with the salted side facing upward. Cook for about $1\frac{1}{2}$ minutes, until the breadcrumbs begin to char. Turn the cutlets, and cook for another $1\frac{1}{2}$ minutes or so.

6 Serve piping hot, with wedges of lemon. If you like, you can trickle a little olive oil over the cutlets when serving them.

MENU SUGGESTIONS

A pasta course of *Spaghetti alla siciliana*, *Pasta con le sarde alla palermitana* or *Penne col sugo di cavolfiore* to begin. Accompany the veal with *La frittedda*, *Broccoli stufati al vino rosso* or *Patate in umido*.

Costolette di vitello profumate all' aglio e rosmarino

SAUTÉED VEAL CHOPS WITH GARLIC AND ROSEMARY

These are our familiar, classic Milanese veal chops, revised in Palermo to suit Sicilian taste. They are breaded and fried in the standard manner, but they are also flavoured with a touch of garlic and rosemary. The flavouring is not laid on with a heavy hand; there is just enough of it to give an engaging Southern raciness to this fine old Northern dish.

The chops must be pounded and flattened before cooking. If they have a corner bone, have your butcher knock it off before pounding them, so they will flatten evenly; or you can do this at home, chopping it off with a meat cleaver.

For four

2 eggs
4 veal chops, 12 mm ($\frac{1}{2}$ inch) thick, with the corner bone knocked off
2 teaspoons rosemary, chopped very fine
120 g ($4\frac{1}{2}$ oz) dry, plain breadcrumbs, spread on a dish
3 tablespoons vegetable oil
30 g (1 oz) butter
4 cloves garlic, peeled and lightly crushed
Salt
Lemon wedges

1 Break the eggs into a deep dish, and beat them lightly with a fork until the yolks and whites are combined.

2 Flatten the veal chops with a meat pounder. Take one chop at a time, and dip it on both sides into the beaten egg. Let excess egg flow back into the dish, so there is just a filmy coating on the chop. Sprinkle the chop with the rosemary, then turn both sides of the chop in the breadcrumbs. Press the chop flat against the breadcrumbs, using the palm of your hand, tap it two or three times, then turn it and do the other side. Your palm should come away dry, which means the breadcrumbs are sticking firmly to the meat.

3 Choose a sauté pan large enough to contain the chops later without overlapping. Put in the oil, butter, and garlic, and turn on the heat to medium high.

4 When the butter foam begins to subside, put in the chops. If the garlic has turned a warm brown, remove it. If it has not, watch it while cooking, and remove it as soon as it does colour; do not let it turn blackish brown.

5 When the chops have formed a nice golden crust on one side, turn

them over, and when you have a crust on both sides, transfer them to kitchen paper to drain. Sprinkle with salt, and serve promptly, with lemon wedges.

MENU SUGGESTIONS

Begin with *La paniscia novarese*, *Maccheroncini alla boscaiola* or *Rigatoni alla napoletana coi peperoni freschi*. Accompany the meat with any vegetable; a particularly apt choice would be *Carote con i capperi*, *Cavolfiore al pomodoro* or *Zucchine gratinate*.

Nodini di vitello con sughetto di acciughe

VEAL CHOPS WITH ANCHOVY SAUCE

These are simple sautéed veal chops served with a little sauce of butter, garlic, anchovies, and parsley. It takes less than 10 minutes to do, because while the chops cook, the sauce can be prepared. Do not overcook the chops, or, like all overdone veal, the meat will become dry.

For four

8 tablespoons vegetable oil
4 veal loin chops, 18 mm ($\frac{3}{4}$ inch) thick
60 g (2 oz) plain flour, spread on a plate
40 g (2 oz) butter
$1\frac{1}{2}$ cloves garlic, peeled and chopped rather course
2 flat anchovy fillets, chopped fine
2 tablespoons chopped parsley
Salt
Freshly ground black pepper

1 In a sauté pan that will be able to contain all the chops in a single layer, heat up the vegetable oil over medium-high heat.

2 Pat the chops with kitchen paper to absorb any moisture, and dredge them on both sides in the flour. When the oil is very hot, slip them into the pan and cook them, turning them from time to time.

3 While the chops are cooking, put the butter and garlic into a very small saucepan over medium heat.

4 As soon as the garlic turns pale gold, put in the anchovies and parsley. Cook for 20 or 30 seconds, stirring and mashing the anchovies with a wooden spoon, then turn off the heat.

5 When the chops are done – about 8 minutes should be sufficient to cook them to a light brown outside and a rosy pink in the centre – sprinkle with a little salt and a grinding of pepper, turn them quickly once or twice, and transfer to a warm serving dish or to individual plates. Spoon the sauce over the meat, and serve at once.

MENU SUGGESTIONS

Begin with *Spinaci e riso in brodo*, *Spaghetti col sugo di cipolle* or *Spaghetti alla siciliana*. Accompany the chops with *I topinambur al pomodoro*, *Fagiolini verdi e carote stufati con mortadella* or *Zucchine trifolate con le cipolle*.

Ossobuchi in bianco

BRAISED SHIN OF VEAL

Unlike the classic Milanese recipe for *ossobuco*, these veal shins are cooked without vegetables or tomatoes. This is why they are called *in bianco*, a term universally used in Italian cooking for juices or sauces that are not tinged with tomato and are therefore 'white'.

These are cut a little thinner than the Milanese shins, about 25 to 37 mm (1 to $1\frac{1}{2}$ inches). They cook at slow heat entirely on top of the stove, until they are tender enough to be cut with a fork. The pan juices are fragrantly deglazed at the end with lemon peel and parsley. As with all shin of veal recipes, try to get the hind shin, which is meatier and far more tender. They should be cooked in a pan that can contain them in a single layer, each slice resting flat on the bottom of the pan. If you do not have a single pan large enough, use two smaller ones (and refer to page 13 for suggestions on how to divide the ingredients).

The ideal accompaniment for these *ossobuchi* is *Puré di patate* (*The Classic Italian Cookbook*, page 329).

For six

$\frac{1}{3}$ cup olive oil
60 g (2 oz) butter
2 hind shins of veal, sawed into slices no more than 37 mm ($1\frac{1}{2}$ inches) thick, skin left on (this makes approximately 10 slices)
125 g ($4\frac{1}{2}$ oz) plain flour, spread on a dish
Salt
Freshly ground black pepper
325 ml ($\frac{5}{8}$ pint) dry white wine
2 tablespoons lemon peel chopped very fine, with none of the white pith attached
5 tablespoons parsley, chopped fine

1 Heat up the oil and butter in a large sauté pan over medium-high heat.
2 Dredge all the veal slices in the flour, on both sides. When the butter foam begins to subside, put them into the pan. They may fit snugly, but without overlapping, in a single layer.
3 Brown the meat well on both sides. Season liberally with salt and freshly ground pepper, and turn the shin slices over once. Add the white wine, and cover the pan tightly. Turn the heat down so that the juices in the pan bubble lazily at the gentlest of simmers. The meat must cook very slowly, until it becomes tender – about 2 to $2\frac{1}{2}$ hours.
4 After 10 or 15 minutes, when there is very little liquid in the pan, add 6 tablespoons warm water. Check the pan from time to time, and add more warm water as needed.
5 The meat is done when it comes away from the bone and is tender enough to be cut with a fork. When done, transfer the shins to a warm dish.
6 Put the lemon peel and chopped parsley into the pan, and turn up the heat to medium. Cook for about a minute, stirring with a wooden spoon and scraping loose any cooking residue stuck to the pan. Boil down any excess liquid.
7 Return the slices of shin to the pan and very briefly turn them in the pan juices. Serve at once with all the pan juices poured over them.

Note This dish may be made in advance but, like all veal dishes, *ossobuco* dries out when reheated. However, if necessary, it can be made earlier the same day that it will be served and does not need to be refrigerated. I would not encourage anyone to cook it a day or two in advance and keep it in the refrigerator. Reheat *ossobuco* in the same pan it was cooked in, covered, over low heat, for 10 or 15 minutes, until the meat is warmed all the way through. If the juices in the pan are not sufficient for reheating, add 1 or 2 tablespoons warm water.

MENU SUGGESTIONS

To begin: *Maccheroncini alla saffi*, *Le piccagge col pesto di ricotta*, *Tortelloni di biete* (from my first book, page 140), or *I pizzoccheri*. With the veal: *Cavolfiore fritto con la pastella di parmigiano*, *Porri al burro e formaggio* or *Crocchette di patate alla romagnola*.

Spiedini all' uccelletto

SKEWERED VEAL AND SAUSAGE WITH SAGE AND WHITE WINE

These are called *all' uccelletto* in Italian because they are done the way one roasts *uccelletti*, little birds: with *pancetta* and sage. The skewered meat is browned in a pan, then cooked with white wine. The deglazed cooking juices at the end provide just a spoonful or two of sauce for each skewer.

Many cooks use liver along with the veal, which adds a nice gamy flavour, but by the time the veal is done the liver is usually dried out and tough. Instead of liver, I like sausage, which contributes its share of tastiness to the dish and turns out perfectly cooked.

The happiest end for these 'birds' would be to rest them upon a bed of polenta; but a plain rice pilaf would do very nicely too.

For six

660 g ($1\frac{1}{4}$ lb) mild sausage, such as *luganega*, cut into pieces 37 mm ($1\frac{1}{2}$ inches) long
20 whole sage leaves, preferably fresh
450 g (1 lb) veal, all solid meat, preferably from the leg, cut into 37-mm ($1\frac{1}{2}$-inch) cubes
225 g (8 oz) *pancetta* in a single slice, unrolled and cut into pieces 37 mm ($1\frac{1}{2}$ inches) long
Approximately 12 skewers, not more than 150 to 200 mm (6 to 8 inches) long
3 tablespoons vegetable oil
12 tablespoons dry white wine

1 Alternate the meat on the skewers in the following sequence: 1 piece of sausage, 1 sage leaf, 1 piece of veal, 1 piece of *pancetta*. As you get to the end you may run short of some of the ingredients, but make sure there is at least one of each of them on every skewer. If using dried sage, do not attempt to skewer it because it will crumble. Put it in loose in the pan later.

2 Choose a 225- to 280-mm (9- to 11-inch) sauté pan, depending on the length of the skewers. Put in the oil, and turn on the heat to medium. When the oil is hot, slip the skewers (and the dried sage if you are using it) into the pan. Brown the meat well on all sides. If the skewers will not all fit into the pan at the same time, put in as many as will fit without overlapping; brown those, then remove them, and finish the rest.

3 Return all the browned meat to the pan. Add the wine, and turn up the heat to high for just a few seconds. When the wine begins to bubble, reduce the heat to minimum and cover the pan.

4 Cook for about 25 minutes, turning the skewers from time to time. They are done as soon as the veal is tender when pricked with a fork. Should there be any liquid in the pan, apart from the fat, uncover, turn up the heat, and boil it away.

5 Transfer the skewers to a warm dish with a slotted spoon or spatula. Tip the pan slightly, and with a spoon remove all but about 3 tablespoons fat. Pour 6 tablespoons water into the pan, and boil it away over medium heat while scraping loose with a wooden spoon the cooking residue from the bottom of the pan. Pour the sauce over the skewers, and serve at once.

MENU SUGGESTIONS

A first course of *Zuppa di riso col cavolo stufato*, *Spaghetti col sugo di cipolle*, or *Penne con spinaci e ricotta*. Accompany the *Spiedini* with *Cavolo stufato alla veneziana*, *Carote con i capperi* or *Patate alla boscaiola*.

Bocconcini di vitello ai sapori e funghi

BRAISED HERB-FLAVOURED VEAL MORSELS WITH MUSHROOMS

This is a stew with a fine bouquet of flavours. In it one finds garlic, rosemary, sage, and parsley, and they produce a stew that is less subdued, more aromatic than the ones we usually make with veal. There is also white wine, which is customary, and there are tomatoes, which are less so.

When the stew is nearly done, it is mixed with sautéed fresh mushrooms, whose light, almost neutral taste pleasantly adjusts the balance of flavours in the dish.

For six

45 g ($1\frac{1}{2}$ oz) butter
2 tablespoons vegetable oil
680 g ($1\frac{1}{2}$ lb) shoulder of veal, cut into 37 mm ($1\frac{1}{2}$-inch) cubes
1 onion, chopped fine
1 large clove garlic, peeled and chopped fine
1 tablespoon plain flour
8 tablespoons dry white wine
110 g (4 oz) tinned Italian plum tomatoes, cut up, with their juice
1 or 2 sprigs fresh rosemary or 1 teaspoon chopped dried rosemary
4 or 5 fresh sage leaves or 2 or 3 dried whole leaves
2 tablespoons chopped parsley
Salt
Freshly ground black pepper
225 g (8 oz) fresh, firm mushrooms

For sautéing the mushrooms

15 g ($\frac{1}{2}$ oz) butter
1 tablespoon vegetable oil

1 Choose a sauté pan that can contain all the meat and mushrooms together. Put in the butter and oil, and turn on the heat to medium. When the butter foam begins to subside, put in the meat and, raising the heat to high, brown the pieces evenly on all sides. (If all the veal does not fit loosely in the pan at one time, do it in batches, removing each batch from the pan as it is done. When every piece has been browned, put them all back into the pan.)

2 Add the chopped onion and garlic, and cook, stirring frequently, until they are lightly coloured.

3 Sprinkle the flour over the contents of the pan, and stir thoroughly, always at high heat, for 30 or 40 seconds.

4 Add the white wine, stir, and let it bubble away for a few seconds.

5 Add the chopped tomatoes with their juice, 225 ml (scant $\frac{1}{2}$ pint) water, rosemary, sage, parsley, about 3 large pinches of salt, and a few grindings of pepper. Turn the heat down to medium low, and cover the pan. Cook at a very gentle simmer, stirring occasionally, for 1 hour, or until the meat is tender enough to be cut with a fork.

6 While the meat is cooking, prepare the mushrooms. Wash them rapidly in cold water, dry them thoroughly with kitchen paper, and cut them into irregular 12-mm ($\frac{1}{2}$-inch) pieces.

7 In a frying pan just large enough to contain the mushrooms in a single layer, heat up 15 g ($\frac{1}{2}$ oz) butter and the tablespoon of oil over medium heat.

When the butter foam begins to subside, add the mushrooms, and raise the heat to high. Sprinkle lightly with salt and pepper.

8 Cook the mushrooms at very lively heat, turning them frequently. As soon as they stop throwing off liquid, and the liquid they have lost has evaporated from the frying pan, they are ready to be added to the pan where the veal is cooking. Do not add the mushrooms to the meat until it has cooked for at least 30 minutes. In fact, they can be added when the meat has almost finished cooking, and has only 5 or 10 minutes to go. When you put the mushrooms in, mix them thoroughly with the contents of the pan. Serve at once when the meat is done.

Note The entire dish may be prepared several hours in advance on the same day that it is to be consumed. It makes a very good dish for a buffet.

MENU SUGGESTIONS

To begin: *Risotto col sedano*, *Penne con spinaci e ricotta*, or *Tonnarelli col rosmarino*. It is not necessary to have a vegetable accompaniment, but if you were to have one, an agreeable choice would be *Fiori di broccoli fritti*, *Porri al burro e formaggio*, or *Zucchine trifolate con le cipolle*.

Rotolo di vitello con spinaci

VEAL AND SPINACH ROLL

The stuffing for this rolled roast of veal is a classic one of spinach sautéed with onion and *pancetta* or prosciutto. It is spread on the flat, thin veal like jam on a sponge roll; the meat is then tightly rolled up and slowly pan-roasted with a little white wine. At the end the pan juices are rounded out with some cream to make a few spoonfuls of sauce. When the roast is cut, the alternating layers of spinach and veal make a very attractive spiral pattern. It is juicy and tender, and tastes every bit as good as it looks.

Everything about this recipe is perfectly straightforward and simple but for one problem: getting a single slice of veal weighing 450 g (1 lb) cut or pounded to a thickness of no more than 10 mm ($\frac{3}{8}$ inch). (It works out to about 515 to 580 sq cm (80 or 90 sq inches) of meat.) The breast of veal, which works so well in other recipes (*The Classic Italian Cookbook*, page 215), does not lend itself easily to this one because it is uneven in thickness. What you need is a cooperative butcher to cut a large slice from the shoulder, the rump, or best of all, the top round. If you end up with two slices to make up the quantity you need, they can be tightly sewn, edge to edge, with thin trussing string. Not a very orthodox solution, but nonetheless a practical one.

For four

- 680 g ($1\frac{1}{2}$ lb) fresh spinach
- Salt
- 45 g ($1\frac{1}{2}$ oz) butter
- 2 tablespoons vegetable oil
- $\frac{1}{2}$ small onion, chopped fine
- 110 g (4 oz) *pancetta* or prosciutto or unsmoked bacon (see page 24), chopped very fine
- Freshly ground black pepper
- 450 g (1 lb) veal, in a single slice, cut or pounded to a thickness of no more than 10 mm ($\frac{3}{8}$ inch) (see introductory remarks above)
- 8 tablespoons dry white wine
- 6 tablespoons double cream

1 Pull the leaves from the spinach, discarding all the stems. Soak the spinach in a basin of cold water, dunking it several times with your hands. Carefully lift out the spinach, and pour out the water together with the sand that has settled to the bottom of the basin. Refill the basin with fresh cold water, and repeat the whole procedure, soaking the spinach, changing the water, until you see there is no more sand.

2 Cook the spinach in a covered pan, over medium heat, with a pinch of salt and just the water that clings to the leaves. Do not overcook; 2 or 3 minutes after the liquid they shed comes to the boil should be sufficient.

3 Drain, and as soon as the spinach has become cool enough to handle, squeeze as much moisture out of it as you can with your hands. Chop the spinach very fine, and set aside.

4 Put 15 g ($\frac{1}{2}$ oz) butter, 1 tablespoon oil, all the onion, and all the *pancetta* into a small sauté pan. Over medium heat, cook until the onion turns a rich golden brown.

5 Add the chopped spinach, salt, and 1 or 2 grindings of pepper. Cook for just 20 or 30 seconds, stirring constantly, then turn off the heat. Do not add any more butter or oil, even if it seems to be insufficient. It isn't.

6 Lay the veal flat on a work surface. Spread the spinach mixture over it, distributing it evenly. Check the way in which the grain of the meat runs; roll up the veal tightly, making sure the grain is parallel to the length of the roll. When you slice the roll after it has been cooked, you should be cutting across the grain to get even, compact slices. Tie the roll securely with kitchen string, in several places, like a salami.

7 Choose a pot in which the veal roll will fit snugly, preferably oval in

shape. Put in it the remaining butter and oil, and turn on the heat to medium high. As soon as the butter foam begins to subside, put in the veal roll and brown the meat well all over.

8 Add a little salt and pepper, turn the roll once or twice, then add all the wine. When the wine has bubbled away for half a minute or so, turn the heat down to low and cover the pot, with the lid slightly askew.

9 Turn the meat over from time to time. Cook for about 1½ hours, until the meat is tender when pricked with a fork. There should be no liquid left in the pot, except for some concentrated cooking juices.

10 Add the cream, turn up the heat, and loosen any residue from the bottom of the pan with a wooden spoon. Turn off the heat as soon as the cream thickens a little and colours a medium brown.

11 Transfer the meat to a chopping board or large dish. Cut it into thin slices and remove the trussing string. Arrange the slices on a serving dish, pour the sauce over them, and serve at once.

MENU SUGGESTIONS

Start with *Passatelli di carne in brodo*, *Conchiglie con bacon, piselli e ricotta* or, from my first book, *Gnocchi* with Tomato Sauce (page 167). To accompany the roast: *Funghi stufati*, *Cipolline stufate coi topinambur* or *Finocchi al burro e formaggio* (from *The Classic Italian Cookbook*, page 322).

Spalla di vitello brasata

BRAISED SHOULDER OF VEAL WITH WHITE WINE

This particularly tasty veal belongs to that vast international family of braised meat dishes known to nearly every home kitchen in Italy and France. The unique character of this recipe comes from the treatment of the vegetables and herbs, which are briskly sautéed instead of slowly wilted, and from browning the meat directly over the sautéed vegetables. The result is a more distinctive herbal and earthy flavour in the sauce and in the meat itself.

If you have a food processor, all the vegetables and herbs can be chopped very fine in it at one time.

For four to six

1 medium carrot, chopped fine
1 medium onion, chopped fine
50 g (1¾ oz) chopped celery root
½ teaspoon rosemary leaves, chopped fine
4 to 5 fresh sage leaves, chopped fine, or 3 dried whole sage leaves, crumbled fine
60 g (2 oz) butter
4 tablespoons vegetable oil
900 g to 1·1 kg (2 to 2½ lb) boneless shoulder of veal, rolled and securely tied
1 teaspoon strong Dijon mustard, dissolved in 225 ml (scant ½ pint) dry white wine
2 tinned Italian plum tomatoes, drained and chopped
Salt
Freshly ground black pepper

1 Preheat oven to 180°C/350°F/Mark 4.

2 Choose a heavy flameproof casserole, with a tight-fitting cover, that will contain the shoulder of veal snugly. Put in all the chopped vegetables and herbs, the butter and the oil. Place it over medium-high heat and cook, stirring frequently, until you find the fat has separated from the vegetables, and these have wilted and diminished in bulk.

3 Put the meat into the pot, and brown it well all over. Do not worry if the vegetables become deeply coloured, but do not let them burn.

4 Add the wine and mustard and the chopped tomatoes. Add salt and pepper liberally. When the liquids in the pot have begun to simmer, cover tightly and place in the middle of the preheated oven.

5 Cook for approximately 1¼ to 1½ hours, until the meat is very tender when pricked with a fork. Turn the meat every 15 or 20 minutes. If you find there is not enough cooking liquid in the pot, add 2 or 3 tablespoons warm water. When the meat is nearly done, if there is too much watery liquid in the pot, raise the temperature another 20°C/50°F for the last 10 or 15 minutes of cooking.

6 When done, place the meat on a chopping board, and cut it into thin slices. Arrange the slices, slightly overlapping, on a warm dish. Taste a little piece for seasoning and, if it lacks salt, add salt to the juices in the pot. Pour all the contents of the pot over the meat, and serve at once.

MENU SUGGESTIONS

Either of the two *lasagne* recipes on pages 151–4, or *Le pappardelle del Cantunzein*, would make a good beginning, or *Risotto con la luganega* (from my first book, page 161). Serve a mildly flavoured vegetable with the meat such as *Carciofini gratinati*, *Funghi fritti alla moda dei porcini* or *Zucchine trifolate con le cipolle*.

Punta di vitello arrosto

ROAST BREAST OF VEAL

If anyone still has doubts that the meat closest to the bone is the tastiest, this succulent breast of veal should provide all the proof necessary.

It is pan-roasted in the Italian manner, that is, very slowly, on top of the stove, with no other liquid than a small quantity of cooking fat, a little wine, and its own juices. It is far simpler to do than any of the stuffed dishes one usually makes with breast of veal, and it produces an impressive roast with a rich brown colour, and unbelievably tender, savoury meat. This particular dish does not call for a fancy grade of veal: the breast is a fairly inexpensive cut that most good supermarkets carry. This is a perfect example of what delectable results can be accomplished with modest materials and simple good cooking.

For four

30 g (1 oz) butter
2 tablespoons olive oil
3 whole cloves garlic, peeled
1 teaspoon dried rosemary leaves or 2 sprigs fresh rosemary
Salt
Freshly ground black pepper
12 tablespoons dry white wine
1·6 kg ($3\frac{1}{2}$ lb) breast of veal, in one piece, with bones in

1 Choose a sauté pan or flameproof casserole that will be able to contain the meat lying flat. Put in the butter, oil and garlic, and turn on the heat to medium.

2 When the butter foam begins to subside, put in the meat, with the skin side facing the bottom. Add the rosemary and brown the meat well on one side, then on the other.

3 Add salt and pepper, turn the meat two or three times, then add the white wine. Let the wine bubble away for about 1 minute, then turn the heat down to very low, and cover the pan, setting the lid slightly askew.

4 Turn the meat from time to time while it cooks. If you find it sticking, loosen it with the help of a tablespoon or two of water. Make sure you keep the heat low. The veal is done as soon as it is very tender when pricked with a fork, and has turned a lovely brown all over. It should take about 2 to $2\frac{1}{2}$ hours.

6 Tip the pan, and draw off most of the fat. Put in 2 or 3 tablespoons water, and, over medium heat, as the water boils away loosen the cooking residue from the bottom of the pan, scraping it with a wooden spoon.

7 Pour the pan juices over the meat, and bring to the table at once. Carve the meat into thin slices, cutting it on a slant, towards the bone.

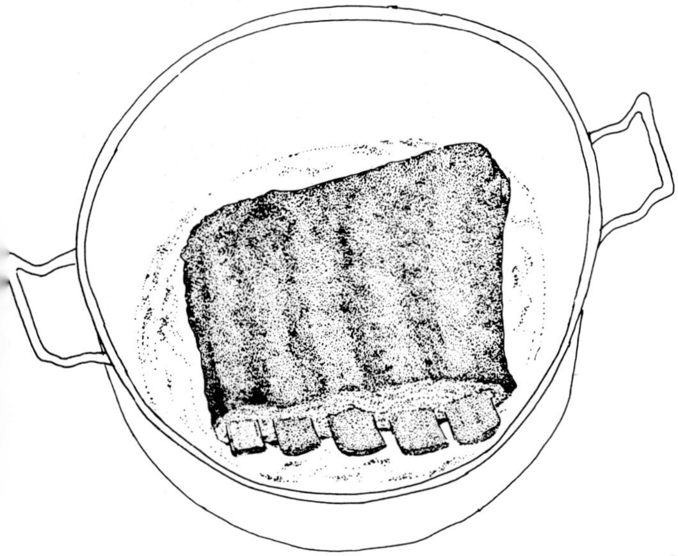

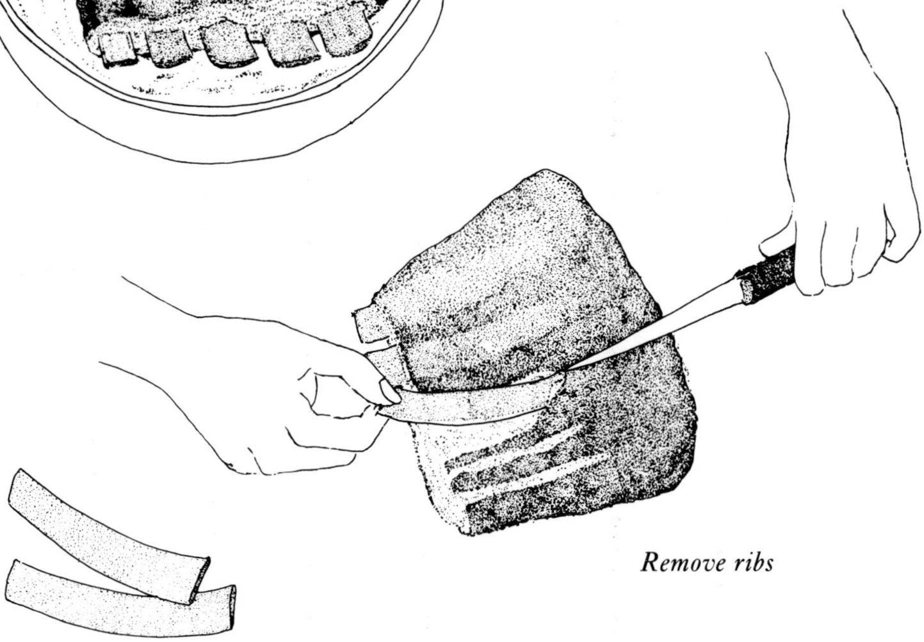

Remove ribs

MENU SUGGESTIONS

Any first course that does not have fish may precede this roast. An elegant and rich pasta would be particularly appropriate, such as *Maccheroncini alla saffi* or *Le lasagne coi carciofi*. The most suitable vegetable accompaniment would be a fried vegetable: *Topinambur fritti*, *Fiori di broccoli fritti*, *Cavolfiore fritto con la pastella di parmigiano*, *Funghi fritti alla moda dei porcini* or, from my first book, *Finocchi fritti* (page 324). Another nice vegetable would be *Porri al burro e formaggio*.

Agnello in fricassea

PAN-ROASTED LAMB CHOPS IN WHITE WINE WITH EGG AND LEMON SAUCE

This lamb, like the chicken fricassee on page 262, is finished with an uncooked coating of beaten egg and lemon, which thickens on contact with the hot meat.

The preliminary precedure is the slow-cooked Italian pan-roasting method, in which the meat is first browned, then cooked with the minimum amount of liquid to keep it going, in this case, white wine and the meat's own fat and juices.

If you have become tired of grilling lamb chops, this is a dish you will enjoy cooking – and eating.

For four

2 medium onions, sliced very thin
45 g (1½ oz) *pancetta*, cut into thin strips, or smoked bacon (but only if *pancetta* is absolutely unobtainable)
15 g (½ oz) lard (vegetable oil may be substituted, but lard produces a finer, lighter flavour)
4 loin lamb chops, about 1·1 kg (2½ lb)
⅛ teaspoon grated nutmeg
Salt
Freshly ground black pepper
8 tablespoons home-made meat broth (see page 18) or ½ bouillon cube dissolved in 8 tablespoons warm water
225 ml (scant ½ pint) dry white wine
1 egg yolk
2 tablespoons lemon juice

1 Choose a sauté pan that can contain all the chops in a single layer. Put in the onion, *pancetta*, and lard, and cook over medium heat.

2 When the onion has coloured lightly, add the lamb chops, and raise the heat to medium high. Brown the chops well on both sides. The onion will turn deep brown, but should not turn black.

3 Add the nutmeg, 3 large pinches of salt, a liberal grinding of pepper, and the broth. Let the broth bubble away until it evaporates; scrape loose any cooking residue stuck to the bottom of the pan, and turn the chops over once.

4 Put in the white wine, turn the heat down to medium low, and cover the pan, setting the lid slightly askew. Cook at gentle heat for about 1½ hours, until the meat of the chops is very tender.

5 When done, the chops will have shed much of their fat, which you will find, liquefied, floating on top. Tip the pan, and, with a spoon, draw off and discard all but about 2 tablespoons of it.

6 In a small bowl, lightly beat the egg yolk with the lemon juice. Pour this over the chops, off the heat, turning the chops so they become coated on both sides with sauce. Serve at once.

Note The egg and lemon must be added just before serving, while the meat is still hot, but *off the heat*. If the chops have cooled before you are ready to add the sauce, warm them up slowly in their cooking juices, turn off the heat, and finish them with the sauce.

MENU SUGGESTIONS

A first course of *Risotto primavera*, *Maccheroncini alla boscaiola* or *Tonnarelli col rosmarino*. To accompany the meat: *Fettine croccanti di melanzana*, *Carciofini fritti* (from my first book, page 294), or *Zucchine fritte con la pastella* (from my first book, page 337). Any fried vegetable will be a good choice.

Stufatino di agnello con l'aceto

LAMB STEW WITH VINEGAR AND FRENCH BEANS

Of all meat dishes, I think I get most pleasure from a good stew, and this is one of my favourites. As in all proper stews, the meat becomes succulently tender, but it has something more – a very fresh and lively taste that comes from the vinegar and the long, slow cooking with French beans. It transforms shoulder of lamb into a fine, sprightly dish that should appeal even to those who are not usually fond of lamb.

For four to six

½ onion, chopped
6 tablespoons olive oil
900 g (2 lb) boned shoulder of lamb, cut into 37- to 50-mm (1½- to 2-inch) cubes
Salt
Freshly ground black pepper
8 tablespoons good wine vinegar
450 g (1 lb) fresh French beans, ends snapped off, and rinsed in cold water

1 Choose a flameproof casserole that will later be able to contain all the meat and French beans. Put in the chopped onion and olive oil, and sauté over medium-high heat.

2 When the onion turns pale gold, put in as many pieces of lamb as will fit comfortably without crowding. Turn up the heat, and brown the meat on all sides. When the meat has been nicely browned, remove it, and add the pieces that remain to be done.

3 When all the meat has been well browned, put it all back into the casserole. Add salt, pepper, and the vinegar, and raise the heat to maximum high. Stir for about 45 seconds, then turn the heat down to very low.

4 Add the French beans, and a little more salt and pepper, and cover the casserole. Cook at a very gentle simmer for about $1\frac{1}{2}$ to 2 hours, or until the meat is very tender when pricked with a fork. It should not be necessary to add any liquid, but if you find at some point that there are not enough juices left for the meat to continue cooking without sticking, add a little warm water, up to 4 tablespoons. Bear in mind, however, that at the end the natural cooking juices and the oil should be the only liquids in the casserole.

5 Serve at once directly from the casserole, or transfer to a warm serving dish.

Note The entire dish may be prepared in advance and reheated, but the flavour will be best protected if it is done within the same day, and not refrigerated.

MENU SUGGESTIONS

Begin with *Spinaci e riso in brodo*, *Spaghetti alla carbonara* or *Penne col sugo di cavolfiore*. Follow with a salad of *Rape rosse al forno*, *Le patate in insalata* or any raw greens.

Spezzato d'agnello con peperone e prosciutto

LAMB STEW WITH WHITE WINE, HAM, AND PEPPER

Like most Italian stews, this one starts out with meat browned in hot fat, then cooked slowly in its own juices and a little wine. It has a refreshingly different ending, where raw sweet pepper and strips of ham are added to the stew when it has already become tender. The cooking continues just long enough to soften the pepper while retaining the freshness of its fragrance. A very pleasing final balance results between the vivacity of the recently added peppers and ham, and the long-steeped herb-enriched flavours of the meat.

For four to five

900 g (2 lb) boneless lamb, from the shoulder, neck, or shin
6 tablespoons vegetable oil
2 medium cloves garlic, peeled
½ teaspoon rosemary
4 or 5 fresh sage leaves, or 2 or 3 dried whole sage leaves
8 tablespoons dry white wine
Salt
Freshly ground black pepper
1 red or green pepper
110 g (4 oz) boiled unsmoked ham, cut into thin strips

1 Cut the lamb into cube-like pieces about 37 to 50 mm (1½ to 2 inches) on a side.

2 Put the oil, garlic, rosemary, sage leaves, and lamb pieces into a sauté pan. Over medium-high heat, cook for about 15 minutes, turning the lamb pieces, until these are nicely browned on all sides.

3 Add the white wine, turning the heat to high. Let the wine bubble for a few seconds, while you turn the lamb. Turn the heat down to medium low, add 3 or 4 large pinches of salt, a liberal grinding of pepper, and cover the pan. Set the cover slightly askew.

4 Cook for 1 hour to 1 hour 15 minutes, until the meat is tender and the wine has evaporated. Turn the meat from time to time. If you find that all the liquid has evaporated before the lamb is done, add a couple of tablespoons water.

5 While the lamb is cooking, strip the pepper of its skin, using a swivel-action potato peeler and a light hand. Split the pepper open, remove and discard all the seeds and pulpy core, and cut it into stubby strips, about 12 mm (½ inch) wide and 37 mm (1½ inches) long.

6 When the lamb is tender when pricked with a fork and the wine has evaporated, add the strips of pepper and ham to the pan. Cover, and cook for an additional 15 minutes or so, until the pepper is tender. If, at this point, the moisture from the pepper has thinned out the cooking juices in the pan, uncover, raise the heat, and boil away the excess liquid. Transfer all the contents of the pan to a warm serving dish and serve at once.

MENU SUGGESTIONS

A first course of *Riso con la verza*, *Le piccagge col pesto di ricotta* or

Tonnarelli col rosmarino. No vegetable accompaniment. Follow with a salad of *Rape rosse al forno; Le patate in insalata;* or *Finocchio in insalata* (from my first book, page 350).

Costolette di maiale con i funghi

BRAISED PORK CHOPS WITH MUSHROOMS

There is no better way to cook pork than to braise it, and Italian cooks are unsurpassed masters of the art. Two of their most successful methods are to cook it with white wine and tomatoes, and to cook it with milk. This recipe combines both, except that cream takes the place of milk. The result is a truly succulent dish of chops. They are served with sautéed mushrooms, which sit well with pork, and this happy alliance is further enhanced by the redolent earthy fragrance of dried wild boletus mushrooms.

For four

30 g (1 oz) dried imported boletus mushrooms
6 tablespoons vegetable oil
900 g (2 lb) pork chops, preferably middle loin, cut 12 mm ($\frac{1}{2}$ inch) thick
8 tablespoons dry white wine
110 g (4 oz) tinned Italian plum tomatoes, seeded but not mashed, and drained
8 tablespoons double cream
Salt
Freshly ground black pepper
225 g (8 oz) fresh, firm mushrooms

1 Soak the dried mushrooms at least 30 minutes in advance in a bowl with 450 ml ($\frac{3}{4}$ pint) warm water. Proceed to rinse them and to filter the water, as described on page 191. Cut up the mushrooms in large pieces, and set aside. Also set the filtered water aside.

2 Choose a sauté pan large enough to contain the chops in a single layer, put in 3 tablespoons vegetable oil and turn on the heat to medium high.

3 When the oil is hot, slip the chops into the pan, and brown them well, first on one side, then on the other.

4 Add the white wine, and let it bubble for just a few seconds.

5 Add the tomatoes, cream, 2 or 3 large pinches of salt, a liberal grinding of pepper, and the cut-up reconstituted wild mushrooms. Turn the heat

down to medium low. When the liquid settles to a gentle simmer, cover the pan.

6 Cook for 45 minutes to 1 hour, depending on the thickness and quality of the chops, until the meat is very tender when pricked with a fork. Turn the chops from time to time.

7 While the chops are cooking, put the reserved filtered mushroom water in a small saucepan, and boil it down to about 6 tablespoons.

8 Rinse the fresh mushrooms rapidly under cold running water. Wipe them thoroughly dry with a soft cloth or kitchen paper, then cut them into very thin slices lengthways, without detaching the caps from the stems.

9 Choose a sauté pan in which the mushrooms will fit without being too tightly packed. Put in the remaining 3 tablespoons oil, and turn on the heat to high.

10 When the oil is hot, put in the mushrooms. Stir them frequently, adding a little salt and pepper. When the liquid they throw off has boiled away, add the reduced water from the wild mushrooms. Continue stirring. When all the liquid has evaporated, turn off the heat.

11 When the pork chops are tender, add all the mushrooms to their pan. Turn the chops, stir the mushrooms in the sauce, and cover the pan. Cook for another 5 to 8 minutes at medium-low heat, turning the chops from time to time. Serve at once.

MENU SUGGESTIONS

Begin with *Risotto col sedano*, *Fettuccine con le zucchine fritte*, or *Fettuccine al gorgonzola* (from my first book, page 114). With the chops: *Coste di biete saltate* or *Cavolfiore fritto con la pastella di parmigiano*.

Costolette di maiale alla modenese

PORK CHOPS, BRAISED WITH SAGE AND TOMATOES, FROM MODENA

Modena is celebrated for two things: pork products and fast cars. While a Maserati may not always come out on top, the Modenese touch with pork can't be beaten. The recipe is one of the simplest and tastiest ways of doing pork chops I've ever found. As with all recipes that call for sage (see page 23), if you are using dried sage, sniff it first. If it is very pungent, cut down on the quantity; if bland, use a little more.

For four

30 g (1 oz) butter
1 tablespoon vegetable oil
4 pork loin chops, preferably end loin, 12 mm (½ inch) thick
60 g (2 oz) plain flour, spread on a dish
6 to 8 fresh sage leaves or 3 or 4 whole dried leaves
Salt
Freshly ground black pepper
180 g (6 oz) tinned Italian plum tomatoes, cut up, with their juice

1 In a sauté pan just large enough to contain the chops later without overlapping them, heat up all the butter and oil over medium-high heat.

2 Dredge the chops in flour on both sides. When the butter foam begins to subside, put in the chops and the sage.

3 Brown the chops nicely on each side for about 2 minutes.

4 Add 2 or 3 pinches of salt, a grinding of pepper, and the chopped tomatoes with their juice. Cover the pan, turn the heat down to medium low, and cook for about 1 hour, or until the meat is tender when pricked with a fork. The sauce should be quite dense. If it is not, turn up the heat for a few moments and reduce it rapidly.

5 Tip the pan, and with a spoon remove all but about 1 tablespoon of fat. Serve at once.

MENU SUGGESTIONS

Begin with *Zuppa dei poveri con la rucola*, *Spaghetti alla carbonara* or *Penne col sugo di cavolfiore*. Avoid any first courses with tomato sauce. To accompany the chops: *Funghi fritti alla moda dei porcini* or *Patate alla boscaiola*.

Costolette di maiale ai due vini

PORK CHOPS BRAISED WITH MARSALA AND RED WINE

Pork will take kindly to almost any treatment except fast cooking. Here loin chops are braised in a mixture of two wines, a young red wine and Marsala. The aromatic intensity of Marsala is balanced by the vivacity of the red wine, producing a flavour that is both rich and lively. The pork takes beautifully to it. Any decent red wine will do for this, but for the most interesting results it would be desirable to have the tartness of a young, firm wine. A good Barbera from Piedmont, such as Barbera d'Asti, would be perfect.

I like pork to cook a long, slow time, until the meat falls easily off the bone. How long, however, depends on the quality of the pork. Here, as elsewhere, it is a good idea not to leave all the decisions to the timer, but to test the meat from time to time and make up your own mind when it is ready.

For four

4 tablespoons olive oil
15 g (½ oz) butter
4 pork loin chops, about 18 to 25 mm (¾ to 1 inch) thick
60 g (2 oz) plain flour, spread on a plate
1½ cloves garlic, peeled and chopped
1 tablespoon tomato purée, dissolved in 8 tablespoons dry Marsala and 8 tablespoons young red wine (see introductory remarks above)
Salt
Freshly ground black pepper
¼ teaspoon fennel seeds
1 tablespoon chopped parsley

1 In a sauté pan able to contain all the chops in a single layer, put in the oil and butter, and turn on the heat to medium.

2 Pat the chops with kitchen paper to absorb any dampness. Dredge them in flour on both sides, giving them a tap to shake off excess flour.

3 When the butter foam in the pan begins to subside, slip in the chops. Brown them well on both sides.

4 Add the garlic, but do not let it rest on top of the meat, stir it into the cooking fat. When the garlic has turned light gold, add the mixture of the 2 wines with the dissolved tomato purée. Season with 2 or 3 large pinches of salt and a liberal grinding of pepper. Add the fennel seeds.

5 When the wine has bubbled away for about 1 minute, cover the pan tightly, and turn the heat down to minimum.

6 Cook for about 1 hour, or until the meat is very tender. Turn over the chops from time to time. When nearly done, add the parsley, mixing it into the cooking juices, and turn the chops.

7 Transfer the chops to a warm dish. Tip the pan, and remove all but 2 or 3 tablespoonfuls fat, drawing it off with a spoon or small ladle.

8 Add 6 tablespoons water to the pan, and turn up the heat to high. Boil away the water while scraping loose with a wooden spoon any cooking residue stuck to the bottom of the pan. When you have a small amount of dense, dark sauce, pour it over the meat, and serve at once.

MENU SUGGESTIONS

Start off with *Zuppa di riso col cavolo stufato*, *Risotto primavera* or *Fusilli alla pappone* (from my first book, page 90). Accompany the meat with *La frittedda* or *Coste di biete saltate*.

Arrosto di maiale ubriaco

DRUNK ROAST PORK

This 'tipsy' pork loin braises slowly in enough wine to cover it. It becomes extraordinarily tender, and acquires, when done, a beautiful dark, deep mahogany colour. It is, of course, perfectly safe to serve to children, since the alcohol completely evaporates in cooking.

For six

3 medium carrots
1·1 kg (2½ lb) boned pork loin
1 tablespoon vegetable oil
2 tablespoons butter
15 g (½ oz) plain flour, spread on wax paper or on a large plate
2 tablespoons *grappa* or good dry grape brandy
350 ml (⅔ pint) Barbera or other sturdy dry red wine
⅛ teaspoon nutmeg
2 bayleaves
Salt
Freshly ground black pepper

1 Peel and wash the carrots, and cut them lengthways into sticks a little less than 12 mm (½ inch) thick.

2 Tie up the pork loin tightly, and fasten securely in several places with cotton twine.

3 Take a long, pointed, and fairly thick tool, such as a meat probe, a knife-sharpening steel, or a heavy chopstick, and pierce the meat in several places at both ends. Keep the holes about 37 mm ($1\frac{1}{2}$ inches) apart and parallel. Stuff carrot sticks into every hole. (**Note** This adds to the visual appeal of the roast when it is sliced, but if you have problems with it, you can omit the step and put the carrots directly into the pot.)

4 Choose a braising pot or flameproof casserole, possibly oval in shape, just large enough to contain the meat later. Put in the oil and butter and turn on the heat to medium high.

5 Dredge the meat in the flour, and when the butter foam in the pot begins to subside, put in the meat. As it browns in one spot turn it until it is well browned all over.

6 Add the *grappa*. After a few seconds, when it has boiled away, pour in the wine. There should be enough wine nearly to cover the meat. If 350 ml ($\frac{2}{3}$ pint) is not enough, add more.

7 Add the nutmeg, bayleaves, several large pinches of salt, and a liberal grinding of pepper. Give the meat one or two turns. When the wine comes to the boil, turn the heat down to minimum, and cover the pot tightly, placing a double sheet of aluminium foil between the lid and the pot. Cook at very slow heat for at least 3 hours, occasionally turning the meat.

8 After $2\frac{1}{2}$ hours' cooking, check to see how much liquid there is left. If there is a substantial amount, remove the foil, set the lid slightly askew and raise the heat slightly.

9 The meat is done when it is very tender when prodded with a fork. It will be quite dark, and there will be a small quantity of dense, syrupy sauce. Cut the meat into thin slices and arrange them so they slightly overlap on a warm serving dish. Spoon all the sauce over them, along with any bits of carrot that may have slipped out while slicing the meat. Serve at once.

MENU SUGGESTIONS

A first course of *Rigatoni alla napoletana coi peperoni freschi*, *I pizzoccheri* or, from my first book, *Paglia e fieno alla ghiotta* (page 112). To go with the roast: *Carciofini gratinati* or *Asparagi e funghi passati al burro*.

Stufatino di maiale alla boscaiola

BRAISED PORK WITH WILD MUSHROOMS AND JUNIPER BERRIES

This tender, savoury pork is a veritable anthology of fragrances from the woods and the herb garden: wild mushrooms, juniper, marjoram, bay. When I first tried it, over *polenta*, it reminded me of the great game and *polenta* feasts we used to have on the Lago di Garda, when I was in my teens.

The cooking method here is that of a classic braised pot roast, except that the meat is cut into stewing-sized pieces. There is very little for the cook to do, beyond getting all the ingredients into the pot and waiting for the meat to become tender. Although this is a delicious enough dish on its own, it is absolute perfection when served on a bed of steaming *polenta* (see *The Classic Italian Cookbook*, page 175).

The best part of the pig for this recipe is the hand.

For four

25 to 30 g (¾ to 1 oz) imported dried wild mushrooms
½ small onion, chopped fine
6 tablespoons olive oil
680 g (1½ lb) boned hand of pork, cut into pieces about 25 mm (1 inch) thick and 50 mm (2 inches) square
8 tablespoons dry white wine
2 tablespoons good wine vinegar
3 flat anchovy fillets, chopped
¼ teaspoon marjoram
1 or 2 bayleaves, chopped if fresh, crumbled if dried
20 juniper berries, crushed with a mallet or meat pounder
Salt
Freshly ground black pepper

1 Soak the mushrooms for 30 minutes or more in a small bowl with 350 ml (⅔ pint) lukewarm water. When they have finished soaking, carefully lift out the mushrooms without disturbing the water. Rinse them in several changes of cold water to rid them of any grit still clinging to them. Chop them into not too fine pieces, and set aside. Filter the water in which they have soaked through a fine wire strainer lined with kitchen paper, and reserve.

2 Choose a sauté pan or flameproof casserole that can later contain all the meat in no more than two layers, put in the onion and oil, and cook over medium heat.

3 When the onion becomes translucent, put in the pork. Turn the heat up to medium high, and brown the pieces of meat all over.

4 Put in the wine and the vinegar, raise the heat a little, and let them bubble away for a minute or two.

5 Put in the chopped mushrooms, their strained water, the chopped anchovies, the marjoram, the bayleaves and the crushed juniper berries. Stir all the contents of the pan, and turn the heat down to low. Put in 2 or 3 healthy pinches of salt, a liberal grinding of pepper, stir again, and cover the pan tightly.

6 Cook at a very gentle simmer for $1\frac{1}{2}$ to 2 hours, or until the meat is tender when pricked with a fork.

7 When the meat is done, if the juices in the pan are thin and runny, uncover, and turn up the heat to medium high. Reduce the juices until the fat separates from them.

8 Transfer the meat to a warm dish. If there is an excessive amount of fat in the pan, tip it slightly and draw off the excess fat with a ladle or spoon. Pour the juices and all the contents of the pan over the meat, and serve at once.

MENU SUGGESTIONS

If serving with *polenta*, instead of a pasta, precede with slices of prosciutto and melon, or, from my first book, *Carciofi alla romana* (page 286). Otherwise, you could start with *Zuppa di riso e cavolo rapa*, *Conchiglie con bacon, piselli e ricotta* or *Le lasagne col carciofi*. Accompany with *Porri al burro e formaggio*, *Fiori di broccoli fritti*, or other fried vegetables.

Costicine di maiale ai ferri

GRILLED MARINATED SPARERIBS

In Italy there are farmhouses, now become restaurants, whose fare consists of stout country soups or hand-made pasta, salamis and hams cured in their own attics, and assorted meats grilled or spit-roasted over wood fires. There, and perhaps nowhere else, you would be likely to have these spareribs. They are remarkably good because grilling quickly drains them of fat, and crisps the meat, giving it a leaner, fresher taste than other methods of cooking ribs.

The ideal way to do them would be on a spit. I do not have one, but I have found a first-rate substitute in a V-shaped roasting rack with sides that tilt and adjust to any angle. Placed over the grilling pan, it works somewhat like a spit, because it lets air circulate all around the meat. I am not gadget-minded, but I love this rack. Cradle racks, with detachable sloping sides, are inexpensive, and if you do much roasting, it is one of the most helpful things one can have.

These ribs are first marinated in olive oil, garlic, and rosemary. Allow at least 1 hour for the flavours of the marinade to sink into the meat, then another 25 minutes for cooking. Ribs should be juicy but well done.

For four

6 tablespoons olive oil
3 cloves garlic, peeled and chopped very fine
1 tablespoon rosemary, chopped fine
Salt
Freshly ground black pepper
1·35-kg (3-lb) rack of pork spareribs, in one piece
A roasting spit or a V-shaped (or cradle) roasting rack

1 Put the olive oil, garlic, rosemary, a liberal amount of salt and freshly ground pepper into a small bowl, and beat together very briefly with a fork.

2 Put the spareribs on a dish, and pour the marinade over them, rubbing it over the meat with your fingertips, or brushing it on with a pastry brush. Allow to stand at room temperature for at least 1 hour.

3 Turn on the grill 15 minutes before starting to cook, placing the grilling pan 175 to 225 mm (7 to 9 inches) away from the source of heat.

4 Put the V-shaped or cradle roasting rack on the grilling pan. Place the meat in it, adjusting the angle of the side grills so that air circulates freely all round the ribs. (Or position the ribs on your spit, if you have one.) Brush the meat with any of the marinade left in the dish, slide the meat under the grill, and cook for about 25 minutes. Turn the meat every 6 minutes.

5 Serve piping hot.

MENU SUGGESTIONS

A good beginning would be *Minestrone alla novarese*, *Riso con la verza*, *Spaghetti alla carbonara*, or *I pizzoccheri*. Accompany the spareribs with *Sedano in umido*, *Broccoli stufati al vino rosso* or *Zucchine saltate all'origano*.

Costicine di maiale alla trevigiana

PAN-ROASTED SPARERIBS FROM TREVISO

This is a more succulent, more expansive way of doing spareribs than the preceding recipe but I have no favourite; sometimes I prefer the one, sometimes the other. A little fickleness is a good thing in the kitchen; it does away with monotony.

Here the ribs are browned in hot oil, then cooked with garlic, sage, and white wine. They are pan-roasted, that is, slow-cooked in a covered pan without other liquid. They are served with the degreased cooking juices over polenta or mashed potatoes. This deeply warming, most satisfying dish is a speciality of *la cucina trevigiana.* I was given the recipe by my assistant, Maria Daffré, a rather special product of Treviso herself.

For four

- 8 tablespoons vegetable oil
- 1·35-kg (3-lb) rack of spareribs, cut into single ribs
- 3 cloves garlic, peeled and sliced very thin
- 2 tablespoons chopped fresh sage or 2 teaspoons chopped dried whole sage leaves
- 225 ml (scant ½ pint) dry white wine
- Salt
- Freshly ground black pepper

1 In a sauté pan large enough to contain all the spareribs without crowding, heat the oil over medium-high heat.

2 When the oil is hot, put in the spareribs and brown them on all sides.

3 Add the garlic and the sage. When the garlic colours lightly, add the wine, raise the heat and let the wine bubble away for a few seconds.

4 Moderate the heat, add salt and a liberal sprinkling of pepper, and cover the pan. Cook for about 40 minutes, turning the ribs from time to time, until the fleshiest part of the ribs is tender.

5 When done, transfer the spareribs to a warm dish. Tilt the pan and remove about one third of the fat. Leave more fat than you usually would when degreasing because you will need it to season the *polenta* or mashed potatoes that should accompany the spareribs. Add 8 tablespoons water and, over high heat, scrape loose the cooking residue from the bottom of the pan while boiling away the liquid. You should end up with a dark, dense sauce. Pour it through a strainer over the spareribs. Serve at once with *polenta* (page 175 in *The Classic Italian Cookbook*) or *Purè di patate* (page 329 in the same book).

MENU SUGGESTIONS

See those for the preceding spareribs recipe.

Salsicce col cavolo nero

SAUSAGES WITH RED CABBAGE

I like most kinds of cabbage with all kinds of meat. This savoury and sweet combination of sausage and red cabbage is a particularly happy one. The cabbage and the sausages are cooked separately at the beginning, the former in olive oil, the latter in their own fat. They are then put together and, as they finish cooking, engage in a reciprocal assimilation of flavours.

For four

1½ cloves garlic, peeled and chopped
8 tablespoons olive oil
680 g (1½ lb) red cabbage, sliced into fine strips
450 g (1 lb) *luganega* sausage or other good-quality mild, coarse-grain sausage, cut into 75-mm (3-inch) lengths
Salt
Freshly ground black pepper

1 Put the garlic and olive oil into a large sauté pan and, over medium heat, sauté the garlic until it turns deep gold.

2 Add all the cabbage, turning it a few times so that it is all coated with oil and the garlic is evenly distributed. Continue to cook at medium heat in the uncovered pan, stirring from time to time.

3 While the cabbage is cooking, brown the sausages in a small frying pan. Pierce them in a few places with a fork, and the fat that spills through these puncture holes will be all the cooking fat you need. Turn them as they cook until they are nicely browned all over, then remove them from the pan and set aside.

4 When the cabbage is nearly done – it should be much reduced in bulk, and limp, though not yet completely soft – add several large pinches of salt, some pepper, and the browned sausages. Continue cooking for another 20 minutes, turning the sausages and cabbage from time to time. Serve piping hot.

MENU SUGGESTIONS

Start with *Zuppa dei poveri con la rucola*, *Minestrina di broccoli e manfrigul* or *Tonnarelli col rosmarino*. Follow with *Insalata di borlotti e radicchio* or with any mixed green salad.

Salsicce con le cipolle

SAUSAGES WITH SMOTHERED ONIONS

Onions, tomatoes, peppers – it sounds like a cliché of Italian cooking. But a little change in proportions, a light-handed touch, and you have one of those dishes so sweet and fresh it can never fail to please. Here the classic trio is combined with sausage, preferably the mild *luganega* sausage available in many good Italian delicatessens.

If there is any leftover sausage, cut it into small pieces, and combine it with its own cooking fat to form the base of a tasty *risotto*. Or crumble it and toss it with pasta, together with butter and cheese. Or drain it well of fat, and add it to a *frittata* (page 288), together with some grated Parmesan cheese.

For four

4 tablespoons vegetable oil
225 g (8 oz) onion, sliced very fine
225 g (8 oz) tinned Italian plum tomatoes, chopped, with just a little of their juice
Salt
Freshly ground black pepper
450 g (1 lb) *luganega* or German bratwurst or other good, mild sausage, cut into 100- to 125-mm (4- to 5-inch) lengths
1 green pepper, peeled, seeded and cut into thin strips

1 Put the oil and onion into a sauté pan, cover, and cook over medium heat. When the onion wilts and becomes much reduced in bulk, uncover the pan, and turn up the heat to medium high. Sauté the onion, stirring occasionally, until it becomes deep gold in colour.

2 Add the tomatoes, a little salt, a grinding of pepper, stir well, and reduce the heat to medium. Cook at a steady simmer for 20 minutes or so, until the fat separates from the tomato.

3 Add the sausage, puncturing the skin in a few places with a fork. Add the strips of green pepper, cover the pan, and cook for 20 minutes longer, turning the sausage from time to time.

4 Tip the pan, and draw off two thirds of the fat with a spoon or ladle. (Do not discard the fat; if there is leftover sausage you will be able to use it in other preparations [see introductory remarks above].)

5 Serve at once, with plenty of good crusty bread.

Note The entire dish may be cooked in advance – even a day or two beforehand. Refrigerate if not serving it the same day. Do not degrease it until after reheating.

MENU SUGGESTIONS

Follow those in the preceding sausage recipe.

Salsicce col vino rosso e i funghi secchi

SAUSAGES WITH RED WINE AND DRIED WILD MUSHROOMS

Nothing could agree more with sausage than the aroma of wild mushrooms, and the happiest end for both is to come to rest on a bed of *polenta* or mashed potatoes (*The Classic Italian Cookbook*, pages 175 and 329).

For four to six

30 g (1 oz) dried boletus mushrooms
1 tablespoon olive oil
8 tablespoons dry red wine
680 g (1½ lb) *luganega* sausage (or bratwurst or other sausage), cut up into 100- to 125-mm (4- to 5-inch) lengths

1 Soak the mushrooms at least 30 minutes in advance in a bowl with 450 ml (¾ pint) warm water. Then proceed to rinse them and to filter the water, as described on page 191. Do not cut up the mushrooms.

2 Choose a sauté pan in which the sausage will fit in a single layer, put in the oil and the sausage and, over medium heat, brown the sausage well all over.

3 Add the red wine, and turn the heat down so that the wine bubbles at a gentle simmer. Turn the sausage from time to time.

4 When the wine has evaporated completely, add the reconstituted wild mushrooms and the filtered water.

5 Cook, always at a gentle simmer, turning the sausage and mushrooms occasionally, until the water has completely evaporated. At the same time, scrape loose the cooking residue from the bottom of the pan, using a wooden spoon.

6 Tip the pan and draw off the floating fat with a spoon or small ladle. If serving the sausage over *polenta*, mashed potatoes or rice, remove only part of the fat. If serving alone, remove as much of the fat as possible.

MENU SUGGESTIONS

If served with *polenta* or rice, no soup or pasta is called for. Precede with *Pisci d'ovu* or *Carciofi alla giudia* (from my first book, page 293). Otherwise, start with *Minestrina di broccoli e manfrigul* or *Penne con spinaci e ricotta*. A nice vegetable accompaniment would be *Erbette saltate per la piadina*.

Piccata di fegato di vitello al limone

SAUTÉED CALVES' LIVER WITH LEMON

Practically everyone familiar with Italian cooking is acquainted with *Piccata al limone* – thin veal *scaloppine*, sautéed, and sauced with a little lemon juice. Here is a very similar procedure applied to thin slices of calves' liver. You must use very fresh calves' liver, cut evenly in slices no more than 6 mm ($\frac{1}{4}$ inch) thick, and as free of gristle as possible. This is not always easy to get, but it is one of the rewards of a diligently nurtured relationship with a good butcher, something all serious cooks must establish, unless they prefer to become vegetarians.

The cooking here is very, very fast. There is no time for meditation or rereading the recipe, because thin slices of liver cook in less than 1 minute in very hot fat. If possible, this is an even finer dish than the version with *scaloppine*. It is unquestionably one of the freshest and lightest things one can do with liver.

For four

450 g (1 lb) choice calves' liver, cut into slices no more than 6 mm ($\frac{1}{4}$ inch) thick
4 tablespoons vegetable oil
45 g ($1\frac{1}{2}$ oz) butter
110 g (4 oz) flour, spread on a plate
Salt
Freshly ground black pepper
3 tablespoons freshly squeezed lemon juice

1 If some of the thin, stiff skin is still on the liver, remove it. It would shrink while cooking and keep the slices from lying flat in the pan. Also remove any of the larger white gristly tubes that may be present.

2 Put the oil and butter into a good-sized sauté pan, and turn on the heat to medium high. Heat the fat until the butter foam subsides and the butter turns a very faint brown.

3 Rapidly dredge the liver on both sides in the flour, and slip as many slices into the pan as will fit loosely. Cook the liver for about $\frac{1}{2}$ minute on each side, then transfer to a warm dish, and sprinkle with salt and pepper. If the slices are a little thicker than 6 mm ($\frac{1}{4}$ inch), cook them slightly longer. The liver should be a moist pink inside. To make sure, cut into a slice while cooking and see.

4 When all the liver is done, add the lemon juice to the pan. The heat should still be at medium high. Stir very quickly once or twice. Slip in all the liver, and turn the slices for a few brief moments. Transfer at once to a warm serving dish, pour all the juices from the pan over the meat, and serve immediately.

MENU SUGGESTIONS

Begin with *Risotto primavera*, *Maccheroncini alla saffi* or *Fettuccine all'Alfredo* (from my first book, page 111). Accompany with *Cipolline stufate coi topinambur*, *Coste di biete saltate* or *Zucchine trifolate con le cipolle*.

Rognoncini di agnello saltati con cipolla

SAUTÉED LAMB KIDNEYS WITH ONION

This is an unorthodox way of doing lamb kidneys that succeeds in removing every trace of that somewhat sharp taste many people find objectionable. You will find that in this recipe the kidneys are cooked in two stages, and the liquid thrown off during the first stage is discarded. One might think this procedure would toughen them, but it does not. Lamb kidneys are particularly tender to begin with. Here they acquire a firmer textural quality than in some other cooking methods, but it is quite agreeable, like that of very fresh mushrooms.

For four

16 to 18 lamb kidneys
6 tablespoons vinegar
6 tablespoons olive oil
1 onion, chopped fine
45 g ($1\frac{1}{2}$ oz) butter
3 tablespoons parsley, chopped fine
Salt
Freshly ground black pepper

1 Split the kidneys in half and wash briefly under cold running water. Put them into a bowl with enough water to cover and add the vinegar. Let them soak for at least 30 minutes. Drain and pat thoroughly dry with kitchen paper.

2 Cut the kidneys in very thin slices that look a bit like sliced mushroom caps. When you reach the whitish core, slice around it and discard the core.

3 Put the kidneys into a large sauté pan and cook them over medium heat for 2 minutes or so, stirring them almost constantly, until they throw off their dark red liquid. The kidneys will have lost their raw colour and turned greyish.

4 Turn off the heat and drain the kidneys, discarding all the liquid in the pan. Put the kidneys in a wire strainer or colander and rinse them quickly in cold running water. Drain them well.

5 Rinse the pan and wipe it dry. Put the olive oil and onion into it, and turn on the heat to medium high. When the onion becomes translucent, put in the kidneys and the butter. After a few moments add the parsley. Cook the kidneys for a minute or two, stirring them frequently. Add salt and 2 or 3 grindings of pepper, stir once or twice, and serve immediately.

MENU SUGGESTIONS

A first course of *La paniscia novarese*, *Maccheroncini alla boscaiola*, or *Fettuccine con le zucchine fritte*. With the second, *Topinambur fritti, Fettine croccanti di melanzana* or *Purè di patate* (from my first book, page 329).

Trippa e fagioli

TRIPE AND BEANS

The wave of interest in good cooking that in recent years has begun to move across the country has brought back with it foods and ingredients that had been almost completely banished from our tables. Of these none deserves its rehabilitation more than tripe. The tenderness and delicate flavour of tripe, when well prepared, cannot be equalled by far more expensive cuts of meat. And, for those who watch calories, tripe has so little fat that it produces one third or less the amount of calories of roast beef, while yielding the same amount of protein.

The following combination of tripe with beans is an immensely satisfying one, and, in closely related versions, it is a great favourite in those two bean-loving regions of Italy, Tuscany and the Veneto.

For six

1 whole carrot
1 stick celery
1 whole peeled onion
900 g (2 lb) tripe, possibly honeycomb
60 g (2 oz) butter
6 tablespoons olive oil
½ onion, chopped very fine
½ stick celery, chopped very fine
½ carrot, chopped very fine
3 medium cloves garlic, peeled and cut into 2 or 3 pieces
½ teaspoon chopped rosemary
2 tablespoons chopped parsley
225 ml (scant ½ pint) dry white wine
3½ teaspoons salt
12 or more grindings of pepper
360 g (12 oz) tinned Italian plum tomatoes, coarsely chopped, with their juice
225 ml (scant ½ pint) home-made meat broth (page 18) or ½ bouillon cube dissolved in the same quantity of water
680 g (1½ lb) fresh cranberry beans (unshelled weight) **or** 225 g (8 oz) tinned *cannellini* **or** 180 g (6 oz) dry white kidney beans, cooked as directed on page 346
100 g (3½ oz) freshly grated Parmesan cheese

1 Choose a large, heavy flameproof casserole with a tight-fitting lid, put in the whole carrot, the celery stick and the whole onion, add 4 litres (7 pints) water, and bring to the boil.

2 Wash the tripe thoroughly in running water, put it into the casserole, cover, and when the water returns to the boil cook for 20 minutes.

3 Lift out the tripe and transfer it to a chopping board. Discard the rest of the contents of the casserole. As soon as the tripe is cool enough to handle, cut it into strips no more than 6 mm ($\frac{1}{4}$ inch) wide. The length does not matter.

4 Preheat the oven to 180°C/350°F/Mark 4. Rinse the casserole, put in the butter, olive oil, and chopped onion. Sauté the onion lightly over medium heat until faintly gold in colour, then add the chopped celery and carrot, and sauté lightly for about a minute.

5 Add the garlic, rosemary, parsley, and cut-up tripe. Cook for 2 or 3 minutes, stirring everything from time to time. Add the wine, turn up the heat, and cook for about 30 seconds or until the liquid has boiled away.

6 Add the salt and pepper, stir thoroughly, then add the cut-up tomatoes with their juice, and the broth, and bring to the boil. Cover the pot and place it in the middle level of the preheated oven. Cook for at least 3 hours, checking the contents every 20 minutes to make sure there is still sufficient cooking liquid in the pot. If the liquid has evaporated, add about 6 tablespoons water. After 3 hours the tripe should be cooked. It is done when it is tender enough to be easily cut with a fork. Test it and taste it. Continue cooking, if necessary, until it is sufficiently tender.

7 Fresh beans must be cooked before the tripe is done. If you are using precooked or tinned beans they can be added at step 9, when the tripe has finished cooking.

If using fresh beans, shell the beans, rinse them in cold water and put them in a pot with enough water to cover by about 37 mm ($1\frac{1}{2}$ inches). Do *not* add any salt.

8 Bring the beans to a very slow boil, then cover the pot. If the beans are very fresh and young they will cook in about 45 minutes. Otherwise they may take as much as 1 to $1\frac{1}{2}$ hours. When tender, turn off the heat and let them rest in their own cooking liquid.

9 When the tripe is done, remove it from the oven. If you are using fresh beans, add the beans plus 4 tablespoons of their cooking liquid. If not, add the drained precooked or tinned beans. Cover the casserole and simmer over medium-low heat for 5 to 10 minutes.

10 Off the heat mix in all the grated Parmesan cheese. Serve from the casserole, piping hot.

MENU SUGGESTIONS

No soup or pasta is required. If you wish, you can start with an appetiser, such as *Cappelle di funghi ripiene*, *Insalata di spaghetti* or, from my first book, *Peperoni e acciughe* (page 32). Follow with a salad of *Rape rosse al forno*, *Finocchio in insalata* (from my first book, page 350) or mixed raw vegetables.

Pollo al limone

ROAST CHICKEN WITH LEMON

If this were a still-life by Picasso instead of a recipe, it could be entitled 'Chicken with Two Lemons'. That is all there is in it; no fat, no fancy bed of vegetables, no basting. After you have put the chicken in the oven, you turn it over just once. The chicken, the lemons and the oven do all the rest. When it is done you will have one of the juiciest, tenderest, most exquisitely flavoured birds you have ever tasted. Were I to choose a dish to show how the simplest cooking can also be the most sublime, I would take this one.

For four

1 young chicken, weighing about 1·1 kg ($2\frac{1}{2}$ lb)
Salt
Freshly ground black pepper
2 whole lemons

1 Preheat the oven to 180°C/35°F/Mark 4.

2 Wash the chicken thoroughly in cold water, both inside and out. Remove all the bits of fat hanging loose. Let the chicken sit for about 10 minutes on a slightly tilted dish, until all the water has drained out of its cavity. Dry it well internally and externally with kitchen paper.

3 Sprinkle a liberal amount of salt and freshly ground pepper on the chicken, rubbing it into all its surfaces and into its interior, using your fingertips.

4 Rinse the lemons in cold water, and dry them off with kitchen paper. Soften them up gently, pressing them between your two palms, and rolling them back and forth a few times. Perforate each lemon in at least twenty places with a trussing needle, a round toothpick, or any tool of similar thickness.

5 Place both lemons in the chicken's cavity. Close up the opening with toothpicks or trussing needle and string. Run a string from one leg to the other, tying it at both knuckle ends. Do not pull the legs tightly together; leave them in their natural position. The chicken swells while it cooks, and the string is only to keep the thighs from spreading and stretching and splitting the skin at the inner folds.

6 Put the chicken into a roasting tin, breast downwards. Do not add cooking fat of any kind. This bird is self-basting, so you need not fear it will stick to the pan. Place it in the upper third of the preheated oven.

7 After 15 minutes, turn the chicken, with breast facing up. Be careful not to break the skin. If it is kept intact, the chicken will swell like a balloon, which leads to a beguiling presentation later at the table. Should it deflate, however, it does not affect the flavour in the least, which, after all, is all that really matters.

8 Cook for another 20 minutes, then raise the heat to 200°C/400°F/ Mark 6 and cook for an additional 15 minutes. There is no need to turn the chicken again.

9 Whether the chicken is all puffed up or not, it is a nice touch to bring it whole to the table and leave the lemons inside until it is carved and opened. Serve it with all the juices that run out, because they are perfectly delicious. The lemons will be shrivelled up, but be careful about picking them up and squeezing them, for they may squirt.

MENU SUGGESTIONS

Begin with *Spaghetti alla nursina*, *Penne con spinaci e ricotta*, *Tortellini verdi* or *Crespelle alla fiorentina* (from my first book, page 152). With the chicken: *Asparagi e funghi passati al burro*, *Fagiolini verdi e carote stufati con mortadella* or *Zucchine trifolate con le cipolle*.

Pollo in umido col cavolo nero

CHICKEN BRAISED IN RED CABBAGE

Here the cut-up chicken cooks smothered in red cabbage, which keeps its flesh moist and sweet. By the time the chicken is done, the cabbage has dissolved into a delectable tender mass that serves as the accompanying sauce.

For four

1½ medium onions, sliced thin
6 tablespoons olive oil
2 cloves garlic, peeled and quartered
450 g (1 lb) or more red cabbage, shredded very fine
1 roasting chicken, weighing about 1·1 kg (2½ lb), cut into 8 pieces
8 tablespoons good red wine
Salt
Freshly ground black pepper

1 Choose a sauté pan broad enough to contain all the chicken pieces in a single layer, put in the sliced onion, the olive oil, and the garlic, and sauté over medium heat until the garlic turns a rich deep gold.

2 Add the shredded cabbage, and cook, uncovered, always at medium heat, for 6 to 7 minutes. Stir it thoroughly once or twice.

3 Put in the chicken pieces, sliding them under the cabbage so that they rest, skin down, in a single layer on the bottom of the pan.

4 Add the wine, salt, and a liberal amount of pepper, cover the pan and continue to cook at medium heat. To balance the natural sweetness of the cabbage, add salt a little more freely than normal. From time to time, turn the chicken pieces over and stir the contents of the pan. The chicken will be done in 40 to 45 minutes, or when tender when pricked with a fork. The cabbage will no longer be recognisable as such. It will be much reduced and will have the consistency of a thick, pulpy sauce.

Note This dish turns out particularly well in one of those handsome flameproof earthenware casseroles imported from Italy. This is the original cook-and-serve pot of the Italian country kitchen, and there is no more appealing or practical container in which to bring a fricassee or similar dish to the table.

MENU SUGGESTIONS

Start with *Zuppa dei poveri con la rucola*, *Spaghetti alla carbonara* or *Fettuccine con le zucchine fritte*. No vegetable accompaniment is necessary. Follow with any salad of mixed raw vegetables, or with *Insalata di lattuga e gorgonzola*.

Pollo in tegame al limone

PAN-ROASTED CHICKEN WITH LEMON JUICE

Nearly all Italian chicken dishes have these things in common: they are quick, uncomplicated, and make a judiciously sparing use of seasonings. Their appeal is equally great for those who eat them and those who prepare them, because they tax neither the palates of the former nor the patience of the latter. The following recipe is a straightforward fricasseed chicken lightly enhanced by the tangy fragrance of fresh lemon.

For four to six

1 chicken weighing 1·1 to 1·35 kg ($2\frac{1}{2}$ to 3 lb)
2 tablespoons vegetable oil
15 g ($\frac{1}{2}$ oz) butter
1 sprig fresh rosemary or 1 teaspoon dried rosemary leaves
3 whole cloves garlic, peeled
Salt
Freshly ground black pepper
6 tablespoons dry white wine
2 tablespoons freshly squeezed lemon juice
5 or 6 thin julienne strips of lemon peel

1 Cut up the chicken into six or eight pieces, and wash them under cold running water. Do *not* dry them. Put the chicken pieces skin side down in a sauté pan in which they will fit without overlapping. Over medium-high heat, dry and lightly brown the chicken on all sides. No cooking fat is required at this point: the moisture clinging to the washed chicken pieces and their own fat will suffice. You must watch them, however, and turn them before they stick to the pan.

2 When the chicken is lightly browned on all sides, add the oil, butter, rosemary, garlic, salt and pepper. Cook for 2 to 3 minutes, turning the chicken pieces once or twice.

3 Add the wine, turn the heat up a little and let the wine bubble for half a minute or so. Then turn the heat down to medium low and cover the pan. Cook until the chicken is tender, testing one of the thighs with a fork. It should take about 40 to 45 minutes.

4 Turn off the heat, and transfer just the chicken pieces to a warm serving dish.

5 Tip the pan, and with a spoon remove all but 2 tablespoons fat. Add the lemon juice and lemon peel, turn the heat on to medium low, and stir with a wooden spoon, scraping loose any cooking juices that have stuck to the pan. Pour this light sauce over the chicken, and serve at once.

MENU SUGGESTIONS

To begin: *Zuppa di lattughe ripiene*, *Risotto col sedano* or *Maccheroncini coi piselli e i peperoni*. With the chicken serve *Cavolfiore gratinato con la balsamella*, *Insalatina tenera con la pancetta* (do not serve this if you served lettuce soup first) or *Zucchine gratinate*.

Pollo in fricassea alla marchigiana

FRICASSEED CHICKEN WITH EGG AND LEMON SAUCE

The name is but one of the things an Italian *fricassea* shares with a French *fricassée*. They are dishes that move along parallel paths – you start by browning the meat, continue the cooking with a little liquid, and finish with a sauce combining egg yolks and lemon juice. But at this point the two kinds of fricassee branch off to emerge with distinctly different characters. Unlike the French, *la fricassea alla marchigiana* has no liquid left for sauce at the end. Moreover, the egg is not allowed to cook even slightly: it is simply spun and wrapped about the chicken; it is the sizzling heat of the chicken that pulls it close in a clinging, satiny coat.

This method is applied not only to chicken but to lamb (page 236), rabbit, and even to vegetables.

For four to six

60 g (2 oz) butter
½ medium onion, chopped very fine
1 chicken weighing 1·1 kg (2½ to 3 lb), cut into serving portions
Salt
Freshly ground black pepper
225 ml (scant ½ pint) home-made broth (page 18) or more if needed, or 1 bouillon cube dissolved in the same quantity of water
4 tablespoons freshly squeezed lemon juice
1 teaspoon flour
2 egg yolks

1 Choose a sauté pan that will contain all the chicken pieces in a single layer. Put in the butter and onion, and sauté over medium heat.

2 When the onion turns pale gold, put in the chicken, increase the heat a little, and brown all the pieces well on both sides.

3 Add salt, 2 or 3 grindings of pepper, and all the broth. Turn the heat down so that the chicken will cook at the gentlest of simmers. Turn the pieces from time to time. At this slow pace, the chicken should be done in about 45 minutes. Test it for tenderness by pricking the thighs with a fork. There is no need to cover the pan if it is a fairly young, small chicken. With an older and heavier bird, set a lid on slightly askew.

4 If it becomes necessary, add 1 or 2 tablespoons broth during the cooking. But when the chicken is done there should be no broth left in the pan. If there is any, raise the heat and boil it away quickly, turning the chicken pieces frequently. Then turn off the heat.

5 Put the lemon juice into a bowl, and dissolve the flour in it, adding it little by little. Add the egg yolks. Beat with a whisk or fork until the mixture is well amalgamated. Pour it over the chicken, turning all the pieces quickly so that they are evenly coated. Serve at once.

MENU SUGGESTIONS

Begin with *Zuppa primavera*, *Passatelli di carne in brodo* or *Le lasagne coi carciofi*. Accompany with *Cavolfiore fritto con la pastella di parmigiano*, *Cipolline stufate coi topinambur* or *Coste di biete alla parmigiana* (from my first book, page 317).

Il pollo ripieno

STUFFED BONED CHICKEN

This is something you want to undertake when you are not too concerned about time, and are in a mood to enjoy working with your hands. The reward is a dish as elegant in flavour as it is in appearance.

Boning the chicken is the only tricky work involved, but it is not as hard as it may sound (see pages 265–7). It can be done in advance, and stuffing and cooking it can be put off until the following day.

The stuffing is similar in composition to some of the meatballs I make. There is minced beef, parsley, garlic, Parmesan and a mush made of milk-soaked bread. Once the chicken is stuffed and trussed up, it is browned and slowly pan-roasted with wine, cooking fat and its own juices. It is served sliced, either hot or cold.

For six

50 g ($1\frac{3}{4}$ oz) crumb (the soft, crustless part of the bread), diced into 25-mm (1-inch) pieces
8 tablespoons milk
450 g (1 lb) lean minced beef
2 tablespoons parsley, chopped very fine
1 small clove garlic, chopped fine
Salt
Freshly ground black pepper
60 g (2 oz) freshly grated Parmesan cheese
1 young roasting chicken [about 1·1 kg ($2\frac{1}{2}$ lb)], boned as directed on pages 265–7
A trussing needle and string or any heavy-duty sewing thread
6 tablespoons vegetable oil
15 g ($\frac{1}{2}$ oz) butter
8 tablespoons dry white wine

1 Put the diced crumb and the milk into a small bowl or deep dish and allow to soak for about 10 minutes.

2 Put the minced beef, parsley, garlic, 2 teaspoons salt, a few grindings of pepper and grated cheese in a bowl, and mix thoroughly.

3 Lightly squeeze the soaked crumb in your hand so that, while still saturated, it no longer drips. Add the crumb to the beef, and with your hands knead all the ingredients together until they are blended into a smooth, uniform mixture.

4 Lay the boned chicken skin side down on a board or work top. Take some of the stuffing from the bowl and fill the places in the legs where the bones used to be. Take the rest of the stuffing and shape it into an oval mass about as long as the chicken. Put it in the centre of the chicken, and bring the chicken skin round and over it, covering it completely. One edge of the skin should overlap the other, but by no more than 25 mm (1 inch). Mould the shape with your hands so that it returns as closely as possible to its original chicken appearance.

5 Sew up the chicken, starting at the neck and working down towards the tail, looping the stitches over the edge of the skin. It is difficult to do a perfectly neat job at the tail end, but do the best you can, making sure that you have sewn up all the openings.

6 Heat up the oil and butter in a flameproof casserole, preferably oval-shaped, over medium heat. When the butter foam begins to subside, put in the chicken, the side with the stitches facing down. Brown it well, without pushing it about too much, then turn it and brown the other side.

7 Put in the wine, letting it boil away for a minute or so. Sprinkle lightly with salt, and cover the pot, setting the lid slightly askew. Do not cover tightly or the chicken will steam-cook. Turn the heat down to medium low. The chicken should be cooked in about 1 hour, during which time you should turn it once or twice.

8 Transfer the chicken to a chopping board or a dish and let it cool for a few minutes.

9 Remove all but 1 or 2 tablespoons of fat from the pot. If any cooking residue has stuck to the bottom, add 1 or 2 tablespoons water, turn the heat up to high, and while the water evaporates scrape the residue loose. Pour these cooking juices into a small sauceboat.

10 At the table, carve the chicken into thin slices, starting at the neck end. Pour a tiny bit of sauce over each slice when serving.

Note The chicken can be boned a day in advance.

This dish can also be served cold, in which case omit the sauce.

MENU SUGGESTIONS

Avoid first courses with pungent sauces: if serving the chicken hot, try *Maccheroncini alla saffi*, either of the two *lasagne* on pages 151–4 or *Tortellini di prezzemolo* (from my first book, page 137). Accompany with *Carciofi e patate passati al forno*, *Funghi stufati* or *Pisellini alla fiorentina* (from my first book, page 328).

BONING A WHOLE CHICKEN

A chicken with all its bones removed makes a beautiful natural casing for any kind of stuffing. Moreover, it is fun to bring it to the table, its chicken shape less angular, more voluptuous, but intact, and cut it with aplomb into perfect, solid, boneless slices.

There is nothing mysterious about boning a chicken. Almost anyone endowed with patience and a small, sharp knife can figure it out for himself. Nearly all of a chicken's carcass – backbone, ribs, and breastbone – conveniently comes out in one piece when it has been loosened from the flesh. The thigh and drumstick bones must be removed separately, and you must start with those. The wings are not worth fussing with; their bones can be left in place.

What one must be careful about is never to cut or tear the skin (except, of course, for the single long incision at the back that one must make to get at the bones, and which will later be sewn up). Chicken skin is wonderfully strong and elastic when intact. But any breach will spread into a yawning gap. To prevent puncturing the skin, always keep the cutting edge of the knife facing the bone you are working on. Do not worry too much about what happens to the meat.

When you have finished boning, you will be faced with what looks like

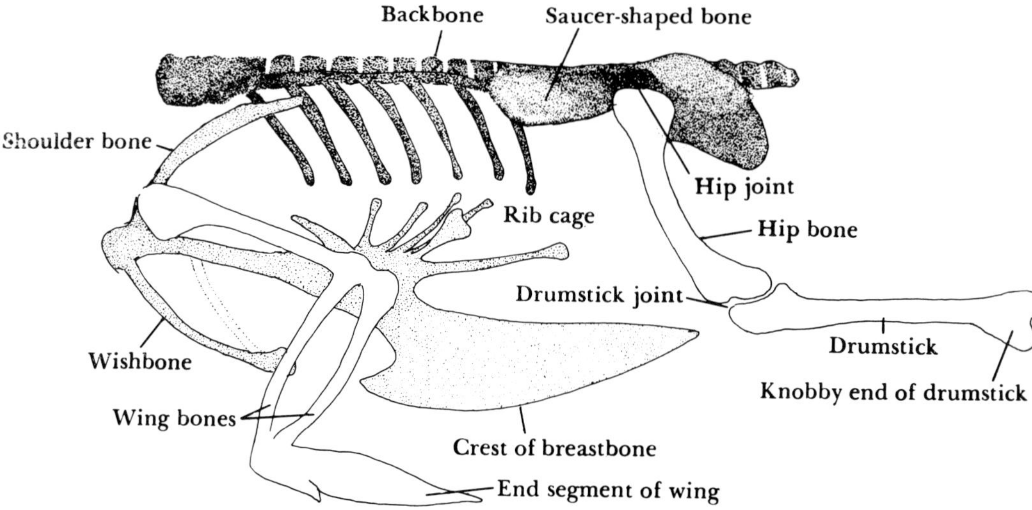

a hopelessly confused and floppy mass that in no way resembles a chicken. Do not panic. When the stuffing goes where the bones used to be, the bird will fill out in all the right places and look absolutely lovely.

1 Choose a very sharp, short knife. Place the chicken, breast down, on the worktop, and make a straight cut from the neck all the way down to the tail deep enough to reach the backbone.

2 Work on one side of the bird at a time, moving from neck to tail. Detach the flesh from the bones, prying it loose with your fingers, and, where necessary, cutting it from the bone with the knife. Always angle the knife edge towards the bone and away from the skin.

3 Past the midway point, approaching the small of the back, you will find a small saucer-shaped bone filled with meat. Pull the meat away with your fingertips, cutting it loose, where necessary, with the knife. A bit further on you will come to the hip joint. Loosen as much of the meat around it as you can, using your fingers. Then, with poultry shears, sever the joint from the carcass.

4 With one hand, hold the end of the leg. With the other, pull the meat away from the hip bone. When you come to long white filaments – the tendons – detach them from the bone with the knife.

5 The next joint you come to will be that connecting the hip bone to the drumstick. Hold the hip bone in one hand, the drumstick in the other, and snap off the hip bone at the joint. Remove the hip bone completely, using your knife to scrape it loose from any meat still attached to it. Always watch out for the skin, taking care not to tear it or pierce it.

6 Now the drumstick bone must be removed. Start from the thick, fleshy end. Loosen the meat from the bone, pulling it away with your fingers where it will give, cutting it loose where necessary with the knife. Cut the tendons from the bone, leaving them attached to the flesh. Be careful not to split the skin as you approach the knobby end of the drumstick. As you continue to pull the meat away from the bone, you will find this part of the chicken turning itself inside out like a glove.

7 About 12 mm ($\frac{1}{2}$ inch) up from the drumstick's knob, make a circular cut, cutting skin, meat, and tendons clear through to the bone. Grasp the bone by the knob end, and push it back through the leg until it slips out.

8 Return to the upper part of the back. Pulling with your fingers, and scraping along the bone with the knife, free the flesh from the rib cage of the carcass until you reach the breastbone. Leave the skin attached to the crest of the breastbone for the time being.

9 Joined to the wing you will find the shoulder bone. Pry the meat loose from it, using fingers and knife, as before, then cut the bone off at the joint where it meets the wing, and remove it. Cut off with the poultry shears the end segment of the wing. Do not bother to remove the wing bones.

10 Bone the other side of the bird, following the same procedure, until the chicken is attached to the carcass only at the crest of the breastbone.

11 Turn the chicken over so that the breast is facing you, and the carcass is resting on the worktop. Pick up the two loose sides of the chicken and lift them away from the carcass, holding them with one hand. With the knife, carefully free the skin from its hold on the crest of the breastbone. You must be most careful here, because the skin is very thin where it is attached to the bone, and easily slit. Keep the edge and point of the knife turned away from the skin, scraping along the surface of the bone. Discard the carcass, and proceed to stuff the chicken.

Note This entire operation may be completed a day before you are ready to stuff the chicken.

Anatra arrosto

ROAST DUCK

The duck in this recipe starts out very much like a Chinese bird, but it ends up with a taste and texture that are indisputably Italian.

As in some Chinese recipes, the duck is given a brief dunking in boiling water, and then is quickly gone over with a hair dryer. The first step opens up the pores in the skin, the second ensures that they stay open during the cooking. As a result, while the bird roasts in the oven, the fat melts and slowly runs out through the open pores, leaving the flesh tender and succulent, but not greasy, and the skin deliciously crisp. This procedure is not applicable to wild ducks, but only to those commercially grown duck-lings thickly engirdled with fat. The gravy is produced by the duck's own cooking juices, flavoured with a traditional mixture of sage, rosemary, and the mashed duck liver. Since a duck does not have quite as much liver as we need for this preparation, you must add to it either chicken liver or, if you can get it from your butcher, an extra duck liver.

The marvellous thing about this duck, apart from its fine flavour, is that it never turns out either dry or greasy.

For four

1 teaspoon rosemary leaves, chopped very fine
$1\frac{1}{2}$ teaspoons chopped or crumbled sage leaves
2 tablespoons salt
1 tablespoon freshly ground black pepper
60 g (2 oz) duck liver, or duck and chicken liver (see comments above), chopped fine
Duck, weighing 2 to 2·25 kg ($4\frac{1}{2}$ to 5 lb), preferably fresh
A hand-held hair dryer

1 Mix the rosemary, sage, salt, and pepper, and divide the mixture into two equal parts.

2 Put the chopped liver and one of the two halves of the above herb mixture into a bowl, and mix well.

3 Fill a pot with enough water to cover the duck later, and bring it to the boil.

4 Preheat the oven to 250°C/450°F/Mark 8.

5 If the bird still has its gizzard, remove and discard it. When the water comes to the boil, put in the duck. After the water returns to the boil, leave the duck in the pot another 5 to 7 minutes, then remove it.

6 Drain the bird well, and dry it thoroughly inside and out with kitchen paper. Take a hand-held hair dryer, and direct hot air over the whole skin

of the duck, for 6 to 8 minutes. This is to keep the pores wide open and ease the outflow of fat while roasting.

7 Rub the half of the herb mixture that does not contain liver over the skin of the duck.

8 Spread the herb and liver mixture inside the bird's chest cavity.

9 Put the duck on a roasting rack, breast up, and place the rack in a shallow roasting tin. Tuck the tail up with a toothpick so that the filling does not spill out. Place in the upper third of the preheated oven.

10 After about 30 minutes, turn the oven down to 190°C/375°F/Mark 5, and cook the duck for at least 1 more hour, until the skin is crisp.

11 Remove the duck from the oven, and transfer it temporarily to a deep dish. Remove the toothpick at the tail, and let all the liquid inside the cavity run into the dish. Collect this liquid and put it into a small saucepan, together with 4 tablespoons fat from the roasting tin.

12 Scrape away the herb and liver mixture adhering to the inside of the duck's cavity, and add it to the saucepan. Over very low heat, stir the contents of the saucepan until you have a fairly dense gravy.

13. Detach the duck's wings and drumsticks, and cut the breast into four pieces, or several thin slices, if you prefer. Put it all on a warm serving dish, spoon the gravy over it, and serve immediately. If you like to carve your duck at the table, you can serve the gravy separately in a sauceboat.

MENU SUGGESTION

Spaghetti alla nursina, *Le lasagne coi funghi e prosciutto* and *Le pappardelle del Cantunzein* would be good starters. Accompany with *Asparagi e funghi passati al burro*, *Porri al burro e formaggio* or *Zucchine trifolate con le cipolle*.

DISHES FOR SINGLE-COURSE MENUS AND FOR BUFFETS

Piatti Unici

THE dishes in this section are particularly suited for use outside the traditional two- or three-course structure of an Italian meal. Some of these are ideal for a light luncheon or as the principal course of a meal where they need only be accompanied by salad or fruit. Any one of them, or a combination of two or more, can be served buffet style at a party. (See individual recipes for additional suggestions.)

Their number is small, but their range is extensive. There are dishes of great elegance, such as the asparagus with prosciutto, the timbale of mushrooms, the artichoke pie. There are dishes from the country kitchens, such as the *pizza rustica* and *pizza di scarola*. There is one – stuffed pancakes – that manages to combine sophistication and earthiness. There are two *spaghetti frittate* that are novel and fun. Not all of these dishes need to be served hot. The beautiful tuna and spinach loaf is always served cold, and any of the *frittate* may be served either warm or at room temperature.

What they all have in common is a sense of freedom. They are to be enjoyed with your family or with a crowd, at a glittering holiday table or at a casual weekend in the country, in any way that falls in with your plans.

Polpettone di tonno e spinaci

TUNA AND SPINACH LOAF

Of the many things Italians do with their fine tinned tuna, this is one of the loveliest in appearance and flavour. The tuna is combined with spinach, anchovies, eggs, and cheese, and simmered tightly wrapped in muslin. When cold it is sliced like a salami.

If you want the dish to be pretty and decorative, here is a simple way to do it. When you cut the cooked loaf, arrange the beautiful green slices on a dish so that they slightly overlap, like roof tiles. Depending on the dimensions of the dish, you will end up with one or more parallel rows of overlapping slices. Over each slice place a thin slice of lemon, cut in half, and over the lemon place a thin, perfectly round carrot disc.

For six to eight

680 g (1½ lb) fresh spinach
Salt
100 g (3½ oz) tinned Italian or Spanish tuna packed in olive oil
4 flat anchovy fillets
1½ slices good-quality white bread, trimmed of crust
8 tablespoons milk
2 eggs
50 g (1¾ oz) freshly grated Parmesan cheese
30 g (1 oz) breadcrumbs
Freshly ground black pepper
Muslin
6 tablespoons olive oil
2 teaspoons freshly squeezed lemon juice
1 lemon and 1 small carrot for decoration (optional)

1 Pull the spinach leaves from their stems and soak them in a basin in several changes of cold water until they are thoroughly free of soil.

2 Cook the spinach in a covered pan with just the moisture clinging to the leaves and a pinch of salt. When tender, after 10 minutes' cooking or more, depending on how fresh and young it is, drain the spinach and let it cool.

3 Take a fistful of spinach at a time, and squeeze it firmly until no more liquid runs out. When all the spinach has been squeezed dry, chop it very fine, and put it into a mixing bowl.

4 Drain the tuna, and chop it fine, together with the anchovy fillets. Add it to the bowl.

5 Put the bread and milk into a deep dish, letting the bread soak thoroughly.

6 Break the eggs into the mixing bowl containing the chopped spinach and tuna. Add the grated Parmesan cheese, breadcrumbs, salt and a generous amount of pepper.

7 Squeeze the bread in your hands, letting all the milk run out, chop it and add it to the mixing bowl with the other ingredients. Mix thoroughly with a wooden spoon or spatula.

8 Turn the mixture out onto your worktop, and form it into a sausage shape about 62 mm ($2\frac{1}{2}$ inches) thick. Wrap it in four thicknesses of muslin, tying it securely at both ends.

9 Put the roll into a flameproof oval casserole where it will fit snugly. Add enough water to cover, place a lid on the pot, and cook over moderate heat for 35 minutes. It should cook at a slow but steady boil.

10 Remove the roll carefully from the pot, lifting it at both ends with spatulas or large forks. Allow to cool slightly. Remove the muslin and let the loaf cool completely.

11 Cut it into slices about 9 mm ($\frac{1}{8}$ inch) thick, season these with the olive oil and lemon juice, and serve.

MENU SUGGESTIONS

(See introductory remarks, page 270.) This is an ideal dish to have in a buffet, but it can also be an elegant, delicate appetiser, served before the first course, in an elaborately conceived sit-down meal. Or, in a seafood dinner, it can replace pasta or *risotto*, and immediately precede the fish course. It also makes a fine luncheon dish, followed by a salad of tomatoes and cucumbers, or *Insalata di arancia*.

Involtini di asparagi e prosciutto

ASPARAGUS AND PROSCIUTTO BUNDLES

Even down-to-earth Italian cooks like to have fun from time to time dressing up familiar ingredients in fancy wraps. That is the case here. Choose thick, juicy asparagus at the peak of the season, parboil them, place slices of fontina alongside them, and wrap them in prosciutto. Gratiné them until the cheese melts. It makes rather a pretty package, but it is also a most delectable mingling of flavours.

If you cannot find good-quality fontina, you can use slivers of Parmesan instead; in this case use boiled ham instead of prosciutto, because Parmesan and prosciutto together would be too salty for the asparagus.

For six

18 choice, thick, fresh asparagus
225 g 8 oz) Italian fontina cheese
225 g (8 oz) prosciutto, sliced thin
90 g (3 oz) butter (plus butter for greasing an oven dish)

1 Trim, peel, rinse and cook the asparagus as described on page 112, steps 1 and 2. Do not overcook. Drain the asparagus when it is tender but still crunchy and allow to cool.

2 Preheat the oven to 200°C/400°F/Mark 6.

3 You are going to be making six bundles containing 3 whole asparagus each. You will need, therefore, to divide into six equal parts the ingredients that go into the bundles, according to the directions that follow. Cut the fontina into thin slices, using a swivel-action vegetable peeler or a cheese-slicing tool. It does not matter if the slices are irregular, as long as they are fairly even in thickness. Divide the slices into six separate and equal little mounds.

4 Divide the sliced prosciutto into six equal piles of slices.

5 Set aside 45 g ($1\frac{1}{2}$ oz) butter, and divide it into six equal dollops.

6 Take 3 asparagus and place a prosciutto slice under them. Take all but 2 slices of fontina from one of the six mounds, and put it in between the asparagus stalks. Put in one of the small dollops of butter. Wrap the asparagus, using all the prosciutto slices from one of the six piles. Do not worry if the wrap is not perfectly neat, as long as it is fairly even in thickness, not too bunched up in spots. Proceed thus until all six bundles are done. The only ingredients left over at this point are 2 fontina slices from each mound, 12 in all, and some butter.

7 Choose an oven dish that will contain all the asparagus in a single

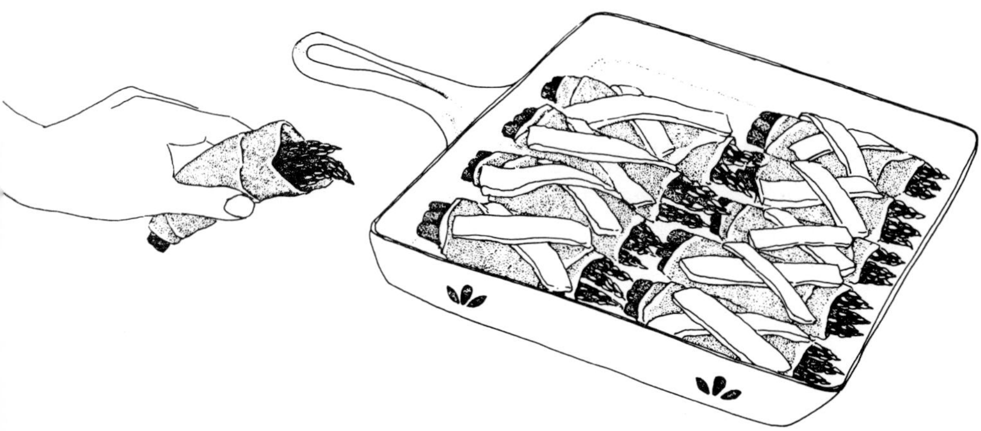

layer, without overlapping. Lightly grease the bottom of the dish with butter. Put the asparagus bundles in the pan. Over each bundle place 2 slices of fontina, criss-crossed. Use the remaining butter to dot all the bundles in several places.

8 Place the dish on the uppermost rack of the preheated oven. Leave it in for 20 minutes, or long enough for the cheese to melt and form a lightly coloured crust.

9 Allow to rest for several minutes before serving. After serving each bundle, baste it with the juices from the pan. Provide good crusty bread.

MENU SUGGESTIONS

(See introductory remarks, page 270.) In Italy, when the first asparagus of spring arrives it is precious enough to replace the meat course. You could follow suit and serve these after a fine course of pasta, such as *Le pappardelle del Cantunzein* or *Fettuccine all'Alfredo* (from my first book, page 111).

Pasticcio di fagiolini verdi

FRENCH BEAN MOULD

A pasticcio is two different things in Italian. In everyday life, outside the kitchen, it is a 'mess', in the sense of 'How did I ever get into this *pasticcio*?' When produced on purpose by a cook, it is a mixture of cheese and vegetables, meat or cooked pasta, bound by eggs or béchamel, or both. It is baked, usually, but not invariably, without a pastry crust.

A well-known example of *pasticcio* is that made with macaroni (see *The Classic Italian Cookbook*, page 93). The one here is made with French beans, and contains both béchamel and eggs. For a substantial dish, its flavour is fresh and light, and when unmoulded, it has a delectable appearance that tallies with its taste.

For six

450 g (1 lb) fresh French beans
45 g ($1\frac{1}{2}$ oz) butter
Salt

Béchamel sauce (page 16) of medium density, made with 300 ml ($\frac{1}{2}$ pint) milk, 30 g (1 oz) butter, 30 g (1 oz) plain flour, $\frac{1}{8}$ teaspoon salt

3 eggs
3 tablespoons freshly grated Parmesan cheese
$\frac{1}{8}$ teaspoon nutmeg
A 1·5- to 1·7-litre ($2\frac{3}{4}$- to 3-pint) soufflé mould
60 g (2 oz) fine, dry, plain breadcrumbs

1 Snap both ends off the French beans, pulling away any strings. Soak them a few minutes in cold water, then drain well and cut them into pieces approximately 25 mm (1 inch) long.

2 Choose a sauté pan broad enough to contain the French beans in a closely packed single layer. Put in 30 g (1 oz) butter, the French beans, 2 or 3 pinches of salt, and just enough water to cover. Cook over medium-high heat, turning the beans from time to time. When all the water has evaporated, sauté the beans in the butter for a minute or two, then turn off the heat.

3 Preheat the oven to 190°C/375°F/Mark 5.

4 Make the béchamel sauce, following the instructions on page 16, but using the quantities indicated in the list of ingredients above.

5 Break the eggs into a large mixing bowl, and beat them lightly. Whisk in the grated cheese and nutmeg, add the French beans and the béchamel, and mix all the ingredients thoroughly.

6 Smear the inside of the soufflé mould with butter, and sprinkle with enough breadcrumbs to coat lightly the bottom and sides. Turn the mould upside down and tap it to shake away the excess crumbs. Pour all the contents of the mixing bowl into the mould.

7 Place the mould on the uppermost rack of the oven, and bake for 45 minutes, or until a light crust forms on top.

8 To unmould the 'pudding', run a knife along its side while it is still hot, loosening it from the mould. Cover it with the flat side of a plate, hold the plate tightly against the mould and, grasping both with a towel, sharply flip over. The French bean mould should slip out easily onto the plate without much shaking. This is not a difficult thing to do at all, but if you feel uneasy about it you can serve the pudding by spooning it directly from the mould. In either case, let it cool for several minutes before serving.

MENU SUGGESTIONS

(See introductory remarks, page 270.) This could fit into the traditional sequence of an Italian meal, where it would replace the pasta and become the first course. It can precede any kind of roast or fricassee, but it is particularly pleasing when it is followed by a fish course, especially one with sauce, such as *Il pesce in brodetto* or *Pesce da taglio in salsa*.

Timballo di funghi

TIMBALE OF MUSHROOMS

This is an elegant and savoury monument to the mushroom. In this dish the caps and stems are cooked differently. The caps are breaded and crisply fried; some are used to line the bottom of the mould, and some to crown the pie when it is unmoulded. The filling is composed of the stems (sautéed and cooked with tomatoes) which alternate with the fried caps and with layers of cheese. In Italy this *timballo* would be made with fresh *funghi porcini*, wild boletus mushrooms. In this recipe I have used dried wild mushrooms, which combine with the cultivated mushrooms to recapture some of the original *porcini* flavour.

A *timballo* is a traditional Italian mould, drumlike in shape. It also refers to the dish prepared in the mould, and there are as many different kinds of *timballi* as there are things that can be minced, dressed, and baked. I have used a soufflé dish, which is shorter and broader, but works in exactly the same manner.

This is not at all a difficult dish to produce, but it certainly takes time. However, it can be made a day ahead, kept in its ceramic mould after baking, and reheated a short while before serving.

Six to eight

45 g (1½ oz) dried imported wild mushrooms
900 g (2 lb) very choice firm white fresh mushrooms with good-sized caps
2 eggs
120 g (4¼ oz) dry, plain breadcrumbs, spread on a dish
290 ml (½ pint) vegetable oil
6 tablespoons olive oil
1 small clove garlic, peeled and chopped fine
2 tablespoons chopped parsley
Salt
Freshly ground black pepper
110 g (4 oz) tinned Italian plum tomatoes, drained and chopped fine
225 g (8 oz) Italian fontina cheese, sliced very thin
50 g (1¾ oz) freshly grated Parmesan cheese
A 1-litre (1¾-pint) ceramic or glazed terracotta soufflé mould
Butter for greasing the mould

1 Soak the dried mushrooms for 30 minutes or more in a bowl with 600 ml (1 pint) lukewarm water. When they have finished soaking, lift them out carefully without disturbing the water. Rinse them several times in cold water.

2 Filter the water in which the mushrooms have been soaked through a

fine wire strainer that has been lined with kitchen paper. Put the water into a small saucepan, put in the wild mushrooms, and cook over medium heat until the liquid has been completely boiled away. Turn off the heat and reserve for later. (While the mushrooms are soaking in the bowl, it will save time if you proceed with cleaning and preparing the fresh mushrooms as directed in the following steps.)

3 Rinse the fresh mushrooms rapidly in cold running water. Drain them well, and separate the caps from the stems. Wipe the caps dry with a soft cloth or kitchen paper.

4 If the caps are tightly closed, with edges curling inwards, cut off a thin slice straight across the bottom of the caps, making the bottoms flat. These slices will look like rings. Cut them in two, and set them aside. Leave the rest of the caps whole.

5 Cut the stems into the thinnest possible lengthways slices, and put them together with the trimmings from the bottoms of the caps.

6 Break the eggs into a deep dish, and beat them lightly with a fork until the yolks and whites are combined.

7 Dip the mushroom caps into the eggs, letting excess egg flow back into the dish.

8 Turn the caps in the breadcrumbs, tapping the crumbs onto them to make certain they stick.

9 When all the caps have been coated in egg and breadcrumbs, put half the vegetable oil into a small frying pan. Turn the heat on to medium high. When the oil is hot, start frying the caps, a few at a time. When they have formed a fine, golden crust on one side, turn them; when both sides have a nice crust, transfer them to kitchen paper to drain. Then put in another batch of caps.

10 When you have finished frying half the caps, you will find that the oil has turned black. This is from the breadcrumbs. Turn off the heat, carefully pour out and discard the oil, and wipe the pan clean with kitchen paper. Put in the remaining fresh vegetable oil, and finish frying the mushroom caps.

11 In a medium-sized sauté pan put the olive oil and the chopped garlic, and over medium heat sauté the garlic until pale gold. Add the sliced mushroom stems and cap trimmings, and the chopped parsley. Raise the heat to high and cook for about 3 minutes, turning the mushrooms frequently.

12 Add the cooked wild mushrooms, 2 or 3 large pinches of salt and a few grindings of pepper. Stir once or twice, then add the chopped tomatoes. Cook for about 5 minutes more, always at lively heat, stirring from time to time. When you see the fat separate from the tomato, turn off the heat. Taste and check seasoning.

13 Preheat the oven to 180°C/350°F/Mark 4.

14 Grease the inside of the soufflé dish with butter and cover the bottom with a layer of fried mushroom caps, their bottoms up. Sprinkle very lightly with salt. Cover with a layer of fontina slices, then with some of the mushroom stems and tomato, then sprinkle with Parmesan cheese. Repeat the operation, beginning with another layer of fried mushroom caps. Top off the pie with the last of the caps, bottoms always up.

15 Bake in the upper third of the preheated oven for 25 minutes.

16 When done, allow to cool for about 10 minutes. Run a knife along the sides of the mould to loosen the *timballo*. Put a dinner plate, bottom up, over the top of the mould. Grasp both plate and mould tightly together, and turn the mould upside down over the plate. Use a towel to hold them if the mould is too warm to be handled comfortably. Lift the mould away, leaving the *timballo* standing on the plate. Cool another 5 to 10 minutes before serving. You should have no problem in unmoulding but if you feel very apprehensive about it, you may prefer to settle for serving the *timballo* directly from the mould. In this case, remember to change the direction in which the mushroom caps face when filling the mould: they should be placed with bottoms facing *away* from you.

Note If preparing this dish in advance, after cooking the *timballo*, do not unmould it. Let it cool, then refrigerate it overnight covered with film wrap. Bring it to room temperature before reheating. Reheat it in a 150°C/300°F/Mark 2 oven for 15 minutes, and unmould it as soon as you are able to handle it, following the directions above.

MENU SUGGESTIONS

(See introductory remarks, page 270.) A rich and satiating dish that in an ordinary meal could take the place of a roast. It would then be preceded by an appetiser, such as sliced prosciutto with melon, or by a light *risotto*, such as *Risotto col sedano*. Or, if served in moderate quantity, it could be used as an elegant vegetable accompaniment for a fine roast.

Torta di carciofi

GLOBE ARTICHOKE PIE IN A FLAKY CRUST

One of the interesting things about this lovely vegetable pie is the pastry crust. It is a type of *pasta frolla*, Italian flaky pastry. Instead of the eggs that usually go into *pasta frolla*, this one has ricotta. It is very light, very flaky, and takes little time and no special skills to make.

The filling is absolutely delicious. Its principal constituent is globe artichokes, sliced very thin and braised on a bed of sautéd carrot and onion. It is rounded out with eggs, ricotta, and Parmesan cheese. The pie should be unmoulded before serving. If you have no problems with unmoulding, use a ceramic soufflé dish of about 1½-litre (2½-pint) capacity; or you can make life easier for yourself, and bake it in a springform tin.

For four to six

The filling

4 medium globe artichokes
Juice of ½ lemon
4 tablespoons olive oil
2 tablespoons chopped onion
3 tablespoons chopped carrot
1 tablespoon chopped parsley
Salt
Freshly ground black pepper
50 g (5 oz) ricotta
50 g (2 oz) freshly grated Parmesan cheese
2 eggs

1 Trim the globe artichokes, following the basic method described on page 151. Do not detach the stem, but peel away the green rind all the way down to the pale and tender core. Snap off all the hard outer leaves, exposing the tender artichoke heart. Trim away all the dark green tops from the remaining leaves. You want to avoid any tough unchewable bits of artichoke in the filling. Cut the artichokes in half in order to remove the choke and prickly inner leaves, then slice them into the thinnest possible slices lengthways. Put them in a bowl with enough water to cover and the juice of half a lemon.

2 Put the oil, onion, carrot, and parsley into a sauté pan, and over medium heat sauté, until the onion turns light gold.

3 Drain the artichokes, and rinse them under cold water to wash away the acid lemon flavour. Put them into the sauté pan, stirring and coating them with oil for about a minute.

4 Add salt and a few grindings of pepper, stir once, add 8 tablespoons water, and cover the pan. Cook until tender but not mushy. Depending on the youth and freshness of the artichokes, this should take from 7 to 15

minutes. If you find that the liquid has evaporated before the artichokes are done, add a little more water, but there should be no water in the pan when the artichokes are cooked. If there is, uncover the pan, raise the heat, and boil it away rapidly.

5 Pour all the contents of the pan into a bowl, and allow to cool completely.

6 When cool, mix in the ricotta and grated Parmesan cheese.

7 Break the eggs into a deep dish, beat them lightly with a fork, then mix them into the bowl. Taste and check seasoning.

Making the pastry and completing the pie

180 g (6 oz) flour
110 g (4 oz) butter, completely softened at room temperature
150 g (5 oz) ricotta
½ teaspoon salt
Additional butter and flour for greasing the baking tin
A 200-mm (8-inch) springform tin or a 1½-litre (2½-pint) soufflé dish (see introductory remarks above)

1 Preheat oven to 190°C/375°F/Mark 5.

2 Mix the flour, butter, ricotta and salt in a bowl, using your fingers or a fork.

3 Turn out the mixture onto a work surface, and knead for 5 to 6 minutes until the dough is smooth.

4 Divide the dough into two unequal parts, one twice as large as the other.

5 Roll out the larger piece of dough to a thickness of no more than 8 mm (⅓ inch). To avoid problems in transferring this to the tin, roll out the dough on a lightly floured sheet of cardboard or paper.

6 Grease the tin or soufflé with butter. Sprinkle lightly with flour, and turn it over to shake off excess flour.

7 Slip the sheet of pastry into the tin, covering the bottom and letting it come up the sides. Smooth it with your fingertips, pressing down and thinning any thick folds.

8 Transfer all the contents of the bowl with the artichoke mixture into the tin. Level off the filling with a spatula.

9 Roll out the remaining portion of the dough into a circular sheet, again over a floured piece of cardboard or paper. Slip it over the pie, covering it completely. Trim away any excess pastry, leaving on the sides a border of 12 mm (½ inch), and fold that border over the pastry that lines the sides. Pinch all around the edge with your fingertips to seal it well.

10 Place in the uppermost level of the preheated oven and bake for 45 minutes, until the pie is lightly browned on top.

11 If baked in a soufflé dish, unmould it by inverting it onto a serving dish, then invert it again, exposing its browned top.

Serve lukewarm or at room temperature. Do not refrigerate if preparing it several hours ahead of time.

MENU SUGGESTIONS

(See introductory remarks, page 270.) This pie can replace the pasta, soup or *risotto* before almost any meat course, save those, of course, that already have vegetables, such as some stews. It is also an elegant prelude to a fine fish course, like *Orate al limone e maggiorana*.

Pizza di scarola

ESCAROLE PIE

Like *pizza rustica* (page 284), this is less a pizza than it is a pie. In this particular instance, a vegetable pie, made with escarole.

Escarole is a kind of lettuce related to chicory, with crisp, open, wavy leaves that from a pale green at their ruffled tips fade to a creamy white at the base. While rather bland when raw, it has an appealingly tart, earthy taste when cooked. It is excellent in soup (see *The Classic Italian Cookbook*, page 55), or in a cooked salad.

In the filling for this pie, cooked escarole is sautéed with olive oil, garlic, olives, and capers. Later, anchovies and pine nuts are added. The dough used to enclose the filling is a simplified but savoury bread dough that goes through one brief rising.

Pizza di scarola can be made very deep or shallow, depending on taste, and, of course, on the dimensions of the pan. I like it shallow, which gives me a greater proportion of crusty dough to filling. For this recipe, I use a 250-mm (10-inch) round tin, which produces a pie about 50 mm (2 inches) deep. One can also use a square tin 200- to 225-mm (8- to 9-inch) sides. A difference of up to 25 mm (1 inch), one way or the other, is not critical.

For six to eight

The dough

300 g (10 oz) plain flour
1 teaspoon salt
Freshly ground black pepper
15 g (½ oz) fresh yeast or ½ packet active dry yeast, dissolved in 225 ml (scant ½ pint) lukewarm water
30 g (1 oz) lard, softened at room temperature or partly melted in a small pan

The filling

1·35 kg (3 lb) escarole
Salt
8 tablespoons olive oil
2 large cloves garlic, peeled and chopped
10 black (Greek) olives, stoned and each cut up into 4 to 6 pieces
3 tablespoons capers, preferably tiny, of which half should be chopped
7 flat anchovy fillets, cut into 12-mm (½-inch) pieces
30 g (1 oz) *pinoli* (pine nuts)

1 Pour the flour onto a work surface, and shape it into a mound. Make a hollow in the centre of the mound and put into it the salt, a few grindings of pepper, the dissolved yeast and the lard.

2 Knead thoroughly for about 8 minutes. The dough should be quite soft but, if you have difficulty in kneading it, add another tablespoon or two of flour. If you have a food processor, all the kneading can be done in the processor, using the steel blades.

3 Shape the dough into a ball, and put it into a lightly floured bowl. Cover the bowl with a damp, doubled-up towel, and put it in the middle level of a turned-off oven. If your oven does not have a gas pilot, preheat it to 50°C/100°F, turn it off, then put in the dough. Let it rise for 30 to 40 minutes.

4 Discard any of the escarole's bruised or blemished outer leaves. Cut up or tear the rest into small pieces, about 50 mm (2 inches) long. Soak them in a large basin or a sink filled with cold water, changing the water frequently.

5 Bring 3 to 4 litres (5¼ to 7 pints) water to the boil, add some salt, and drop in the drained escarole. Cook until tender, up to 20 minutes or so, depending on the freshness and youth of the vegetable.

6 Drain the escarole. As soon as it is cool enough to handle, gently squeeze more moisture out of it with your hands, and set aside.

7 Put the olive oil and chopped garlic in a large sauté pan (about 11 inches), and turn on the heat to medium. When the garlic turns pale gold, add all the cooked escarole, lower the heat to medium low, and sauté the escarole for 10 minutes or so, turning it from time to time.

8 Add the pitted olives and both the chopped and whole capers. Sauté for a minute or two, turning all the ingredients in the pan. If there is liquid in the pan, raise the heat and boil it away. Then remove the pan from the heat.

9 Mix in the anchovies and pine nuts. Taste and check the salt. Transfer all the contents of the pan to a bowl, and set aside to cool.

10 If you have not already done so, remove the dough from the oven. Then turn on the oven to 190°C/375°F/Mark 5.

11 Divide the dough into two unequal parts, one twice the size of the other.

12 Dust a large sheet of waxed paper or foil with flour. On it, roll out the larger piece of dough until it is large enough to cover the bottom of a baking tin and line its sides as well. It should work out to a thickness of not much more than 6 mm (¼ inch).

13 Grease the inside of the tin with butter. Pick up the sheet of paper or foil with the dough on it, and turn it over into the tin, covering both the sides and bottom of the tin. Peel away the sheet. Smooth the dough, flattening and evening out any particularly bulky creases with your fingers.

14 Put all the escarole filling into the pan, and level it off.

15 Roll out the remaining piece of dough until it is large enough to cover the pie. Place it over the filling in the tin and press its edge against the edge of the dough lining the tin. Make a tightly sealed seam, folding any excess dough over towards the centre of the pie.

16 Place the pan in the uppermost level of the preheated oven. Bake for 45 minutes until the pie swells slightly and turns a very pale gold.

17 If using a springform tin, remove the sides of the tin. When the pie is cooler and firmer, slide it onto a serving dish. If using another type of tin, as soon as it is cool enough to handle, put a plate upside down over it, and turn the tin over, letting the pie slip onto the plate. Then turn the pie over between two plates, so that it is right side up again.

Serve lukewarm or at room temperature. Do not refrigerate.

MENU SUGGESTIONS

(See introductory remarks, page 270.) Escarole pie makes a nice country-style lunch, needing little more than to be followed by a good salad, possibly real garden tomatoes with fresh basil. It can also be served as a first course, replacing pasta, before a hearty meat course such as *Farsumauru-il braciolone*.

Pizza rustica

PORK AND CHEESE PIE

Pizza rustica has absolutely nothing in common with pizza except the name. It is a meat-and-cheese pie whose filling is baked in sweet egg pastry, *pasta frolla*. The meat is an assortment of pork products – prosciutto, cooked sausages, salami, etc. – and the cheeses are lean ones such as ricotta and *scamorza* (mozzarella). In the Abruzzi, people also add hard-boiled eggs but I find the filling rich enough without them.

The combination of sweet pastry with salty filling may seem somewhat startling, but they are not at odds with each other. It is in fact a most pleasing and sparkling coupling of flavours. This recipe uses half the amount of sugar usually called for, which I would find excessive. There is also mention of cinnamon in traditional recipes, but I loathe cinnamon, so the less said about that the better.

For six

The sweet egg pastry (*pasta frolla*)

240 g ($8\frac{1}{2}$ oz) plain flour
2 egg yolks
A tiny pinch salt
110 g (4 oz) butter, cut up into small pieces
3 tablespoons ice water
30 g (1 oz) granulated sugar

Mix all the ingredients, and knead them together briefly, preferably on a cold surface, such as marble. As soon as they are well amalgamated into a compact dough, wrap the dough in waxed paper or film wrap and put it in the refrigerator. Leave it in the refrigerator for at least 1 hour before proceeding with the rest of the recipe. It can be refrigerated for up to 4 or 5 hours.

All the mixing and kneading can be done in a food processor, if you have one. Put all ingredients into the beaker and spin the steel blades on and off until balls of dough form on them. When you take the dough out of the processor, shape it into a single ball before you wrap it and refrigerate it.

The filling

2 egg yolks
350 g (12 oz) whole-milk ricotta
110 g (4 oz) prosciutto or ham, or salami, chopped not too fine
110 g (4 oz) *mortadella*, chopped not too fine
110 g (4 oz) whole-milk mozzarella, cut up in small pieces
2 tablespoons freshly grated Parmesan cheese
Salt
Freshly ground black pepper

A litre ($1\frac{3}{4}$-pint) soufflé dish or similar ceramic ovenproof dish

Butter for greasing

The refrigerated egg pastry from the above recipe

1 Put the egg yolks into a bowl, and beat them briefly with a whisk.

2 Add the ricotta, and beat until it becomes rather creamy.

3 Add the chopped meats, the mozzarella, the grated cheese, a liberal amount of salt, and several grindings of pepper. Mix all the ingredients thoroughly.

4 Preheat oven to 190°C/375°F/Mark 5.

5 Thickly grease the inside of the baking dish with butter.

6 Cut off about one third of the pastry dough. Over a sheet of aluminium foil or waxed paper, roll it out into a round shape large enough to line the bottom of the baking dish, and come a little way up the sides. Turn the dough over into the dish, peeling the sheet away from the dough. Fit the dough into the bottom of the dish, spreading it evenly.

7 Cut off another third of the dough, and always over foil or waxed paper, roll it into rectangular strips about as wide as the baking dish is deep. Line the sides of the dish with these strips. You can overlap where necessary; where there are gaps, they can be filled by pressing into them little bits of dough, handling them like putty. Smooth with your fingers, evening off any thicker layers. Press the dough where the sides meet the bottom into a tightly sealed seam.

8 Pour all the filling from the bowl into the dish. Press it lightly to force out any air bubbles trapped in it.

9 Roll out the rest of the dough into a disc large enough to cover well the top of the pizza. Place it over the filling, and press its edges tightly against the dough lining the sides of the dish, making sure of a tight seal. Trim away the dough along the sides wherever it comes up higher than 12 mm ($\frac{1}{2}$ inch) above the top of the pizza; fold the rest of it down. Smooth all rough connections with a moistened fingertip.

10 Place in the upper level of the preheated oven. Bake for 45 minutes, until the top has turned a light golden brown. Do not open the oven door during this time. If after 45 minutes the crust seems to you to require a little more browning, turn up the thermostat to 200°C/400°F/Mark 6, and bake for another 6 to 8 minutes.

11 When cool enough to handle, the pizza may be unmoulded by being inverted onto a plate (see description of this procedure in step 16 of the recipe for *timballo di funghi*; page 276.) It is also very nice served directly from the baking dish.

Pizza rustica may be served while still warm or at room temperature, but not piping hot. It will keep for one day without refrigeration, at normal room temperature.

MENU SUGGESTIONS

(See introductory remarks, page 270.) Here is a dish that can be the centrepiece of a rustic meal, as the name itself – *pizza rustica* – suggests. As a starter you could serve *Arrosticini all'abruzzese*, *Minestrina di broccoli e manfrigul* or *Spinaci e riso in brodo*.

Tortino di crespelle

PANCAKES STUFFED WITH TOMATOES, PROSCIUTTO, AND CHEESE

This interesting dish combines the fine, light texture of pancakes – *crespelle* – with a robust filling that reminds one of pizza.

It is assembled and baked in a dish or tin, somewhat in the manner of *lasagne*. There is a flat layer of pancake, then a little stuffing, another pancake, more stuffing, and so on. The layers of pancakes should not exceed eight or nine; if you need to make larger quantities than the recipe calls for, plan on using more than one baking tin.

Makes enough for four servings with 8 to 9 crespelle

The pancakes

8 tablespoons milk
40 g ($1\frac{1}{2}$ oz) plain flour
1 egg
A tiny pinch of salt
25 to 30 g ($\frac{3}{4}$ to 1 oz) butter
A 200-mm(8-inch) frying pan or pancake pan

1 If you have a favourite method for making pancakes, make nine, using the quantities of milk, flour, egg and salt listed in the ingredients above to make the batter; or make the pancakes following the directions below.

2 Put the milk into a mixing bowl. Add the flour, shaking it through a wire sieve, and beat with a fork or a whisk until the milk and flour are smoothly blended.

3 Break the egg into the bowl, and add a very small pinch of salt. Beat thoroughly until all ingredients in the batter are well mixed.

4 Put a very small amount of butter into the frying pan, and turn on the

heat to medium low. As the butter melts, rotate and tilt the pan, evenly coating the bottom.

5 When the butter is fully melted, but before it colours, pour 2 tablespoons batter into the centre of the pan. Immediately lift the pan from the heat and tip in several directions, in a seesaw motion, to spread the batter evenly over the whole bottom.

6 Return the pan to the heat. Cook until the pancake has set and its underside has turned a light, creamy brown. Turn it over with a spatula, and brown it very lightly on the other side, then transfer it to a dish.

7 Do the rest of the pancakes in the same manner, adding a small amount of butter to the pan each time before you pour in the pancake.

The sauce

3 tablespoons olive oil
1½ cloves garlic, peeled and chopped
1½ tablespoons chopped parsley
150 g (5 oz) tinned Italian plum tomatoes, cut up, with their juice
Salt

1 Sauté the olive oil and garlic in a small pan over medium heat until the garlic turns pale gold. Add the parsley, stir once or twice, then add the cut-up tomatoes with their juice.

2 Put in a little salt, stir thoroughly, and cook at a gentle simmer for about 6 to 8 minutes. If there was too much liquid with the tomatoes, you may have to turn up the heat for a minute or so to reduce it.

Assembling and baking the dish

A 225-mm (9-inch) round cake tin
8 g (¼ oz) butter
50 g (1¾ oz) prosciutto or unsmoked ham, shredded very fine
25 g (¾ oz) freshly grated Parmesan cheese
50 g (1¾ oz) whole-milk mozzarella, chopped very fine

1 Preheat the oven to 200°C/400°F/Mark 6.

2 Grease the cake tin with the butter.

3 Place the largest of the pancakes on the bottom of the tin. Coat the pancake very lightly with some of the tomato sauce. You should be using one-eighth of the sauce, because you will be doing this eight times. It may not appear to be much sauce, but you will find it quite savoury when it is done.

4 Sprinkle a little of the ham, Parmesan and mozzarella over the sauce, and cover with another pancake. Continue thus until you have used up all the pancakes and the filling. You should have just a little sauce left with which to dab the topmost pancake, and a little grated Parmesan to sprinkle on top.

5 Place in the preheated oven on the uppermost rack. Bake for 15 minutes.

6 Transfer to a serving dish. Do not turn the tin over onto the dish; slide the *tortino* out of the tin, loosening it with a spatula. Serve either hot or at room temperature.

MENU SUGGESTIONS

(See introductory remarks, page 270.) In a meal, this is a satisfying, filling dish that does not need much support from other courses. A good way to lead up to it would be with *La carne cruda come a canelli* or *Arrosticini all'abruzzese*. And, if you want a vegetable with it, *Coste di biete saltati* would be very nice, as would any fried vegetable. Do follow with a refreshing, mixed green salad.

Frittata con le cipolle

ITALIAN OMELETTE WITH ONIONS

Ever since writing about *frittate* in *The Classic Italian Cookbook*, I have heard from many cooks who have become enthusiastic converts to this Italian way with eggs. As I had hoped, most have taken the basic method and used it as a vehicle for an inventive variety of fillings. Here I would like to return to one of the most fundamental and earthiest *frittate*. Like a large part of Italian cooking, it rests on a foundation of browned onion. If you want it to, it will support almost any structure of vegetables, herbs, meat, or even shellfish, that you may wish to lay upon it. Anything may be added, but nothing need be. It is complete and satisfying just as it is.

(For a discussion of *frittate*, see *The Classic Italian Cookbook*, page 277.)

For four to six

450 g (1 lb) red onions (or English onions, if red onion is not available), very finely sliced
6 tablespoons olive oil
5 eggs
60 g (2 oz) freshly grated Parmesan cheese
Salt
Freshly ground black pepper
45 g ($1\frac{1}{2}$ oz) butter

1 Put the onion and the olive oil in a large frying pan or sauté pan, and

cook the onion very slowly over low heat until gradually it wilts, becomes greatly diminished in bulk, and eventually attains a rich golden-brown hue.

2 Off the heat, tip the pan, move all the onion to one side, and let the oil drain and collect in a puddle on the other side of the pan. (**Note** The onion may be cooked up to this point several hours ahead of time.)

3 Break the eggs into a bowl, and beat them until the yolks and whites are lightly blended.

4 Add the onion to the bowl, using a slotted spoon or spatula to transfer them from the pan so that the oil will all be left behind.

5 Add the grated cheese, a liberal amount of salt and a few grindings of pepper to the bowl. Mix all the ingredients thoroughly.

6 Melt the butter in a 300-mm (12-inch) frying pan over medium heat. Do not let the butter heat long enough to become coloured. As soon as it begins to foam, pour the contents of the bowl into the frying pan, stirring them with a fork in the bowl while pouring. Turn the heat down to very low.

7 After about 15 minutes of very slow cooking, when the eggs have set and thickened, and only the surface is runny, place the frying pan under the grill. Remove it after 1 minute or less, when the 'face' of the *frittata* has set, but not browned.

8 Loosen the *frittata* with a spatula, and slide it onto a round dish. Cut it like a pie, into serving wedges.

MENU SUGGESTIONS

(See introductory remarks, page 270.) For a light lunch, the *frittata* alone is sufficient, followed by a salad. It can also be preceded by a simple soup, such as *Minestrina di broccoli e manfrigul.*

Frittata con le patatine fritte

OMELETTE WITH PAN-FRIED POTATOES

Here is a simple and offbeat variation on the onion *frittata* theme. The potatoes are diced into tiny cubes so that they are mostly fine, crackling crust when they are browned. They are then combined with sautéed onions for the *frittata* mixture. It is an engaging pairing of the tender and the crisp.

For four to six

6 tablespoons vegetable oil
300 g (10 oz) potatoes, peeled, rinsed, and diced into very fine 6-mm ($\frac{1}{4}$-inch) cubes
$1\frac{1}{2}$ medium onions, sliced as fine as possible
30 g (1 oz) butter
6 large eggs
Salt
Freshly ground black pepper

1 Choose a frying pan or sauté pan large enough to contain all the potatoes in a single layer without overlapping. Put in the oil, and turn on the heat to medium high.

2 When the oil is quite hot, put in the potatoes. Turn them at first to coat them evenly with oil, then spread them in an even layer, and do not stir them except to check, after a little while, if they have formed a nice brown crust on their underside. When they do, turn them and cook until they have formed a golden brown crust all over. With a slotted spoon or spatula, transfer the potatoes to a plate covered with kitchen paper to drain.

3 Put the sliced onion in the same pan, containing still the same oil in which the potatoes were cooked. Over medium heat add some salt and sauté the onions until they are tender and turn a rich gold. Transfer them to a dish, using a slotted spoon or spatula to drain them well of oil.

4 Pour out the oil from the pan, and clean the pan thoroughly.

5 Break the eggs into a mixing bowl, and beat them lightly with a fork. Add the potatoes, onions, salt, and a few grindings of pepper and mix well.

6 Melt the butter in the pan over medium heat. Do not let the butter become coloured but as soon as it begins to foam, pour the contents of the bowl into the pan, spreading evenly with a fork. Turn the heat down to very low. Finish cooking as directed in the preceding recipe for *frittata*, steps 7 and 8.

MENU SUGGESTIONS

(See introductory remarks, page 270.) Like any *frittata*, this is an ideal dish for a light lunch. It could also be chosen to precede one of the tastier fish dishes, such as *Tonno in agrodolce alla trapanese*. It is very good eaten cold; you should try it next time you make up a picnic basket.

Frittata di spaghetti

SPAGHETTI FRITTATA

The obvious thing to say about a *frittata* that uses cooked *spaghetti* is, what a wonderful way to use leftover pasta! It is indeed, but in my experience leftover pasta is an exceedingly rare commodity. In any event, this is such a marvellous dish that it is well worth cooking pasta especially for it. If you are cooking *spaghetti* ahead of time with the intention of using them later in a *frittata*, the moment the pasta is cooked and drained it must be tossed and coated with butter, otherwise it will turn into a solid, gummy mass.

The recipe below, which illustrates the basic technique, uses the purest of *spaghetti* dishes, one dressed simply with butter, cheese, and parsley. It is the best one to start with, to get the feeling, look, and taste of the finished dish. Then you can improvise as you like, adding basil or fried aubergine, fried courgette or some leftover peppers and tomato sauce (see *Salsa rossa*, *The Classic Italian Cookbook*, page 25). Virtually any ingredient that goes well with *spaghetti* goes well with this *frittata*.

I particularly like the appearance of the dish, which comes out looking like a pie, with the tangled *spaghetti* strands fixed into a lovely swirling pattern. It is served cut into wedges, a job that is most neatly executed with a pizza-cutting wheel. This *frittata* comes from Naples, a city whose inspired cuisine has not travelled well abroad where it is as little understood as it is much maligned.

For four to six

- 225 g (8 oz) *spaghetti* or 175 to 200 g (6 to 7 oz) leftover cooked *spaghetti*
- 45 g ($1\frac{1}{2}$ oz) butter for the *spaghetti*, plus 15 g ($\frac{1}{2}$ oz) for the *frittata*
- 30 g (1 oz) freshly grated Parmesan cheese
- 2 tablespoons chopped parsley
- 3 eggs
- Salt
- Freshly ground black pepper
- A 275- to 300-mm (11- to 12-inch) frying pan or sauté pan

1 Cook the *spaghetti* in at least 3 litres ($5\frac{1}{4}$ pints) salted boiling water until very firm to the bite. They should be a little more *al dente* – more underdone – than usual because they will undergo further cooking.

2 Drain, and toss the *spaghetti* in a bowl together with 45 g ($1\frac{1}{2}$ oz) butter, the grated cheese and the parsley. Allow the *spaghetti* time to cool.

3 Break the eggs into a deep dish or small bowl and beat them lightly, together with salt and pepper.

4 Add the beaten eggs to the *spaghetti*, and mix thoroughly.

5 Melt 15 g ($\frac{1}{2}$ oz) butter in the pan over medium heat. When the butter foam begins to subside, put in the *spaghetti*, spreading to an even thickness over the entire bottom of the pan.

6 Cook for 3 to 4 minutes without touching the pan. Then tilt the pan slightly, bringing the edge closer to the centre of the heat source. After about 1$\frac{1}{2}$ minutes – always keeping the pan very slightly tilted and its edge near the centre of the heat – rotate the pan a shade less than a full quarter turn. Cook for another minute or so, and continue turning and cooking until you have come round full circle. This procedure is necessary in order to cook the *frittata* evenly; otherwise it will be overcooked in the middle and undercooked at the edges. To see if it is cooked properly, lift up an edge of the *frittata* with a spatula, and make sure that the underside has formed a nice golden crust.

7 Take a round dish at least as large as the pan, place it upside down over the pan, then turn the pan over, letting the *frittata* plop onto the dish. Now slide the *frittata* back into the pan, with its uncooked side facing the bottom. Repeat the cooking procedure described in step 6, until the second side of the *frittata* has also formed a fine golden crust.

8 Transfer it from the pan to a chopping board and cut into wedges. Like nearly all *frittate*, it may be served hot, lukewarm, or at room temperature. But please, not just out of the refrigerator.

MENU SUGGESTIONS

(See introductory remarks, page 270.) In the simplest of the versions given above, the *frittata* can precede any roast or stew, particularly lamb or chicken. If elaborated with the addition of other ingredients, it stands best alone, as a luncheon dish, followed by salad.

Frittata di spaghetti farcita

STUFFED SPAGHETTI FRITTATA

This *frittata* is similar in approach to the basic *spaghetti frittata* in the preceding recipe. The one substantial difference is that here there are two layers of *spaghetti* separated by a filling of sautéed onion, tomato, mozzarella, and salami. It is as colourful as it is tasty, and, of course, somewhat more substantial than a straightforward *frittata*. As I suggested in the previous recipe, should you have the inclination to experiment, try it the way it is given here first, and when you have seen how it works, you can devise a great variety of fillings, and give the dish a style that is your own.

For six

225 g (8 oz) *spaghetti*
30 g (1 oz) butter for the *spaghetti*, plus 30 g (1 oz) for the *frittata*
30 g (1 oz) freshly grated Parmesan cheese
2 tablespoons parsley, chopped fine
3 tablespoons olive oil
2 tablespoons chopped onion
110 g (4 oz) tinned Italian plum tomatoes drained and cut up
Salt
50 g ($1\frac{3}{4}$ oz) mozzarella diced very, very fine
60 g (2 oz) mild Italian salami, diced or chopped very fine
3 eggs
Freshly ground black pepper
275- 300-mm (11- to 12-inch) frying pan or sauté pan

1 Cook the *spaghetti* in at least 3 litres ($5\frac{1}{4}$ pints) salted boiling water until very firm to the bite. The pasta will undergo further cooking, so it should be even more *al dente* – more underdone – than usual.

2 Drain, and toss the *spaghetti* with 30 g (1 oz) butter, half the grated Parmesan cheese, and the chopped parsley. Set aside for later.

3 Put the olive oil and the onion into a small sauté pan or saucepan. Over medium heat cook the onion until it turns golden brown.

4 Add the cut-up drained tomatoes and a little salt, and cook for about 15 minutes, stirring from time to time. Turn off the heat.

5 When the tomatoes have cooled, mix in the diced mozzarella and salami.

6 Break the eggs into a deep dish or small bowl, and beat them lightly, adding 2 or 3 grindings of pepper.

7 Add the beaten eggs to the pasta, and mix well.

8 Put 30 g (1 oz) butter into a frying pan, and turn on the heat to medium high. When the butter foam begins to subside – but before it starts to darken – take half the pasta and spread it evenly over the whole bottom of the pan. Then spread the tomato filling over the pasta, stopping just short of the edge. Sprinkle the remaining grated Parmesan over it. Cover with the remaining half of the *spaghetti* in an even layer, spreading out to the edges of the pan.

9 Turn the heat down to medium, and cook for about 4 minutes without touching the pan. Then tilt the pan slightly, bringing the edge closer to the source of the heat. After a minute or so, rotate the pan a little, less than a quarter turn, and continue cooking and turning, always keeping the pan

slightly tilted, until you have come round full circle. Check on the underside of the *frittata* by lifting its edge gently with a spatula, to see if it has formed a fine, golden crust all round. If it has not, cook a little longer where needed.

10 Turn on the grill, and run the pan under the grill for just a few minutes, until the top side of the *frittata* has formed a lightly coloured crust.

11 Transfer the *frittata* to a chopping board, cut into pie-shaped wedges, and serve while still warm.

MENU SUGGESTIONS

(See introductory remarks, page 270). A little more filling than the previous *frittate*, this would be an excellent choice for a country-style buffet, a very satisfying luncheon dish or a late-night snack for hungry insomniacs.

VEGETABLES

Le Verdure

Carciofini gratinati

GRATIN OF GLOBE ARTICHOKES

Gratin dishes are not only a graceful way to present vegetables, but they also favour the development of interesting, subtly articulated expressions of flavours. This particular gratin, in which the earthy assertiveness of artichoke is rarefied and sublimated by butter, Parmesan, and the oven's enveloping heat, is a good example.

As with so many dishes that come out of the oven, always allow a few minutes for the heat to abate and the taste of the food to come through.

For four

4 large or 6 medium globe artichokes
½ lemon
An ovenproof dish
60 g (2 oz) butter
Salt
60 g (2 oz) freshly grated Parmesan cheese

1 Trim the globe artichokes and cut them into wedges, following the instructions on page 151. The half lemon is for rubbing the cut surfaces of the artichokes so that they do not discolour.

2 Bring 3 litres (5¼ pints) water to the boil. Put in the artichokes and cook for 5 to 7 minutes from the time the water returns to the boil. The artichokes should be fairly tender, but firm enough to offer some resistance when pierced with a fork. Drain and leave to cool.

3 Preheat the oven to 190°C/375°F/Mark 5.

4 Cut the artichoke wedges lengthways into very thin slices.

5 Smear the bottom of the baking dish with butter, and cover it with a layer of artichoke slices. Sprinkle very lightly with salt and grated cheese, and dot with butter. Repeat the entire operation, building up layers of artichokes until there are none left. Sprinkle the topmost layer generously with cheese, and dot with butter.

6 Bake in the upper third of the preheated oven for 15 to 20 minutes, or until a light crust forms on top. Allow to settle for several minutes before serving.

MENU SUGGESTIONS

A gratin of artichokes will go well with just about any meat course that calls for a vegetable accompaniment. It is a particularly effective foil for those dishes with concentrated, lively flavours, such as *Fettine di manzo farcite*, *Scaloppine piccanti* or *Arrosto di maiale ubriaco*.

Carciofi e patate passati al forno

GRATIN OF GLOBE ARTICHOKES AND POTATOES

If you see some lovely artichokes in the market, and you already have potatoes in the house, this is a good recipe to bear in mind. It makes a very satisfying vegetable dish, ample enough to serve up to six people, with the most expensive component, the globe artichoke, held down to a minimum. In this combination, the artichokes supply most of the flavour, the onions impart sweetness, the potatoes give body and texture.

The artichokes are first cooked slowly with onions. They are then baked with potatoes sliced no thicker than chips, and finished with a topping of Parmesan cheese. When served in a handsome baking dish, they make an understated but rather elegant appearance.

For six

4 fresh, tight globe artichokes of medium size
1 lemon
75 g ($2\frac{1}{2}$ oz) butter
$1\frac{1}{2}$ medium onions sliced very thin
Salt
3 medium potatoes, peeled and sliced thin
Freshly ground black pepper
50 g ($1\frac{3}{4}$ oz) freshly grated Parmesan cheese

1 Trim the artichokes, cut them into wedges, and discard the choke,

following the instructions on page 151. Do not discard their stems, but trim away the green rind all the way down to the paler, tender core.

2 Put the trimmed artichokes and stems into a bowl, cover with cold water, and squeeze into it the juice of 1 lemon. Stir, and leave to soak until needed.

3. Choose a sauté pan large enough to contain all the ingredients. Put in it 39 g (1 oz) butter and all the onion, and over medium heat slowly cook the onion until deep gold. Turn off the heat.

4 Drain the artichoke wedges and stems. Rinse them in fresh cold water to remove all traces of lemon flavour. Cut the wedges into very thin slices lengthways. Cut the stems in half, lengthways, or, if rather thick, in four parts.

5 Put all the artichokes and stems into the pan with the onion. Sprinkle with salt, add 8 tablespoons water, and cover the pan with the lid just slightly askew. Over medium heat cook until the artichokes are tender when pricked with a fork, about 10 to 20 minutes, depending on their freshness. Turn them from time to time.

6 Preheat the oven to 200°C/400°F/Mark 6.

7 When the artichokes are done, uncover, and put in the sliced potatoes. Mix well for about a minute, then remove from heat.

8 Choose an oven dish in which all the ingredients will fit to a depth of not more than 37 mm (1½ inches). Put into it the artichokes, potatoes, and all the contents of the sauté pan. Distribute the mixture evenly, adding more salt and one or two grindings of pepper. Dot the top with the remaining 45 g (1½ oz) butter.

9 Place in the upper level of the preheated oven. After 15 minutes, take out the dish, mix its contents well, and put it back into the oven. In another 15 minutes or so, when the potatoes are cooked, sprinkle the top with all the grated cheese. Continue baking for several more minutes until the cheese melts and forms a very light crust. Allow to settle for a few minutes before serving.

MENU SUGGESTIONS

These artichokes and potatoes would be an excellent accompaniment to *Filetto al barolo*, *Rotolo di vitello con spinaci* or *Pollo in tegame al limone*.

La frittedda

SMOTHERED GLOBE ARTICHOKES, BROAD BEANS AND PEAS FROM PALERMO

There are six weeks in spring, between April and May, when in Sicilian homes people make *frittedda*, one of the most heavenly vegetable dishes known to any cuisine. The essential quality of *frittedda* is freshness – the freshness of artichokes, broad beans, and peas when they are very young and just picked. I have seen this dish done in Palermo when the vegetables were so tender they cooked in scarcely more time than it took to stir them into the pot.

If you grow your own vegetables, you can make perfect *frittedda* following this recipe. If you do not have a vegetable garden, you can adopt the careful compromises suggested, and obtain a very close and most enjoyable likeness of the original. One of the key ingredients in this and many other Sicilian dishes is wild fennel. If you cannot find this, use the leafy tops of fennel or fresh dill.

For six

3 medium globe artichokes, very fresh, with no discolorations
1 lemon, cut in half
900 g (2 lb) young, fresh, small broad beans (unshelled weight) or 300 g (10 oz) frozen broad beans
450 g (1 lb) fresh, small peas (unshelled weight) or 150 g (5 oz) frozen *petit pois* thawed
25 g ($\frac{3}{4}$ oz) wild fennel or 30 g (1 oz) fennel leaves or 15 g ($\frac{1}{2}$ oz) fresh dill
1$\frac{1}{2}$ medium red onions, sliced thin
8 tablespoons fruity olive oil
Salt

1 Trim the globe artichokes as directed on page 151. Strip the artichokes down to their tender hearts, and take care to cut off all the dark green tops of the leaves. Cut the artichokes into 12-mm ($\frac{1}{2}$-inch) wedges, removing the choke and prickly inner leaves. Rub all the cut parts with lemon to keep them from discolouring.

2 Shell the broad beans, if using fresh, and discard the pods.

3 Shell the peas, if using fresh, and discard the pods.

4 Rinse the wild fennel, fennel tops or the dill in cold water. Chop them into a few large pieces.

5 Put the sliced onion and the olive oil into a pot large enough to contain all the ingredients later. Turn on the heat to medium or medium low and

cook, uncovered, until the onion becomes soft and translucent. It must cook rather slowly. Stir occasionally.

6 Put in the wild fennel (or its substitute) and the artichoke wedges. Cover the pot. After 5 minutes inspect the contents of the pot. If the artichokes look very dry to you, add 3 tablespoons warm water. All this depends on the freshness and tenderness of the artichokes. If they are at their prime, the oil and the vapours in the pot from the onion and fennel are sufficient to cook them. If you are in any doubt, a little water will do no harm.

7 When the artichokes are half done (after about 15 minutes, always depending on their freshness) add the fresh broad beans, and the fresh peas, and follow the same method you used for the artichokes: add 2 or 3 tablespoons warm water whenever you are in doubt that there is sufficient moisture in the pot. Keep the cover on during the entire time the vegetables are cooking. When all the vegetables are tender, add salt to taste.

(**Note** *If you are using fresh broad beans and frozen peas:* cook the broad beans first for about 10 minutes, if they are very small, 15 or 20 if they are larger and tougher; then put in the thawed peas, and cook another 4 to 5 minutes.

If you are using frozen broad beans and frozen peas: put both in when the artichokes are just about done, and cook for another 4 to 5 minutes.

If you are using fresh peas and frozen broad beans: put in the peas when the artichokes are half done; when both the peas and artichokes are very nearly tender, add the frozen broad beans, and cook for another 4 to 5 minutes.)

Serve when done, but allow a few minutes for the heat to dissipate and the flavours to emerge. Do not serve cold.

MENU SUGGESTIONS

Except for stews and other braised dishes cooked with vegetables, this is a dish that fits well alongside any meat course. Try matching it with those that have some Sicilian character, such as *Scaloppine ammantate*, *Cotolette alla palermitana* or *Costolette di maiale ai due vini*.

Topinambur fritti

FRIED SLICED JERUSALEM ARTICHOKES

Among the New World's gifts to Europe's cooking, which includes such priceless ones as the tomato, beans, corn and potatoes, the Jerusalem artichoke is among the least prominent. But it is very nice to have nonetheless.

While its flavour may distantly recall that of artichoke hearts, it is really unique and all its own. It can be cooked in a number of ways, with other vegetables or by itself, and it is excellent in salads, raw and sliced paper thin. Frying is one of the most successful treatments. It needs no preliminary blanching. Just trim the artichoke, slice it into slim rounds, and slip it into the pan. Its flavour and fine texture take beautifully to frying; it turns very crisp on the outside, while becoming surprisingly tender and staying sweet within.

For further discussion about Jerusalem artichokes and more recipes, see *The Classic Italian Cookbook*, pages 299–301.

For four

450 g (1 lb) Jerusalem artichokes
Enough vegetable oil to come *at least* 6 mm ($\frac{1}{4}$ inch) up the sides of the frying pan
Salt

1 Pare the artichokes with a potato peeler. A swivel-action peeler does this job best. If, unlike me, you do not object to the stiffness of the skins, you can omit peeling them, but brush the artichokes thoroughly clean under cold running water.

2 Cut the artichokes into very thin chiplike slices. Wash them in several changes of cold water. This is done to rinse away not only traces of soil but some of the starch. Thoroughly pat dry with kitchen paper or a towel.

3 Heat up the oil in the frying pan over high heat. When it is very hot, slip in as many of the artichoke slices as will fit loosely. When they turn a nice russet brown on one side, turn them and brown them on the other side. With a slotted spatula or skimmer transfer them to kitchen paper to drain. When all the batches of artichokes are done, sprinkle with salt to taste, and serve at once.

MENU SUGGESTIONS

Most fried vegetables are welcome in any menu, and the sweet-tasting Jerusalem artichoke is compatible with virtually any course, of fish or meat. Try it with *Salsicce con le cipolle*, *Rognoncini di agnello saltati con cipolle* or *Gamberi dorati*.

Cipolline stufate coi topinambur

BRAISED SPRING ONIONS AND JERUSALEM ARTICHOKES

One always finds spring onions used for flavouring, but they are also a fine cooking vegetable. To discover how good they can be on their own, try them the way leeks are done in the recipe on page 327.

Here, the onions are slow-cooked in butter, and combined with Jerusalem artichokes. Both are tender, both are sweet, each in a different way that points up and complements the other.

For four to six

450 g (1 lb) Jerusalem artichokes
8 medium bunches spring onions
45 g ($1\frac{1}{2}$ oz) butter
Salt
Freshly ground black pepper

1 Peel the artichokes with a small, sharp paring knife. Wash them in cold water, and pat dry thoroughly. Cut into very thin slices, about 6mm ($\frac{1}{4}$ inch) thick, and set aside.

2 Trim the roots off the spring onions, and remove one or two of the outer leaves if bruised and discoloured. Do not discard the green tops. Wash in cold water, pat dry, and cut the spring onions across in half, so that from each you get two shorter pieces about 100 mm (4 inches) long. If some of the bulbs are very thick divide them in half lengthways.

3 Melt the butter in a sauté pan. Put in the spring onions, turn them in the butter, lower the heat to medium, and add 8 tablespoons water. Cook slowly until all the liquid evaporates, turning the spring onions from time to time.

4 Add the sliced artichokes, a large pinch or two of salt, and a liberal grinding of pepper. Turn and mix all the contents of the pan, and add another 8 tablespoons water. Cook until all the liquid evaporates and the artichokes are tender. Test the artichokes from time to time with a fork. If they are very fresh, they may become tender before all the liquid evaporates, in which case turn up the heat and boil it away quickly. If, on the other hand, they are still very firm when there is no more liquid in the pan, add 2 or 3 tablespoons water and continue cooking. When done – it may be approximately 20 minutes – taste and check seasoning. Serve hot.

MENU SUGGESTIONS

Use this to compensate for earthy flavours in the meat course, or to complement those that are more understated. Examples of good pairings: with *Farsumauru-il braciolone*, *Rotolo di vitello con spinaci* or *Costolette di maiale con i funghi*.

I topinambur al pomodoro

SMOTHERED JERUSALEM ARTICHOKES WITH TOMATO AND ONION

Jerusalem artichokes have a sweet and not very forthcoming flavour, which receives a most appetising boost in this preparation.

What we have done here again are the underpinnings of so many Italian dishes – onions and garlic sautéed in olive oil, tomatoes, and parsley. It is wonderful how much one can build on them, from sauces for pasta, to stews, roasts, fish soups, and an infinity of vegetable dishes. The difference between good and clumsy Italian cooking is the lightness and freshness with which you handle these materials. Judiciously dosing the oil, lightly colouring the garlic, using good, solid tomatoes and not overcooking them, and, most important of all, not blurring and thickening the keen edge of their flavours by heating them over and over, as restaurants do, or lazy cooks.

For six

680 g ($1\frac{1}{2}$ lb) Jerusalem artichokes
4 tablespoons olive oil
1 small onion, sliced very fine
1 clove garlic, peeled and chopped
2 tablespoons chopped parsley
50 g ($1\frac{3}{4}$ oz) tinned Italian plum tomatoes, chopped, with their juice
Salt
Freshly ground black pepper

1 Peel the artichokes with a paring knife or a swivel-action peeler. Rinse them in cold water. Cut them up into pieces about 25 mm (1 inch) thick.

2 Put the oil and onion into a sauté pan, and turn on the heat to medium high.

3 When the onion turns a deep gold, put in the garlic. Stir rapidly for a few seconds, then add the parsley, continuing to stir a few more brief moments.

4 Add the tomatoes with their juice. Stir, turn the heat down to medium, and cook at a steady simmer for 2 to 3 minutes.

5 Put in the cut-up Jerusalem artichokes, 2 or 3 large pinches of salt, a liberal grinding of pepper, stir thoroughly and turn the heat down to low. Cook for about 30 to 45 minutes, until the artichokes are very tender when pricked with a fork.

Note The entire dish may be cooked several hours or a day in advance, but it should be reheated just once.

MENU SUGGESTIONS

It goes well with any savoury meat course that is not heavily sauced with tomatoes. Among others, I would serve it with *Il bollito rifatto alla moda di papi*, *Cotolette alla palermitana* or *Nodini di vitello con sughetto di acciughe*.

Asparagi e funghi passati al burro

SAUTÉED ASPARAGUS AND MUSHROOMS

The asparaus for this dish is cut up in diagonal pieces so it will cook rapidly, and maintain a firm, almost crunchy consistency. The approach, even the textures and appearance of this preparation, recall Chinese stir-fried vegetables. It is another example of the mysterious kinship between these two cuisines from opposite ends of the world. But there is no mystery about the taste: it is fresh, spontaneous, and thoroughly Italian.

For six

450 g (1 lb) fresh asparagus	Salt
225 g (8 oz) fresh mushrooms	Freshly ground black pepper
45 g (1½ oz) butter	

1 Trim the asparagus spears of all the small 'leaves' that sprout below the tips. Wash the spears in cold water and pat dry thoroughly with kitchen paper.

2 Cut the spears into diagonal pieces, starting at the tips and working down towards the butt end of the stalk. Use as much of the stalk as feels tender, and discard the rest. To compensate for different thicknesses of asparagus, space the cuts about 25 mm (1 inch) apart on medium-sized spears, a little closer together on thicker spears, and farther apart on skinnier ones.

3 Wash the mushrooms rapidly under cold, running water, and pat thoroughly dry. Any mushroom whose cap is no more than 25 mm (1 inch) across should be kept whole. Larger ones must be cut in half, lengthways, and if very large, into four.

4 Choose a sauté pan that can later contain the asparagus and mushrooms closely packed, and even slightly overlapping, but in more or less a single layer. Put in the butter and melt it over medium heat. Put in the asparagus with a couple of pinches of salt, raise the heat to medium high, and cover the pan. Cook for about 2 minutes, slightly longer if the asparagus is not terribly fresh and tender. Stir once or twice.

5 Uncover the pan, raise the heat to its highest setting, and put in the mushrooms with some salt and a few grindings of pepper. Stir constantly, and cook for 2 minutes or so, until any liquid the mushrooms may throw off has evaporated.

6 Taste and check seasoning. Serve at once while the mushrooms are still a clear white. If you wait or reheat this dish, it will become flabby and lose its crisp colour contrast as the mushrooms turn dark.

VARIATION WITH JERUSALEM ARTICHOKES

For six

450 g (1 lb) asparagus
450 g (1 lb) Jerusalem artichokes
60 g (2 oz) butter
Salt
Freshly ground black pepper

1 Trim and slice the asparagus as described in steps 1 and 2 of the preceding recipe.

2 Peel the Jerusalem artichokes, using a paring knife or swivel-action peeler. Rinse them in cold water, and cut them into very thin slices, little more than 3 mm ($\frac{1}{8}$ inch) thick.

3 Melt the butter in a medium-sized sauté pan over medium heat. Put in the sliced asparagus and Jerusalem artichokes, and add several pinches of salt and a liberal grinding of pepper. Turn the vegetables with a long fork or spoon for about 30 seconds, until they are lightly coated with butter.

4 Add 8 tablespoons water. Cook for 6 to 7 minutes, stirring from time to time, until all the water has bubbled away and the vegetables are tender. If, when the water evaporates, the vegetables are still hard, add a little more water to continue the cooking.

5 When the vegetables are done there should be no more water left in the pan; if there is, boil it away rapidly. Let the vegetables brown very briefly in the butter, stirring them once or twice. Taste and check seasoning. Serve at once; do not reheat or let the vegetables sit in the pan once they are done.

MENU SUGGESTIONS

Whether done with mushrooms or with Jerusalem artichokes, this is an ideal accompaniment for roasts, such as *Arrosto di maiale ubriaco*, *Pollo al limone* or *Anatra arrosto*.

Fagiolini verdi e carote stufati con mortadella

FRENCH BEANS AND CARROTS WITH MORTADELLA

Here is an attractive dish. The carrots are cut into skinny sticks to match the French beans, and the spindly look of both is broken up by small, lumpy cubes of *mortadella* or ham. They are all cooked together in butter.

It is a combination that is just as much fun for the palate as it is for the eye, mingling the fresh vegetable taste of the beans, the sweetness of the carrots, and the lusty flavour of the pork.

For four

225 g (8 oz) fresh French beans, as young and small as you can find
2 or 3 medium carrots
Salt
50 g ($1\frac{3}{4}$ oz) *mortadella* sausage, diced into 6-mm ($\frac{1}{4}$-inch) cubes
45 g ($1\frac{1}{2}$ oz) butter

1 Snap both ends off the French beans, pulling away any strings. Soak them for a few minutes in cold water, then drain well.

2 Peel the carrots, wash them in cold water, and cut them into sticks of approximately the same size as the French beans.

3 Choose a sauté pan in which all the ingredients will fit without over-crowding. Put in the beans, carrot sticks, one or two large pinches of salt, the diced *mortadella*, and the butter. Cook over medium heat, stirring frequently, for about 2 minutes.

4 Cover the pan, and cook for a few minutes, the exact time depending on how young and fresh the vegetables are. Test them. When they are tender but still a little crunchy, they are done. Taste and check the salt, and serve at once.

Note If you cannot find *mortadella*, you can substitute ham, or very good-quality salami, if it is not highly spiced and garlicky.

MENU SUGGESTIONS

Good with all roasts, and most veal dishes. It adds a cheery splash of colour to the soft hues of *Pollo al limone*, and to the fine, subdued *Ossobuchi in bianco*.

Polpettone di fagiolini alla genovese

FRENCH BEAN AND POTATO PIE, FROM GENOA

A *polpettone* anywhere else in Italy is a meat loaf. In Genoa, it is a baked mixture of French beans and potatoes. It is known as a rich man's *polpettone* or a poor man's *polpettone*, depending on whether the French beans or the potatoes predominate.

I call it a pie because it is baked in a pie dish, and it comes out looking much like a crustless pie or shortcake. Given good French beans, it is nearly impossible for it not to turn out well. It is made by mixing boiled beans and potatoes into a batter with cheese, eggs, and marjoram, and baking in a medium oven for 1 hour. *Polpettone* will fit into any menu scheme, as an appetiser, vegetable dish, second course, or as part of a buffet.

For six

225 g (8 oz) boiling potatoes
450 g (1 lb) fresh French beans
Salt
A food mill
2 eggs
100 g ($3\frac{1}{2}$ oz) freshly grated Parmesan cheese
Freshly ground black pepper
1 teaspoon marjoram
A 225-mm (9-inch) round cake tin or pie dish
Olive oil
Plain, dry breadcrumbs

1 Wash the potatoes, and put them unpeeled into abundant cold water to boil.

2 Snap both ends off the French beans, and wash in cold water.

3 Bring 3 litres ($5\frac{1}{4}$ pints) water to the boil in another pot, add 2 tablespoons salt and the French beans. Cook, uncovered, at a moderate boil, until the beans are tender but quite firm. It may take 6 minutes or more, depending on their youth and freshness. Drain at once when done.

4 Cut up the beans into large pieces. Put the disc with the largest holes into the food mill, and press the French beans through it, into a bowl.

5 As soon as the potatoes are done, drain them, peel them, and pass them through the food mill into the bowl with the French beans.

6 Break both eggs into the bowl, add the grated cheese, salt, a few grindings of pepper, and the marjoram. Mix all the ingredients well.

7 Preheat the oven to 180°C/350°F/Mark 4.

8 Lightly grease the baking dish or tin with olive oil. Sprinkle all the

surfaces of the dish with breadcrumbs, then turn it over and shake away the loose crumbs.

9 Put the bean-and-potato mixture into the dish, distributing it evenly. Top with a light sprinkling of breadcrumbs; over them pour a thin and evenly spread stream of olive oil.

10 Place in the upper third of the preheated oven, and bake for 1 hour. Allow to cool a few minutes before serving.

MENU SUGGESTIONS

Serve *polpettone* with any braised meat or simple roast that is not accompanied by its own vegetables. A lovely combination would be with *Pollo al limone* or with *Piccata di fegato di vitello al limone*.

This may also be served as a light first course, replacing pasta or soup.

Fiori di broccoli fritti

FRIED BROCCOLI FLORETS

The florets are blanched first, then fried with a coating of breadcrumbs. They turn out tender but firm, with a very fine, crisp crust.

For four to six

680 g ($1\frac{1}{2}$ lb) fresh broccoli
Salt
1 large or 2 smaller eggs
120 g ($4\frac{1}{4}$ oz) fine, dry plain breadcrumbs, spread on a dish
Enough vegetable oil to come 12 mm ($\frac{1}{2}$ inch) up the side of the pan

1 Cut off the broccoli florets at their base where they meet the stalks. Set the stalks aside, but do not discard them (see note below).

2 Rinse the florets gently in cold water.

3 Bring 2 litres ($3\frac{1}{2}$ pints) water with a large pinch of salt to the boil. When it boils, put in the florets. From time to time moisten any part of a floret that floats above the water line, or it will become yellowish. When the water begins to boil again, remove the florets with a slotted spoon, drain well, and set aside to cool.

4 When cool, cut the large florets lengthwise into pieces about 25 mm (1 inch) thick, to make all the pieces more or less uniform in size so that they will cook evenly.

5 Break the egg or eggs into a soup dish, and beat lightly with a fork.

6 Dip the broccoli, one piece at a time, into the beaten egg, allowing excess egg to flow back into the dish. Then dredge the broccoli in the breadcrumbs, patting lightly with your fingertips to make sure the pieces are firmly breaded. As each piece is dipped in egg and coated with bread, put it into a dish until all the florets are ready for frying.

7 Heat up the oil in a medium-sized frying pan over medium-high to high heat. When hot, slip in as many broccoli pieces as will fit loosely in a single layer. When they have formed a nice golden crust on one side, turn them. When done on both sides, transfer them to kitchen paper to drain, and sprinkle with salt. Serve hot.

Note The stalks are delicious, and may be served the same day, or within a day or at most two, raw in a salad, or cooked as a vegetable dish. To prepare them for cooking or for a salad, you must first cut off the tough butt end of the stalks, and pare away all the dark green skin.

Cooking the stalks

Drop the peeled stalks into 2 to 3 litres (3½ to 5¼ pints) boiling salted water. Cook for about 7 minutes, or until tender, but still crunchy. Drain, split the thickest stalks, and serve lukewarm seasoned with olive oil and salt. Or serve when cold, seasoned with olive oil, a little vinegar, and salt. Another excellent way to prepare them is to sauté them with garlic (see *The Classic Italian Cookbook*, page 310).

Serving the stalks raw

After peeling them, as instructed above, rinse them in cold water, pat dry thoroughly, and cut them lengthways into bite-sized strips about 6 mm (¼ inch) thick. Season with salt, pepper, good olive oil, and a touch of wine vinegar.

MENU SUGGESTIONS

The fried florets can accompany a savoury, earthy fish or meat course, such as *Orate al limone e maggiorana*, *Pesce spada al salmoriglio* or *Stufatino di maiale alla boscaiola*.

The cooked stalks go well with *Bistecchine di manzo alla cacciatora*, *Costolette di vitello profumate all'aglio e rosmarino*, or *Piccata di fegato di vitello al limone*.

The raw stalks are useful wherever a fresh, crunchy green salad is required.

Broccoli stufati al vino rosso

SMOTHERED BROCCOLI IN RED WINE

If you expect, as I always did, to have broccoli turn out crunchy and bright green, you will be disappointed, as I was the first time, at the appearance of this dish. The broccoli is so limp and dull-looking that, before tasting it, you will think something has gone terribly wrong. You will find, however, that it tastes absolutely delicious, in a way intriguingly different from any broccoli you have ever had. What happens is that through long cooking in the bath of red wine, the broccoli surrenders its crisp green identity in exchange for an intense new set of flavours, drawn from the tartness of the olives, the sweetness of the onions, and the zest of the anchovies. It works.

For four to six

680 g ($1\frac{1}{2}$ lb) fresh broccoli
225 g (8 oz) onion, sliced very thin
60 g (2 oz) black Greek olives, cut in half and pitted
4 flat anchovy fillets, roughly cut up
50 g ($1\frac{3}{4}$ oz) fresh Parmesan cheese, cut into thin slivers
Salt
6 tablespoons olive oil
225 ml (scant $\frac{1}{2}$ pint) sturdy dry red wine

1 Cut away about 12 mm ($\frac{1}{2}$ inch) from the tough butt end of the broccoli stalks. Separate the florets from the stalks. With a sharp paring knife, peel off the dark green skin on the stalks and stems and cut the stalks, lengthways, into strips about 6 mm ($\frac{1}{4}$ inch) thick. Divide the larger floret clusters in two.

2 Take a large sauté pan, and cover its bottom with a thin layer of onion slices. Over this spread a layer of broccoli stalks. Dot with a few olives, some bits of anchovy, and a few slivers of Parmesan. Sprinkle with a little salt. Just a small pinch will do, because the olives, anchovy, and Parmesan are already salty. Moisten with a thin stream of olive oil.

3 Repeat this entire procedure, alternating layers of sliced onion with broccoli stalks, moistening them each time with a little olive oil. Save the broccoli florets for the top layer.

4 When all the ingredients have been used up, add the red wine. Cover, and cook for 1 hour over low heat, or until all the wine has evaporated. Do not stir. Serve promptly when done, and do not set aside and reheat.

MENU SUGGESTIONS

This goes well with a simple but not too timid meat course: *Cotolette alla palermitana*, *Costicine di maiale ai ferri*, or *Costolettine di agnello fritte* (from my first book, page 239). I also enjoy making a meal of this alone, with lots of good bread and a tart, tender sheep's milk cheese to follow.

Cavolo stufato alla veneziana

SMOTHERED GREEN CABBAGE FROM VENICE

The people of the Veneto have found many tasty things to do with cabbage, and this is one of them. The finely shredded cabbage is cooked very slowly in a covered pot in the vapour of its own escaping moisture, in some olive oil, and with a tiny amount of vinegar. No other liquid is necessary. The Venetian term for this method is *sofegao*, which is exactly translated by 'smothered'. The cabbage becomes very tender, almost dissolving, with that satisfying sweetness of slow-cooked cabbage, here faintly punctuated by the light, sour accent of vinegar.

For four to six

900 g (2 lb) green cabbage
1 large onion, chopped
8 tablespoons olive oil
3 to 4 cloves garlic, peeled and chopped
Salt
Freshly ground black pepper
1 tablespoon wine vinegar

1 Remove and discard the first few outer leaves of the cabbage. Shred the cabbage very fine. (The food processor does this perfectly and in no time.)

2 Put the onion and olive oil into a deep sauté pan, and turn on the heat to medium. Sauté the onion until it turns deep gold, then add the garlic.

3 Sauté the garlic for a minute or two, then add all the shredded cabbage. Stir and turn the cabbage for several minutes until it is all wilted.

4 Add salt, a few grindings of pepper, and the vinegar. Cover the pan, and turn the heat down to minimum.

5 Cook for at least $1\frac{1}{2}$ hours, or until very tender. Turn it every once in a while. Taste and check seasoning. Some like it served piping hot. I prefer to let it rest for just a few minutes after it has done.

MENU SUGGESTIONS

This is very good with pork and with grilled meats. It would be excellent with thick, juicy hamburgers. Try it with *Spiedini all'uccelletto* or with *Salsicce col vino rosso e i funghi secchi.*

Carote con i capperi

CARROTS WITH CAPERS

The coupling of carrots and capers makes an intriguing match. The tart corrective of the capers is just what the carrots need to add a little zip to their otherwise passive sweetness. And their gentleness, in turn, tempers the tonic bite of the capers. Choose young, tender carrots. The starchy taste of older carrots is all right in soups and stews, but it would repress the lively sparkle of this dish; and young carrots will cook so much faster.

For four

450 g (1 lb) young choice carrots
4 tablespoons olive oil
$1\frac{1}{2}$ cloves garlic, peeled and chopped
2 tablespoons chopped parsley
Salt
Freshly ground black pepper
2 tablespoons capers

1 Peel the carrots, and rinse them in cold water. Drain well.

2 You want the carrots to be no thicker than your forefinger. If they are very small, they may already be that size. If not, cut them lengthways in half, or if necessary in quarters.

3 Choose a sauté pan that can contain all the carrots without overcrowding. Put in the olive oil and garlic, and turn on the heat to medium high.

4 When the garlic turns a rich gold colour, add the carrots and the parsley. Stir the carrots for a few moments, until they are well coated with

oil. Then add 4 tablespoons water. When the water has completely evaporated, add another 4 tablespoons. Continue adding water at this rate, whenever it evaporates, until the carrots are done. It should take about 20 to 30 minutes, depending on the youth and freshness of the carrots; they should be tender but firm. Pricking with a fork will tell you how they are coming along, and at the end taste to make sure. There should be no more water in the pan when the carrots are done. If there is some, let it evaporate quickly. Allow the carrots to brown lightly.

5 Add salt, taking into account the saltiness of the capers, and a little pepper. Turn the carrots once or twice, then add the capers. Cook another minute or two, stirring frequently; serve at once.

Note The carrots may be cooked a few hours in advance, but kept out of the refrigerator. Add the capers only when reheating. The dish will have a fresher flavour, however, if cooked just before serving.

MENU SUGGESTIONS

I love these carrots with *Costolette di vitello profumate all'aglio e rosmarino*, but this dish will enliven any grilled meat or simple roast. It would be excellent served with *Arrosto di agnello pasquale col vino bianco* (from the first book, page 235).

Cavolfiore al pomodoro

CAULIFLOWER WITH TOMATO

The sauce used here is a very light-handed one of tomatoes cooked only a few minutes with that inseparable trio, oil, parsley, and garlic. The taste of the tomatoes comes through transparently sweet and fresh, most enjoyable with the cauliflower.

For four to six

1 young head cauliflower, about 450 to 680 g (1 to $1\frac{1}{2}$ pounds)
8 tablespoons olive oil
3 cloves garlic, peeled and chopped fine
2 tablespoons parsley, chopped fine
350 g (12 oz) tinned Italian plum tomatoes, drained and coarsely chopped
Salt
Freshly ground black pepper

1 Wash the cauliflower in cold water, trim away the base of the stem, and pull off and discard all the tough, large outer leaves. Cut it into four wedges.

2 Bring 3 to 4 litres ($5\frac{1}{4}$ to 7 pints) unsalted water to the boil. Put in the cauliflower and when the water returns to the boil, cook for 3 to 4 more minutes, then drain.

Note The cauliflower may be cooked up to this point even a day in advance.

3 Separate the cauliflower florets into small clusters, with a bit of stem attached to each.

4 Put the olive oil and garlic into a good-sized sauté pan and, over medium heat, sauté the garlic until it colours lightly.

5 Put in the parsley, stirring rapidly two or three times.

6 Put in the chopped tomatoes. Cook in the uncovered pan for 10 minutes over medium heat, keeping the tomatoes bubbling gently at a steady simmer. Stir well from time to time.

7 Put in the cauliflower, 2 or 3 large pinches of salt, a few grindings of pepper, and stir well. Cook until tender, for 6 to 8 minutes, always at medium heat, turning the cauliflower frequently. Serve piping hot.

MENU SUGGESTIONS

Combine with any hearty meat dish in which there is no tomato sauce. A very successful coupling would be with *Costicine di maiale alla trevigiana*, where the savouriness of the meat and the sweet freshness of the vegetable are in perfect accord.

Cavolfiore fritto con la pastella di parmigiano

FRIED CAULIFLOWER WITH PARMESAN CHEESE BATTER

Parmesan cheese helps to make wonderful frying batters. It is an ideal bonding agent, because it melts without becoming runny or rubbery. And, of course, it contributes its own incomparable savoury taste. This batter produces a fluffy, tender crust which is ideal for frying vegetable pieces such as cauliflower. If you are pleased with it, try it with broccoli or wedges of fennel. Remember that the vegetables must be boiled first.

For six to eight

1 small, young head of cauliflower [about 680 g (1½ lb)]
8 tablespoons lukewarm water
40 g (1¼ oz) plain flour
30 g (1 oz) freshly grated Parmesan cheese
Salt
1 egg
Enough vegetable oil to come 6 mm (¼ inch) up the sides of the pan

1 Cook the cauliflower in abundant unsalted boiling water. Remove when tender but still very firm, after 20 minutes or more, depending on the cauliflower.

2 Detach the floret clusters at the base of their stems. Separate into individual florets, and cut each of these, lengthways, in two. Sprinkle lightly with salt.

3 Put the lukewarm water into a bowl, and add the flour to it gradually, shaking it through a wire strainer (not a flour sifter). Beat constantly with a fork while adding the flour.

4 Add the Parmesan cheese and a small pinch of salt. Stir well.

5 Break the egg into a deep dish, beat it lightly with a fork, then mix it into the batter in the bowl.

6 Put enough vegetable oil into a medium-sized sauté pan to come at least 6 mm (¼ inch) up its sides. Turn on the heat to high. When a speck of batter dropped into the pan stiffens and instantly floats to the surface, the oil is hot enough for frying.

7 Dip 2 or 3 pieces of cauliflower into the batter, pick them up gently, letting excess batter flow back into the bowl, and slip them into the pan. Add more pieces to the pan, but do not overcrowd it.

8 When the cauliflower has a nice, golden crust on one side, turn it over. When both sides have formed a crust, transfer it to kitchen paper to drain, or to a cake-cooling rack set on a dish. Put in more freshly dipped pieces of cauliflower as space is made for them in the pan.

9 Sprinkle the fried cauliflower with salt. When it is all done, serve at once.

MENU SUGGESTIONS

This fried cauliflower goes especially well with pork and chicken. It is ideal with *Costolette di maiale con i funghi* and *Pollo in fricassea alla marchigiana*.

Cavolfiore gratinato con la balsamella

GRATIN OF CAULIFLOWER WITH BÉCHAMEL SAUCE

Some perfectly respectable dishes have been appropriated by institutional or cafeteria cooking and given a bad name. Cauliflower with white sauce is one of them. It is a shame, because it can be an exquisite dish, deserving a place at the most fastidious table.

Take a young sweet cauliflower, use only real, freshly grated Parmesan, and bake with a generous amount of fine, smooth, silken béchamel. What you will end up with is anything but ordinary, and you will be helping to repair the damage that has been done to the reputation of a blameless, charming dish.

For four to six

1 medium, young head cauliflower
Salt
Béchamel Sauce (page 16), of medium density, made with 450 ml (¾ pint) milk, 60 g (2 oz) butter, 45 g (1½ oz) plain flour, ¼ teaspoon salt
60 g (2 oz) freshly grated Parmesan cheese
⅛ teaspoon grated nutmeg
30 g (1 oz) butter

1 Wash the cauliflower, cut it into wedges, and cook it following the directions in the recipe for *cavolfiore al pomodoro*, page 313. Drain it and allow to cool.

2 Cut the cauliflower into bite-sized slices, about 12 mm (½ inch) thick. Sprinkle lightly with salt, and set aside.

Preheat the oven to 200°C/400°F/Mark 6.

3 Make the béchamel sauce, following the instructions on page 16. When the sauce reaches medium density, remove from the heat and mix in all but 2 tablespoons of the grated cheese, and all the nutmeg.

4 In a bowl, gently mix the sliced cauliflower with the béchamel.

5 Smear a baking dish with butter. Put in the cauliflower and all the béchamel from the bowl. The dish should be large enough so that the layer of cauliflower is not more than 37 mm (1½ inches) thick. Sprinkle on top the remaining grated cheese. Dot with butter.

6 Bake in the uppermost level of the oven for 20 minutes, or until a light brown crust is formed. Remove from the oven, and allow it to rest for about 10 minutes before serving. The fine, mild flavours of this dish emerge when the heat subsides.

MENU SUGGESTIONS

I would have no hesitation in serving this next to an elegant meat course such as *Filetto al barolo* or a magnificent whole braised shin of veal (see *Lo 'schinco'*, from my first book, page 219). It is also very good with any of the tastier chicken dishes, for example, with *Pollo in tegame al limone*.

Sedano in umido

BRAISED CELERY WITH TOMATOES, ONIONS, AND PANCETTA

The fresh, herbal fragrance of celery makes it a valuable element in many braised dishes, and, when it is given the starring role in a dish of its own, it rises splendidly to the part. In this recipe, all the braising liquid comes from the celery's own moisture, the onions, and the tomatoes. For cooking, I prefer the stalks to the hearts, because they have more tang. Save the hearts and eat them on another occasion in *pinzimonio* - raw, dipped in olive oil, and salt and pepper, see page 343.

For four to six

450 to 560 g (1 to $1\frac{1}{4}$ lb) meaty, unblemished sticks celery
6 tablespoons vegetable oil
$2\frac{1}{2}$ medium onions, sliced very thin
60 g (2 oz) *pancetta*, cut into thin strips, or green bacon
180 g (6 oz) tinned Italian plum tomatoes, chopped, with their juice
Salt
Freshly ground black pepper

1 Cut the sticks of celery into pieces about 75 mm (3 inches) long. Peel away or snap off as many of the strings as possible. Split the broadest pieces in half, lengthways. Rinse them all thoroughly in cold water.

2 Choose a 200- or 225-mm (8- or 9-inch) flameproof casserole or sauté pan. Put in the oil and sliced onion, and over medium heat cook the onion until it wilts and and colours faintly.

3 Put in the *pancetta*, and cook it briefly until the fat becomes translucent.

4 Put in the tomatoes and their juice, the celery, several pinches of salt,

2 or 3 grindings of pepper, and stir everything well. Cover, and cook at medium heat until the celery is tender – about 25 minutes or more, depending on the celery.

5 If, when the celery is done, the juices in the pan are rather runny, uncover, raise the heat to high, and boil them down for a few moments, stirring constantly.

MENU SUGGESTIONS

Use it as an earthy accompaniment with an equally earthy meat course, avoiding any that is sauced with tomato. A natural combination would be with *Costicine di maiale ai ferri*. Also try it with *Stufatino di maiale alla boscaiola* or *Pollo in tegame al limone*.

Coste di biete saltate

SAUTÉED SWISS CHARD STALKS

Of all greens there is none better endowed than Swiss chard to keep pace with the resourceful fancy of an Italian cook. Its leaves can be used in stuffings for pasta, roasts, or fish; they can be boiled for a cooked salad, seasoned with oil, salt and pepper, and a splash of lemon; or sautéed like spinach; the sweet-tasting stalks are magnificent fried, or in gratin dishes.

In this recipe the stalks are boiled, then sautéed with olive oil and garlic. Their delicate taste and fine texture are in refreshing juxtaposition to the aromas of the preparation.

Do not discard the leaves. Use them, as early as possible, in one of the ways alluded to above.

For four

170 g (5½ oz) Swiss chard stalks, cut into pieces about 37 mm (1½ inches) long
3 tablespoons olive oil
2 cloves garlic, peeled and chopped
2 tablespoons chopped parsley
Salt
Freshly ground black pepper

1 When the stalks have been trimmed of all their green tops and cut into

37 mm ($1\frac{1}{2}$-inch) lengths, rinse them in cold water, then drop them into 3 litres ($5\frac{1}{4}$ pints) salted boiling water. Cook until tender when pierced with a fork, about 30 minutes or more, depending on the stalks. Drain and set aside.

2 Put the olive oil and garlic into a 200- or 225-mm (8- or 9-inch) frying pan or sauté pan, and turn on the heat to medium.

3 As soon as the garlic becomes very lightly coloured, add the cooked stalks, the parsley, salt, and pepper. Turn up the heat to medium high, and sauté the stalks, turning them from time to time, for about 5 or 6 minutes.

4 Transfer all the contents of the pan to a serving dish, and serve promptly.

MENU SUGGESTIONS

The country treatment of these stalks suggests pork for the meat course. For example, *Costolette di maiale con i funghi* or *Costolette di maiale ai due vini*. Also good with chicken fricassees.

Melanzanine con la mozzarella

BABY AUBERGINES WITH MOZZARELLA

Baby aubergines that resemble the small, sweet ones of Sicily are still quite a rare sight in the vegetable markets, but many people are growing their own. They can be used, of course, in any recipe for aubergine, but this one is specially tailored to take advantage of their small size and their sweetness. The aubergines are split in two, cooked slowly in olive oil with a little garlic and parsley, and topped with melted mozzarella.

For six or more

8 tiny aubergines, under 125 mm (5 inches) long and 30 mm (2 inches) thick
$2\frac{1}{2}$ cloves garlic, peeled and chopped
2 tablespoons chopped parsley
Salt
Freshly ground black pepper
30 g (1 oz) plain breadcrumbs
6 tablespoons olive oil
225 g (8 oz) whole-milk mozzarella, cut into slices or strips no thicker than 6 mm ($\frac{1}{4}$ inch)

1 Cut off the green tops from the aubergines, and rinse them in cold water. Split them in half lengthways.
2 Score the flesh of the aubergines in a criss-cross pattern. Cut deeply into the flesh, but do not go through the skin on the other side.
3 Choose a sauté pan large enough to contain all the aubergines in a single layer. (If you need two pans, increase the quantity of olive oil to 8 tablespoons.) Lay the aubergines in the pan, skin side down, flat side facing up.
4 In a small bowl, put the garlic, parsley, a liberal amount of salt and pepper, the breadcrumbs and 1 tablespoon olive oil. Mix well.
5 Spoon a little of the mixture over each aubergine. Spread it evenly with your fingertips, forcing some into the crevices of the criss-cross cuts.
6 Pour the remaining olive oil in a thin stream, partly over the aubergines, partly into the pan.
7 Cover, and turn on the heat to medium low. Cook until the flesh of the aubergines is creamy tender, 20 minutes or more.
8 Cover each aubergine with mozzarella, and turn up the heat to medium. Cover, and cook until the mozzarella has melted.
Serve warm, but not piping hot.

MENU SUGGESTIONS

This dish is substantial enough to replace the pasta course. It could precede any meat that is both savoury and uncomplicated, such as *Farsumauru-il braciolone* or *Costolette di vitello profumate all'aglio e rosmarino*. Or it could be served alone as a light luncheon, along with good bread, and followed by a tomato and basil salad.

Fettine croccanti di melanzana

CRISP-FRIED AUBERGINE SLICES

Vegetarians can be very nice people, I am told, but some of their bad restaurants have done unspeakable things to aubergines, such as that soggy, greasy slab that is sometimes called a vegetarian cutlet. Well, here is a recipe for *real* aubergine cutlets.

The aubergines are sliced very thin, coated with a light egg-and-breadcrumb batter – just like veal cutlets *alla milanese* – and fried. That is all it takes to make them turn out crisp, crackling, and delicious.

For four to six

1 medium aubergine [560 to 680 g ($1\frac{1}{4}$ to $1\frac{1}{2}$ lb)]
Salt
1 egg, beaten in a bowl with $\frac{1}{4}$ teaspoon salt
225 g (8 oz) fine, dry breadcrumbs, spread on a dinner plate or on wax paper
Enough vegetable oil to come 25 mm (1 inch) up the side of the pan

1 Peel the aubergine and cut off its green stem. Cut the aubergine in two crossways, thus dividing it into stubby halves about 90 mm ($3\frac{1}{2}$ inches) long. Cut both halves lengthways into thin slices no more than 3 mm ($\frac{1}{8}$ inch) thick. The most manageable way to hold the aubergine while slicing it is to stand it on end, resting the flat cut side against the chopping board.

2 Spread the aubergine slices in slightly overlapping rows on a board or large dish. Sprinkle each row with salt before lapping the next row over it. Prop the board or dish at a slight angle to allow liquid released by the aubergine to run off. Allow to stand for 30 to 45 minutes.

3 Pat the aubergine slices dry with kitchen paper. Dip each slice into the beaten egg, then dredge in the breadcrumbs. Press the breadcrumbs onto the aubergine with the flat of your hand until your hand feels dry and the breadcrumbs are firmly stuck to the surface of the aubergine.

4 Heat up the oil in a frying pan over medium-high heat. When it is quite hot, slip in the breaded aubergine slices and turn the heat down to medium. Do not put in any more slices than will fit comfortably without overlapping. Fry and turn the aubergine until it is crisp on both sides. When crisp, remove with a long fork or slotted spatula, and transfer to a dish lined with kitchen paper to drain. As the first batch is done, add more until all the aubergine is done. Sprinkle with salt, and serve piping hot.

MENU SUGGESTIONS

Whenever you are in doubt about what to serve with a meat course that has a tricky sauce or pronounced flavour, you can always turn confidently to these crisp aubergines. They will get on well with anything. Try them with *Agnello in fricassea*, *Rognoncini di agnello saltati con cipolla* or *Pollo in umido col cavolo nero*.

Melanzane e peperoni fritti

DEEP-FRIED AUBERGINES AND PEPPERS

Do not be disappointed if the vegetables in this recipe do not turn out crackling crisp. They are not supposed to. Deep-frying, here, is used to cook the aubergine and peppers long enough to make them tender, and to intensify their flavours. After they have been fried and drained, they are bathed with olive oil in which a little garlic has been very faintly browned.

For four or more

1 medium aubergine [about 680 g (1½ lb)]
Salt
4 sweet red peppers
Enough vegetable oil to come 12 mm (½ inch) up the sides of the pan
6 tablespoons olive oil
2½ cloves garlic, peeled and chopped fine
3 tablespoons chopped parsley
Freshly ground black pepper

1 Rinse the aubergine in cold water, and peel it. Cut off the green top.

2 Cut the peeled aubergine into cubes no larger than 37 mm (1½ inches).

3 Put the diced aubergine into a pasta colander set over a deep dish. Sprinkle very liberally with salt. Allow to rest for at least 1 hour.

4 After the aubergines have sat in the colander for an hour, rinse them in cold water to remove the salt. Then take a few pieces at a time in your hands, squeeze out some of the remaining moisture, and lay them all out on kitchen paper to dry.

5 Cut the peppers into strips lengthways, following their deep folds. Scoop out and discard the cores and seeds. Peel the strips with a swivel-action peeler, and cut them into pieces 37 to 50 mm (1½ to 2 inches) long.

6 Put enough vegetable oil in a sauté pan to come at least 12 mm (½ inch) up the sides of the pan. Turn on the heat to medium high. When the oil is hot (when a piece of aubergine goes in, it must be ringed with sizzling bubbles), put in as much of the aubergine as will fit without being crowded. Cook until golden brown all over, then transfer to kitchen paper to drain. Sprinkle with salt, very lightly.

7 When you have done all the aubergines, turn the heat up to high, and put in as much of the pepper as will fit loosely in the pan. Cook very briefly, first on one side, then the other, until lightly browned. The peppers should

be tender but firm, not too yielding. Transfer to kitchen paper to drain, and sprinkle lightly with salt.

8 Put the olive oil and garlic into a small saucepan, and turn on the heat to medium. As soon as the garlic becomes lightly coloured, add the parsley, stir once or twice quickly, and take the pan off the heat.

9 Put all the fried aubergines and peppers into a deep serving dish or bowl. Pour over them the olive oil from the saucepan, and toss well. Taste and check salt, and add 1 or 2 grindings of pepper to taste.

MENU SUGGESTIONS

If served while still warm, this can accompany, and add life to, grilled or boiled beef or chicken. Serve also with *Il bollito rifatto alla moda di papi* or *Cotolette alla palermitana*. Served at room temperature, with a crusty slice of bread, it makes a delicious appetiser.

Polpettine di Melanzane

FRIED AUBERGINE PATTIES

Can there be any vegetable more resourceful than the aubergine? One is always discovering new and irresistible ways in which it may be prepared. In these meatless patties, which are among the most appealing I have ever come across, aubergine is the star of the show. It is first baked, then peeled, drained of its liquid, chopped, and formed into patties with an assortment of tasty ingredients such as garlic, parsley, egg and cheese.

Apart from the baking time for the aubergine, it takes no time at all, and is as good as it is easy to do. These patties are subject to many variations. Two of the most interesting ones are given below, after the basic recipe.

For four to six

- 1 large or 2 medium-small aubergines [about 900 g (2 lb)]
- 40 oz (1¼ oz) fine, dry, plain breadcrumbs
- 3 tablespoons parsley, chopped fine
- 2 cloves garlic, peeled and chopped fine
- 1 egg
- 3 tablespoons freshly grated Parmesan cheese (optional)
- Salt
- Freshly ground black pepper
- Enough vegetable oil to come 12 mm (½ inch) up the sides of the pan
- 60 g (2 oz) plain flour, spread on a plate

1 Preheat the oven to 200°C/400°F/Mark 6.

2 Rinse the aubergines in cold water, and place them on the uppermost rack of the preheated oven. Cook for about 40 minutes, depending on their size. Test them with a toothpick; if it penetrates easily the aubergines are done.

3 Remove them from the oven, and as soon as they are cool enough to handle, peel them, and cut them up in large pieces, about six pieces for each aubergine. Put the pieces in a colander to drain. You will find a considerable amount of liquid running off and you can accelerate the process by squeezing the pieces gently. It should take no more than 10 minutes altogether.

4 Chop the aubergines very fine, and mix in a bowl together with the breadcrumbs, parsley, chopped garlic, egg, and the optional grated cheese. Add salt and pepper to taste. If you have opted for the grated cheese, take its saltiness into account when seasoning. Mix thoroughly until all the ingredients are well amalgamated.

5 With your hands, shape the mixture into patties about 50 mm (2 inches) in diameter and 12 mm (½ inch) thick. Place them on a dish.

6 Put enough vegetable oil into a frying pan to come at least 12 mm (½ inch) up the sides of the pan and turn on the heat to high.

7 When the oil is very hot, dredge the patties on both sides in the flour, and slip them into the pan. Do not crowd them. When they have formed a nice dark crust on one side, turn them. When both sides are crusted, transfer them to kitchen paper to drain. Serve hot or at close to room temperature. Do not reheat or refrigerate.

AUBERGINE PATTIES, VARIATION 1

The fried patties from the basic recipe
3 medium onions, sliced very fine
6 tablespoons olive or vegetable oil
350 g (12 oz) tinned Italian plum tomatoes, chopped with their juice
Salt
Freshly ground black pepper

1 Choose a sauté pan large enough to contain all the fried patties in a single layer. Put in the onion and the oil, and over medium-low heat cook the onion until it turns a rich gold.

2 Add the tomatoes, and adjust the heat so that they cook at a slow, intermittent bubble. Cook until the tomato separates from the oil, about 15 to 20 minutes. Add salt and a few grindings of pepper.

3 Put in the fried aubergine patties, and turn them a few times in the onions and tomato sauce until they are well heated through. Serve at once.

AUBERGINE PATTIES, VARIATION 2

The fried patties from the basic recipe
An oven dish large enough to hold all the patties in a single layer
Butter, enough to grease the pan
1 whole-milk mozzarella, cut into 6-mm ($\frac{1}{4}$-inch) thick slices

1 Preheat the oven to 200°C/400°F/Mark 6.

2 Lightly grease the oven dish with butter, and place the fried patties in the dish, in a single layer, edge to edge, but without overlapping.

3 Cover each patty with sliced mozzarella, and place the dish on the uppermost rack of the preheated oven. When the mozzarella melts, remove from the oven and serve promptly.

MENU SUGGESTIONS

These patties take the place of meat. They can be served as a light luncheon, followed by a salad of baked beetroots or beetroot tops, or a mixed salad with a varied assortment of raw greens and vegetables. For a more complete meal, they can be preceded by a pasta, such as *Spaghetti col sugo di cipolle*, *Penne col sugo di cavolfiore* or, from my first book, *Spaghetti 'ajo e ojo'* (page 88).

Erbette saltate per la piadina

SAUTÉED GREENS FOR PIADINA

A combination of both mild and slightly bitter greens is necessary to the success of this mixture. Savoy cabbage and spinach are the mild components, *cime di rapa* the bitter. In place of spinach you can use Swiss chard, if it is available. In fact, it would be an improvement. If you cannot find *cime di rapa* – it comes in long clusters of skinny leaves topped with pale yellow buds – substitute dandelion greens or experiment with other bitter field greens. The amount you use depends on its sharpness, and you can adjust the basic proportions given above to achieve a balance of mildness and bitterness pleasing to your taste.

For six

450 g (1 lb) fresh spinach or Swiss chard (see introductory remarks above)
225 g (8 oz) turnip tops (*cime di rapa*) (see introductory remarks)
450 g (1 lb) Savoy cabbage
Salt
4 tablespoons olive oil
3 to 4 cloves garlic, peeled and chopped
Freshly ground black pepper

1 Detach the spinach (or Swiss chard) at the base of the stems. Soak it in a basin of cold water to remove all traces of soil. Change the water several times, first removing the spinach each time, until you see that no more soil is settling at the bottom of the basin.

2 At the same time, but in a separate basin, follow the same procedure for washing the *cime di rapa*.

3 Remove and discard the darkest outer leaves of the Savoy cabbage, and cut off the butt end of the stem. Cut the cabbage into four parts.

4 Bring 3 to 4 litres ($5\frac{1}{4}$ to 7 pints) water to the boil, add 1 tablespoon salt, and put in the *cime di rapa*. Put on the lid slightly askew, and cook for 8 to 12 minutes, depending on freshness and tenderness. Drain and set aside. If using Swiss chard, cook it in exactly the same manner, stalks included. The Savoy cabbage is also cooked in the same manner *except* that you do not put any salt in its cooking liquid. The cabbage will take about 15 to 20 minutes to cook, until the thickest part of its leaves is easily pierced by a fork.

5 Cook the spinach in a covered pan with just the water that adheres to its leaves and $\frac{1}{2}$ tablespoon salt. Cook until tender, 10 minutes or more, depending on how young and fresh it is. Drain and set aside. (To avoid scrubbing more pots than is necessary you can cook all the greens in the same pan, but at separate times, of course, and with fresh changes of water each time.)

6 Gently but firmly squeeze all the moisture you can out of all the greens. Chop them all together, not too fine.

7 Put the oil and garlic into a medium sauté pan, and sauté until the garlic colours just lightly.

8 Put in the chopped greens, turning them with a fork so that they are all evenly coated, adding salt and pepper. Sauté over medium heat for about 10 minutes, turning the greens frequently. Taste and check seasoning. Serve hot.

Note You can prepare the greens up to step 7, just before they are to be sautéed, several hours ahead of time, but within the same day. Do not refrigerate.

MENU SUGGESTIONS

Although these greens are meant to go with *piadina*, it would be a pity to pass them up just because you have not made *piadina*. They are delicious on their own, particularly as a vegetable accompaniment to any pork dish. They are perfect with sausages, either simple browned sausage or *Salsicce col vino rosso e i funghi secchi*.

Porri al burro e formaggio

BRAISED LEEKS WITH PARMESAN CHEESE

Leeks are one of the most gentle and delicate members of the onion family. They are very good in soups and braised with other vegetables. This delicious preparation is a reminder of how fine they can be.

For four

4 good thick leeks or 6 medium ones
45 g (1½ oz) butter
Salt
3 tablespoons freshly grated Parmesan cheese

1 Remove from the leeks any leaves that may be yellowed or withered. Cut off the roots from the bulbous end. Do not cut off or discard the green tops. Cut each leek in half lengthways.

2 Wash the leeks very thoroughly under cold running water, spreading the tops with your hands to make sure any hidden bits of grit are washed away.

3 Put the leeks into a shallow casserole or sauté pan. A long, narrow shape of pan is ideal, but it does not matter too much, as long as the leeks lie flat and straight.

4 Add the butter and 6 tablespoons water (adding more water if there is not sufficient to cover), cover the pan, and cook over medium-low heat for 15 to 25 minutes, depending on the freshness and thickness of the leeks, until they are tender when pricked with a fork. Turn them from time to time.

4 When tender, uncover the pan, turn up the heat, and boil away all the liquid. The leeks should become lightly browned in the process. Before removing from the heat, add the grated cheese, mixing it in with the leeks. Transfer to a warm dish and serve at once.

Note You can use exactly the same procedure, with excellent results, to cook spring onions.

MENU SUGGESTIONS

Leeks or spring onions done in this manner will go well with virtually any meat course, but what they get on really famously with is veal. Try them with *Scaloppine piccanti*, *Ossobuchi in bianco* or *Punto di vitello arrosto*.

Insalatina tenera con la pancetta

SMOTHERED LETTUCE WITH PANCETTA

Lettuce, of course, is not just a salad green. It is a vegetable, which can be used, like other vegetables, in soups, stews, and sautéed dishes. There is a special red chicory from Treviso that is delicious grilled, and in Genoa they use lettuce as a wrapper for meat stuffing (see page 89).

Here, tender lettuce is smothered in a pan together with oil, sautéed *pancetta*, and onion. Sweet onion, savoury *pancetta*, and the gentle tartness of lettuce combine flavours in very appealing harmony.

For four

680 g ($1\frac{1}{2}$ lb) round lettuce
2 tablespoons vegetable oil
1 small onion, chopped fine
30 g (1 oz) *pancetta* or green bacon, chopped fine
Salt

1 Detach nearly all the lettuce leaves from the head. Save just the hearts to use in a salad on another, but not too distant, occasion.

2 Soak the leaves in a basin or sink filled with cold water. Drain, and change the water several times. When thoroughly clean, shake off all the water, using a salad spinner or any other method for drying lettuce.

3 Cut or tear each leaf into two or three pieces, depending on its size, and set aside.

4 Put the oil, onion, and *pancetta* into a sauté pan, and, over medium heat, sauté until the onion becomes a rich gold colour. Stir occasionally.

5 Add as much cut-up lettuce as will not overfill the pan. As it cooks and diminishes in bulk, add the rest. Cover the pan. Cook for 30 to 40 minutes, until the thick, central rib of the leaf is just tender. If the lettuce has thrown off some liquid, uncover the pan, raise the heat, and boil it away. Serve at once. Do not reheat or refrigerate.

MENU SUGGESTIONS

A mild yet earthy dish that would go best with a course such as *Bistecchine di manzo alla cacciatora*, *Scaloppine ammantate* or *Pollo in tegame al limone*.

Verdure miste al forno

MIXED BAKED VEGETABLES

This is a cheerful, comforting dish. The only flavours present are the vegetables' own, concentrated and intermingled in the oven's dry heat. Yet each vegetable clearly retains its own texture and identity. The most appropriate oil to use here would be a green, fruity olive oil. If you are not prepared to be prodigal with olive oil because a good one is so expensive and hard to come by, the dish will work out quite satisfactorily with vegetable oil. You will want some good crusty French bread to accompany this.

For six

4 medium red potatoes
3 sweet and meaty peppers, red, yellow or green
3 round tomatoes or 6 plum tomatoes, fresh, firm, and ripe
4 medium onions
4 tablespoons fruity olive oil or vegetable oil (see remarks above)
2 tablespoons salt
Freshly ground black pepper

1 Preheat oven to 200°C/400°F/Mark 6.

2 Peel the potatoes and cut them into wedges about 25 mm (1 inch) thick.

3 Cut the peppers into lengthwise sections, following their folds. Scrape away and discard all the seeds and the pulpy core to which they are attached. Remove as much of the peppers' skin as you can, using a swivel-action peeler and a light touch.

4 Cut the tomatoes into six to eight wedge-shaped sections. If you are using plum tomatoes, cut them in half lengthways.

5 Peel the onions and cut them into four sections each.

6 Wash all the vegetables in cold water, and drain well. Put them into a baking dish in which they will fit comfortably. If they are too tightly packed, they will steep and turn soggy in their own vapours.

7 Add the oil, salt, and one or two grindings of pepper. Place the dish in the upper third of the preheated oven. Turn the vegetables every 10 minutes or so. The dish is done when the potatoes are tender, after about 25 to 30 minutes. Do not worry if some of the vegetables become slightly charred at the edges. It is quite all right, and even desirable. If after 20 minutes you see that the tomatoes have thrown off an excessive amount of liquid, you may turn up the oven to 230°C/450°F/Mark 8 or higher for the remaining cooking time.

8 When done, transfer the vegetables to a warm dish, using a slotted spoon. You do not want too much oil in the dish. If there are any bits stuck to the sides or bottom of the baking dish, scrape them loose and add them to the dish. These are choice morsels. Serve at once.

MENU SUGGESTIONS

Choose a meat course that is savoury but not overwhelming. You do not want to be distracted in your enjoyment of the vegetables. I would recommend *Cotolette alla palermitana*, *Spiedini all'uccelletto* or, from my first book, *Arrosto di agnello al ginepro* (page 236).

Funghi fritti alla moda dei porcini

FRIED MUSHROOMS

This is the way we fry wild boletus mushrooms in Italy, especially those small ones found in pine woods which we call *pinaroli*. It is a very good way to fry cultivated mushrooms. It cannot quite endow them with the flavour of the wild boletus, but it does wonderful things for their texture.

For four

350 g (12 oz) fresh, firm mushrooms
Enough vegetable oil to come at least 6 mm ($\frac{1}{4}$ inch) up the sides of the pan
1 extra large egg
Salt
Freshly ground black pepper
150 g (5 oz) plain, dry breadcrumbs, spread on a plate

1 Rinse the mushrooms rapidly under cold running water. Dry them thoroughly with a soft cloth or kitchen paper.

2 Cut them lengthways into slices less than 12 mm ($\frac{1}{2}$ inch) thick. Do not detach the caps from the stems. Do not cut them and set them aside for later, or they will discolour.

3 Put the oil into a frying pan, and turn on the heat to high.

4 Break the egg into a deep dish, add a little salt and 1 or 2 grindings of pepper. Beat the egg lightly with a fork.

5 When the oil is very hot, dip the mushrooms in the egg, letting excess egg flow back into the dish. Dredge them, one piece at a time, in the breadcrumbs, on both sides. Slip them into the pan. Do not overcrowd.

6 When they have turned a deep golden brown on one side turn them over. When both sides become nicely coloured, transfer them to kitchen paper to drain, or onto a cooling rack over a dish. Add more mushrooms to the pan as room is made for them. When they are all done, sprinkle with salt and serve at once.

MENU SUGGESTIONS

It would be difficult to find a meat course that would not profit from the presence of fried mushrooms – save those dishes that already have mushrooms in them. Combinations that are particularly pleasing are with *Spalla di vitello brasata*, *Agnello in fricassea* and *Anatra arrosto*.

Funghi Stufati

SMOTHERED MUSHROOMS

In Italian cooking mushrooms are usually inseparable from olive oil, garlic, and parsley. This Milanese recipe starts out with oil and garlic, but substitutes rosemary for parsley and adds a few minutes' slow cooking with tomatoes.

As an optional procedure, you can use dried wild mushrooms to produce a more intense and woody flavour. It is not an indispensable step, however. Even without wild mushrooms, you will find this a fragrant and tasty dish.

For four

20 g ($\frac{2}{3}$ oz) dried imported boletus mushrooms (optional)
450 g (1 lb) fresh, firm mushrooms
6 tablespoons olive oil
1½ cloves garlic, peeled and chopped
½ teaspoon chopped rosemary
Salt
Freshly ground black pepper
110 g (4 oz) tinned Italian plum tomatoes, cut up, with their juice

1 (Proceed to step 3 if not using wild mushrooms.) Soak the dried mushrooms in a small bowl in 350 ml ($\frac{2}{3}$ pint) lukewarm water for at least 30 minutes. When they have finished soaking, lift them out carefully, without stirring the water. Rinse them several times in cold water. Cut them up in large pieces, and set aside.

2 Filter the water in which the mushrooms have soaked through a wire strainer lined with kitchen paper, and reserve.

3 Wash the fresh mushrooms rapidly under cold running water. Wipe them thoroughly dry with a soft towel or kitchen paper.

4 Cut the mushrooms lengthways in half or, if large, in quarters. Do not detach the caps from the stems.

5 Put the oil and garlic into a large sauté pan, and turn on the heat to medium high.

6 When the garlic begins to colour lightly, add the rosemary, the optional wild mushrooms, and their filtered water. (If you are not using wild mushrooms, proceed immediately to step 7.) Cook at lively heat, stirring from time to time, until the mushroom liquid has completely evaporated.

7 Add the cut-up fresh mushrooms, salt, and a liberal grinding of pepper. Turn up the heat to high, and cook, stirring frequently, until most of the liquid the mushrooms throw off has evaporated.

8 Add the tomatoes with their juice, turning the heat down to low. Stir well, then cover the pan. Cook for 10 minutes, taking care that the mush-

rooms do not stick to the bottom of the pan. If this should happen, loosen them with a couple of tablespoons of warm water.

9 Serve promptly.

Note You may complete the cooking a few hours in advance and reheat the mushrooms, uncovered, just before serving. Do not refrigerate.

MENU SUGGESTIONS

Do not couple these mushrooms with meat courses that have a tomato sauce, or stews or braised dishes that are done with vegetables. They would be a good accompaniment for *Messicani di vitello*, *Rotolo di vitello con spinaci* or *Il pollo ripieno*.

Patate alla boscaiola

POTATOES BAKED WITH MUSHROOMS

This is a recipe from Liguria, the Italian Riviera, a land where potatoes, garlic, and mushrooms are justly venerated. Here, we have all three. In Liguria the dish would be made with wild boletus mushrooms. A similar, if not identical, result, can be achieved by mingling, as we do in many other recipes of this book, fragrant dried wild mushrooms with the fresh cultivated variety.

For four

25 g ($\frac{3}{4}$ oz) dried boletus mushrooms
450 g (1 lb) small, new potatoes
225 g (8 oz) fresh, firm mushrooms
8 tablespoons olive oil
2 cloves garlic, peeled and chopped very fine
2 tablespoons chopped parsley
Freshly ground black pepper
Salt

1 Soak the dried mushrooms at least 30 minutes in advance in a small bowl with 350 ml ($\frac{2}{3}$ pint) warm water. Afterwards, rinse them, and filter the water in which they have soaked, as described on page 191.

2 Put the reconstituted mushrooms and their filtered water into a small saucepan, and turn on the heat to medium high. Cook until all the liquid has boiled away, and set aside. Preheat the oven to 200°C/400°F/Mark 6.

3 Peel the potatoes, rinse them in cold water, and cut them in slices no thicker than 6 mm ($\frac{1}{4}$ inch).

4 Rinse the fresh mushrooms rapidly in cold running water, then wipe them thoroughly dry with a soft cloth or kitchen paper. Cut them lengthways, without detaching the caps from the stems, in slices the same thickness as the potatoes.

5 Choose an oven dish in which all the ingredients will fit without being piled up any deeper than 37 mm ($1\frac{1}{2}$ inches). Put in the olive oil, garlic, potatoes, the wild and fresh mushrooms, the parsley, and a few liberal grindings of pepper. Mix everything well, and level off the contents of the dish. Place the dish in the uppermost level of the preheated oven.

6 Bake for 15 minutes, then add 2 or 3 large pinches of salt, and mix all the ingredients well. Bake for 15 minutes more, or until the potatoes are tender.

Allow to rest for a minute or two and remove some of the excess oil before serving. Do not prepare in advance or reheat.

MENU SUGGESTIONS

This dish should be paired with a meat course of equal substance and character. *Bistecchine di manzo alla cacciatora*, *Agnello in fricassea* or *Costolette di maiale alla modenese* would all be good choices.

Crocchette di patate alla romagnola

POTATO AND HAM FRITTERS

These are the kind of fritters we might have in Italy at a farmhouse lunch, along with a roast bird or a stew or cold meats such as prosciutto or homemade salami.

The batter is a simple one that uses ingredients invariably present in an Italian home. It contains mashed boiled potatoes, egg, Parmesan cheese, and a few bits of prosciutto, *mortadella*, or mild salami. It is lightly spiced with a small, quickening pinch of nutmeg.

For six

450 g (1 lb) boiling potatoes
1 whole egg plus 1 yolk
180 g (6 oz) prosciutto or other ham or *mortadella* or salami, chopped very fine
50 g ($1\frac{3}{4}$ oz) freshly grated Parmesan cheese
$\frac{1}{8}$ teaspoon nutmeg
Salt
Freshly ground black pepper
Enough vegetable oil to come 6 mm ($\frac{1}{4}$ inch) up the sides of the pan
90 g (3 oz) plain flour, spread on a dish

1 Wash the potatoes and boil them, unpeeled, in abundant water. When done, drain them and skin them while still hot, or as soon as you are able to handle them. Pass them through a food mill, or any other potato-mashing tool.

2 With a fork lightly beat the egg and the extra yolk in a mixing bowl. Add the chopped prosciutto, or other meat, and the Parmesan cheese, and mix well. Add the mashed potatoes, mix, then add the nutmeg, salt and pepper, and mix all the ingredients again thoroughly. Taste and check seasoning.

3 Take a little of the mixture at a time in your hands and shape into small patties about 50 mm (2 inches) across and no more than 12 mm ($\frac{1}{2}$ inch) thick.

(**Note** You can prepare everything up to this point several hours in advance, as long as the fritters will be fried later on the same day. Do not refrigerate.)

4 Heat up the oil in a medium frying pan over high heat.

5 Turn the potato patties one at a time in the flour, pressing them lightly with your hands. Shake off excess flour, and slip them into the pan when the oil is very hot. When they have formed a crust on one side, turn them. When the other side forms a crust, transfer them to kitchen paper to drain. Serve while hot.

MENU SUGGESTIONS

These fritters are country fare, and are delicious served with a spit-roasted chicken. They would also be most enjoyable with *Stufatino di manzo con i piselli*, *Salsicce con le cipolle*, or, from my first book, *Coniglio in padella* (page 271).

Patate con le acciughe

PAN-ROASTED POTATOES WITH ANCHOVIES

Nowhere else in Italy do they do so many interesting things with potatoes as on the Riviera. This is one of them. The potatoes are roasted in an open pan, in oil that has been flavoured with anchovies. At the end they are flavoured with a little garlic and parsley. Ideally, the garlic should be as fresh and sweeet as that of the Genoese coast. Indispensable in this preparation is a good, fruity olive oil.

For four to six

680 g ($1\frac{1}{2}$ lb) mature potatoes, preferably red
6 tablespoons olive oil
30 g (1 oz) butter
2 flat anchovy fillets, chopped
Salt
Freshly ground black pepper
$1\frac{1}{2}$ cloves garlic, peeled and chopped
3 tablespoons chopped parsley

1 Peel the potatoes, and cut them into slices no more than 6 mm ($\frac{1}{4}$ inch) thick.

2 Let the sliced potatoes soak in a bowl of cold water for at least 5 minutes; then drain them and pat them thoroughly dry with kitchen paper.

3 Choose a sauté pan that will later be able to contain all the potatoes in a layer about 37 mm ($1\frac{1}{2}$ inches) thick. Put in the oil, butter, and chopped anchovy fillets. Turn the heat on to medium, and sauté the anchovies for a few seconds, mashing them a little and stirring with a wooden spoon.

4 Put in the potatoes, with 2 or 3 pinches of salt and a grinding of pepper. Turn them so all the slices are coated with the hot butter and oil.

5 Cover the pan, and cook for 7 to 8 minutes, turning the potatoes from time to time.

6 Uncover, and continue cooking for another 15 minutes or so, until the potatoes are tender. Turn them while cooking, from time to time. The slices should form a very light brown crust.

7 When the potatoes are nearly done, put in the garlic and parsley, and stir well. Cook for another minute or so, then serve at once.

MENU SUGGESTIONS

One could make a meal just with these potatoes, a small loaf of good bread, and a bottle of a young and lively white wine. But they can and do accompany a great variety of meat courses. Try them with *Messicani di vitello*, *Arrosto di maiale ubriaco*, *Pollo in fricassea alla marchigiana*.

Patate in umido

STEWED POTATOES WITH ONIONS AND TOMATOES

Before the distinctions between seasons became partly blurred by the presence in the markets of vegetables from greenhouses or warmer climates, this immensely satisfying dish was typical of Italian winter menus. Even during the most sullen month of the year, one could always count on potatoes, onions and tinned peeled tomatoes to make a warm, sunny dish.

Here the onions are sliced and sautéed in olive oil until they are golden and soft, tomatoes are added and cooked very briefly, then they are joined by the cut-up potatoes. For fragrance and colour you can add green peppers, a most agreeable, even if not seasonal, touch. If you really must, you can substitute vegetable oil for olive oil, but the result will certainly not be as good. You can use any kind of potato, but if new potatoes are available they are to be preferred for their sweetness and tenderness. The amount of tomato and onion can vary to suit your taste; a little more of one or less of the other will work equally well.

This is a dish that is as hearty as a good meat stew, without the meat. It begs for good firm bread to go with it and help take up all the delicious juices.

For six

225 g (8 oz) onions, sliced very thin
6 tablespoons olive oil or vegetable oil or a combination of both
1 green pepper, seeds and core removed, cut into 12-mm ($\frac{1}{2}$-inch) wide strips (optional)
300 g (10 oz) tinned Italian plum tomatoes, cut up, with their juice
Salt
Freshly ground black pepper
680 g ($1\frac{1}{2}$ lb) potatoes, peeled, washed, and cut into 25-mm (1-inch) cubes

1 Put the onions and the oil into a sauté pan, and cook over medium heat until the onions wilt and turn light gold. If using green pepper, put it in at the same time as the onions.

2 Add the cut-up tomatoes with their juice, salt, and a few grindings of pepper, and turn the heat down to low. Cook the tomato at a slow, intermittent bubble, for about 15 minutes or so, until it separates from the oil.

3 Add the potatoes, and turn the heat down very low. Cover the pan. Cook the potatoes until they are tender when pricked with a fork, after about 30 minutes, depending on the potatoes. Taste and check salt. Serve while hot.

Note The entire dish may be prepared in advance and reheated, if done within the same day. Do not keep overnight, and do not refrigerate.

MENU SUGGESTIONS

This dish should accompany a tasty but uncomplicated meat course. For example, *Bistecchine di manzo alla cacciatora*, *Cotolette alla palermitana*, or *Spalla di vitello brasata*. It is particularly good served with boiled short ribs of beef.

Zucchine gratinate

GRATIN OF COURGETTES WITH TOMATO AND HERBS

There is a rich garden flavour to this dish that the gratin treatment helps to bring out.

The courgettes are sliced thin and cooked separately with olive oil and garlic. The garlic is not browned so that it contributes more sweetness than pungency. A simple tomato sauce is prepared, with marjoram and parsley. Courgettes and tomatoes are then put together in layers, sprinkled with Parmesan, and baked. The whole dish can be done early on the day it will be served, and reheated in the oven. Do not refrigerate.

For six

680 g ($1\frac{1}{2}$ lb) fresh, firm courgettes, soaked, scrubbed and trimmed as instructed on page 160
4 tablespoons olive oil
$1\frac{1}{2}$ cloves garlic, peeled and chopped
1 medium chopped onion
225 g (8 oz) tinned Italian plum tomatoes, cut up, with their juice
$\frac{1}{8}$ teaspoon marjoram
1 tablespoon chopped parsley
Salt
Freshly ground black pepper
2 tablespoons freshly grated Parmesan cheese

1 Preheat oven to 200°C/400°F/Mark 6.

2 Cut the courgettes into very thin disc-like slices.

3 Put 2 tablespoons olive oil and all the garlic into a sauté pan and turn the heat on to medium high. As soon as the oil is hot, and before the garlic

colours, put in all the courgette slices. Cook, uncovered, stirring from time to time, until the courgettes are limp. Turn off the heat.

4 In a small saucepan, put the chopped onion and the remaining 2 tablespoons olive oil. Over medium heat, cook until the onion becomes translucent. Add the cut-up tomatoes with their juice and the marjoram, and continue to cook, uncovered, for 15 to 20 minutes, or until the oil and the tomatoes separate. Turn off the heat, and stir in the parsley, 2 or 3 large pinches of salt and a few grindings of pepper.

5 Smear the bottom of an oven dish with a little bit of oil from the saucepan. Spread half the courgettes in an even layer on the bottom of the dish. Cover with half the sauce from the saucepan, and sprinkle with a tablespoon grated cheese. Cover this with a layer of the remaining courgettes, on top of which you will spread the rest of the sauce and sprinkle the remaining Parmesan.

6 Place the dish in the uppermost level of the oven, and bake for 20 minutes, or until the surface has dried somewhat. Allow to settle for about 10 minutes before serving.

MENU SUGGESTIONS

Avoid pairing this gratin of courgettes with any meat dish that has a tomato sauce, or, like some stews, that already has vegetables in it. It would be an enjoyable accompaniment to *Costolette di vitello profumate all'aglio e rosmarino*, *Pollo in tegame al limone* or, from my first book, *Polpettone alla toscana* (page 211).

Zucchine trifolate con le cipolle

SAUTÉED COURGETTES WITH ONIONS

How this dish is done can be described in few words: thin rounds of courgettes are cooked over rapid heat in a sauté pan with butter and browned onions. But there is something more at work here. It is the gift Italian cooks possess of taking an ingredient just so far as is needed to release its simple goodness – and stopping there. This is pure Italian cooking at its best. To understand it, no wordy mediation is required. It only wants to be tried.

For four to six

5 medium zucchini [about 680 g ($1\frac{1}{2}$ lb)]
45 g ($1\frac{1}{2}$ oz) butter
2 medium onions, sliced very thin
Salt

1 Scrub the courgettes thoroughly under cold running water until their skin feels very smooth. If the skin is blemished or feels gritty, scrape away or lightly peel off the top layer. Slice the courgettes as thin as possible. If you have a food processor it will do the job perfectly. If you are slicing by hand make the slices as uniform as possible but do not get tense over it. An extra 3 mm ($\frac{1}{8}$ inch) is not going to make any difference.

2 Put the butter and onion into a broad sauté pan and cook uncovered over medium heat until the onion turns a nice golden brown.

3 Add the sliced courgettes and 2 or 3 large pinches of salt, and turn up the heat to high. Stir frequently. Do not cover. The cooking time can vary greatly, depending on how young and fresh the courgettes are, but they are done when they turn a light brown at the edges and are tender, but not mushy. Small, freshly picked courgettes may be done in less than 5 minutes; old, brawny ones may need 20 minutes or more. Taste from time to time. Serve promptly when done.

Note Although this dish is at its best the moment it is done, it can be prepared a few hours before and reheated. Do not refrigerate, however, and do not keep it overnight.

MENU SUGGESTIONS

Except for those dishes that already have in them a conspicuous onion presence, or other vegetables, these sautéed courgettes are an amiable and invariably successful accompaniment for any meat course. Try them with *Fettine di manzo farcite*, *Agnello in fricassea*, or *Pollo al limone*.

Zucchine saltate all'origano

SAUTÉED COURGETTES WITH OREGANO

This is a quick way to do courgettes – simply sauté them in olive oil. The oregano adds the frank, forward taste of the sunny cooking of the South.

For four to six

680 g ($1\frac{1}{2}$ lb) courgettes, preferably small young ones, very firm and fresh
8 tablespoons olive oil
3 cloves garlic, peeled and chopped not too fine
Salt
Freshly ground black pepper
$\frac{1}{4}$ teaspoon oregano

1 Soak the courgettes for 10 minutes in a basin of cold water. Then scrub them under cold running water until the skin feels clean and smooth. If the skin is flabby or blemished, and still feels a bit gritty, scrape away or lightly peel off the thin top layer.

2 Cut off and discard both ends from all the courgettes. Slice the courgettes into very thin discs, and set aside.

3 Choose a sauté pan deep enough to contain all the sliced courgettes without piling them up more than 25 or 37 mm (1 or $1\frac{1}{2}$ inches) high. Put in the oil and garlic, and turn the heat on to medium.

4 When the garlic has coloured lightly, add the courgettes, 2 or 3 large pinches of salt, some pepper, and the oregano. Turn the heat up to medium high, and cook, uncovered, stirring frequently. If the courgettes are as fresh as they ought to be, they will be done in less than 10 minutes. They should be tender but still a little firm. Drain away most of the oil before serving, leaving just enough to coat the courgettes, and for a crusty piece of good bread to mop up.

Note This dish can be prepared entirely in advance, several hours before serving. Do not refrigerate. Reheat gently just before serving.

MENU SUGGESTIONS

Except for stews with vegetables, and dishes that already have oregano, any meat course will benefit from the spirited, tasty presence of these courgettes. Interesting combinations would be with *Brasato di manzo con le cipolle*, *Costicine di maiale alla trevigiana* or *Anatra arrosto*.

SALADS

Le Insalate

Dressing an Italian Salad

ITALIAN salad dressing is olive oil, salt, and wine vinegar.

Sometimes I hear people discuss the proportion of oil to vinegar as though it were a numbers game: 2 to 1, 3 to 1, 5 to 1, all one needs is to come up with the winning combination. Unfortunately, no such formula exists. So much depends on the density and fruitiness of the oil, and the aroma and sharpness of the vinegar. Yet it is so easy to make a good salad once one understands the rôle that each of its components plays.

The central and commanding one is that of the greens and vegetables. The character and richness of the oil supplies the all-enveloping setting for it. The vinegar, along with any other flavouring that may be used, is 'up front', spotlighting and calling attention to the production. It follows that any shortcomings in the oil will impoverish the show, while an excess of vinegar will steal it.

One cannot overestimate the importance of using a good, intensely fruity olive oil, and using it liberally. Without it there cannot be a successful salad, as Italians understand it. Italians will never taste a salad and exclaim, 'What a wonderful dressing!' but they do say, 'What marvellous oil.'

As an old proverb has it, one must be miserly with the vinegar. If you let it run away with you, its fierceness will upset the lightly balanced harmonies of the dish. For an Italian salad, vinegar should be natural wine vinegar, usually made from red wine, without any herbal embellishments.

Pepper is an optional addition. It does not appear too frequently, and when it does, it is used with discretion. It is always black pepper, because it has so much more aroma than the white, and, of course, it is freshly ground.

Garlic is a flavouring that can be exciting on rare occasions, but tiresome when brought on too often. Its presence should be an offstage one, as employed in the savoy cabbage salad on page 343.

Either parsley or basil will do most salads some good. Parsley is particularly nice with cucumbers, and basil never fails to enhance the taste and appearance of a tomato salad. Mint is a little more special, and is rarely used, but it is most successful in a citrus salad, such as the one on page 345.

Freshly squeezed lemon juice is sometimes a substitute for vinegar, quite refreshing with summer salads, It is particularly welcome on tomatoes, cucumbers, or carrots shredded very fine.

A very special vinegar, *aceto balsamico di Modena*, is beginning to find its way out of Italy in extremely limited quantities. It is made from the boiled-down must of white Trebbiano grapes, and aged in a series of barrels of different woods, of gradually diminishing size. By law it must be at least ten years old, but home-made *aceto balsamico* is often aged fifty years or more. It is a mellow, sweet-and-sour vinegar, with a heady fragrance. A minute quantity added to ordinary vinegar is sufficient in a salad. Waverley Root, in *The Food of Italy*, gives an interesting and well-researched account of *aceto balsamico*.

There is one type of salad, called *pinzimonio*, in which no vinegar or lemon is used. It is a dip of olive oil, coarse salt, and black pepper for raw fennel, celery, sweet peppers, or tender, young artichokes. *Pinzimonio* is a play on the verb *pinzare*, to pinch. *Monio* is borrowed from *matrimonio*, matrimony. One tears off – 'pinches' – a piece or leaf of the vegetable, and swirls it around in the small bowl, 'marrying' it with the dip.

Dressing a salad in Italy is done at the table, just before serving it, and there is nothing fussy about it. Choose a bowl ample enough to give all the greens or vegetables room to move around. Pour the salt, oil, and vinegar directly over the greens in the bowl. Toss thoroughly to distribute the dressing evenly but gently, especially in the case of tender field greens and soft lettuce, which can bruise easily. Taste and check the seasoning.

Verza cruda in insalata

RAW SAVOY CABBAGE SALAD

This is a favourite salad during the winter months when fresh, tender lettuce greens are not easily found in Italy. The Savoy cabbage is shredded fine, as ordinary cabbage is for coleslaw. Before seasoning it with the customary olive-oil-and-vinegar dressing, it is tossed with garlic-smeared crusts of bread.

For six or more

1 Savoy cabbage, about 900 g (2 lb)
2 cloves garlic, peeled and lightly crushed
2 pieces of bread crust, about 25 mm (1 inch) long
Salt
Freshly ground black pepper
Olive oil
Wine vinegar

1 Pull off the green leaves from the cabbage; discard, or save to add to a vegetable soup. Shred all the white leaves very fine, and put them in a salad bowl.

2 Briskly rub the garlic against the bread crusts. Discard the garlic, and put the crusts into the salad bowl.

3 Toss thoroughly, and leave to stand for 45 minutes to 1 hour.

4 Ten minutes or so before serving the salad, dress with salt, pepper, a liberal amount of olive oil and a dash of vinegar. Toss thoroughly. Discard the crust. Taste and check the seasoning.

MENU SUGGESTIONS

This is an earthy winter salad that best follows such robust meat courses as *Stufatino di maiale alla boscaiola*, *Farsumauru – il braciolone*, *Brasato di manzo con le cipolle*.

Insalata di lattuga e gorgonzola

COS LETTUCE SALAD WITH GORGONZOLA AND WALNUTS

Cheese and nuts are good things to bring together. In Emilia-Romagna we sometimes have a little Parmesan with walnuts at the beginning of the meal, to start the salivary juices flowing; or it can close the meal, and help finish off a bottle of Amarone, or Sforzato from Valtellina.

Here, we have walnuts and Gorgonzola paired in a salad. It is a salad that fits perfectly into the traditional Italian meal sequence, after the meat course. Or it can be a satisfying light lunch, in the contemporary English style. Serve, in either case, with good, crusty bread.

For six to eight

1 head cos lettuce [about 450 g (1 lb)]
5 tablespoons olive oil
1 tablespoon good wine vinegar
½ teaspoon salt
Freshly ground black pepper
110 g (4 oz) Gorgonzola
60 g (2 oz) shelled walnuts, chopped very coarse

1 Pull off and discard any of the lettuce's bruised or blemished outer leaves. Detach the rest from the core, and tear them by hand into bite-sized pieces. Soak in several changes of cold water. Dry thoroughly.

2 Put the olive oil, vinegar, salt, and a few grindings of pepper into the salad bowl. Beat them two or three times with a fork.

3 Add half the Gorgonzola, and mash it well with a fork.

4 Add half the chopped walnuts, all the lettuce, and toss thoroughly. Taste and check the seasoning.

5 Top with the remaining half of the Gorgonzola, cut into small nuggets, and the rest of the chopped walnuts.

Insalata di arancia

ORANGE AND CUCUMBER SALAD

When I was teaching mathematics near Milan, I used to share the drive to school with a colleague, a Sicilian gentleman, professor of Italian. To relieve his nostalgia for Sicily, he would frequently talk, as we rode, of the food he used to have at home. The descriptions of the pastas, the vegetables, the glorious sweets were so intense that for those few minutes they seemed to pull a little life and colour out of the lugubrious skies of the grim, grey city where we were both exiles.

One of the dishes that enchanted me most is this bright, cheery salad of oranges and cucumbers, scented with lemon juice and fresh mint leaves. I have served it often since, especially after a fish course, when one most appreciates its sweet, refreshing, cleansing taste.

For four

1 cucumber
1 large orange
5 or 6 small red radishes
A few fresh mint leaves
Salt
Olive oil
Freshly squeezed juice of $\frac{1}{2}$ lemon

1 If the skin of the cucumber is waxed, peel it. If not, scrub it under cold running water. Wipe dry. Cut the cucumber into the thinnest possible rounds and put them into the salad bowl.

2 Peel the orange, taking care to remove all the white pith. Cut the orange into thin, round slices. Cut these in half or, if the orange is very large, in four sections, and pick out all the seeds. Put all the orange into the bowl.

3 Rinse and scrub the radishes, but do not peel them. Cut them into very thin rounds. Add to the bowl.

4 Tear the mint leaves into small pieces, and add them to the salad bowl.

5 Dress with salt, olive oil, and lemon juice. Toss thoroughly, and serve at once.

Insalata di borlotti e radicchio

CRANBERRY BEANS AND CHICORY SALAD

There is a delicious tart red chicory native to Treviso, near Venice, which comes into season for a brief time in winter. One celebrated way of serving it is grilled, with olive oil, salt, and pepper. Another is raw, in a salad, together with cooked dried cranberry beans. The combination of the warm, yielding flesh of the beans with the bittersweet snap of the raw chicory is delightful.

Red radicchio is not easily found in this country, though it is becoming increasingly popular in good markets. I have also found that the recipe is very successful with chicory. It has the right texture, and enough bitterness to provide the necessary contrast with the lovely marbled, pink cranberry beans. Unfortunately, fresh cranberry beans are very rarely available here. They are sometimes in the market in early summer (when chicory itself is hard to find!). However, at other times, you can use dried or tinned beans. If you cannot find cranberry beans at all, try this with other beans, such as *cannellini*.

For four

900 g (2 lb) fresh cranberry beans (unshelled weight) or 180 g (6 oz) dried or 600 g ($1\frac{1}{4}$ lb) tinned, drained
450 g (1 lb) red radicchio or chicory
Olive oil
Wine vinegar
Salt
Freshly ground black pepper

If using fresh beans

Shell the beans, place them in a pot with enough cold, unsalted water to cover by about 50 mm (2 inches). Bring the water to a gentle simmer, cover the pot, and cook over moderate heat until tender, about 45 minutes to 1 hour.

If using dried beans

Soak the beans overnight in enough cold water to cover by about 50 mm (2 inches). The following day drain the beans, and cook exactly as directed for the fresh, above.

If using tinned beans

Drain and discard all the liquid from the tin. Warm up the beans in about 6 tablespoons water, in a covered pot, over moderate heat. As soon as they are warm, drain, and they are ready to use.

1 Cut the radicchio or chicory crossways into strips about 6 mm ($\frac{1}{4}$ inch) wide. Rinse in cold water, and dry thoroughly.

2 Put the warm drained beans and the cut-up chicory into the salad bowl. Dress with a liberal amount of olive oil, a little vinegar, salt, and plenty of freshly ground black pepper. Toss thoroughly, and serve at once.

Rape rosse al forno

BAKED BEETROOTS

The very best way to cook beetroots is to bake them. It concentrates their flavour to an intense, mouth-filling sweetness that will be a revelation to those who taste them for the first time and who are used to bought ready-cooked beetroots or, worse still, ones from a jar. Sliced, dressed with olive oil, salt, and vinegar, they are one of the most delicious salads one can make.

If you can, buy raw beetroots with their tops. Both the stems and the leaves are excellent boiled and served as salad. Look for tops with small leaves, which are younger and more tender. The spindly red stems strewn among the lush green leaves are lovely to look at, and the contrast between the crunchiness of the former and the tenderness of the latter is delightful.

For four

1 bunch fresh raw beetroots (about 4 to 6, depending on size)
Salt
Olive oil
Wine vinegar

1 Cut off the tops of the beetroots at the base of the stems, but do not discard (see following recipe). Trim the root ends of the beetroots.

2 Rinse the beetroots in cold water. Wrap them all together in aluminium foil, making sure it is very tightly sealed.

3 Put them on the upper rack of the oven, and turn the thermostat to 200°C/400°F/Mark 6. They should be done in about 1½ to 2 hours, depending on their size. To test them, run a fork into them; they should be tender but firm. When done, remove them from the oven, and from the foil.

4 While they are still warm, but cool enough to handle, pull away the blackish skin around them. Cut them into thin slices.

5 When ready to serve, season them with salt, olive oil, and good red wine vinegar. They can be served while still slightly warm, or at room temperature. They are best the day they are done, and not refrigerated, but, if necessary, they can be prepared a day or two ahead of time, and kept peeled, but whole, in plastic wrap in the refrigerator. Bring them to room temperature well before serving.

Cime di rape rosse in insalata

BEETROOT TOPS SALAD

For four

Stems and leaves from 3 or more bunches of beetroots
Salt
Olive oil
Freshly squeezed lemon juice

1 Pull the leaves from the stems. Snap the stems in two or three pieces, pulling away any strings as you do so.

2 Rinse both stems and leaves in cold water.

3 Bring 3 to 4 litres ($5\frac{1}{4}$ to 7 pints) water to boil, add salt, and as soon as it returns to the boil, put in the stems. After 8 or 9 minutes (a little longer if the stems are large and thick), put in the leaves. They will be done when tender, after about 5 minutes or less. Drain thoroughly.

4 When they have cooled, but are still slightly warm, dress with salt, olive oil, and a dash of freshly squeezed lemon juice. Serve at once.

Note The stems and leaves do not keep, and should not be refrigerated after cooking. If you have just one bunch of beetroots on hand, a nice mixed salad can be made with the sliced baked beetroots and the boiled stems and leaves.

Le patate in insalata

ITALIAN POTATO SALAD

Some years ago in New York, I had a call from a young man, introducing himself as a friend of friends, who had been away from Italy for some while. I invited him to dinner and, having learned that for a long time he had been surviving on restaurant food, I asked him if there was any dish he had a special yearning for. He said yes, there was something he had been craving almost from the first day he had been abroad. Could I please make a boiled potato salad? I was amused, but not astonished. The right potatoes, properly boiled, and seasoned simply, without gimmickry, are as good as anything possibly can be.

In an Italian potato salad, do not look for onions or eggs or any of the other curiosities one finds in a delicatessen's salad. Apart from seasoning, all there is is potatoes. But they must be good boiling potatoes, their flesh waxy smooth and compact, their colour, when cooked, warm and creamy, like maize. They should be boiled until tender, but without the least trace of sogginess. And the first step in seasoning is the most critical. They must be splashed with wine vinegar when they are hot and absorbent, ready to soak up the vinegar's aroma; at the same time their warmth will vaporise it, and blur the sharpness of its acetic edge.

For four

680 g (1½ lb) new or mature boiling potatoes (Desirée or red, but not King Edward), all of a size
Red wine vinegar
Salt
Fruity, green olive oil

1 Rinse the potatoes in cold water. Put them into a pot, unpeeled, with enough water to cover by at least 50 mm (2 inches). Bring to the boil, and cook until tender, but not too soft. It will take 35 minutes, or less if you are using small, new potatoes. Try not to test them too frequently with the fork, or their punctured skin will let the potatoes become soggy.

2 When done, pour out the water from the pot, but leave the potatoes in. Over medium heat, move the potatoes around by shaking the pot back and forth, for a few moments. This will cause excess moisture to evaporate.

3 Peel the potatoes as soon as you are able to handle them.

4 Cut them in slices about 6 mm (¼ inch) thick, and put them into a serving bowl. Add 3 tablespoons vinegar immediately, and toss the potatoes gently, being careful not to break up the slices too much.

5 When ready to serve, add salt and a liberal amount of olive oil. Taste and check seasoning, adding more vinegar if necessary.

Serve while still a little warm or at room temperature. Do not refrigerate. Do not keep for the following day.

DESSERTS

I Dolci

Crema pasticcera

ITALIAN CUSTARD CREAM SAUCE

Crema pasticcera is the basic custard sauce used as a filling in many Italian desserts, and most notably in *Zuppa inglese* (page 352). It can also be served on its own, in individual bowls, accompanied by biscuits. It is firmer and has more body than the sauce the French call *crème anglaise* because it is thickened with flour. Many cooks who have had frustrating experiences with flour think there must be some magic involved in cooking with it. All it really requires is the patience to cook it long enough, without boiling it, to give flour time and just sufficient heat to dissolve in the sauce without leaving a trace of graininess, or of pasty, floury taste. There is nothing mysterious about it. When a sauce is lumpy or has a doughy flavour, it means the flour has been cooked too fast or not thoroughly enough or both.

Although I am accustomed to using a heavy-bottomed saucepan for making *crema pasticcera*, if you are worried about how to keep the heat under control try using a double boiler; but make sure the water in the lower half of the boiler stays at a brisk boil.

Makes about 500 ml (scant pint)

3 egg yolks
150 g (3 oz) icing sugar
50 g (1¾ oz) flour
450 ml (¾ pint) milk
Grated peel of ½ lemon

1 Put the egg yolks and sugar into a heavy saucepan or in the upper half of a double boiler. Off the heat, beat the eggs until they are pale yellow and creamy. Add the flour gradually, beating in no more than 1 tablespoon at a time.

2 In another pan bring all the milk just to the brink of the boil, when the edge begins to be ringed with little bubbles.

3 Add the hot milk very gradually to the egg-and-flour mixture, always off the heat. Stir constantly to avoid lumps.

4 Put the saucepan over low heat (or over the lower half of the double boiler, in which the water has been brought to the boil). Cook for about 5 minutes, stirring steadfastly with a wooden spoon. Do not let the mixture come to the boil; it is all right, however, for an occasional bubble to break slowly through the surface. The *crema* is done when it clings to the spoon with a medium-dense creamy coating.

5 Remove from the heat, and stir for a few minutes until the bottom of the pan cools off a little. Mix in the grated lemon peel.

Zuppa inglese

Everyone always wants to know why this popular Italian dessert is called *inglese*, English. I have heard a number of explanations, all equally plausible. We will probably never know for sure. What is more useful, I think, is to understand why it is called a *zuppa*, soup. The reason is that the cake is so steeped in custard it has the consistency of the bread soaking in peasant soups. And, like a soup, it should be eaten with a spoon.

In Italy, *Zuppa inglese* would be flavoured with a combination of rum and *alchermes*. *Alchermes* is a flowery and lightly spiced liqueur whose red colour comes from crushed dried cochineal insects. It is not imported here, but *Zuppa inglese* just would not be the same if its dose of spirits did not include something red and aromatic. I use a cherry brandy that is not quite as sweet as some cherry brandies can be and imparts what seems to me to be an appropriate warmth. But you can experiment with various combinations of rum and cordials until you hit upon the flavour that suits you best.

In assembling the dessert it is important to have the Madeira cake cut and the spirits mixture ready before you make the custard cream sauce, so that you can use the sauce the moment it is done.

For six servings

The custard cream sauce from the preceding recipe [approximately 500 ml (scant pint)]

300 g (10 oz) Madeira cake, cut into 6-mm ($\frac{1}{4}$-inch) thick slices

A combination of the following spirits: 4 tablespoons cherry brandy, 2 tablespoons cognac, 2 tablespoons Drambuie, 1 tablespoon rum (see note in introductory remarks)

60 g (2 oz) cooking chocolate

Optional topping: 30 g (1 oz) chopped toasted almonds

1 Choose a deep dish or bowl, from which you will be serving the *zuppa*. Smear the bottom of the dish with about 4 to 5 tablespoonfuls of the hot custard cream sauce.

2 Line the bottom of the dish with a layer of sliced Madeira cake.

3 Dip a pastry brush into the spirits mixture and saturate the layer of Madeira cake with it.

4 Thickly cover the layer with one third of the remaining custard cream.

5 Preheat oven to 130°C/250°F/Mark ½.

6 Mount another layer of Madeira-cake slices over the previous one, and soak it with spirits.

7 Put the chocolate into a small saucepan, and place it in the preheated oven to melt (or follow your usual procedure for melting chocolate).

8 Divide the remainder of the custard cream into two parts. Mix the melted chocolate into one of the parts, and spread this over the cake in the bowl.

9 Add another layer of sliced Madeira cake to the dish, soak it with the remaining spirits, and cover with the last of the custard cream. Top with the optional chopped toasted almonds.

10 Refrigerate for 2 to 3 hours before serving. Serve chilled. If refrigerating for a longer period, cover the dish.

Torta di mandorle

ALMOND CAKE

Every cook in Emilia-Romagna believes herself to be in possession of the best recipe for almond cake. Some use whole eggs, others only egg yolks, some peel the almonds, others not. There are those who favour a crumbly cake instead of a soft one. Actually they are all really very good. My recipe uses only egg whites, and I like it as well as any. It produces a firm but not crumbly cake, and a rather light one too, considering it is a nut cake. It can be topped with freshly whipped cream, or it can be divided into two layers and the cream spread thickly in between. It is also perfectly good just as it is.

Makes six to eight servings

300 g (10 oz) unpeeled almonds
260 g (9 oz) granulated sugar
8 egg whites
½ teaspoon salt
Peel of 1 lemon, grated without digging into the white pith beneath
190 g (3 oz) plain flour
A 200- or 225-mm (8- or 9-inch) springform tin
Butter for greasing the tin

1 Preheat the oven to 180°C/350°F/Mark 4.

2 Grind the almonds very fine, but not to a paste, using a blender, the food processor or – the old-fashioned way – a mortar and pestle.

3 Add the sugar to the ground almonds, mixing them thoroughly.

4 Beat the egg whites together with the salt until they form stiff peaks.

5 Add the sugar-and-almond mixture and the grated lemon peel to the egg whites, a little at a time, mixing them in gently but well. The egg whites may deflate a bit, but if you do the mixing with care, there will be no significant loss of volume.

6 Add the flour, shaking it through a wire strainer, a little at a time. Again, mix very gently.

7 Thickly grease the baking tin with butter. Put the cake mixture into the tin, giving the tin a little shake to level off the mixture.

8 Bake in the middle level of the preheated oven for 1 hour. At the end of that time, pierce the centre of the cake with a toothpick. If it comes up dry, the cake is done.

9 Remove the spring-locked sides of the tin, and let the cake cool completely before serving. It can be kept in a tin box, and will stay fresh for a long time.

Torta di noci

WALNUT CAKE

A walnut cake is as delicious as it is uncomplicated. It has a rich and concentrated flavour, and a modest slice can be amply satisfying. It is a perfect cake for morning coffee or afternoon tea. If served after dinner, it would go well with a dollop of freshly whipped cream on top of each portion.

There can be nothing better than very high-quality walnuts in the shell. Buy them if you are absolutely sure of the reliability of your source. But often you do not know what you are getting when you buy unshelled walnuts. Extracting all the kernels is tedious work, and it is particularly frustrating if a high percentage of them are shrivelled or rancid. It may be preferable to buy shelled walnuts, or loose kernels from a nut shop, if they will permit you to taste them first to make sure they are not rancid.

Makes about eight portions

110 g (4 oz) butter, softened at room temperature
150 g (5 oz) granulated sugar
1 egg
2 tablespoons rum
Peel of 1 lemon, grated without digging into the white pith beneath
1½ teaspoons baking powder
225 g (8 oz) shelled walnuts, chopped very fine in a blender or food processor, but not reduced to a paste
120 g (4¼ oz) plain flour
A 200- or 225-mm (8- or 9-inch) layer-cake tin or springform tin

1 Preheat oven to 180°C/350°F/Mark 4.

2 Set aside 15 g (½ oz) butter for greasing the tin later. Put the rest into a bowl and mash it with a wooden spoon until it is uniformly creamy.

3 Add the sugar, a little at a time, mixing it thoroughly into the butter with the spoon.

4 Add the egg, the rum, lemon peel, and baking powder. Mix thoroughly until all ingredients are well amalgamated.

5 Add the chopped walnuts, a little at a time, incorporating them thoroughly into the mixture.

6 Add the flour, shaking it through a wire strainer, mixing it uniformly with the other ingredients, until you have a fairly dense and evenly blended cake mixture.

7 Grease the inside of the cake tin, sprinkle lightly with flour, and turn it over, giving it a tap to shake loose excess flour. Put in the walnut mixture, pressing it down and levelling it off with a spatula.

8 Place the tin in the uppermost rack of the preheated oven. Bake for 1 hour.

9 If you are not using a springform tin, loosen the sides of the cake from the tin while it is still warm, and invert it onto a plate. Then invert it again onto a serving plate. The flavour of the cake improves if served the following day. It does not need to be refrigerated. Put it in a tin box if keeping it for several days.

La ciambella di nonna polini

MY GRANDMOTHER'S PASTRY RING

In Romagna, as in the rest of Italy, there are very few cakes one bakes at home. *Ciambella* is one of these, and it is, in fact, Romagna's most traditional dessert. As with other home-nurtured traditions, there is a slightly different version for every household. Some use aniseed along with, or in place of, lemon peel, others add white wine to the mixture. Each is as 'authentic' as the next. This is the one my grandmother used to make, and like all tastes one grows up with, it is the one I like the best.

There are many ways one uses *ciambella*. The old, country way is to dunk it, at the end of the meal, into a sweet, fruity local wine, *Cagnina*. It is the favourite way of the students at my classes in Bologna. One manages to soak up a not inconsiderable amount of wine this way, but it does no harm since *Cagnina* is very low in alcohol. You could try it here with a German Spätlese or Auslese wine.

It is also served, a little more elegantly and with less disastrous consequences for a tablecloth, sliced, with *crema pasticcera* (page 351) spread over it.

The other principal use of *ciambella* is at breakfast, taken with *caffè latte*. This is Italy's breakfast coffee, a little weaker than espresso, diluted with warm milk.

Makes eight to ten portions

110 g (4 oz) butter
500 g (1 lb 2 oz) plain flour
150 g (5 oz) granulated sugar
$2\frac{1}{2}$ teaspoons cream of tartar
1 teaspoon bicarbonate of soda
1 small pinch salt
Grated peel of 1 whole lemon (do not grate deeper than the coloured surface skin)
4 tablespoons lukewarm milk
2 eggs
A heavy baking tray, lightly buttered and dusted with flour

1 Preheat oven to 190°C/375°F/Mark 5.

2 Gently melt the butter in a little saucepan without letting it get too hot.

3 Put the flour into a large bowl. Add the sugar, melted butter, cream of tartar, soda, salt, grated lemon peel, and warm milk. Add the first egg. As you add the second egg, let the white run into the bowl first. Before adding the yolk, remove a teaspoonful of it, and set it aside. You will use it later to 'paint' the ring.

4 Mix all the ingredients thoroughly, then turn out onto a board or other work surface and knead for a few minutes. Shape the dough into a large sausage roll about 50 mm (2 inches) thick, and make it into a ring, pinching the ends of the roll together to close the ring.

5 Brush the surface of the ring with the teaspoon of egg yolk you set aside earlier, and score it with a few shallow diagonal cuts.

6 Place the ring in the centre of the buttered and floured baking tray. Bake in the upper level of the preheated oven for 35 minutes. It should nearly double in size.

7 Set on a rack to cool. It tastes best when served the following day.

La crostata di mamma

A SIMPLE FRUIT TART

This is one of those crusty, plain, infallible desserts devised by home cooks who are not fancy bakers. A fruit preserve is spread over a bed of biscuit dough, it is topped with a criss-cross, diamond-shaped pattern made with pencil-thin rolls of the same dough, and popped into the oven. It is as good as the fruit you use, and with home-made preserves it can be wonderful. My mother used to make it with *amarena*, morello cherry. If you do not make your own preserves, buy a top quality brand made of whole fruit, and not oversweetened.

Makes about six to eight servings

250 g (9 oz) plain flour
110 g (4 oz) granulated sugar
A tiny pinch of salt
110 g (4 oz) butter, heated until it melts, then cooled
2 tablespoons milk
Grated peel of $\frac{1}{4}$ lemon
2 egg yolks
A heavy standard-sized baking tray
Butter and flour for greasing and dusting the tray
110 g (4 oz) good-quality apricot or peach preserve

1 Preheat oven to 180°C/350°F/Mark 4.

2 Mix the flour, sugar, and salt in a bowl, then pour it into a mound on a work surface.

3 Make a hollow in the centre of the mound, and put in the melted

butter, milk, lemon peel, and egg yolks. Push the walls of the mound together to close up the hollow, and knead well for a few minutes, until all the ingredients have been well amalgamated into a soft, smooth, compact dough. Wrap in plastic film and refrigerate for at least 30 minutes.

4 Lightly grease the baking tray. Dust it with flour, and turn it over to shake loose the excess flour.

5 Remove the dough from the refrigerator, take slightly more than half of it, place it between two sheets of waxed paper, and roll it out into a rectangular or round shape, whichever you prefer, a little less than 12 mm (½ inch) thick. Peel off the top sheet of waxed paper, turn the dough over onto the baking tray, and remove the second sheet of waxed paper. Spread the fruit preserve over the dough, leaving an uncovered margin of less than 12 mm (½ inch) all round.

6 With the remaining dough make several long, skinny rolls, about 8 mm (⅓ inch) thick. Place these rolls over the tart in a lattice-work pattern, criss-crossing the surface of the tart from edge to edge, leaving small, diamond-shaped spaces where they intersect. You can join two or more lengths of each roll, if necessary. The mending will not show after the tart is baked. Run a roll all round the edge of the tart, pressing it into place like window putty.

7 Bake in the upper level of the preheated oven for 25 to 30 minutes, until the dough turns a light golden brown. Transfer to a cooling rack.

Torta di pere alla paesana

A COUNTRY CAKE WITH FRESH PEARS

This is so modest and elementary a cake it could almost be called naïve. It comes straight out of old country kitchens, devised by cooks who knew nothing of the aristocratic art of the pastry maker. It contains a minimum of such rich things as butter and eggs, and I find it as good as it is light and simple.

For six

2 eggs
4 tablespoons milk
200 g (7 oz) granulated sugar
A tiny pinch of salt
200 g (7 oz) plain flour
900 g (2 lb) fresh pears
A 225-mm (9-inch) layer-cake tin
30 g (1 oz) butter
60 g (2 oz) dry, plain breadcrumbs

1 Preheat oven to 180°C/350°F/Mark 4.
2 Beat the eggs and milk together in a bowl.
3 Add the sugar and salt, and continue beating.
4 Add the flour, mixing it thoroughly with the other ingredients.
5 Peel the pears. Cut them in half, and scoop out the seeds and core. Cut them into thin slices, no more than 25 mm (1 inch) broad. Add them to the bowl, mixing them well with the other ingredients.
6 Grease the baking tin with butter, and sprinkle the breadcrumbs on it. Turn it upside down, and tap it or shake it lightly to get rid of all the loose crumbs.
7 Put the cake mixture into the tin, levelling it off with the back of a spoon or a spatula. Dot the surface with butter.
8 Bake it in the upper level of the preheated oven for 45 minutes, or until the top has coloured lightly.
9 Remove the cake from the tin as soon as it is cool and firm enough. It may be served lukewarm or cold.

Torta casereccia di polenta

POLENTA SHORTCAKE WITH DRIED FRUIT AND PINE NUTS

The cornmeal gives away this cake's origin, which is the Veneto region, more specifically Treviso. Like many other fruit and nut cakes around the world, it is traditionally made for the year-end holiday season. It is rather substantial stuff, and a small portion, at the end of a meal, can be quite satisfying. It is also good with afternoon tea.

Although it may seem to be too heavy to rise without the assistance of any other agent than the one egg, it does indeed come up to around 50 mm (2 inches) – high enough for this rich and dense dessert.

It can be quite good served with a spoonful or two of fresh whipped cream on top.

Makes six to eight portions

200 g (7 oz) coarse-grained cornmeal
1 teaspoon salt
1½ tablespoons olive oil
110 g (4 oz) granulated sugar
45 g (1½ oz) pine nuts
45 g (1½ oz) raisins

110 g (4 oz) dried figs cut up into 6-mm ($\frac{1}{4}$-inch) pieces
30 g (1 oz) butter plus sufficient butter to grease the tin
1 egg
2 tablespoons fennel seeds
120 g ($4\frac{1}{4}$ oz) plain flour
A 225-mm (9-inch) round cake tin
2 to 3 tablespoons fine, dry, plain breadcrumbs

1 Bring 450 ml ($\frac{3}{4}$ pint) water to the boil in a medium-sized saucepan. Reduce the heat to medium and add the cornmeal in a thin stream. (I pick up a handful at a time and let it run through the fingers of a partly clenched fist.) Stir constantly with a wooden spoon. When all the cornmeal has gone in, add the salt and oil. Continue to stir for about 15 minutes or so, until the mush thickens and pulls easily away from the sides of the pan. Turn off the heat.

2 Preheat the oven to 200°C/400°F/Mark 6.

3 To the *polenta* in the saucepan add the sugar, pine nuts, raisins, figs, butter, egg, and fennel seeds. Mix thoroughly. Add the flour and continue to mix until all the ingredients are well amalgamated.

4 Smear the sides and bottom of the cake tin with butter. Sprinkle in the breadcrumbs until all the buttered surfaces of the tin are well coated with them. Turn the pan over to shake away all the loose crumbs.

5 Fill the tin with the cake mixture, levelling it off with a spatula. Bake in the upper level of the oven for 40 minutes.

6 While the cake is still warm, turn it over on a plate, lift the tin away, then turn it over again onto another plate. (This procedure can be eliminated if you own one of those baking tins with a removable rim.) Serve after the cake has cooled completely.

Torta di ricotta

RICOTTA CHEESECAKE

This Neapolitan cake is quite different from what one thinks of as cheesecake in England. The latter belongs to a creamy, rich, and somewhat heavy category of desserts, while this one is firmer in texture, yet lighter and more aromatic. English cheesecake is usually open faced. This one is completely enclosed in pastry.

English ricotta too is often very different from the Neapolitan variety, and in order to adapt it to the requirements of this recipe, which calls for a substantial quantity of ricotta, I have found it necessary to subject it to a little manipulation. The problem is that here ricotta is homogenised. When baking, the liquid separates from the cheese, and leaks into the pastry shell, making it soggy. The solution is to cook the ricotta first, forcing most of the liquid out and evaporating it. Then wrap it in muslin, and hang for at least 30 minutes, letting it drain almost completely dry.

No other problems should come up in making this very nice and uncomplicated cake. The pastry is the same sweet egg pastry used in *Pizza rustica*, page 284. If you already know how to make *pâte sucrée*, and think you would be more comfortable using your own version, by all means do so.

The aromatic element in this dessert is Strega, a sweet, yellow Italian liqueur, with a cool, herbal flavour. It is widely distributed and should be easily obtainable.

Makes about eight servings

Sweet egg pastry from the recipe for *pizza rustica*, page 284
950 g (2 lb) ricotta
7 g ($\frac{1}{4}$ oz) butter
A springform tin 200 mm (8 inches) in diameter and 62 mm ($2\frac{1}{2}$ inches) deep, or a layer-cake tin of the same size
3 eggs, separated into yolks and whites
110 g (4 oz) candied citron, diced
3 tablespoons granulated sugar
2 tablespoons Strega liqueur
Muslin

1 Prepare the dough for sweet egg pastry as directed on page 284, and refrigerate for about 1 hour, wrapped in waxed paper.

2 Put the ricotta into a 250-mm (10-inch) frying pan or sauté pan, and turn on the heat to medium high. Cook the ricotta for about 10 minutes, stirring it almost constantly.

3 Pour out any liquid that may remain in the pan, and wrap the ricotta in muslin. Tie it securely, and suspend it over a bowl. Let it hang over the bowl for at least 30 minutes, to drain it as much as possible of the liquid it still contains.

4 Preheat the oven to 180°C/350°F/Mark 4.

5 Take the pastry dough out of the refrigerator, and cut off one third of it. Put this piece between two sheets of waxed paper, and roll it out into a round sheet a little larger than the bottom of the tin.

6 Smear the inside of the tin with butter.

7 Peel off the upper sheet of waxed paper from the rolled-out pastry disc. Turn the pastry dough over into the tin, peeling the other sheet of

paper away from it. Fit the dough into the bottom of the tin, lining it evenly and allowing excess dough to come up the sides.

8 Roll out another third of the pastry between two sheets of waxed paper, into a more or less square shape. With scissors, cut the dough, still held between the waxed paper, into rectangles about 55 mm ($2\frac{1}{4}$ inches) wide. Taking one rectangle at a time, peel off the top sheet of paper and turn the dough over onto the tin, facing and lining the sides. Peel off the paper still sticking to the dough. Join the dough to the edge of the pastry lining the bottom, overlapping slightly and evening off any irregularities with your fingertips. Smooth the dough against the sides of the tin, lining them completely.

9 Remove the ricotta from the muslin and put it into a bowl. Add 2 egg yolks, and all the citron, sugar, and liqueur. Mix thoroughly with a fork until all the ingredients have been well amalgamated.

10 Beat the 3 egg whites in a separate bowl until they form stiff peaks. Add to the mixture in the other bowl, folding in gently but thoroughly.

11 Empty out the contents of the bowl into the tin and level off.

12 Roll out the remaining third of pastry dough between two sheets of waxed paper into a disc large enough to cover the cake. Peel off the top sheet of paper, and turn the dough over onto the cheese mixture in the pan. Peel off the other sheet of paper. Join the dough to the pastry dough lining the sides of the tin, using your fingers to make a tight-fitting connection.

13 Lightly beat the remaining egg yolk, and brush it over the dough topping the cake.

14 Place the tin in the uppermost level of the preheated oven. Bake for at least 50 minutes, or until the top of the cake becomes a rich pinkish gold.

15 If using a springform tin, remove the sides as soon as you take it out of the oven. When the cake is cool and firm enough, slide it off the bottom onto a plate. If using a layer-cake tin, wait until the cake is cool and firm; then place a plate upside down over the tin, and turn the cake over onto the plate. Place another plate over the cake, and turn it over again, so that it is right side up.

Bombolette di ricotta

RICOTTA FRITTERS

The only problem I have ever had with these ricotta fritters is making enough of them. They are so light and crisp, and so easily disposed of that no one ever seems to be shy about taking another, and another, and they are soon gone.

They are simplicity itself to make, which should appeal to those who like to have fun with desserts but get nervous when they have to spend time on a complicated production.

For four

225 g (8 oz) ricotta
2 eggs
40 g ($1\frac{1}{2}$ oz) plain flour
25 g ($\frac{3}{4}$ oz) butter, softened to room temperature
Grated peel of 1 lemon (do not grate deep enough to reach the pith)
Salt
Enough vegetable oil to come 12mm ($\frac{1}{2}$ inch) up the sides of the pan
110 g (4 oz) honey

1 Put the ricotta into a bowl, and beat it with a whisk until it is rather creamy.

2 Break the eggs into a soup dish or small bowl, and beat them lightly with a fork. Add them to the ricotta, beating in with a whisk.

3 Put in the flour, a little at a time, beating it into the ricotta with the whisk. Add the butter, lemon peel, and a tiny pinch of salt, beating all the ingredients until they are well amalgamated.

4 Set the batter aside, and let it rest at room temperature for at least 2 hours, but no more than $3\frac{1}{2}$.

5 Put the oil into a frying pan, and turn on the heat to medium high. When the oil is quite hot (test it with a drop of batter – if it instantly floats to the surface, the oil is ready), put in the batter, a tablespoonful at a time. A fast and easy method is to push it off the spoon, using the rounded corner of a rubber spatula. Do not overcrowd the pan.

6 When the fritters are golden brown on one side, turn them and brown the other side. If they are not puffing up into little balls, the heat is too high. Turn it down a little.

7 When the fritters are nicely browned all over, transfer them with a slotted spoon or spatula to kitchen paper to drain. Repeat the procedure with any remaining batter.

8 When all the fritters are done, place them on a serving dish, pour the honey over them, and serve while still hot.

Fave dei morti

ALL SOULS' DAY BISCUITS WITH ALMONDS AND PINE NUTS

All Souls' Day is a religious holiday in November, when the memory of the departed is honoured in Italy with brief masses and long weekends. And the making of desserts. These biscuits are one among many versions of the traditional sweet of the day. They have a satisfying chewy consistency, an agreeable bittersweet nutty taste, and a homely character not lacking in charm. They are called *fave* because people used to shape them to look like a broad bean, with a faint hollow in the centre. Sculpting biscuits is not my favourite pastime, and since it does not influence in the least the way they taste, I just roll them into little flattened balls.

Makes about 30 biscuits

225 g (8 oz) shelled almonds
2 rounded tablespoons *pinoli* (pine nuts)
75 g ($2\frac{1}{2}$ oz) plain flour, plus additional flour for dusting the baking tray
75 g ($2\frac{1}{2}$ oz) granulated sugar
15 g ($\frac{1}{2}$ oz) butter, softened at room temperature, plus butter for greasing the baking tray
Grated peel of $\frac{1}{2}$ lemon
1 tablespoon *grappa* or other grape brandy
1 egg

1 Drop the almonds into boiling water. Remove them after 15 seconds, draining them well. Put all the almonds into a damp tea-towel, and rub them vigorously with the towel. This should skin most of them. If any are left with the skin still on, squeeze them out of it with your fingers.

2 Pat the almonds thoroughly dry with kitchen paper, then chop them together with the *pinoli*. Do not chop them excessively fine. The pieces should be about as large as a grain of rice.

3 Preheat the oven to 140°C/275°F/Mark 1.

4 Put the chopped almonds and *pinoli* into a mixing bowl together with the flour, sugar, softened butter, grated lemon peel, *grappa* and egg. Mix thoroughly, and knead for a few minutes with your hands. At first the mixture will be dry and brittle, but as you knead, it becomes more elastic.

5 Grease an oven tray and sprinkle it lightly with flour. Turn it over and give it a tap to shake off any loose floor.

6 Moisten your hands with water. Pull off a small piece of dough and roll it between the palms of your hands, flattening it slightly. Put it on the baking tray. Leave about 50 mm (2 inches) space between each piece.

Proceed in this manner until you have used up all the dough. Always work with moistened hands, and as they become sticky, rinse them clean.

7 Place the baking tray on the uppermost rack of the preheated oven. After 20 minutes, turn up the thermostat to 150°C/300°F/Mark 2. Bake for another 10 minutes, then remove and cool.

When cold, these biscuits will keep a long time in a tin. They are very nice served with chocolate ice cream.

Pere cotte con crema e cioccolato

COOKED PEARS WITH CUSTARD CREAM SAUCE AND CHOCOLATE

This dessert is a sumptuous treatmeant for pears. After they have been cooked in sugar and water, they are placed under a velvety cloak of custard cream sauce edged with melted chocolate. They are finished with a web of spun caramel filaments cast over the top.

The favourite cooking pear in Italy is the William or Bartlett, but if you should want to make the dish in late winter, you will probably be using the Anjou. I have tried it with one and with the other, and it is equally good with both.

For four

The pears

2 unblemished and not overripe pears
75 g (2½ oz) granulated sugar
2 strips of lemon peel
45 g (1½ oz) cooking chocolate

The custard cream sauce

Follow the directions on page 351 using the following quantities:

2 egg yolks
50 g (1¾ oz) icing sugar
2 tablespoons plain flour
280 ml (½ pint) milk
The grated peel of ½ lemon

The caramelised sugar

50 g ($1\frac{3}{4}$ oz) granulated sugar
2 teaspoons water

1 Peel the pears, cut them in half lengthways, and scoop out the seeds and core.

2 Choose a sauté pan just large enough to contain the pears laid flat in a single layer. Put in the pears, with their flat sides facing the bottom of the pan. Add 75 g ($2\frac{1}{2}$ oz) sugar, the 2 strips of lemon peel, and enough water to come two-thirds of the way up the sides of the pears.

3 Turn on the heat to medium high, and cook the pears until tender but firm. It will take 10 minutes or more, depending on the ripeness of the pears. Turn them gently from time to time while cooking. If all the water evaporates while they are still hard, add a little water to continue the cooking.

4 When the pears are tender but firm when pricked with a fork, turn up the heat to high, and boil away any liquid left in the pan. When the sugar become a medium brown colour, transfer the pears to a deep serving dish. Arrange them with their flat sides down and their tips meeting in the centre of the dish, forming a crosslike pattern.

5 Prepare the custard cream sauce with the ingredients listed above, following the directions on page 351.

6 When the sauce is done, wait until it is lukewarm, then pour two-thirds of it over the pears.

7 Put the cooking chocolate into a small saucepan. Melt the chocolate in 130°C/250°F/Mark $\frac{1}{2}$ oven (or follow your usual procedure for melting chocolate).

8 Mix the melted chocolate with the remaining custard cream. Pour the mixture along the edge of the dish, letting some of it run into the hollows between the pears, but not covering too much of the cream-shrouded pears.

9 Put 50 g ($1\frac{3}{4}$ oz) granulated sugar and 2 teaspoons water into a small saucepan, and turn on the heat to medium high. Melt the sugar completely and continue cooking until it becomes a caramelised brown. Do not stir with a spoon, but tilt the pan from time to time. When the sugar has become caramelised, let it cool briefly, but not too long or it will solidify. You should be able to pick it up with a spoon, forming thin, brittle threads. Quickly spoon the spun sugar over the pears.

Serve slightly chilled, but not straight out of the refrigerator.

Mele renette al forno con gli amaretti

BAKED APPLES WITH MACAROONS

Macaroons, with their nutty bitter-almond flavour, are a delicious accompaniment to baked apples. Here, the apples are baked whole with a macaroon-and-butter stuffing, and served very prettily afterwards with a macaroon cap on top.

Amaretti (Italian macaroons) come wrapped in pairs, which accounts for the distinction made in the instructions below between 'pairs' and 'singles'. In Italy we would use the rennet apple, firm, full of flavour and fine-fleshed. Any apple will turn out well in this preparation, but the less starchy and flabby it is to start with, the happier you will be with the results.

For four

4 firm, juicy apples
5 pairs of *amaretti* (Italian macaroons)
60 g (2 oz) butter, completely softened at room temperature
50 g ($1\frac{3}{4}$ oz) granulated sugar
8 tablespoons water
8 tablespoons dry white wine
4 single *amaretti*

1 Preheat the oven to 200°C/400°F/Mark 6.

2 Wash the apples in cold water. Core them from the top, with any suitable tool, from an apple corer to a vegetable peeler, but take care not to go all the way through the bottom. Leave a scooped-out centre well at least 12 mm ($\frac{1}{2}$ inch) broad. Prick the apples' skin in many places, every 25 mm (1 inch) or so, with the point of a knife.

3 Place the 5 double macaroons within a folded-up sheet of waxed paper, and pound them with a mallet, meat flattener, heavy knife handle, or whatever, until they are coarsely crushed. They should not become pulverised.

4 Mix the crushed macaroons thoroughly with the softened butter. Divide the mixture into four equal parts, using them to stuff the cavities of the apples, packing them tight.

5 Place the apples in a baking tin, right side up. Sprinkle a tablespoon of sugar over each, and pour the water and white wine over them.

6 Put the pan on the uppermost rack of the preheated oven, and bake for 45 minutes.

7 When done, gently transfer the apples with a large metal spatula to the serving dish or to individual plates.

8 There will be some liquid left in the pan. Dip the four single macaroons

in the liquid, but not long enough for them to become soggy and break up. Use each macaroon to cap the openings of the apples.

9 If the baking tin is not suitable for cooking over direct heat, transfer its contents to a saucepan. Place the pan over high heat. When the liquid has become syrupy, pour it over the apples.

Serve at room temperature. They may be refrigerated if cooked 2 or 3 days in advance, but bring to room temperature before serving.

Castagne alla romagnola col vino rosso

CHESTNUTS BOILED IN RED WINE

Chestnuts boiled in wine are a country dish from my particular part of the country, Emilia-Romagna. It is fitting that the chestnut season is in winter because this is a very warming dish to have, late on a cold evening, sitting by the fire, in the company of friends and with a bottle of young, rough red wine. I remember my father cautioning us that the combination of chestnuts and wine would make us giddy. Although there is nothing about a chestnut that makes wine more inebriating, there is no question that a bite of one leads irresistibly to a sip of the other. And wine calls for more chestnuts. And so on. Fair warning.

The only problem a chestnut ever gives anyone is peeling it. My family's old method of slitting the chestnuts before cooking is the best solution I have found to this problem. It is a horizontal slit, which splits the shell around the middle for about two-thirds the circumference of the chestnut. Here is how it is done. Start the cut on the flat side of the nut, just before the edge. Work your way round, slitting the shell on the bulging belly side of the nut, and continue the cut just past the other edge and over onto the flat side. When cooked, the shell and inner skin will lift away without too much trouble.

For four

450 g (1 lb) fresh chestnuts (look for the larger, heavier chestnuts with glossy shells)

225 ml (scant $\frac{1}{2}$ pint) dry, full-bodied red wine

Salt

2 bayleaves

1 Rinse the chestnuts in cold water, then pat them dry.

2 Slit the shells as directed in the introductory paragraph above. Do not cut into the meat.

3 Put the chestnuts, wine, a tiny pinch of salt, and the bayleaves into a pot with just enough water to cover. Cover the pot, and turn on the heat to medium.

4 After 1 hour, uncover the pot, and allow all but 1 or 2 tablespoonfuls liquid to evaporate. Serve at once, preferably from the pot, or in a warm bowl.

Crema fredda di uva nera

CHILLED GRAPE PUDDING

This is a refreshingly fruity dessert that takes hardly any more time, fuss, or skill to prepare than those artificial commercial concoctions. Its authentic grapy flavour is a delight.

For four

450 g (1 lb) black grapes
2 tablespoons plain flour
2 tablespoons granulated sugar
8 tablespoons cold whipping cream

1 Pull off all the grapes from their stems, and rinse them in cold water.

2 Insert the disc with the smallest holes into your food mill, and strain all the grapes through the mill and into a bowl. If you prefer to use the blender or the food processor, first remove the seeds from the grapes. Crushed seeds release a bitter oil.

3 Put 225 ml (scant $\frac{1}{2}$ pint) of the strained or puréed grapes into a small saucepan. Add the flour, shaking it through a wire sieve. Mix thoroughly, until the flour is completely and uniformly incorporated with the grapes.

4 Add the sugar to the grapes in the bowl, stirring until it has completely dissolved.

5 Slowly pour the contents of the bowl into the saucepan, mixing thoroughly all the while.

6 Place the saucepan over low heat. Stir constantly. When the grape mixture begins to simmer, cook for 5 more minutes. Keep the simmer from

coming to the boil, and stir constantly. The mixture will become rather dense.

7 Pour everything into a bowl, and allow to cool completely at room temperature. Then spoon the pudding into four individual glass bowls and place them in the refrigerator. Chill for at least 3 hours before serving, or even overnight.

8 Just before serving, whip the cream until it stiffens, and divide it up among the four bowls, topping the pudding.

Mango e fragole al vino bianco

MANGOES AND STRAWBERRIES MACERATED IN WHITE WINE

There are no mangoes in Italy, but there are marvellous sweet, fragrant peaches. I have never been fortunate enough to find such perfect peaches elsewhere, but mangoes are a good substitute. Their succulence and colour are strongly reminiscent of peaches, although there is a spicy finish to their flavour and a certain flabbiness to their texture that are distinctly different. The mangoes I prefer are the small mottled ones, but any ripe mango will do. They are usually least expensive just when they are at their best, ripe and tender to the touch. If they are very firm, they will need two or three days' ripening at home, at room temperature, until they give slightly under thumb pressure.

For six

2 small ripe mangoes or 1 large one
350 g (12 oz) fresh strawberries
2 tablespoons granulated sugar
1 whole lemon, with unblemished skin
225 ml (scant $\frac{1}{2}$ pint) naturally sweet white wine such as Moscato, Vin Santo, Sauternes, or an Auslese Riesling

1 Peel the mangoes with a small paring knife. Slice the flesh loose from the large stone. Cut the mango into bite-sized cubes of about 25 mm (1 inch). Put them into a serving bowl.

2 Rinse the strawberries in cold water. Remove stems and leaves. If very

small, leave them whole; if large, slice them in half lengthways. Add them to the bowl.

3 Put the sugar into the bowl. Grate into it the entire peel of the lemon, taking care not to dig into the bitter white pith below the skin. Add the wine.

4 Mix all the fruit very gently, so as not to bruise it.

5 Refrigerate for 1 to 2 hours before serving.

Note If preparing this dish more than 2 hours ahead of time, keep the strawberries in reserve. Add them only up to 2 hours before serving, or they will become mushy.

Macedonia di uva bianca e nera

MACÉDOINE OF WHITE AND BLACK GRAPES

This is a beautiful fruit salad. The contrast of the divided purple globes of the black grapes with the cool elongated ovals of the white grapes is of a pure and elemental elegance. It is a joy to eat because there are no seeds to swallow or spit out. And it is extraordinarily good and refreshing. I have found that people enjoy it at least as much as rich and more elaborate desserts. The only fussy part is removing the seeds of the black grapes. The method described below works well, and is quite quick.

For six to eight

450 g (1 lb) seedless white grapes
450 g (1 lb) large black grapes
1 whole lemon, with unblemished skin
3 tablespoons granulated sugar
Freshly squeezed juice of 3 oranges

1 Rinse both the white and black grapes in cold water.

2 Detach the white grapes from their stems and put them into a serving bowl.

3 Detach the black grapes from their stems and put them into a dish. Hold each grape with the stalk end facing up; with a sharp knife cut the grape horizontally around its middle. Cut it all the way round, but not all

the way through. With you fingertips, hold the upper half of the grape above the cut; with the other hand twist off the bottom half. You will now have two separate and nearly equal halves. From the exposed centre of one of the halves you will see seeds protruding. Pick them out, discard them, and put both seedless halves of the grape into the serving bowl. Continue thus until all the seeds of the black grapes have been removed.

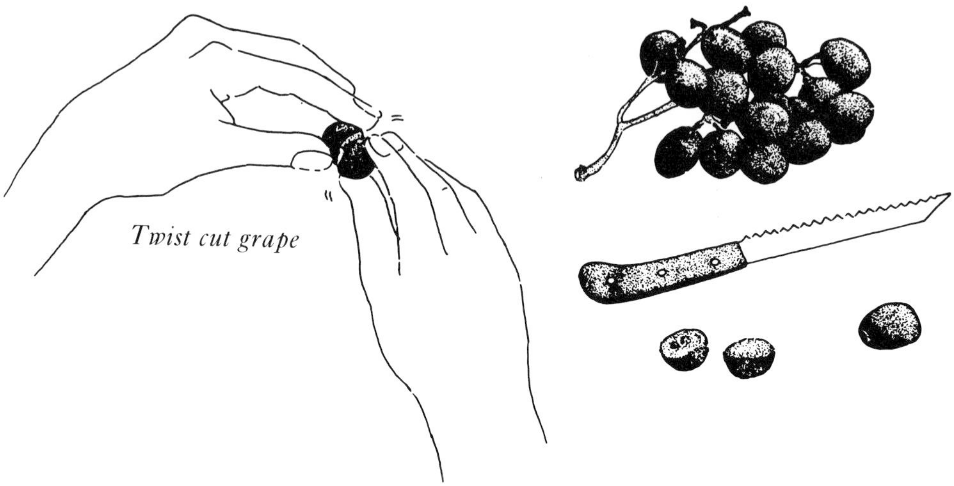

Twist cut grape

4 Grate the whole peel of the lemon into the bowl, taking care not to dig into the white bitter pith just below the skin.

5 Put the sugar into the bowl.

6 Add the orange juice to the bowl. There should be just enough juice to cover the grapes. If it is not sufficient, squeeze a little more.

7 Mix thoroughly, and refrigerate for 2 to 3 hours before serving. Do not keep overnight, because the grapes may begin to ferment and turn sour.

ICE-CREAM

Of all man's activities none has been so genially conceived and so perfectly realised as sitting an hour or two on a summer afternoon in Italy at an outdoor café, eating ice-cream. There is perhaps no other pleasure we can take that is so kindly protective of those endangered attributes of happiness: indolence and well-being.

Italian summer afternoons cannot be duplicated, but the ice-cream can. Home-made ice-cream can come very close to the smoothness, lightness and flavour that make these luscious sweets one of the most delightful rewards of travel in Italy. The machines we have available for puréeing and freezing natural ingredients are so efficient and so simple to use that it is nearly impossible for anyone to fail. The machine I have used in my recipes is the kind that goes into the freezer, and usually turns itself off when the ice-cream is done. But the old-fashioned hand-cranked models give equally good results. They just require more work.

The flavours that go into ice-cream are limited only by imagination and good sense. I wish I could have included in this sampling the jasmine ice-cream I had in Palermo. It was the single most ravishing experience to which my palate has ever been exposed. I have put in a delicious prune ice-cream that was also a part of my memorable Sicilian ice-cream revels. There are other fruit recipes, of which I particularly recommend the one with fresh strawberries.

And then there are those two basics of the Italian ice-cream maker's art, hazelnut and custard cream. The hazelnut ice-cream is a pure, smooth concentrate, and, I regret, rather costly because of the quantity of nuts required. The custard cream is as much a universal favourite in Italy as vanilla is in England. It is a rich emulsion of eggs and milk, with a nearly imperceptible tingle of lemon peel. It is the recipe with which anyone trying the taste of Italian ice-cream for the first time should start.

Italian ice-cream is never oversweet, it is always quite smooth, and it is essentially light and soft. It should give way creamily to the pressure of a spoon. To borrow a definition from Mrs Marshall's delightful nineteenth-century *Ices Plain and Fancy*, it should 'convey to the palate the greatest possible amount of pleasure and taste, whilst . . . in no way [being] suggestive of nourishment or solidity.'

It is best when just made, but if you are making it long in advance take it out of the freezer and let it soften in the refrigerator at least 30 to 40 minutes before serving.

Il gelato di crema

CUSTARD CREAM ICE-CREAM

450 ml (1 pint) milk
4 egg yolks
110 g (4 oz) granulated sugar
1 tablespoon water
¼ teaspoon salt
A double boiler of flameproof glass, enamelware or ceramic-lined, but not of aluminium
1 whole lemon peel, grated without digging into the white pith beneath
A home ice-cream freezer

Makes four portions

1 Warm up the milk in a small saucepan over medium heat until the edge is ringed with tiny bubbles. Turn off the heat at once. Do not let the milk boil. Cover the pan, and allow to rest for 10 minutes.

2 While the milk is resting, put the egg yolks, sugar, water, and salt into a mixing bowl. Beat the yolks until they are creamy and pale, and form ribbons.

3 Add the milk to the bowl, a little at a time, stirring it in well with a wooden spoon.

4 Pour the contents of the bowl into the upper half of the double boiler. Place the double boiler over medium heat. Stir the custard cream continuously from the moment the water in the lower half of the pan begins to come to the boil. Within 2 to 3 minutes after the water has started to boil, the custard is done. Do not let the custard itself come to the boil.

5 Transfer the custard cream to a bowl, and stir the lemon peel into it. Let it cool completely, then place in the refrigerator.

6 When the custard has been chilled for at least an hour, place it in your ice-cream freezer, and from there proceed according to the manufacturer's instructions.

7 When the ice-cream is done, place it in a plastic container with an air-tight lid, and put it in the freezer. It will be ready to eat when it has firmed up a little, within 1½ to 2 hours, depending on how cold your freezer is. It should not be extremely hard. If you are making it several hours or a day or two ahead of time, place it in the refrigerator for at least 30 minutes before serving. It should be soft enough to offer little resistance to the spoon.

Gelato di nocciola

HAZELNUT ICE-CREAM

110 g (4 oz) shelled hazelnuts
350 ml ($\frac{2}{3}$ pint) milk
Muslin
2 egg yolks
2 tablespoons granulated sugar
A double boiler
A home ice-cream freezer

Makes three to four portions

1 Toast the hazelnuts under the grill for 4 to 5 minutes, turning them frequently.

2 Skin the nuts by rubbing them one against the other, while still fairly hot. It does not matter if a few patches of skin remain attached to them.

3 Use a blender or a coffee grinder to grind the hazelnuts to a very fine paste, or chop them, and pound them in a mortar. (The food processor, in this case, does not produce quite the right consistency.)

4 Warm up the milk in a saucepan over medium heat until the edge is ringed with tiny bubbles. Turn off the heat at once. Put in the hazelnut paste, mix thoroughly, and cover the pan. Allow to cool completely.

5 Line a strainer with a double thickness of muslin. Set the strainer over a bowl. Pour the hazelnut-and-milk mixture into the strainer, and press as much of it as will go through into the bowl. You will find that, since it is rather thick, only a small amount will pass through. At this point, tie up the ends of the muslin, tightly compressing the nut-and-milk mixture within. Suspend the muslin over the bowl, attaching it to a hook or the knob of a cupboard. Some liquid will continue to drip through. When no more liquid drips, squeeze the muslin gently, forcing through as much of the contents as will come, reduced to a creamy consistency. Add this to the bowl.

6 In another bowl, beat the egg yolks and sugar until the yolks are pale and foamy.

7 Add the strained nut-and-milk mixture to the eggs, mixing it in a little at a time.

8 Pour everything into the top part of the double boiler. Turn on the heat to medium. Stir constantly, and cook for 3 to 4 minutes after the water in the lower half of the pot has started to bubble.

9 Pour into a bowl, and allow to cool completely. When cool, chill in the refrigerator for 30 minutes. Then place the mixture in the ice-cream freezer, and follow the manufacturer's instructions.

10 When done, allow the ice-cream to firm up for about 30 minutes in

the freezer before serving. If preparing it in advance, place it in the refrigerator for 30 minutes before serving, to return it to a creamy consistency.

Gelato di fragola

STRAWBERRY ICE-CREAM

225 g ($\frac{1}{2}$ lb) fresh strawberries
150 g (5 oz) granulated sugar
4 tablespoons cold double cream
A home ice-cream freezer

Makes four portions

1 Pull the leaves and stems from the strawberries. If very large berries, cut them in half. Remove the hard, small white core at the stem end. Rinse in cold water.

2 Put the strawberries, 200 ml ($\frac{1}{4}$ pint + 4 tablespoons) water and sugar into a blender, and purée until liquefied. If using the food processor, put in the strawberries and sugar first, let the blades spin for a few moments, then add the water and finish puréeing.

3 Whip the cream until it thickens a little, but not to the density of whipped cream.

4 Put the cream and the puréed strawberries into a bowl, and stir well. Put the bowl into the refrigerator for 1 hour.

5 Place the mixture in your ice-cream freezer and proceed, following the manufacturer's instructions. When done it will be rather soft, but ready to eat all the same. If you like it firmer, put it in a plastic container with a tight-sealing lid, and leave it in the freezer for 3 to 4 hours. If preparing it much longer in advance, let it soften in the refrigerator for at least 30 minutes before serving.

Gelato di prugna

PRUNE ICE-CREAM

14 to 18 dried prunes, depending on size
2 tablespoons granulated sugar
8 tablespoons cold whipping cream
A home ice-cream freezer

Makes four portions

1 Put the prunes, sugar and 350 ml ($\frac{2}{3}$ pint) water into a saucepan, and bring to simmer. Cover, and cook for 10 to 15 minutes, depending on the size of the prunes.

2 Let the prunes cool, then remove the stones.

3 Put the prunes and all the liquid from the pan into the bowl of a blender and purée. If you are using the food processor, put in the prunes first, run the steel blades for a few moments, then add the liquid and finish puréeing.

4 Whip the cream briefly until it thickens slightly.

5 Mix the cream and prune purée in a bowl, and place in the refrigerator for at least 1 hour.

6 Put the mixture in your ice-cream freezer and proceed according to the manufacturer's instructions. The ice-cream is ready to eat when done, or, if you like it firmer, put it in the freezer in a tightly sealed container for 1 to 2 hours. If preparing it much longer in advance, let it soften in the refrigerator for 30 to 45 minutes before serving.

Gelato di banana al rum

BANANA AND RUM ICE-CREAM

2 bannanas
2 egg yolks
2 tablespoons granulated sugar
4 teaspoons rum
225 ml (scant $\frac{1}{2}$ pint) double cream
A home ice-cream freezer

Makes four portions

1 Skin the bananas, and mash them until they are creamy. They turn out best in the food processor, but you can use a blender, an electric mixer, or even just a fork.

2 Beat the egg yolks and sugar together in a bowl, until the yolks become a pale yellow, frothy cream, forming ribbons.

3 Add the creamed bananas to the egg yolks, mixing them in a little at a time.

4 Mix in the rum.

5 Whip the cream until it swells but is not too stiff, then incorporate it into the egg-and-banana mixture. Refrigerate for about 1 hour.

6 Place the mixture in your ice-cream freezer, following from this point onwards the manufacturer's instructions. When done, the ice-cream is ready to eat. If preparing it in advance, store it in the freezer, but place it in the refrigerator at least 30 minutes before serving.

Gelato di uva nera

BLACK GRAPE ICE-CREAM

130 g ($4\frac{1}{2}$ oz) granulated sugar
450 g (1 lb) black grapes
A food mill
4 tablespoons double cream
A home ice-cream freezer

Makes four portions

1 Put the sugar and 8 tablespoons water into a small saucepan over medium heat, and stir from time to time until the sugar is completely melted. Pour the thin syrup that results into a bowl.

2 Detach the grapes from their stems, and wash them in cold water. Fit the disc with the smallest holes into your food mill, and strain the grapes through the mill and into the bowl with the sugar syrup. Do not worry if a few shreds of grape skin pass through the mill, but makes sure none of the seeds do. Do not use a blender or food processor, which would chop the seeds and release the bitter oil they contain.

3 Whip the cream until it swells, but is not too stiff, then incorporate it into the mixture of sugar syrup and crushed grapes. Refrigerate for 2 hours.

4 Place the mixture in your ice-cream freezer, and follow the instructions given by the manufacturer. The ice-cream is ready to eat and at its best when just done. If you must prepare it in advance, store it in the freezer in a tightly sealed container, but allow it to soften up at least 30 minutes in the refrigerator before serving it.

Il mandarino farcito

FROZEN TANGERINE SURPRISE

An Italian ice is the most refreshing way to bring anything to a close – a rich and complex meal, a day in the sun, a happy evening with friends. And of the Italian ices there is no finer example, I think, than this beautiful, ambrosial tangerine ice.

As you will find in the instructions below, it is very simple to do. It is a blend of fresh tangerine, orange, and lemon juice, scented with grating from the orange and lemon peels, mixed with sugar syrup and an egg white, and frozen in an ice-cream freezer. It cannot fail.

The way this is presented in the *gelaterie* of Rome adds immeasurably to its charm. Each portion is stuffed into the hollowed-out shell of a tangerine, which is then capped with its own previously sliced-off top. This takes a little care in the execution, but it is well worth it.

Makes six to eight frozen tangerines

The ice

200 g (7 oz) granulated sugar
Grated peel of ½ orange, using only the thin, surface skin
Grated peel of ½ lemon, using only the thin, surface skin
Freshly squeezed juice of 2 large tangerines (or 4 small)
Freshly squeezed juice of 1 large orange (or 2 small)
Freshly squeezed juice of 1 medium lemon
1 egg white
A home ice-cream freezer
3 tablespoons rum

1 Put 225 ml (scant ½ pint) water and the sugar into a small saucepan, and turn on the heat to medium. As soon as the sugar has melted, pour the contents of the pan into a mixing bowl.

2 Add the grated orange and lemon peels to the bowl, and the tangerine, orange, and lemon juices. Mix well.

3 Lightly beat the egg white until it begins to foam, then add it to the mixture in the bowl. Mix all the contents of the bowl thoroughly.

4 Put the mixture into the ice-cream freezer, and freeze according to the manufacturer's instructions. If using an automatic machine, disconnect it after 2 hours if it fails to cut itself off.

5 Put the frozen ice into a tight-sealing freezer container. Add the rum, mix thoroughly, close the container, and place in the freezer compartment. The ice will be ready to serve after 1 hour, but it can be kept in the freezer for several days. Before serving, stir the ice to amalgamate some of the rum that may have partly separated from the mixture.

The ice may be served in any conventional container, or stuffed into hollowed-out tangerines, as described below.

The tangerine shells

6 large or 8 small to medium tangerines. Try to choose tangerines that still have a leaf attached to the stem. If they do not, buy or pick enough fresh mint to supply you with about 1 dozen bright, unblemished leaves.

1 Rinse the tangerines under cold running water, taking care not to break off any leaves that may be attached to the stems.

2 Neatly slice off the tops of the tangerines, leaving enough of an opening for you to extract the fruit, and later to stuff the shell. Set the tops aside.

3 With your finger, remove the fruit section from the lower half of the tangerines. Work delicately in order not to tear or puncture the fragile rind. Part of the fruit may be pressed to provide the juice needed in the preparation of the ice above, or it may be used in a fruit salad, or eaten as it is.

4 Put the hollowed-out shells and their tops into the freezer. Freeze for at least 2 hours, or keep in the freezer for as long as necessary until ready to use them.

5 About 45 minutes to 1 hour before serving, spoon the fruit ice into the frozen hollowed-out tangerine shells. There should be enough of the ice in the shell to come up slightly above the rim.

6 If the tops of the tangerines do not have their own natural leaves, place one or two mint leaves on the fruit ice, with their tips draped over the edge of the tangerine rind. Place the tops over the shells, at a slight angle. They should not fit tightly, but should be tipped enough to show some of the fruit ice pushing through the crack left open between the top and the bottom of the tangerine.

7 Place the stuffed tangerines in the freezer and serve after about 45 minutes.

A PASTA GLOSSARY

BEYOND *spaghetti* and *rigatoni*, *fettuccine*, and *lasagne*, there is such a lush growth of pasta names and shapes that even Italians sometimes get lost.

Pasta assumes dozens of different forms, many of which are multiplied by variations in size, thickness, and surface texture. These configurations are not merely decorative. They affect the body, character, the very taste of pasta. They determine how it will be served, because each pasta shape has certain sauces it welcomes, and others it rejects.

Nearly all the commercial pasta described here is available, at one time or another, in well-stocked Italian groceries. Most of the home-made pastas can be reproduced in your kitchen, using the specific recipes and techniques found in this book and in my first, *The Classic Italian Cookbook*. A few others are left to reward gastronomic explorers who will track them down to their native source.

Factory-made Pasta

In Italy we call it *pasta compra*, shop-bought pasta. It is factory-made of hard-wheat flour and water. Although it comes in what appears to be a bewildering assortment of shapes, all of these can be classified as long and narrow or short and broad; flat or tubular; solid or hollow; smooth or ridged.

Bucatini Also known as *perciatelli*. It is thick, hollow *spaghetti*. Its most famous preparation originated in Amatrice, near Rome. *Bucatini all'amatriciana* is served with a sauce made with lard or butter, tomatoes, hot red pepper, *pancetta* and *pecorino romano* cheese. (See my first book, page 89.)

Conchiglie It means 'seashells', and it resembles those oblong shells that are pinched at both ends, have a long, narrow slit of an opening, and are sometimes strung together in necklaces. When they are ridged they are called *conchiglie rigate*. Their cavity is ideal for trapping little bits of meat from a sauce made with ham and peas or crumbled sausages, or from a *bolognese* meat sauce.

Farfalle It means 'butterflies', and they look like little bows. When small they go into soup, while the larger ones are good with a prosciutto-and-tomato sauce.

Fusilli Corkscrew-shaped *spaghetti*. In slightly varying forms also known

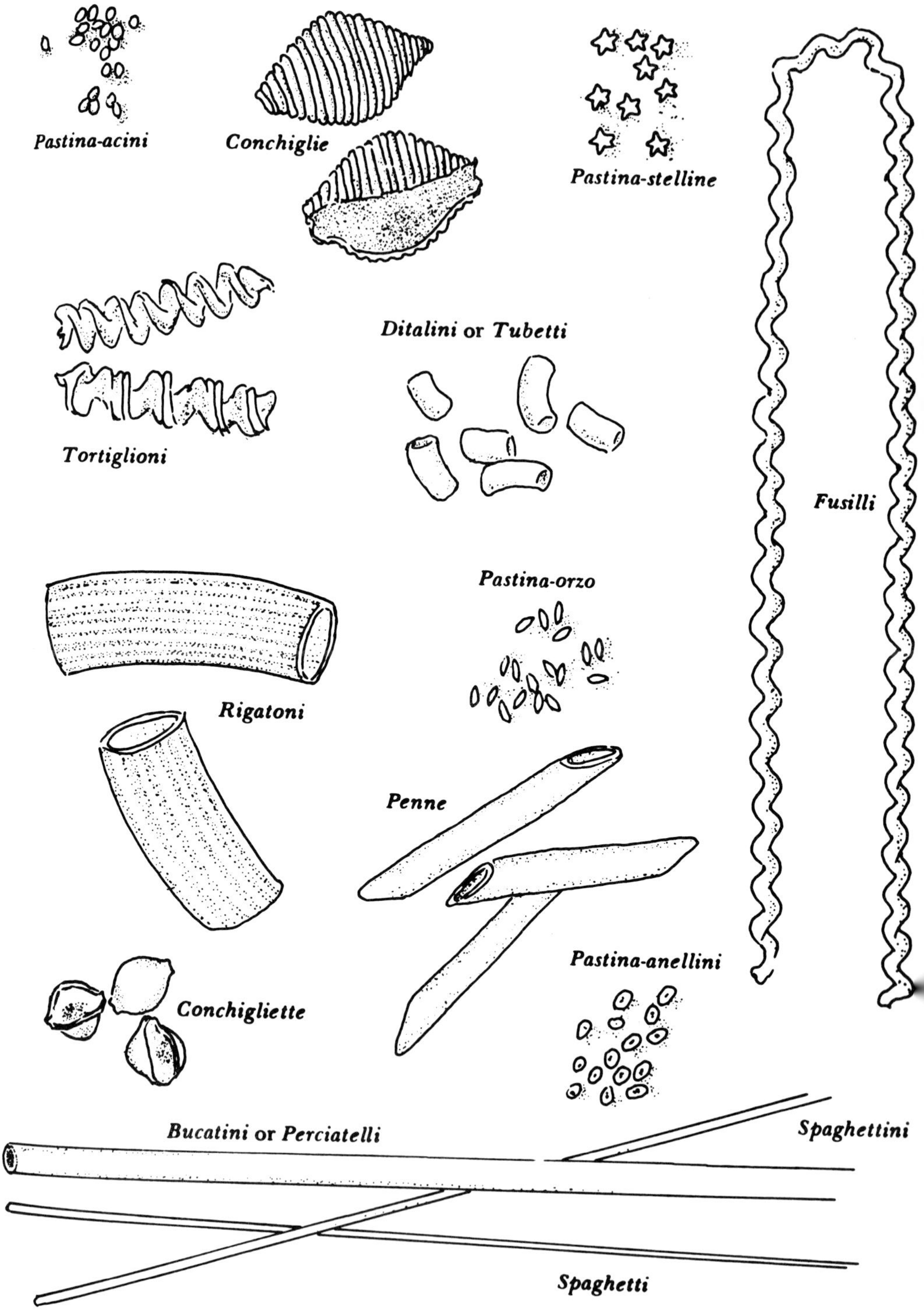
Pastina-acini
Conchiglie
Pastina-stelline
Fusilli
Tortiglioni
Ditalini or Tubetti
Pastina-orzo
Rigatoni
Penne
Pastina-anellini
Conchigliette
Bucatini or Perciatelli
Spaghettini
Spaghetti

as *tortiglioni* or *rotelle*. A shape well suited to thick, clinging, creamy sauces containing bits of meat or such vegetables as courgettes. (See my first book, page 90.) It is not too compatible with fluid tomato or oil-based sauces.

Linguine Flat and long, like a noodle, narrow and slightly tapering at the edges. It is the only pasta I have never been able to like, because it has to an extreme degree the slitheriness I associate with machine-made noodles.

Lumache The word means 'snails'. It is larger than *conchiglie*, but not too dissimilar in shape. It goes well with the same kind of sauces.

Maccheroncini Small, stubby, hollow macaroni. Usually ridged – *rigati* – but sometimes smooth – *lisci*. They agree with a great variety of sauces, but turn out particularly well with those that are a little spicy and contain some ham or other bits of meat. However, *maccheroncini* can be delicious with a simple sauce of tomatoes and fresh basil. The ending *-ini* in the word tells you they are small (while *-oni* means they are large).

Pastina This covers a large variety of miniature pastas, such as *anelli*, *stelline*, *ditalini*, *acini*, etc. It is soup pasta, to be served in a good home-made broth, topped with freshly grated Parmesan cheese.

Penne Means 'quills.' It is shaped like a quill, only much enlarged, and cut diagonally at both end. It is usually smooth, but it is also available ridged, *penne rigate*. The nicest accompaniment for *penne* is a pure tomato sauce made with just butter and tomatoes. But it is a shape one can enjoy with almost any sauce, except perhaps one with seafood.

Rigatoni One of the chewiest and most satisfying macaroni there is. It is stubby, hollow, slightly curved, and ridged. It is a substantial pasta that goes well with a meat sauce. It stays firm even when slightly overcooked, so that it is ideal for gratin dishes (see my first book, page 93).

Ruote di carro Cartwheels. Very popular in the South, especially in Sicily, with aubergines and ricotta. (See page 109.)

Spaghetti and Spaghettini Thin *spaghetti (spaghettini)* tastes best with all olive-oil-based sauces, such as those with aubergines or courgettes, or with clams, mussels, and other seafood (see page 99). One of the most satisfying and fastest preparations for *spaghettini* is the Roman *ajo e ojo*, olive oil with sautéed garlic (see my first book, page 88).

The heavier consistency of *spahetti* gives a closer affinity to butter and cheese sauces, with or without tomato. In Italy it is rarely, if ever, served with meat sauce and, of course, never with meatballs. In Naples, and elsewhere in the South, you may find *spaghetti* and *spaghettini* called *vermicelli* and *vermicellini*. Venetians call them *bigoli*.

Ziti A short tubular shape similar to *rigatoni*, but narrower and unridged. Like *rigatoni*, *ziti* is often served baked. It is not to be confused with *zita* or *mezza zita*, which is long and hollow like *bucatini*, but considerably larger.

Home-made Pasta

HOME-MADE pasta is, with rare exceptions, made with softer flour than macaroni. In Emilia-Romagna it is made with only eggs and flour. On the Italian Riviera they use fewer eggs and add water. In other regions, it is sometimes made without any eggs at all. It is a more tender pasta than macaroni, and the only pasta one can use for many stuffed specialities.

Agnolotti Crescent-shaped dumplings, usually stuffed with meat. A speciality of Piedmont. The classic way to serve *agnolotti* is to cook them, then toss them in a frying pan together with the pan juices from roast game. During the truffle season, in late autumn and winter, they are topped with thin slices of the powerfully fragrant white truffle of Alba.

Cannelloni Another Piedmontese speciality, *cannelloni* are rectangles of noodle dough rolled into a tube shape, stuffed with a meat and béchamel filling, and baked (see my first book, page 127).

Capelli d'angelo Literally, angel hair. Very fine noodles, best served in a good meat broth, with a grating of Parmesan cheese.

Cappellacci Pumpkin-stuffed dumplings. You will find them on menus in country restaurants in Emilia-Romagna, particularly in Ferrara.

Cappelletti Stuffed dumplings made in the shape of peaked 'little hats', which is the literal translation of its name. They are native to the Romagna section of Emilia-Romagna. In the stuffing there are chicken breast, pork, *mortadella*, ricotta, Parmesan, and nutmeg. Traditionally served on Christmas Day in a fine capon consommé.

Casônsèi A speciality of Bergamo and Brescia. It is a sleeve-shaped dumpling stuffed with sausage or salami, spinach, egg yolks, Parmesan, and raisins. Served with sage-flavoured melted butter.

Cavatieddi Made in Apulia with a firm, eggless dough, containing hard-wheat flour. It is rolled by hand into the shape of small seashells. Traditionally, it is boiled together with arugola, and served with olive oil flavoured with garlic and hot pepper.

Fettuccine The Roman version of the egg noodle, a little narrower and thicker than Bolognese *tagliatelle*.

Garganelli Ridged, quill-shaped macaroni of pure egg-noodle dough, made at home on a comb-like instrument (see my first book, page 146). It is still served in restaurants in and near Bologna, most often with a sauce containing cream and prosciutto.

Gasse Small bow-shaped pasta. Served on the Riviera in broth or with pesto. The same shape is called *stricchetti* in Emilia-Romagna, where it is served with a sauce of prosciutto and peas.

Gramigna Looks like very short, curly *bucatini*. It is made at home, of egg-noodle dough, on a machine that looks like a meat grinder. Served in Emilia-Romagna with a sausage-and-cream sauce (see my first book, page 92).

Lasagne Broad strips of egg-noodle dough, baked with béchamel sauce and meat or vegetable fillings. One of the most celebrated versions of *lasagne* is *lasagne verdi*, made with green, spinach pasta and bolognese meat sauce (see my first book, page 122). (Also see other *lasagne* recipes in this book, pages 151–6.)

Maccheroni alla chitarra Square noodles, as thick as they are wide. Made of hard-wheat flour and eggs, and cut on the steel strings of a guitar-like instrument. In Abruzzi it is served with a meat sauce made with chopped lamb. Also in Rome, where it is called *tonnarelli* (see page 143).

Maltagliati Diamond-shaped, short soup noodles made of egg dough (see my first book, page 105). The best pasta to use for bean and vegetable soups.

Manfrigul Home-made egg barley (see page 142).

Orecchiette It looks like little ears, which is precisely what the name means. Made in Apulia of the same dough as *cavatieddi;* it is shaped in the hand, between thumb and palm (see my first book, page 148). Served with a sauce of broccoli, olive oil, and anchovies.

Pansotti Or, as you may see it written in menus on the Riviera, *pansôti*. Triangular dumpling filled with a mixture of five different wild greens, ricotta, eggs, and grated cheese. Traditionally served with *salsa de nõxe*, a creamy walnut sauce.

Pappardelle Broad egg noodles, usually over 12 mm (½ inch) wide. Often they are cut with a fluted pastry wheel to give them a crimped edge. *Pappardelle alla lepre*, served during the hunting season with a sauce of wild hare, is one of the few pasta dishes for which Tuscany is known, and it is well worth looking for. (See my first book, page 105, and this book, page 158, for *pappardelle* recipes.)

Pizzoccheri From Valtellina, near the Swiss border. A short noodle made partly from buckwheat flour, and served with vegetables, melted cheese, and potatoes (see page 165).

Quadrucci Fresh egg pasta cut into 6-mm (¼-inch) squares. Used for soup.

Ravioli The ancestor of all stuffed pasta. Native to the Riviera. The classic stuffing includes escarole, borage, sweetbreads, calves' teat, soft cheese, egg yolks, and marjoram.

Strangolapreti The name, which means 'priest strangler', must derive from some fatal episode of clerical gluttony. The pasta is an innocuous, narrow, *gnocchi*-like nugget, made with eggless, hard-wheat flour dough.

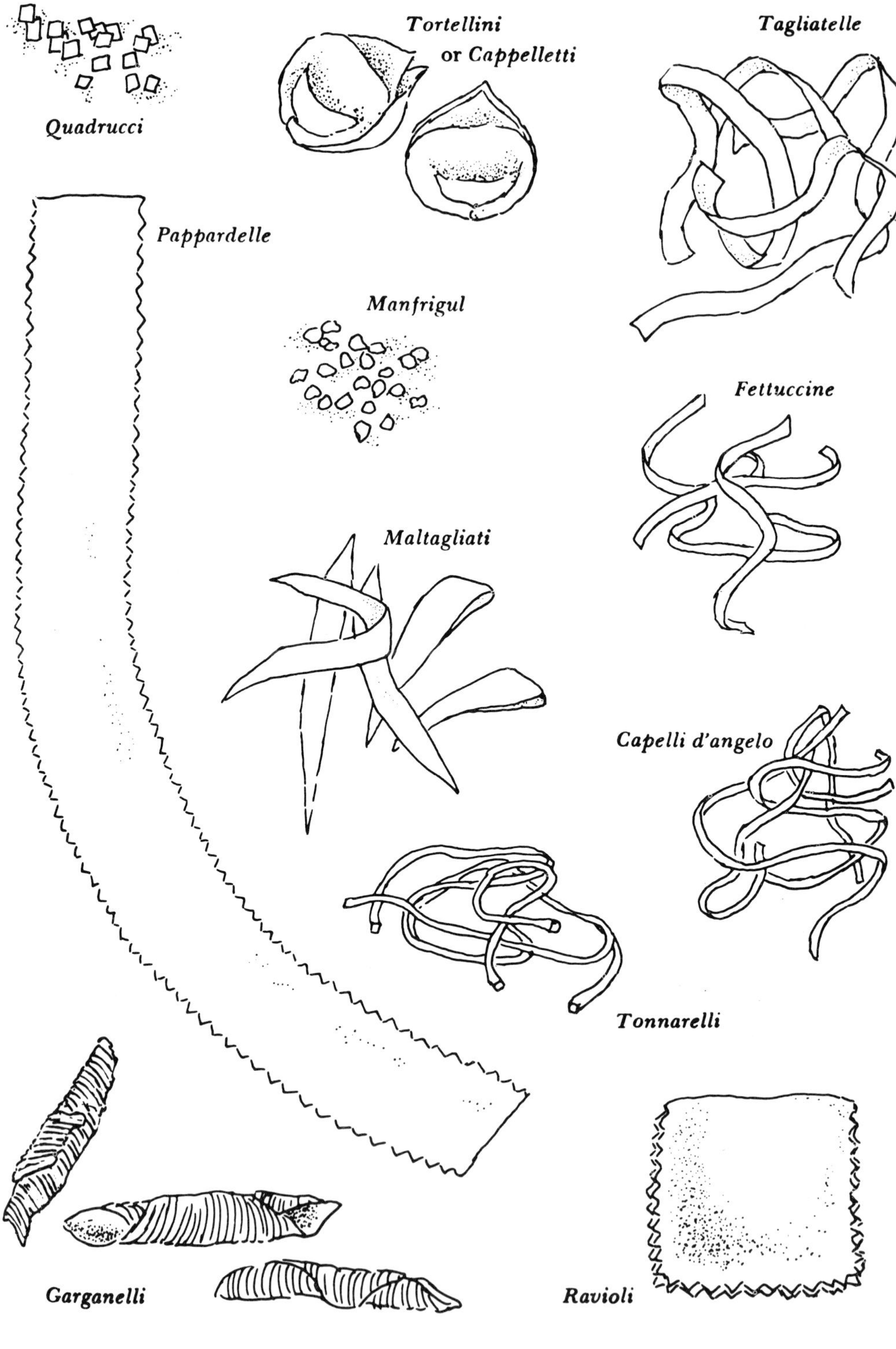
Quadrucci
Tortellini
or Cappelletti
Tagliatelle
Pappardelle
Manfrigul
Fettuccine
Maltagliati
Capelli d'angelo
Tonnarelli
Garganelli
Ravioli

Served with meat sauce, or a sauce containing pork jowl, tomatoes, and hot pepper.

Tagliatelle The classic egg noodle, a speciality of Bologna, where it is served with meat sauce (see my first book, page 110).

Tagliolini Thin noodles for broth, also known as *tagliarini* or *fedelini*. Not quite so fine as *capelli d'angelo*.

Tortelli A *ravioli*-like dumpling, stuffed with greens and ricotta, served with melted butter. A speciality of Parma.

Tortellini A small, ring-shaped dumpling for which Bologna is celebrated. The classic version has a meat stuffing and is served in hot broth, but it can be made with a variety of stuffings, and served with cream and other sauces. (See my first book, pages 137–39, and this book, pages 140–2.)

Tortelloni A large, square dumpling usually stuffed with Swiss chard or spinach. (See my first book, pages 140–44.)

Trenette A narrow noodle made in the Riviera with dough containing a very small amount of eggs. Served with pesto and boiled potatoes (see my first book, page 121).

Troccoli A speciality of Foggia, in Apulia. Very similar to *maccheroni alla chitarra* from Abruzzi, except that the dough is a little softer. It is cut with a special rolling-pin etched with very fine grooves. The pins used to be made by hand, but those are now objects for antique collectors. Modern machine-cut pins are sometimes sold by the roadside to tourists, as decorative souvenirs. *Troccoli* are served with meat sauce.

Trofie A short, tiny, spiral-shaped pasta. It is made entirely by hand, in a quick, diagonal twisting movement as the hand rolls the dough against the surface of the table. Great amounts of *trofie* are made each day by women who work at home to supply the restaurants between Genoa and Recchio. *Trofie* are delicious when served with pesto and boiled small young french beans.

Pasta asciutta One of the most startling questions I have ever been asked came on a radio phone-in programme. A listener wanted to have the recipe for *pasta asciutta*. This is somewhat like asking the recipe for eggs. *Pasta asciutta* is *any* dish of cooked pasta served with a sauce. The term is used in Italian cookbooks, and in restaurant menus sometimes, to distinguish it from *pasta in brodo*, which is any kind of pasta served in broth, instead of with sauce.

Index